SOMETHING ABOUT THE AUTHOR®

Something about
the Author *was named
an "**Outstanding
Reference Source,**"
the highest honor given
by the American
Library Association
Reference and Adult
Services Division.*

ISSN 0276-816X

something ABOUT THE AUTHOR®

**Facts and Pictures about Authors
and Illustrators of Books for Young People**

volume 216

GALE
CENGAGE Learning™

Detroit • New York • San Francisco • New Haven, Conn • Waterville, Maine • London

GALE
CENGAGE Learning™

Something about the Author, Volume 216

Project Editor: Lisa Kumar

Editorial: Laura Avery, Pamela Bow, Jim Craddock, Amy Fuller, Andrea Henderson, Margaret Mazurkiewicz, Tracie Moy, Jeff Muhr, Kathy Nemeh, Mary Ruby, Mike Tyrkus

Permissions: Margaret Abendroth, Savannah Gignac, Aja Perales

Imaging and Multimedia: Savannah Gignac, John Watkins

Composition and Electronic Capture: Amy Darga

Manufacturing: Drew Kalasky

Product Manager: Janet Witalec

Gale
27500 Drake Rd.
Farmington Hills, MI, 48331-3535

LIBRARY OF CONGRESS CATALOG CARD NUMBER 62-52046

ISBN-13: 978-1-4144-4790-2
ISBN-10: 1-4144-4790-6

ISSN 0276-816X

This title is also available as an e-book.
ISBN-13: 978-1-4144-6448-0
ISBN-10: 1-4144-6448-7
Contact your Gale sales representative for ordering information.

Printed in the United States of America
1 2 3 4 5 6 7 14 13 12 11 10

Contents

Authors in Forthcoming Volumes

Below are some of the authors and illustrators that will be featured in upcoming volumes of *SATA*. These include new entries on the swiftly rising stars of the field, as well as completely revised and updated entries (indicated with *) on some of the most notable and best-loved creators of books for children.

*Jim Arnosky ▌ A Vermont-based naturalist, artist, and author, Arnosky blends his interests and talents in children's books about wildlife and nature; his one-hundredth title, *Wild Tracks!: A Guide to Nature's Footprints* was released in 2008. His friendly, informal style is a characteristic of all his writing, which includes "how-to" nonfiction, nature-inspired books such as *Slither and Crawl: Eye to Eye with Reptiles* as well as picture books and nature-based novels such as *Crocodile Safari* and *The Pirates of Crocodile Swamp.*

*Calef Brown ▌ Formerly a freelance illustrator whose work appeared in high-profile periodicals like the *New York Times* and *Newsweek,* Brown turned to writing for children when his hectic, deadline-oriented schedule began to wear thin. Beginning with *Polka-Bats and Octopus Slacks: Fourteen Stories,* Brown's entertaining mix of original poetry and folk-style paintings are also featured in *Flamingos on the Roof, Tippitown,* and *Soup for Breakfast.*

Beth Fantaskey ▌ Fantaskey drew on her love of classic novels by Jane Austen, the Brontës, and others in penning her novel *Jessica's Guide to Dating on the Dark Side,* which combines romance with paranormal themes. In addition to this popular teen read, which focuses on a girl who learns that her birth parents are members of Romanian vampire royalty, Fantaskey references another literary classic in her second YA thriller, *Jekel Loves Hyde.*

Lisa Glatt ▌ Glatt began her writing career penning short fiction and poetry before moving on to novels and children's fiction. Her first novel, *A Girl Becomes a Comma like That,* was praised by many critics, and she treats younger readers to a spunky third-grade heroine in her chapter books *Abigail Iris: The One and Only* and *Abigail Iris: The Pet Project.*

Julia Hoban ▌ Hoban began creating picture books with her mother, artist and children's-book author Lillian Hoban. As her career progressed, however, she turned her focus to older readers, addressing adolescent trauma in highly acclaimed young-adult novels such as *Acting Normal* and *Willow.*

Elle van Lieshout ▌ Van Lieshout is a popular author in her native Netherlands, and frequently collaborates with her husband, Eric van Os. Featuring illustrations by artists such as Paula Gerritsen and Mies Van Lieshout, the couple's gentle stories feature animal characters, and their books *A Nice Party, The Nothing King, The Wish,* and *Lovey and Dovey* have also been translated into English.

*James Proimos ▌ A former advertising copywriter, Proimos now channels his amusingly drawn, boldly colored animated cartoon characters into picture books such as *The Loudness of Sam, Paulie Pastrami Achieves World Peace,* and *The Many Adventures of Johnny Mutton.* In addition to writing books, he has also worked in animation, via television cartoon programs such as *Generation O!, Larry Parka, Polar Pig,* and *The Switch-a-Roonies.*

*Brent Runyon ▌ Runyon's suicide attempt at age fourteen is the subject of his poignant memoir *The Burn Journals,* which describes the painful healing process that occurred after he tried to end his life by setting himself on fire. Although he instantly changed his mind, Runyon did not make it into a nearby shower in time to avoid suffering severe burns over much of his body. Since writing his memoir, he has turned to fiction, producing the well-received teen novels *Maybe* and *Surface Tension.*

*Tanya Lee Stone ▌ A prolific writer, Stone is the author of dozens of nonfiction books for young readers, including titles in the "Regional Wild America," "Wild Wild World," and "Making of America" series. In addition to her nonfiction titles, she has also written illustrated biographies, alphabet books, and the young-adult novel *A Bad Boy Can Be Good for a Girl.*

Rebecca Walsh ▌ Walsh earned respect in the field of children's publishing through her contributions to books by Robert D. San Souci, Nancy C. Wood, and Amy Ehrlich. Her first illustration project, San Souci's *The Well at the End of the World,* retells a British folk story about a royal princess whose homely looks belie a commonsense wisdom. Walsh's evocative and richly toned acrylic-and-water color paintings also bring to life Wood's *How the Tiny People Grew Tall* and Ehrlich's *The Girl Who Wanted to Dance.*

Introduction

Something about the Author (*SATA*) is an ongoing reference series that examines the lives and works of authors and illustrators of books for children. *SATA* includes not only well-known writers and artists but also less prominent individuals whose works are just coming to be recognized. This series is often the only readily available information source on emerging authors and illustrators. You'll find *SATA* informative and entertaining, whether you are a student, a librarian, an English teacher, a parent, or simply an adult who enjoys children's literature.

What's Inside *SATA*

SATA provides detailed information about authors and illustrators who span the full time range of children's literature, from early figures like John Newbery and L. Frank Baum to contemporary figures like Judy Blume and Richard Peck. Authors in the series represent primarily English-speaking countries, particularly the United States, Canada, and the United Kingdom. Also included, however, are authors from around the world whose works are available in English translation. The writings represented in *SATA* include those created intentionally for children and young adults as well as those written for a general audience and known to interest younger readers. These writings cover the entire spectrum of children's literature, including picture books, humor, folk and fairy tales, animal stories, mystery and adventure, science fiction and fantasy, historical fiction, poetry and nonsense verse, drama, biography, and nonfiction. Obituaries are also included in many volumes of *SATA* and are intended not only as death notices but also as concise overviews of people's lives and work. Additionally, each edition features newly revised and updated entries for a selection of *SATA* listees who remain of interest to today's readers and who have been active enough to require extensive revisions of their earlier biographies.

Autobiography Feature

Beginning with Volume 103, many volumes of *SATA* feature one or more specially commissioned autobiographical essays. These unique essays, averaging about ten thousand words in length and illustrated with an abundance of personal photos, present an entertaining and informative first-person perspective on the lives and careers of prominent authors and illustrators profiled in *SATA*.

Two Convenient Indexes

In response to suggestions from librarians, *SATA* indexes no longer appear in every volume but are included in alternate (odd-numbered) volumes of the series, beginning with Volume 57.

SATA continues to include two indexes that cumulate with each alternate volume: the Illustrations Index, arranged by the name of the illustrator, gives the number of the volume and page where the illustrator's work appears in the current volume as well as all preceding volumes in the series; the Author Index gives the number of the volume in which a person's biographical sketch, autobiographical essay, or obituary appears in the current volume as well as all preceding volumes in the series.

These indexes also include references to authors and illustrators who appear in *Gale's Yesterday's Authors of Books for Children, Children's Literature Review,* and *Something about the Author Autobiography Series.*

Easy-to-Use Entry Format

Whether you're already familiar with the *SATA* series or just getting acquainted, you will want to be aware of the kind of information that an entry provides. In every *SATA* entry the editors attempt to give as complete a picture of the person's life and work as possible. A typical entry in *SATA* includes the following clearly labeled information sections:

PERSONAL: date and place of birth and death, parents' names and occupations, name of spouse, date of marriage, names of children, educational institutions attended, degrees received, religious and political affiliations, hobbies and other interests.

ADDRESSES: complete home, office, electronic mail, and agent addresses, whenever available.

CAREER: name of employer, position, and dates for each career post; art exhibitions; military service; memberships and offices held in professional and civic organizations.

MEMBER: professional, civic, and other association memberships and any official posts held.

AWARDS, HONORS: literary and professional awards received.

WRITINGS: title-by-title chronological bibliography of books written and/or illustrated, listed by genre when known; lists of other notable publications, such as plays, screenplays, and periodical contributions.

ADAPTATIONS: a list of films, television programs, plays, CD-ROMs, recordings, and other media presentations that have been adapted from the author's work.

WORK IN PROGRESS: description of projects in progress.

SIDELIGHTS: a biographical portrait of the author or illustrator's development, either directly from the biographee—and often written specifically for the *SATA* entry—or gathered from diaries, letters, interviews, or other published sources.

BIOGRAPHICAL AND CRITICAL SOURCES: cites sources quoted in "Sidelights" along with references for further reading.

EXTENSIVE ILLUSTRATIONS: photographs, movie stills, book illustrations, and other interesting visual materials supplement the text.

How a *SATA* Entry Is Compiled

SATA editors examine a wide variety of published sources to gather information for an entry. Biographical and bibliographic sources are consulted, as are book reviews, feature articles, published interviews, and material sometimes obtained from the biographee's family, publishers, agent, or other associates. Whenever possible, the author or illustrator is sent a copy of the entry to check for accuracy and completeness.

Entries that have not been verified by the biographees or their representatives are marked with an asterisk (*).

Contact the Editor

We encourage our readers to examine the entire *SATA* series. Please write and tell us if we can make *SATA* even more helpful to you. Give your comments and suggestions to the editor:

Editor
Something about the Author
Gale, Cengage Learning
27500 Drake Rd.
Farmington Hills MI 48331-3535

Toll-free: 800-877-GALE
Fax: 248-699-8070

Something about the Author Product Advisory Board

SOMETHING ABOUT THE AUTHOR

AARON, Chester 1923-

Personal

Born May 9, 1923, in Butler, PA; son of Albert (a grocer and farmer) and Celia Aaron; married Margaurite Kelly (a jeweler), April 17, 1954 (divorced, 1973); children: Louis Daniel Segal (stepson). *Education:* Attended University of California, Los Angeles; University of California, Berkeley, B.A., 1966; San Francisco State University, M.A., 1972. *Politics:* "Mixed." *Religion:* Jewish. *Hobbies and other interests:* Garlic farming.

Addresses

Home—P.O. Box 388, Occidental, CA 95465. *E-mail*—chgarlic@comcast.net.

Career

Educator, author, and farmer. St. Mary's College, Moraga, CA, assistant professor, 1972-82, then professor of English, 1983-94; freelance writer, 1967—. Kaiser Permanente, San Francisco, CA, X-ray technician, 1957-58; Alta Bates Hospital, Berkeley, CA, chief X-ray technician, 1957-75; MKI Engineering, San Francisco, technical writer, 1971-72. California Marine Mammal Center, Marin County, volunteer. *Military service:* U.S. Army Armored Infantry, 1943-46.

Member

Authors Guild, Screenwriters Guild.

Chester Aaron (Photograph by Andrea Young. Courtesy of Chester Aaron.)

Writings

YOUNG-ADULT FICTION

Better than Laughter, Harcourt (New York, NY), 1972.
An American Ghost, illustrated by David Lemon, Harcourt (New York, NY), 1973.
Hello to Bodega, Atheneum (New York, NY), 1976.
Spill, Atheneum (New York, NY), 1978.
Catch Calico!, Dutton (New York, NY), 1979.
Gideon, Lippincott (Philadelphia, PA), 1982, reprinted, Zumaya (Austin, TX), 2009.
Duchess, Lippincott (Philadelphia, PA), 1982.

Out of Sight, out of Mind, Lippincott (Philadelphia, PA), 1985.
Lackawanna, Lippincott (Philadelphia, PA), 1986.
Alex, Who Won His War, Walker (New York, NY), 1991.
Home to the Sea, Brown Barn (Weston, CT), 2004.
Willa's Poppy, Zumaya (Austin, TX), 2009.

Author's works have been translated into French and German.

OTHER

The Cowbank (play), produced at University of California, Berkeley, 1955.
About Us (autobiographical novel), McGraw (New York, NY), 1967, reprinted, Creative Arts Book Co. (Berkeley, CA), 2002.
Garlic Is Life: A Memoir with Recipes, Ten Speed Press (Berkeley, CA), 1996.
The Great Garlic Book, Ten Speed Press (Berkeley, CA), 1997.
Garlic Kisses: Human Struggles with Garlic Connections, Mostly Garlic (Milan, OH), 2001, expanded as *Garlic Kisses and Tasty Hugs,* Zumaya (Austin, TX), 2008.
Black and Blue Jew (adult novel), Creative Arts Book Co. (Berkeley, CA), 2002.
Symptoms of Terminal Passion (memoir), El Leon Literary Arts (Berkeley, CA), 2006.
Whispers (adult mystery novel), Zumaya (Austin, TX), 2009.
Murder by Metaphor (adult mystery novel), Zumaya (Austin, TX), 2009.

Contributor of short stories to periodicals, including *Amistad, Coastlines, Highlights for Children, New York Times, North American Review, San Francisco Chronicle,* and *Texas Quarterly.* Contributor of articles to *Organic Gardening.*

Adaptations

Cougar, based on *An American Ghost,* was produced by ABC-TV as a weekend special, 1984, and as a video recording, 1991; *Lackawanna* was optioned for a feature film by Moonlight Productions/ITC Productions.

Sidelights

While Chester Aaron has traveled a number of career paths as an adult—from X-ray technician to college professor to garlic farmer—his desire to become a writer originated in his childhood and has been the thread that unites Aaron's varied life experiences. Although he wrote throughout his life, Aaron was in his mid-forties before he published his first book, the autobiographical novel *About Us,* which recounts growing up in a coal-mining town in Pennsylvania. In his books for younger readers, he draws upon the experience of his youth, earning critical praise for his realistic characters and suspenseful storylines. While the critical reception of Aaron's work has often surpassed its popular success,

his books "belong to the sterling old adventure genre, though with more inner subtleties," according to *St. James Guide to Children's Writers* essayist Naomi Lewis.

After serving in the U.S. Army during World War II, Aaron moved to California and worked at odd jobs while studying creative writing at the University of California, Los Angeles, on the G.I. Bill. Although the stories he submitted for publication usually were rejected, the budding writer was encouraged by professors who felt his powerful writer's voice needed to be heard. With the help of a Hartford Foundation grant, he began work on a praised, but ultimately unpublished novel; discouraged, Aaron set aside his plans to write full time and trained instead as an X-ray technician, a profession he worked at for nearly fifteen years while continuing to write part-time. Finally, in the late 1960s, he published his first book, the critically acclaimed autobiographical novel *About Us.*

Calling *About Us* "a beautiful and original book," *Nation* contributor Donald Fanger described it as "lyrical without mushiness and tough without posing, full of a truth that cannot be abstracted from the words that carry it." Reviewing Aaron's debut in the *Los Angeles Times Calendar,* Richard G. Lillard described the novel as "a rich cross-section of attitudes and conflicts in America during the Depression and World War II," and concluding: "Its radiant insight illuminates a wide circumference of human joy and suffering." Describing *About Us* as a novel about the disintegration of a family, Fanger noted that the plot follows "the scarcely perceptible stages through a pure present tense that becomes gradually complicated with a past and with intimations of a future." As the critic concluded, *About Us* "is a remarkable first novel, able in its authenticity to hear comparison with the best of its kind."

Shortly after the publication of *About Us,* Aaron began teaching at Saint Mary's College in Moraga, California, which gave him more time to pursue writing. Realizing that many of his students were ignorant of the Nazi concentration camps, he knew the time had come to write about the Holocaust. In his 1982 novel *Gideon,* which Lewis labeled a "powerful and important book" in her *St. James Guide to Children's Writers* essay, a brave fourteen-year-old boy survives the Warsaw Ghetto and later the death camp at Treblinka through his own resourcefulness. A contributor to the *Bulletin of the Center for Children's Books* praised the novel as a "moving and terrible story, written with craft and conviction."

Since publishing *Gideon,* Aaron has written several other well-received novels for younger readers. In *Out of Sight, out of Mind,* twin teen psychics become orphaned and their subsequent efforts to present a talk on world peace are thwarted by an aggressive foreign government. *Lackawanna* finds six homeless orphans bonding together as a family during the Great Depression of the 1930s, their sense of invulnerability shattered when one becomes lost while jumping a freight train. *An American Ghost* draws readers back to 1850, as young Albie and his home are washed down river during a flood, his only companion a female cougar seeking shelter so she can give birth to her cubs. Noting the "lasting quality" of these novels, Lewis praised Aaron's work for young readers as containing "an unquenchable spark of optimism, a hopeful energy, [that is] always to be found in the central youthful characters."

Aaron has also dabbled in fantasy for young adults. His novel *Home to the Sea* is the story of Marian Conroy, who, as her body matures, finds herself turning into a mermaid. The novel integrates Aaron's experience with marine mammal rescue, as well. Noting that there is very little magic involved in the "spare narrative," Beth L. Meister wrote in *School Library Journal* that "Aaron creates a believable picture of a girl moving from the normal into the supernatural." A *Children's Bookwatch* contributor felt that Marian's efforts in *Home to the Sea* to find out what the changes in her life mean "will resonate in the hearts of young people."

Since retiring from teaching in 1993, Aaron has continued to live in California, where he now spends much of his time cultivating over eighty different varieties of garlic. His book *Garlic Is Life: A Memoir with Recipes* focuses on his successful attempt to make the transition from retired college professor to garlic farmer, and includes forty recipes. *The Great Garlic Book* is a guide to the many varieties of garlic, and features pictures and growing information. His promotion of garlic and its uses has led to invitations from television and radio shows, and Aaron has also been actively involved with the farming of garlic through Oklahoma's "Garlic Is Life" festival, which was named after his memoir. He was featured in *Newsweek* and interviewed on National Public Radio's *All Things Considered* as a farmer helping garlic to find more respect among food critics, who often disdain the differences among the eighty-seven varieties Aaron has grown.

In addition to his books about garlic, Aaron has penned memoirs and mystery novels for adults. His novel *Whispers* features Eve Gallagher, a journalism student, who writes about the brutal attack of a friend for the college newspaper and is dismissed for being too sensational. Suspicious that her dismissal is a cover-up for the person who committed the crime, Eve continues to investigate the murder, opening up a deep childhood trauma of her own. "There are two interlaced stories in this novel, both equally powerful and disturbing," wrote Mayra Calvani in *Reviewer's Bookwatch*, the critic dubbing Aaron's style "forceful, intelligent and evocative."

Aaron once told *SATA:* "There are several experiences in my seventy-eight years of life that have affected the way I write and the themes and characters that drive my writing of fiction and nonfiction: the extreme pov-

erty of my childhood and youth; the joys and terrors of my parents' childhood and youth (theirs in Russia and Poland, mine in America); the constant presence of love within the family; the passion for education and political activity; my own work in the steel mine and factories; the war and then my experiences in combat, and most of all, perhaps, my participation in the liberation of Dachau—the emotional repercussions as strong today as almost sixty years ago; my meeting early and late in life the icons of left-wing art (writing, music, theater, painting) who were driven to improve the world we lived in (Richard Wright, Bertolt Brecht, Christopher Isherwood, Mai Zetterling, Greta Garbo, to name but a few); my work in hospitals with the sick and injured as an X-ray technician; my twenty-five years as an eccentric college professor who grew progressively more cynical about his colleagues and the education system in general; then as a farmer who found, in that world, a whole new group of themes and characters—a world that in many ways returned me to the world of my childhood in the coal-mining town of Butler, Pennsylvania; along the way, the occasional woman who enriched it all."

Biographical and Critical Sources

BOOKS

St. James Guide to Children's Writers, 5th edition, St. James Press (Detroit, MI), 1999.

PERIODICALS

Bulletin of the Center for Children's Books, June, 1982, review of *Gideon.*

Children's Bookwatch, December, 2004, review of *Home to the Sea.*

English Journal, September, 1986, review of *Lackawanna,* p. 69; October, 1986, review of *Out of Sight, out of Mind,* p. 85.

Horn Book, January-February, 1992, Ann A. Flowers, review of *Alex, Who Won His War,* p. 78.

Instructor and Teacher, May, 1982, Allan Yeager, review of *Gideon,* p. 105; November-December, 1982, Allan Yeager, review of *Duchess,* p. 151.

Los Angeles Times Calendar, July 16, 1967, Richard G. Lillard, review of *About Us.*

Nation, June 26, 1967, Donald Fanger, review of *About Us.*

Newsweek, February 26, 2001, Jerry Adler, "This Bulb's for You: The Humble Garlic Is the Latest 'Heirloom' Veggie," p. 50.

Publishers Weekly, June 4, 1982, review of *Gideon,* p. 67; May 30, 1986, review of *Lackawanna,* p. 69.

Reviewer's Bookwatch, December, 2004, Mayra Calvani, review of *Whisper.*

School Library Journal, April 15, 1982, review of *Gideon,* p. 78; February, 1983, Sylvie Tupacz, review of *Duchess,* p. 72; November, 1985, Ruth Vose, review of *Out of Sight, out of Mind,* p. 93; April, 1996, David A. Lindsey, review of *Lackawanna,* p. 94; October, 1991, Curtis Klause, review of *Alex, Who Won His War,* p. 119; November, 2004, Beth L. Meister, review of *Home to the Sea,* p. 134.

Voice of Youth Advocates, February, 2005, Chris Carlson, review of *Home to the Sea,* p. 488.

Wilson Library Bulletin, April, 1986, Patty Campbell, review of *Lackawanna,* p. 48; May, 1992, Cathi Dunn MacRae, review of *Alex, Who Won His War,* p. 107.

ONLINE

Chester Aaron Home Page, http://www.chesteraaron.com (October 25, 2009).

Autobiography Feature

Chester Aaron

Chester Aaron contributed the following autobiographical essay to *SATA:*

For my eleventh birthday—May 9, 1934—my brother Abe, a writer, sent me a copy of Jack London's *White Fang.* A gift that was to help shape my life. At least my life as a writer.

1934. The Great Depression was fading into history. Once more the miners in North Butler, Pennsylvania, were digging into the earth. In town the Armco Steel Mill and Pullman Standard Car Company belched black smoke again. Kids could sit on the porch of my father's store and count the cars in the trains moving again toward Pittsburgh. The names of those railroads were to reappear fifty years later in *Lackawanna,* a novel for young adults. In 1991, four years after *Lackawanna,* the names of those railroads appeared once more in another young-adult novel, called *Alex, Who Won His War.*

Those names, seen now only in an old movie or some decaying magazine found in a dusty attic, generate for me when I see or hear them vivid memories of my youth and childhood, of an innocence that prevailed before World War II not just in me but in the entire nation: the Pennsylvania Railroad, the Baltimore & Ohio, the Bessemer & Lake Erie, the Delaware Lackawanna. As I speak them now they sing in my ears like the names of the great American rivers: the Mississippi, the Monongahela, the Susquehanna, the Rappahannock, the Delaware. Those names and those memories do not belong in the language of Poland or Russia, where my mother and father were born, or Germany or Italy, where I have visited or lived. They are American. As am I, no matter the European legacy. And I write American stories. Even when I write about foreign places or foreign characters the narrator and his perceptions are, without conscious choice, American. "A golden place, America," my mother would say on Friday nights, as if the words were part of the orthodox prayer ritual. "A place of milk and honey."

*

White Fang arrived on a Tuesday. The following two days I ignored my schoolwork. I played hooky all day Friday so I could hide in our shack in the woods and not worry about being interrupted. The other kids— Roman, Goose, Timmy—were loafing at home or taking early dips in the creek or, like me, playing hooky.

While I lounged in the shack reading *White Fang* they were probably sitting in the back row of the Majestic Theater in Butler, ready to rush the exits at the first sight of Milo Yerkovich, the truant officer.

Just before supper on Friday, I confided to Ray, the one older brother still living at home, that I had finished reading *White Fang.* He was in his work clothes, preparing to walk through the night, along the railroad tracks, to the tire factory. His clothes were clean but they, like his skin and his hair, still smelled of rubber. He whispered, "Did you play hooky today?"

"No," I lied.

He nodded wisely. "In Upper Slobovia that means *yes.*" For the uninformed, Upper Slobovia was a geographic reality in the then-popular cartoon strip, "Li'l Abner."

That night, as the kids and I sat on the bunks in our shack, I told them the story of *White Fang,* reciting it with a dramatic tension almost as effective as London's. Roman and Goose and Timmy sat without moving, their eyes wide. They remained silent for three or four minutes.

Roman broke the silence. "That was better than the radio."

He was right. The story as I told it was indeed better, more exciting, than radio drama. And I had *told* it. *My voice* and *my words* had held them captive. Spellbound. But as good as my story was, its impact did not approach the impact the original writing, the words and sentences and paragraphs Jack London had composed, had had on me. The story, as London had written it, had drawn me to it so insistently that—not just for hours but for days and nights—nothing but the story had existed for me. I'd forgotten parents, brothers, sister, other kids, school. Only the world of polar Alaska existed. The brave and loyal dog, the brave as well as the brutish men, all struggling to survive in ice and snow and wind. For three days and nights, because of the way he had pulled words out of his mind and set them on a page, Jack London's world had been my world. Magic. Pure magic.

"Someday," I promised the kids as well as myself, "I'm going to write stories."

The next day, Saturday, I walked the three miles to town, to the Butler County Library. I returned home with *Call of the Wild, The Sea Wolf,* and *Martin Eden,* all by London, and a collection of his short stories that included one now universally acclaimed classic, "To Build a Fire." For the rest of the spring and all through summer vacation—at our shack, on the porch of my father's store, on the banks of the Connoquenessing Creek—I read Jack London.

Sometimes, too excited to hide the magic inside myself, I read the stories aloud. I read to my mother as she cooked or combed her hair, to my father as he stacked the shelves with canned goods, to my sister, Stella, as she trimmed her nails or sewed her dresses, to the other kids as they played marbles or rested from long swims in the Connoquenessing Creek or interrupted one of our frequent wrestling sessions. Once, on the back porch with Yenta, our own big shaggy dog, I read to her. Flattered by my presence and my attention, Yenta stretched out at my feet, belly-up in total submission. The ideal audience.

*

The nearly 300 houses in our village of North Butler appeared to have been hurled at the steep hills by a mischievous drunken giant, and then, once deposited, they had managed to cling to the mud wherever and however they'd happened to land. We were separated from the tree-lined streets and businesses and factories and Victorian homes of Butler by three miles of birch and oak and elm trees, a dense forest which, we kids had convinced each other, had until recently been home to tribes of Apache and Sioux and Cheyenne savages who had, somehow, relayed their cunning and savagery and durability to us. Not to all of the kids, but to the five of us: Roman, Goose, myself, and, to a lesser degree, Timmy and Bottlenose, a short fat kid who was already working alongside his father in the mines and who could snort like a hog.

In the spring North Butler's dirt roads became rivers of mud. In the winter they were converted to magnificent iced slopes perfect for bobsled races. During late autumn small gardens at the sides of most of the houses were host to enough tomatoes and onions and peppers and lettuce to reduce reliance on my father's store or on the larger markets in town. My mother and father, with their own garden, were convinced that every single vegetable they produced was larger and sweeter and prettier than all others grown by any of their customers foreign—or Pennsylvania—born. An outhouse waited at the far end of the path that started at our back porch, the fabled half-moon cut in the door. Not a single home in North Butler had an inside toilet or bath. Every kid and many adults told progressively horrifying stories about the hazards and traumas awaiting all of us in those cold and hot bug-filled outhouses, stories ranging from the grotesquely comic to the disgustingly tragic. Some of those stories managed to find their way into my first novel, *About Us,* an autobiographical novel about North Butler that is more fiction than fact. I think.

At a certain point I could no longer remember what was true and what was imagined.

Every evening, no matter the season, unless the rain forced us inside, the kids played under the streetlight on the asphalt road in front of our store or in the fields that stretched from the road to the railroad tracks. Pump-pump-pullaway or capture-the-flag or baseball or football or, in the winter, on circular trails stomped in the snow, fox-and-geese.

The men—workers in the mines or railroads around North Butler, or in the steel mills in town—sat on the porch on wooden boxes or metal milk cases or, in winter, gathered on benches around the potbellied coal stove, competing for recognition of their prowess as fighters or workers or hunters or fishermen. Several times each day one or another of the older immigrant workers stopped by to talk to my father, who could speak their Polish or Russian or Czech. The women sought out my mother to have her read, in the same languages, letters sent from the old country. Both my mother and father, peasants themselves, had somehow learned to read and speak a fairly comprehensible English. The other immigrants surrendered to the punishing language, never learning to read or write it.

All in all an apparently perfect childhood for a boy who dreamed of becoming a famous writer. North Butler was not the polar north but its people, its hills and forests and valleys, its dramas, offered more than enough stories to keep a writer productive for many years. About a half century after my childhood a chapter of that first novel was included in an anthology of immigrant literature published by the University of Pittsburgh Press. The title of the anthology: *From These Hills, From These Valleys.*

My North Butler childhood was not ideal. In fact, the farther I travel in time and space from childhood and from North Butler, the more I realize that the imperfections, known and unknown, have taken their toll on my mind if not my body. The pains I suffered then but only identified later, in adult years, have almost (*almost!*) overshadowed the pleasures. When I began to write about my childhood I discovered that what I had considered pleasures fought to remain obscure, distant, like a series of experiences lacking the strength or even the will to survive in clear detail.

I have forgiven if not forgotten the torment of the occasional taunts and attacks by North Butler's grown-ups as well as its kids. *Christ-killer! Sheeny! Kike! Black-headed Jew! I jewed him down!* Forgiven.

But I have neither forgiven nor forgotten the torment of poverty. It haunts me almost daily.

For about ten years, beginning when I was five or six, my father began to lose control of his grocery store and his life. Partly out of his love for humanity and partly

"Mother, Father, and my oldest brother, then one year old," about 1904 (Photograph courtesy of Chester Aaron.)

out of growing resentment of the encroaching, incomprehensible world, he trusted customers who, he knew, would never pay their debts. ("Tell me, what do you do a child comes in he begs for a can of beans for supper?") As he declined slowly into acute despair the store's offerings declined. When I was eight, perhaps nine, I noticed one day that the shelves of the store were literally empty.

Poppa must have had secret resources for Christmas. Early Christmas mornings during the Great Depression my father secretly delivered large boxes of meat and vegetables and bread to the porches of the poorest unemployed workers. My mother and my brothers were aware of his self-destructive charity but how could they denounce him? Wasn't philanthropy etched deeply into the Judaic code? We are our brother's keeper. And our sister's. And our aunt's and uncle's.

My brother Ray, who worked at the tire factory, continued trying to keep the store functioning with offerings from his salary, but the task proved futile, partly be-

cause so much of his earnings went to three other brothers who were struggling through college, or to my mother, whose medical bills were endless.

Before long we were as impoverished as the poorest worker's family. We had no food. I went, with other kids, to trail along behind the occasional coal trains, gathering fallen lumps of coal for our stove. I hiked many miles with my father to pick wild mushrooms and nuts and berries to supplement the potatoes that composed our meals. Potatoes. My mother, artist as well as magician, disguised potatoes so they might look and taste like something other than the lumps of starch they were. The glass cases and ice-cream freezers, to which I used to go with such abandon, were empty of candy bars and ice cream and cold drinks. The doors of the meat locker, empty of ice, stood ajar.

As difficult as it was we never went on welfare, as did almost all of the other families. When our taxes fell due my father insisted on paying them off by working in the hot sun digging ditches, while kids and grown-ups sitting on the porch tried to make sense out of that old Jew's code of morality. What could the police do if Al Aaron didn't pay his taxes? You can't get blood out of a turnip.

Often, on winter nights, covered with old coats and sweaters because all of our blankets had withered away, I would dream of roasted chickens or chocolate bars. They would appear in my dreams with such tangible bulk that I would catch them in my hands and stuff them into my mouth. I would actually taste their sweetness on my tongue. Then I would awake, hands extended in the darkness, the food gone. How often, my stomach aching, I would cry myself to sleep, so hungry that I ignored my shivering.

Two or three times a week Jews drove from Butler, bringing soups and casseroles, cakes and pies, fruits and vegetables. Aware of the touchy and unpredictable pride of my father, they walked past him and went into the kitchen, where the pots and kettles were placed on the table without comment. They praised the tea my mother served them, they talked about the old country, about the synagogue and the new rabbi, and they related funny stories about events in Butler. The visits, the support, given without question or comment, without judgment, was received by my mother with the same generosity with which it had been offered. As they filed back through the store to their cars my father found chores to do in the desolate storeroom.

*

My father never did reclaim his former health or success. The store's shelves continued to offer minimal stock. Eventually outside conditions improved. The Depression gave way. I grew older and began to earn my own money. By the time I was fifteen I had a paper route, carrying fifty pounds of the *Butler Eagle* on my back the three miles from town and then maneuvering the hillsides for another hour or two. Sweating in the summer, freezing in the winter. Giving half of what I earned to my father. He could at least have cigars and cigarettes and chewing tobacco available.

I can never forget those years of anguish. I recall the joys: swimming and ice skating and swinging in birch trees, baseball and football and bobsledding, raiding fruit trees, and gathering around campfires in the lightning bug-saturated summer evenings to roast weiners and potatoes. But sooner or later I succumbed to the inevitable dance of other memories. I still, today, comfortable and well fed and very content with my life, dream now and then of chocolate bars hovering in the surrounding darkness, and I still awaken in tears, reaching out and finding only empty space. I have difficulty eating more than a taste or two of any potato on my plate.

How could I not permit such realities and memories to invade my stories of Americans, young or old, boy or girl? I try, knowing that publishers will not accept and readers will not purchase stories of despair. Perhaps that is why I find it difficult to write comedy, or to dwell on themes that do not include the physical challenges to survive. Perhaps that is why I cannot deny food to any strange dog or cat that arrives at my door or to birds that depend every second of their lives on the mercy of an unpredictable Nature. And perhaps that is why I grow more and more interested, as I grow older, in reading about and working with animals and offering time or money or both to any organization sympathetic to the protection of birds and beasts. Humans can care for themselves and other humans, though they very often refuse the task. In severe distress most animals cannot help themselves. They are forced to depend on the charity of humans, a virtue even more unreliable than the attention of a fickle Nature. They are the ultimate victims. My heart goes out to the beast and the bird more often than it goes out to humanity.

*

My mother had been born in Poland, my father in Russian Georgia. They came to America, with millions of other immigrants, in the opening years of the twentieth century. My five brothers and one sister were almost grown-ups when I was born. I was the baby of the family.

That period rises before me now. It is election day. Few of the people care enough to vote, or think every politician so corrupt there is little choice among them, no matter the office. My mother and father bathe and dress in their very best clothes and walk with solemn pride to the store that serves as their polling station. The idea of having the right to elect your representative, township commissioner or governor or president, is such a triumph of freedom that it is to be treated with respect, with gratitude. Even during his worst days my father, tie worn and badly knotted, shoes unpolished, walked my mother, in her somewhat tattered but freshly washed

"Grandfather and Great-grandfather," Russian Georgia, about 1885
(Photograph courtesy of Chester Aaron.)

and ironed finery, along the dirt road to the polling booth. "America, the golden," my mother reminded us. "You don't know liberty, how sweet it is."

By the time it was my turn to walk to town to be bar mitzvahed my parents were so proud to be considered Americans they were already beginning (though they themselves were then unaware of the process) to surrender the languages and rituals that had set them apart from true Americans. They were turning less frequently to the orthodox Jews in Butler. As a result they were growing farther and farther apart from the seventy or eighty Jewish families in town. Weekly visits to the synagogue gave way to visits only on high holidays, then only to the day or week commemorating the death of beloved parents or brothers or sisters.

My brothers, whenever they came home from college, used words that had little meaning for me but, at the same time, carried a hint of threat, of evil. The sounds of the words were like a vile but nameless medicine I had to swallow. *Nazi* and *Fascist* and *storm troopers* and *concentration camps*. And those names: Adolph Hitler, Benito Mussolini, Julius Streicher, Josef Goebbels.

The jokes and curses I received from the kids could no longer be forgiven so easily. I was driven not just to fight back but to fight and hurt, and even, if necessary, to maim. Driven by a mix of fear and anger I earned the reputation of being a kid it was no longer wise to tease with epithets suggesting Jews were stingy and biblically convicted Christ-killers.

When my father discovered several Nazi swastikas painted on the wall of our store it was I, not Poppa, who struggled to track down the kids, or the men, who might be responsible. Fortunately, it happened to be kids. Two of them. For the first time I used not just my fists but my feet, and a baseball bat. "Fighting fair" was out of the question from that day on.

*

After graduation from high school I was deferred from the draft because four of my brothers were already in the service. The draft board recommended that I stay home with my parents, both of whom were now not just old but ill. And extremely depressed.

The news of the treatment of Jews in Europe grew progressively more terrifying but in a way the treatment here in North Butler—developed in my mother and father's troubled minds perhaps beyond its real significance—was worse. There was reason to expect such a fate in Europe, where hatred of Jews was, as my father intoned, taken in with mother's milk. But swastikas here, in America the golden? Hadn't they proven their devotion to this land? Hadn't they given four of their sons to the defense of this country? Weren't two of

"In combat," Germany, 1943 (Photograph courtesy of Chester Aaron.)

those sons already in combat? Soon, too soon, their fifth and final son, their baby, would be leaving them, would be off to the war.

During my year of deferment I worked in steel mills in Butler and Pittsburgh. Then, on an impulse, I quit my job one day and enlisted in the army. My mother and father wept and pleaded. I could have another year's deferment. Why didn't I wait? But I had to go immediately, before the war ended, before Hitler and the Nazis were conquered. I would regret the loss forever if I did not contribute to their punishment. Fighting ignorant and insensitive kids for their stupid little epithets was no longer enough. I had to kill Germans.

*

I went into the armored infantry, fought in southern Germany, and ended my combat duty in Bavaria.

In the last days of the war, when our unit was rushing along the highway toward the town of Dachau, a gray-orange cloud hovered in the distance. A terrible odor grew stronger as we approached the cloud. It was, I soon realized, the stench of human flesh on fire.

We stormed the gates of Dachau and overwhelmed the few remaining German troops. I helped open the doors of the various gray wooden barracks that contained the living and the dead, one indistinguishable from the other.

We remained at Dachau two days. Those two days changed whatever direction my life, up until then, might have been traveling. I was never the same man.

I still dream about those two days at Dachau. I have struggled to convince myself that I am more than a Jew, I am a man, a human being, like Catholic and Protestant and Muslim men. But it doesn't work. I find myself listening to words of Gentiles, even of those I love, waiting to hear the denunciation that might precede a fist or a rifle butt or knocks at my door in the middle of the night.

*

When I came home from the war I was not quite twenty-two years old. My mother and father were dead.

Veterans at the time, using a new incentive Congress had conceived called the GI Bill, could go to the college of their choice. Not only were all expenses paid but each student received the munificent sum of fifty dollars a month.

In my freshman year at the University of California— Los Angeles I submitted a short story to *Story* magazine's annual contest for college students. I did not win the first prize (publication in *Story*) but I did win an honorable mention, the equivalent of third prize. The honor was appreciated but was later diluted when I read the winning story. I was convinced it was far inferior to mine.

The following semester an instructor named Richard G. Lillard accepted me in his creative-writing workshop. He praised my writing, assured me I had a rare talent. A tough, demanding, almost brutally honest man, he pressed me to continue not just writing more stories but sending them to magazines. Over the next four years every story (approximately thirty) was returned, most with form rejections but several accompanied by notes or letters expressing the editor's appreciation of what they called "your talent."

What was the use of talent if it remained unsuccessful? Unsuccessful meaning unrecognized.

I followed Professor Lillard's recommendation, continuing to write and submit short stories. The writing of fiction became so important that I began to lose interest in education. I dropped out of school several times, worked at a variety of odd jobs, and returned to school for another semester with Professor Lillard. In or out of school, working at odd jobs or studying, I wrote seven and sometimes eight or nine hours a day. My college grades were less than mediocre.

But I did accomplish something. I managed to write an article about a bar of soap I'd picked up at Dachau and had carried in my pack. The soap had been produced by the Germans from the fat melted from the bodies of Jews. Not knowing what else to do with the memory I submitted the single page to the UCLA newspaper, the *Daily Bruin.*

The editor of the *Bruin,* Frank Mankiewicz, informed me that I was a very powerful writer and should certainly continue writing. Several years later mutual friends informed me that Frank Mankiewicz still talked about that 1945 article in the *Daily Bruin.* Perhaps he was right. I should, would, continue writing. But not about Dachau. No more about Dachau. Not then.

*

At the end of the war, after my discharge, one week before I started classes at UCLA, I'd moved to Venice, California, near Santa Monica. One of my first friends was a man named Hans Viertel. He, but more especially his mother, helped stimulate me, educate me, shape me; helped, unknowingly, to foster and enrich that connection between present and past, between America and Europe, between North Butler and California, between childhood and manhood.

Salka Viertel had been an actress in Vienna with the famous director, Max Reinhardt. Her husband had been a notable poet. She'd come to America before the war began, soon after Hitler came to power, to try to find a career in Hollywood. She wrote several movie scripts, including three for Greta Garbo.

Hans invited me, a struggling student/writer, as he was, to his home on Mayberry Road in Santa Monica. I met and loved Salka. She and Hans invited me to many suppers before she insisted I also begin attending her Sunday teas, which Hans called *soirees.* It sounded so debauched.

"Tea" at Mayberry Road meant that during Sunday afternoon and evening I would not only be fed extraordinary European delicacies but I would also meet the most famous and most talented people (American and European) in the arts. All the arts, it turned out, but especially the art of writing and filmmaking.

On good-weather Sundays Salka extended the tea into supper for a select few, which, because of my friendship with Hans, my obvious adoration of Salka, and my willingness to wash dishes, always included me. Actors and actresses, musicians and singers, sculptors and painters and writers, arguing, laughing, crying, performed on the wide lawn or in the sunlit living room that offered the scent of the Pacific Ocean. Though I earned my way in a sense (washing the dishes, cleaning the house) I was one of the hangers-on permitted to sit at the fringe of groups inhabited by Christopher Isherwood, Benoit Brecht, Helena Wiegel, Charles Chaplin, Greta Garbo, Shelley Winters, Vittorio Gassman, James Agee. And many, many others of equal or even greater talent and fame. Once: Sergei Eisenstein.

By now I was coming to Salka's house in the evenings either after classes (if it was one of those seasons I happened to be attending UCLA) or after the completion of one of my many odd jobs (when I wasn't at school).

For an hour or two after supper Salka and I would linger over tea or coffee in the yard or in the house, gossiping and writing. Gossiping meant I listened to Salka's stories about the artists (European and American) who had favored her or been favored by her. Writing meant my reading bits and pieces of a book Salka was then working on and suggesting improvements in language or structure. Had it been published at the time it would have been one of the first Hollywood confessionals, but published many years later (1975? 1980?) it became a modest but enchanting, and very informative, memoir of the joys and sorrows of being an actress and mother and political activist in Europe and Hollywood.

What were my qualifications for such a position? I was by then a writing apprentice of only six or seven years. I was young and energetic and both appreciative of Salka and in awe of her. Many others she could have selected were more qualified, I knew, but I did not realize until later that of those who were qualified none were willing to work for the powerful and alluring Salka for tea and cookies and an occasional supper as compensation.

I met with Salka two evenings every week for about six months. Because a variety of luminaries often dropped in while we worked I heard and even occasionally participated in discussions of art exhibitions, concerts, theater presentations, movies, books.

All of this was occurring during the 1950s, when America, and especially Hollywood, were being intimidated by Senator Joseph McCarthy and the House Committee on Un-American Activities. Little wonder that most of the discussion at Salka's home centered on this political phenomenon. Little wonder, too, that my attitudes about literature were beginning to lean for guidance and support on European models. On those historically approved masters: Chekhov, Gorki, Tolstoy, de Maupassant, Balzac, Zola, and, more current, Levi, Mann, and Silone. Little evidence of interest then among these romantic and brilliant men and women in Hemingway or Faulkner or Fitzgerald. They were so American, only tangentially aware of politics, with that awareness naive, ill-informed. So spoke the mighty Brecht and company. There was some interest in Dreiser, much in Jack London, whose *Iron Heel* was considered a classic denunciation of capitalism. Not the slightest interest in my now personal favorite, Willa Cather.

Those days and evenings on Mayberry Road, that European culture consumed like the finest wine (which, like wine, kept me in a state of constant intoxication), and my own complementary protests against the threatening clouds of atomic war made it impossible for me to write anything that was not "heavy," not related to social action or politics.

Perhaps because of those days in North Butler, and certainly because of those days in Hollywood, I find myself drawn to themes of individuals or families in stress, with social-political over and undertones. Being a Jew in America (*About Us*), young boys in conflict with parents (*Better than Laughter*), a young boy relying on his own mind and body for survival in the wild (*An American Ghost*), young boys and girls caught in the undertows of what I conceive to be an immoral war (*Hello to Bodega*), boys and girls fighting the effects of an ecological disaster (*Spill*), a boy in a corrupt and destructive society (*Gideon*), a young boy struggling to survive after being maimed by family and society (*Duchess*), boys and girls struggling to survive in the Great Depression (*Lackawanna*).

*

During the period when I was working with Salka I was informed by Christopher Isherwood that a new foundation was being established deep in the Santa Monica mountains by a very wealthy man determined to build or buy a career as a patron of the arts. Isherwood pressed me to submit an application. I did, along with a large piece of a novel I was then working on. I was accepted for two consecutive terms, each a year long. The judges: Isherwood, Robert Penn Warren, Aldous Huxley, Thomas Mann, Frank Taylor (a film producer and former editor at Reynal and Hitchcock and, later, at McGraw-Hill). I wondered, given my budding friendship with Isherwood, if I had been judged objectively. He assured me I had been. My manuscript, he said, was so impressive, that the decision by the judges had been unanimous.

My first literary success! A virtual guarantee of imminent publication and praise.

For two years I wrote and rewrote that novel, certain that with my talent already recognized by such world-renowned writers and critics I was to be one of those new young novelists that goad publishers to war with each other to win us into their camps.

The week I left the Huntington Hartford Foundation I sent the novel to New York. I could see the review on the front page of the *New York Times* book section: "Finally! The Great American Novel, Written by an Unknown: Chester Aaron!"

Over the next five months *Axel* was rejected by ten publishers. I hid it in a trunk and haven't looked at it since. In fact, I've long ago lost the trunk.

Why hadn't I been convinced before then, certainly by then, that I was a failure as a writer, that I would never be published? By then I'd been trying for about eight years. I don't know why. Ask me why, after I was born and knew I would eventually die, I didn't stop breathing then?

For about a month after my stay at the Hartford Foundation I burned the frustration out of my heart on the Santa Monica beaches and then began a new project.

Or rather projects, plural. I traveled to San Francisco, where I met a woman who had a two-year-old son by a previous marriage. I could not depend on a writing career to support a family, so when a painter friend who was an X-ray technician assured me that such work offered fair pay and much free time, I began my training.

Hospital work introduced me to a new world. I became engrossed in the power to help people who were sick or in pain. I found the profession exciting, even rewarding. I came to admire nurses (who, of all people in the health care profession, give so much more than they receive) and, if not admire, at least respect physicians, who, without great fanfare, perform what might only be called miracles of healing.

After fifteen years in hospital work (during which I continued to write and continued to be rejected) I was fired for helping to organize X-ray technicians. (There were other reasons, reasons I now consider understandable. Not correct or just but logical. In attacking a wounded lion bare-handed the silly hunter should expect to be mauled.) Now, in 1990, I am not at all surprised that the health care profession had to be rid of me.

*

I was in my forties, trained only to be an X-ray technician. I discovered that I had been blackballed by the hospital and wandered from employment office to employment office searching for work. I was too old to do anything much but grocery checking at Safeway stores.

I had, by this time, published a short story and my first novel (*About Us*) and had just had my first young-adult novel accepted. Through good fortune and friendship and old-boy networks I was hired part-time at Saint Mary's College to teach creative writing. I moved to full time and then, at the age of forty-seven, received tenure. I like teaching so much that I often regret that I'd not gone into the field earlier. But if I had I'd not have engaged the people and animals that evolved into ideas and plots for those and subsequent novels.

During the years at Saint Mary's College, with summers and holidays off, I wrote more than ever. *An American Ghost, Hello to Bodega,* Spill, and *Catch Calico!* followed one after the other, every eighteen months or so. Including *About Us,* they all came out of my life, out of my own experiences.

*

After I joined the faculty at Saint Mary's College of California in 1970 and discovered that my twenty-and twenty-one-year-old students knew nothing about the concentration camps and even considered the Nazis comic lovable clowns, like the characters in the long-running television series *Hogan's Heroes,* I realized that

I no longer had a choice. I *had* to write about the Holocaust. It could not be an adult novel. It had to be a novel for grade-school and high-school students. I was by then, perhaps wrongly, convinced that it is almost impossible to teach, impress, move, a cool, arrogant, self-assured college senior. I had to reach these students before they went off to college, before they learned that it's cool to be cool.

I gave two years of research to the interviewing. I traveled to Israel to complete my research. On my last Friday evening in that country I, an admitted cynic regarding all religions, was guided by friends to the Wailing Wall and, despite my anger and my protests, my hands were pressed to the stones of the remaining wall of the ancient temple. At the touch of the stones I convinced myself I actually saw a spark. I had always rejected theories of racial memory but here I was, on my knees, weeping hysterically.

On my return to Berkeley I had a difficult time describing (not just describing but explaining) my reaction to my son, a self-styled agnostic. I no longer try to explain it to him or myself but accept it as a garden-variety religious experience, which I used to scorn and of which I still, even now, try to be skeptical.

Once I started writing, I wrote day and night for four months.

Gideon, which has been praised by several critics in the United States and England as a classic of its kind, sold less than 5,000 copies in America.

*

I had now written two "Jewish" novels: *About Us* and *Gideon.* Both received high praise, with the *Nation* judging *About Us* one of the ten best novels of the year (1967). They'd gained little attention (even from Jews), and neither had been recommended or required reading in grade-school and high-school classes. They might just as well have not been written.

About this time I read almost everything Philip Roth and Bernard Malamud and other "Jewish" writers had written. They began to bore me. They were missing something. One, they were all about middle-class Jews. Two, they were all placed in urban settings. By now I was living on a sheep ranch, working with animals. Where, I wondered, were the stories about my kind of Jew, the peasant living not in the city but in the country, the Jew who was not a stooped scholar with a Brooklyn accent but the Jewish worker, the impoverished Jew, the Jew who fought with his fists as well as his brain. No one, not even Jews, apparently, wanted to read about such characters. They did not fit the stereotype shaped by both Jew and Gentile.

I vowed to write no more "Jewish" stories or novels, not just because I couldn't write the stories readers wanted to buy or borrow, but because life in America was more than being a Jew or a Black or a Mexican. Life included that (if you happened to be a Jew or a Black or a Mexican), but it went beyond. Otherwise, I felt, such writers should write about Israel or Africa or Spain.

"Write about what you know," I preach to my students. "It's easier and safer." After they've made a lot of false starts and false endings they can go on to try writing about what they don't know, what they've not personally seen or smelled or heard or felt or tasted.

I've followed my own advice in all of my published stories and all but two of my published novels.

Write about what you know. Your own experiences.

The question asked most often, by young and old readers: "Where do your ideas come from?"

My first novel, *About Us,* was published by McGraw-Hill in 1967, shortly after I'd been appointed chief technician in the X-ray department at Alta Bates Hospital in Berkeley. I'd been writing for twenty years.

Actually I'd published a short story, my very first, three years earlier in a very small magazine. *Coastlines* sold about 300 copies. My payment was five free copies. I suspect those five came out of the three hundred.

That short story eventually became the novel *About Us,* the story of a Jewish family in a Pennsylvania mining town during World War II. Over the next twenty years I went on to publish eight more novels, all for young adults. I also published twelve short stories in literary reviews.

Out of my hospital work came, eventually, two short stories and an adult novel which has not gone beyond a second draft but which is in my projects-to-be-completed file. My young-adult novel *Catch Calico!* (E.P. Dutton, 1979) relies heavily on that work in hospitals.

The idea for *Catch Calico!,* like the ideas for almost all of my writing, came out of my own day-to-day activities.

The cat protagonist in the novel, Calico, has rabies. She has bitten an old man who, in the process of dying, introduces his grandson, Louis, to the truths of the death of his own son, Louis's father. Truths, Louis learns, can often be near-lies. Lies are too often essential for survival. A complex message for young adults conveyed through a complex structure. Perhaps the most complex I've attempted. For that reason *Catch Calico!* received mixed reviews, from high praise to low confusion. I believe the novel contains some of my best writing. It was a Junior Literary Guild selection.

Again the connection between three phases of my life: years of hospital work, matured concerns about political issues, my love of animals.

"Emma (Calico)" (Photograph courtesy of Chester Aaron.)

Calico, the character, was based on a cat that had been my companion for many years on a desolate sheep ranch in Sonoma County in northern California. She bit me once when I played too roughly with her. The next day my hand, red and swollen, looked like a lobster claw. Because Sonoma County was a rabies county, with evidence of the disease widespread among foxes and skunks and opossums, and because my cat always lived outside, and because the cat had run off and was not seen again (strange behavior indeed for that cat!), I had to undergo the extremely painful rabies treatment, consisting of daily shots of serum into the abdomen. The routine lasted fifteen days.

I woke up one night in the middle of the treatment period (when the reaction to the shots is most intense) and heard myself muttering, "There's a story here." There was. I began writing it the next morning.

My hospital work helped develop background events that served as a foundation for the novel and, as well, helped give a sense of reality to the picture I painted of a patient enduring the ravages of rabies. My cat was a feral cat, wild and, like all wild animals, unpredictable. But I bore her no ill will. As is usual in most cases where people who live or work with animals are wounded, the fault lies not with the animal but with the insensitive or presumptuous human.

That sense of serving sick and injured people developed during my hospital work led directly to a later decision to volunteer at the California Marine Mammal Center in Marin County, where devoted men and women, young and old, cared for sick and injured seals and sea lions. Working with these beasts, pup and adult, seemed even more satisfying than had my work with humans. Humans have access to all sorts of high-technology care, they can rely on love and sympathy from family and hospital staff. In most cases animals die alone in the water or in the fields, often in pain, receiving care and sympathy usually only if a human intervenes. Too often humans are the source of much of the illness and trauma that animals suffer. Like many others I try to repay my debts to Nature, which has been more than kind to me.

Serving people and aiding and loving animals were automatically incorporated into my attitudes toward literature, my ongoing first love. (A love—not a job, not a hobby, not a casual commitment. A love.) Five of the ten novels I've written include animals, with three of those five being about the intense interaction between animals and humans, an interaction during which each learns from the other.

Out of Sight, Out of Mind was a conscious attempt at science-fantasy. I wanted very much to write about something I could not have experienced. I wanted to play, to fantasize. I had just completed *Gideon* and was very aware of my promise to myself that I would not be labeled a Jewish writer.

It was actually great fun to conceive twins with special powers of extrasensory perception. It was, perhaps, more fun to write, though less satisfying in the end, than several of my novels. I did feel somewhat detached while writing it, perhaps because its characters and events had not steeped in my own life's juices.

"At the California Marine Mammal Center," 1985 (Photograph courtesy of Chester Aaron.)

Although the plot of *Lackawanna* was pure imagination the story did concern itself with the Great Depression (which I had experienced as a child). But I had never lived in New York. I had not traveled across the nation on trains (though, as mentioned, their sights and sounds had composed the resonating music of my childhood and youth in North Butler, Pennsylvania).

While completing research for *Out of Sight, Out of Mind,* I'd run across an article in a 1930 issue of the *New York Times* describing the hundreds of thousands of children, many as young as eight or nine, who had joined the army of hoboes who, in those days, rode the rails all across the nation, who begged and starved and often joined with fellow sufferers in railside jungles for companionship or simple sustenance. According to that article a group of young people who had trailed an adult hobo over the nation's network of rails for an assault he'd made upon them eventually found and killed him. They were apprehended, tried, convicted, sent to prison.

My story parallels that article. In the end, however, I do not punish my young characters. I never do. I can never send my children to prison. I gave my gang motivations and accomplishments much different from that gang in the news article. I also created Deirdre, a female character dearer to my heart than any young woman in any of my stories.

*

In 1970, three years after the publication of *About Us,* just before the publication of *Better than Laughter,* I'd left hospital work to accept the teaching position at Saint Mary's College of California, near Berkeley. The curriculum consisted of a one-month course, every January, requiring heavy concentration on a single topic, intense research, a respectable book list, and more writing than most regular courses required. The instructor could design any kind of course he or she wanted, as long as the work was academically legitimate.

A few years after *Catch Calico!* I started volunteering two mornings a week at the California Marine Mammal Center, helping rescue seals and sea lions that had been stranded on the beaches for reasons ranging from desertion (in the case of pups) to severe illness (from parasites, viral diseases, ingestion of pollutants) to trauma (attacks by sharks, shots by fishermen, collisions with boat or ship propellers).

At the Mammal Center my students and I worked in the open on the coast of the Pacific Ocean. Always, it seemed, in cold winds and heavy rains, luring, wrestling (often the same thing), the stricken animals— occasionally a 2,000-pound bull sea lion—into a carrying cage. We cared for the animals at the center's seaside hospital, feeding them (by hand or by stomach tubes), cleaning their cages (always on the alert for attacks). When the animals recovered (and about seventy percent did) we uncaged some of them at the shore. They dove back into the waves and out to sea. Occasionally we loaded the animals aboard a large seagoing boat and carried them into the ocean so they could find large herds of their own species. Such releases were always excuses for celebrations. When the released animals left the open cage, scuttled across the deck, and leaped into the water we sent them on their way with cheers and toasts from bottles of soda pop.

Twenty students had signed up for the January term. It was, they agreed, a major experience in their lives.

The following January term twenty different students participated in a different course. This time we rescued birds and small mammals, treating them, saving them if we could, and releasing them. We served in this course at the Bird Rescue Center in San Rafael, California. Over the month I observed a young woman who, for her entire life, had feared and hated birds. She joined our group at the recommendation of a psychologist. The director of the Rescue Center gave her personal responsibility for the care of a bald eagle that had been shot by an archer. Almost dead from shock and starvation and dehydration when it was found, the great bird, thanks to the young woman's dedication for one month, worked its way back to health. It is fat and sassy but will never fly again. It is a permanent resident at the center.

The young woman, when it came time to leave the Bird Rescue Center, required a few minutes alone with her bird. Today, in her campus suite, permitted freedom of the entire quarters: two budgies, which perch on the student's shoulder and take food from her mouth. It is difficult to perceive sometimes who feeds whom.

A writer wastes nothing. I have written a story about Samantha and her eagle.

Waste nothing.

How could I not write novels about my childhood in that Pennsylvania coal town, about those two days at Dachau, about my hospital work, about my living near that Audubon Canyon ranch, the bird sanctuary, during the oil spill, about my rabies treatment (thanks to Calico), about my training Border collies to work with sheep after I had worked with the collies? I am still exploiting (in three coming novels) my fifteen years at the hospital, my two years at the Marine Mammal Center. Were I to live a hundred years I'd have enough memories, enough hopes, enough anger, enough love, to write another twenty novels. Not all of them for young adults.

Which brings me to an important point. What distinguishes a novel for adults from a novel for young adults? And why have I chosen to write for young people after having received recognition, and awards, as a writer for adults? Let me answer that question later in this autobiography. (An illustration of how to heighten curiosity and how to justify flashbacks if flashbacks must be used.) In a way, the answer to the question illustrates the relation, or, again, the connection, between my childhood dreams and experiences and my life today.

*

I had been an avid reader before my brother had sent me Jack London's *White Fang*. Thanks to all my brothers, even those not considered intellectuals, and to my sister, Stella, gifts had always been books. And not just fiction. I knew, early on, the pleasure of seeing shelves filled with my own personal collection of books. Occasionally, when I was not outside playing or when I simply had nothing to do, I would pull one of my books, or magazines, from the shelf and read an article or a story that had pleased me or piqued my curiosity weeks or months before. Most of London's works I reread three or four times. But there were others. Often books that had stirred long and quite heated discussions among my brothers and their friends would lie unattended on the kitchen table or in some corner of a room my sister, Stella, called "the parlor."

That was how, at the age of ten or eleven, I came to read Charles Dickens' *Tale of Two Cities* and Eric Remarque's *All Quiet on the Western Front* and Theodore Dreiser's *An American Tragedy*. When I received my first library card at the age of nine the first book I checked out of the library was *Miss Goody Two Shoes*. The graduation from that benign little "do-good" directive to *Wild West Weekly* magazine and the writings of Zane Grey and James Fenimore Cooper and Robert Louis Stevenson occurred after a few months, not years. It was a quick small step, not a slow or delayed leap, to Dickens and Remarque and Dreiser.

Being so devoted to reading, to gathering my own little span of books, did not mean I was a shy or introverted bookworm. I was as daring as any of the other kids when it came to ice skating across melting creeks, climbing birches and swinging like Tarzan one to the other, traveling a hundred yards without touching the ground. After demonstrating my abilities against the Catholic Youth Center's football team in Butler, Father Savage—"My God, Son, how did a boy who looks like you end up with the name of Erin?" "It's spelled *A-a-r-o-n*, Father." "Ah, of course!"—invited me to play for their team. "My Hebrew ruffian," he called me. When North Butler put together a team of boxers to compete against the center's team (our team coached by my brother Ray) I out-boxed and out-slugged a boy who still lives in Butler and who, now a man my age, is still a friend.

And so, despite my love of books, I was never considered odd. In fact, my grabbing at any excuse to read aloud to the other kids, or to talk about certain stories or characters that leaped from one of the books I was reading, gave me an added exotic quality which those

"Feeding a piece of herring to a baby harbor seal, teaching it how to eat" (Photograph courtesy of Chester Aaron.)

semiliterate toughs, who were already smoking, chewing tobacco, drinking beer, digging ditches, and even going down in the mines, secretly admired. Perhaps it was free entertainment, like a ticket to see the bearded lady at a visiting carnival. Whatever the motivation for their attention I enjoyed it. The attention grew to respect, and then virtually a required diversion—"Hey, Chester. Read something to us. Come on. You know, that story about those cowboys," or "That book about that sailor, the one had that ship, who read all the time, he was sort of crazy," or "You still have that book about that explorer who went to the North Pole, Chester? How about you bring it to the shack tonight?"

I began to bring stories I had written. The responses: awed discussions at their homes, prompt selection to the teams, whether the game was baseball or football or capture-the-flag, cookies from their kitchens, candy bars bought at my dad's store, extra weiners, even, once, a black-handled Barlow penknife found in the woods and, by unanimous vote (Meaning no more than three), offered to me as a gesture of goodwill, after, of course, several punches and scornful disdainful jokes about my hitting or my tackling or my silly-looking nose.

No professional critic has ever read my stories or novels and presented me with cookies or a candy bar. If now an editor were to replace that long-lost Barlow knife I would swear allegiance to that publisher forever.

What happened there in that shack in the woods or on the creek bank or on that store porch when the train whistles called across the valley? Something about that crew of listeners converting without the slightest resistance into an attentive audience so impressed me that the sense of its charm, of its importance, of its satisfaction, continued motivating me all through high school, through the army, through college, through the last book or story last week, through today.

*

Here now is that earlier promise to consider the writing of fiction for adults and young adults.

My attitude, my stories, my style, are the same in adult and young-adult fiction, except for one specific area. I use the same vocabulary, the same reliance on clear prose, the same insistence on direct narrative (with as little complexity as possible in the structure) that I learned from Jack London. The one area I permit myself to examine in adult stories, but not in stories for young adults, is sex. My feelings about sex are my own, private and personal, not to be shared with young readers. Let the young, boys and girls, find their own way through that treacherous minefield. They neither need nor deserve guidance from me.

None of those stories I read, or wrote, for the other kids in North Butler were complex. They were all simple stories, with characters either excessively evil or excessively good. The plots were clear and clean, with straight-ahead development not distracted by flashbacks or switches in time or perspectives through the eyes of more than a single character. I have come to require, for my own enjoyment, stories that do not rely on the writer's need to preen, to display his or her own sophistication. It is the role of simple, unpretentious prose to deliver interesting and complex characters acting out an exciting and satisfying drama that clarifies my world, or other worlds that could someday be mine.

How did it start, this involvement in writing for young people? In truth, it was accidental.

After many years of effort I published the novel *About Us*. That was 1967, remember. Through a dear friend at the University of California-Berkeley (Mae Durham Roger, a professor of children's literature) I met Margaret McElderry, then at Harcourt Brace Jovanovich, now at Atheneum. We talked about children's literature. We reminisced, trading our favorite tales. Had I ever written for children? No. Would I like to? Yes. Will you send the manuscript to me? Yes.

The manuscript I sent her a year later needed work, she said. I followed her advice, much of which was identical to my own now-established criteria: a story that pleased me would probably please others. The young boy in me, that young boy from North Butler, Pennsylvania, should perform again for his friends sitting in that shack in the woods.

Margaret McElderry accepted the rewritten manuscript. *Better than Laughter,* my first novel for young adults, was published in 1972. It received very good reviews, went into paperback, and was then published in England and, years later, in Germany. When Margaret McElderry moved to Atheneum I followed her. She and Atheneum published *Hello to Bodega* (1976) and *Spill* (1977).

After my divorce, in the sixties, I lived in Bodega, California, about sixty miles north of San Francisco, near the coast. Bodega is a quiet little town that is that proverbial spot-on-the-highway you can miss if you blink when you drive through it. But a sheep ranch at the edge of that town was my home for more than ten years. During the daily two-hour commute, four days a week, to and from Saint Mary's I had much time to think.

The Vietnam War was still claiming attention and lives. A veteran of World War II, and perhaps more to the left politically than many people, I protested that war. On a ranch near Bodega, a young Vietnam vet was trying to develop a commune that would be a rest-place for whatever renegade youth passed through the area. The war had turned this young man (not yet twenty) into an almost-militant pacifist.

"Observing a baby harbor seal in a wire pen" (Photograph courtesy of Chester Aaron.)

I visited him several times, heard his story, sympathized with him, and gave him what support I could. The community was not yet ready for him and his kind. As self-appointed judges and juries, the local ranch families settled terrible punishment on him and his ranch and his animals. He finally had to give in and give up. Defeated, he moved back to Iowa. I wrote *Hello to Bodega* and tried to tell young readers about the importance of our indulgence of different cultures, about mutual trust and fellowship. It was one of the first Vietnam novels for young people. A critic in the *New York Times* deplored the novel. "We're tired of hearing about that war." She has, I suspect, grown much more tired over the subsequent years.

Spill was inspired by another significant experience in my life. I had been living with my wife and son in Bolinas, California, in the late sixties and early seventies, not far from the Audubon Bird Sanctuary. In that sanctuary, from January through the end of summer, common egrets and great blue herons build their nests high in the redwood trees on the steep hillsides rising from the seacoast. The white and blue birds so fill the trees that the dark foliage seems to have been struck by an ongoing snowstorm. During the oil spill of January 1971, I joined neighbors and friends to try to protect the Bolinas Lagoon, which would be the primary food source for all the herons and egrets about to arrive at the sanctuary.

Volunteers came from all over California to work in cold rain and knee-high muck to try to save the lagoon and the birds. Richmond Oil, the responsible company, and the local utility, Pacific Gas & Electric, sent equipment and workers to try to lessen the impending damage. I witnessed the hatred and resentment that existed between several hippies and hard-hat workers grow into friendship. The process of working together to save the birds, the sanctuary, the lagoon, had broken old visions, had, in many cases, created new ones. That, indeed, satisfied all my needs, as a human, as a father, as a teacher, and, certainly, as a writer.

*

And so something interesting had happened, was happening, to me on my way to becoming a writer of novels for young adults.

When I was invited to classes to discuss *Better than Laughter,* I discovered an audience of readers who not merely expressed their enthusiasm for my own work but expressed as well that voracious hunger for literature (stories) that adds depth and color to their world. Often, required to explain why I created this or that character, or how I'd thought up this or that event, I found myself defining, honing, my own opinions about storytelling, about building tension, about developing character, about creating mood.

Storytelling. Telling a story.

"My current home in Occidental, Sonoma County, California" (Photograph courtesy of Chester Aaron.)

That, for me, is the definition of literature, whether we're talking about the Bible or *The Odyssey* or Ernest Hemingway's *For Whom the Bell Tolls* or the latest best-selling prize-winning novel by Saul Bellow or Joyce Carol Oates.

After *Better than Laughter* came a second novel for young adults, and a third and fourth. The year 1991 will see the publication of the ninth and the tenth. With each new book there were more and more invitations to meet young readers. The responses were not very different from those first responses to *Better than Laughter*. I began to look forward to meeting with young people to discuss literature in general and my books in particular.

There came back to me, as I wrote, all those joys associated with my boyhood. Those early secret sessions when I read the books recommended by a teacher or a librarian and the break from that controlled process to the unrestricted attention to books my brothers were reading. I felt so adult, I remember, and, at the same time, so young. I discovered again, meeting with young readers, that they admit to an unrestrained thrill, they do not censor or sublimate, they yield to the writer,

they willingly suspend disbelief and accept what the writer offers them. If the writer stumbles, or deceives, or concocts lies to describe truths, the young readers will quietly but surely turn away, put the book down, shrug off the writer. Adults are more indulgent, less demanding, quicker to be swayed by fashion and hype, too jaded to permit themselves to be absorbed by simplicity, too adult (and therefore, they think, too sophisticated) to hide beneath the covers at midnight with a flashlight illuminating a silly thing called a *book*.

*

After the relative success of *Better than Laughter* came 1973's *An American Ghost*. It has been published in England and is about to be published in France.

The source of the idea for *An American Ghost?* My own life. One day at the sheep ranch I saw, at the edge of a pond, what I at first thought to be one of the many cats inhabiting the fields and forests. I put my binoculars on it. It was a cougar. It visited and I saw it two more times. I took a deep breath and began to tie ideas together.

An American Ghost is about a boy alone in his frontier home during a storm. After the house is swept by flood-waters off of its foundation and into the Mississippi River, Albie discovers another tenant in the house. A cougar, or mountain lion, that had obviously been in the tree the house had rammed the night before on its way down the river toward the gulf. Albie survives by guile, by intelligence, by courage. He is in a very real sense betrayed by adults at the end of the novel. But the form of the betrayal is an accepted pattern in pioneer America.

Perhaps the cougar in *An American Ghost* can be seen simply as a larger cat than the feline protagonist in *Catch Calico!* The novel, however, required a different story, involving different types of characters in a different historical period. *Duchess,* a story about a boy and his Border collie, is another animal story but, again, dogs offer different opportunities for the writer than do cats, big or little. *Marian,* my current novel-in-progress, relies on my experiences with seals and sea lions. It is also an animal story. Do stories about seals or sea lions, or about dolphins or whales, mine the same emotional terrain as do stories about people and their cats and dogs? I'll soon know.

*

I was sixty-seven years old this year. I am in good health, still teach at Saint Mary's College, and now live in a solar home on a small fruit ranch in Occidental, California. When I'm not traveling I spend weekends and holidays and summers here, planting trees, pruning, building irrigation systems, picking fruit, and feeding birds, wandering deer, several cats. I tell myself that I need a few sheep to keep down the grass in the fields. If I get sheep that will be an excuse to have at least two Border collies.

I am less than twenty miles from Bodega, the birthplace of *Hello to Bodega* and *Duchess.* I have built a large old-fashioned grape arbor. This summer I sat under the arbor one evening observing five deer—a buck, two does, two still-spotted fawns—and I thought of that child in that shack in the Pennsylvania coal country. I swallowed the lump that rose to my throat. Oh how my mother and father—immigrants from Europe, travelers, sufferers, who'd died unfulfilled—oh how they would love it here. They would read my books, help me build and plant, eat our fruit. My mother, who could not stand the sight of a wasted crumb, would be awake day and night, making applesauce, canning peaches and pears and apples, baking pies. "America," they both would say, "a golden place, a place of milk and honey."

Chester Aaron contributed the following update to his autobiographical essay in 2009:

My essay in the *Something about the Author Autobiography Series* published in 1991 ended with the words "milk and honey." This update essay should begin with the word "garlic."

Garlic—the herb and the word itself—has changed not only my physical and literary worlds, but also the quality and after-effects of the tears and cheers those physical and literary worlds have produced.

Between the publication of my first novel, *About Us,* and my eleventh novel, *Alex, Who Won His War*, not one single phrase in one published short story or novel contained the word *garlic.* Then, starting in the early eighties and continuing for the next several years, almost everything I published (or mentioned in interviews on NPR and PBS) was born of my then-current obsession with *Allium sativum.* Garlic.

I should not have been surprised.

After all, hadn't I worked in the garden as a child, alongside my Russian father and my Polish mother, when they planted and harvested their garlic? Didn't I and any of my six siblings who complained about an earache or a toothache have that ear or tooth stuffed with peeled and mashed raw garlic cloves? Didn't we always—whenever any one of us sustained cuts or bruises—submit to hourly swabbing with an ointment of raw garlic cloves pressed into olive oil?

And our food, whether cooked by my mother or my father, always contained garlic. My two favorite dishes (which I still, occasionally, serve to friends willing to risk their marriages): *chalupka* (my Polish mother's stuffed cabbage) and *chkmeruli* (my Russian father's garlic fried chicken).

Abutting and abetting these memories: a still-vivid memory of World War II experiences in Germany. We American troops had penicillin; the Russian soldiers did not. How many times (five? ten?) did I see a wounded

Chester Aaron, 1990 (Photograph courtesy of Chester Aaron.)

Russian soldier pull a garlic clove from his pocket, peel it and rub it—raw—on his wounds? Their recovery rate? Equal to ours and costing far less.

In the late seventies and early eighties I was living on that Bodega, California, sheep ranch that had already provoked and nourished the writing and publication of *An American Ghost* and *Hello to Bodega* and *Spill* and *Catch Calico!* and, as an aftermath, *Duchess.*

I must point out here that though life on that ranch did not provoke the writing and publication of *Gideon* or *Out of Sight, Out of Mind* or *Lackawanna* or *Alex, Who Won His War* it certainly did ease the conception and nourishment of their births.

From my very first year on that ranch (1972), the owner (Louis Albini) and I grew the ordinary garlic available at every supermarket in every city in the United States: the garlic grown in Gilroy, California. Then, one day in the late seventies, a day that would prove to be a life-changer, a neighboring rancher drove his battered pick-up onto Louis Albini's ranch. He offered me a handful of what I thought were small red beets. "Is not bitts," the old rancher said. "Is *chesnok*. Red Toch *chesnok*, Village Tochliavri, Republic Georgia." In Russian (which I had spoken as a child), *chesnok* means *garlic.* When I managed to communicate the fact that my fa-

ther had been born in that village called Tochliavri, the rancher gave me every red-skinned bulb in his hands.

Over the next several days I ate about twenty cloves, raw. I swear to every garlic god that still exists, the taste that followed every clove I chewed returned to me my mother's and father's faces, my mother's and father's voices. How could I not plant cloves of that Red Toch *chesnok* next to, but separate from, the cloves of that white *chesnok* from Gilroy?

I planted the Red Toch garlic in October. Forty cloves. In June I harvested thirty-three huge bulbs, four of which I traded for four bulbs of a garlic another rancher was growing, a garlic that a neighbor called *Hungarian White.* Source? His brother who, traveling in Hungary, had bought the garlic at a village market. The next harvest gave me three varieties of garlic (the Gilroy, the Red Toch, the Hungarian White), each of the three strains different in size and shape and skin color, in size and shape of cloves and bulbs, and in number of cloves to the bulb. And different in taste (a word the definition of which is guaranteed to vary from taster to taster of whatever is being tasted).

Over the next few years (the eighties into the nineties), after I moved to my own farm and traveled to various so-called "Food Events," I met other garlic-farmers (from other states, other countries) growing other vari-

The author, working with his garlic, 1987 (Photograph courtesy of Chester Aaron.)

The author, surrounded by garlic bulbs, 1989 (Photograph courtesy of Chester Aaron.)

eties of garlic. I traded and planted and harvested more varieties of bulbs, and continued trading and planting. One example: a friend (Professor Robin Miller, Brandeis University, just returned from Europe) gave me four bulbs she had collected in a market in, of all places, Transylvania. As of the writing of this essay, my Transylvanian garlic (bulbs having doubled in size, with much larger cloves than the original offered) has protected me and my home from every single vampire that has dared to threaten the neighborhood. The taste, for me: very hot, immediately, with a heat that fades fast, leaving a mild garlic taste that lingers and slowly disappears. I am not talking about the effect on my breath or my body. No one has dared inform me.

The more I traveled, the more markets I visited, the more growers I met, the more I learned about growing garlic, eating garlic, exploiting the health benefits of garlic. (If you have doubts here, please Google "David Mirelman" to see what I mean by *health benefits*.) David (a friend I met at one of the Garlic-is-Life Festivals in Tulsa, Oklahoma) occupies the Besen-Brender chair of Microbiology and Parasitology at the Weizman Institute of Science, Rehevot, Israel.

As of this fall (though I long ago, almost seven years ago, stopped writing a word about my garlic life), I harvested over sixty varieties of garlic from over thirty countries. Almost one and a half tons of garlic. *Har-*

vested means digging in the field, mowing in the field, planting in the field, sweating in the field, enduring the mud in the field, fighting gophers and wild turkeys and wasps in the field. To be able to continue this at the age of eighty-six, I was compelled to double my former quota of raw garlic clove consumption (now eight to ten a day).

It was in the late eighties, after I moved onto my own little farm in this beautiful village of Occidental where I now live (about sixty miles north of San Francisco), that God and a man named Phil Wood (president of Ten Speed Press, Berkeley) led me to the literary exploitation of my exotic obsession. Phil Wood and Ten Speed Press published my memoir *Garlic Is Life* (1996), with beautiful photographs by Suzanne Kaspar, and followed that book in 1997 with *The Great Garlic Book* (photos by Kaspar again). They also published the "Great Garlic Poster," containing Kaspar's stunning photos of about forty of my collected garlic varieties. Those two books and the poster have sold all over the world for almost twelve years. Though *Garlic Is Life* and the poster are now out of print, publication of *The Great Garlic Book* continues. (Ten Speed Press, as of mid-2009, is now a member of Random House Publishers.)

My meteoric and transient fame as a garlic guru took me and my books (not just the garlic books, incidentally) all over the country, to lectures and tastings and garlic festivals. In Tulsa, Oklahoma, a local farmer named Darrell Merrell—motivated by his love for my memoir, *Garlic Is Life*—started an annual presentation of The Garlic-Is-Life Festival. Each of the five years Darrell offered that festival (on the Tulsa campus of the University of Oklahoma), I was the honored guest-lecturer. I met garlic lovers and garlic growers from all over the world at those festivals. But Darrell, who had invested much of his own finances, finally had to call it quits. I continue friendships with many of those garlic lovers I met in that magnificent city and state.

Thanks to tough but tender-hearted Darrell, I met Doug Urig and his wife, Linda, at the first Garlic-Is-Life Festival. The Urigs lived in Collins, Ohio. We became close friends within minutes of meeting and remained close friends until Doug's death three years ago. Over two years Doug's *Mostly Garlic* magazine published several stories born of my new and somewhat bizarre obsession with collecting and planting and harvesting the different varieties of garlic. He went on to publish a collection of those stories (*Garlic Kisses*), which was republished in 2008 in a new format (with a foreword by the Tuscan Chef Marcella Ansaldo) by Zumaya Publications.

Doug died three years ago, Darrell died a year ago. I think of them, always with much love, almost daily. Our conversations and sentiments went far beyond the single topic of garlic. That they both honored my writing even more than my garlic would have pleased my mother and father, peasants though they were.

Having fully exploited my garlic life for literary benefit, I returned, in the late nineties, to the world of fiction. I should say I hoped to return, tried to return. In some cases: failed to return.

The world of publishing, I quickly and dramatically discovered, had changed. So, of course, had I.

Much older now, I wanted to concentrate on adult fiction as well as adult nonfiction (especially two memoirs). I was certain that my previous publication of that one adult novel and those eight young-adult novels and various short stories could only facilitate my return to New York's literary world.

But every manuscript I submitted to publishers in New York was either rejected and trashed or returned unread.

I credited this not to any diminishment of talent or skill or artistry in me, but to the fact that I was no longer relying on high-level literary agents to get me into the offices of editors. Impressed with my own successes at representing myself with Ten Speed Press, I intended to continue representing myself and saving that fifteen or twenty percent that every agent subtracts from monies earned.

Swallowing my false pride, I decided to rely on an agent again to maneuver the publishing bunkers. I composed a curriculum vitae (five pages, with citations of the twelve books published and the honors won in the U.S. and abroad by the books and the author). Confident that my past successes would ease the way, I sent copies of that CV to thirty agents in New York and Los Angeles, confident that ten or fifteen of those agents would leap to represent an author with such a record.

I received one response.

Written in longhand across the first page of the CV I had sent her: "Thanks, but no, thanks."

I called that agent at her New York office. She replied, "Oh yes, Chester Aaron. Let's face it. How old are you now, Mister Aaron?" I said I was seventy-six (this was ten years ago, remember). "Why," she said, "should I waste my time and money on you?"

After publishing a letter including these details in *Poets & Writers* magazine, I received about fifty calls, e-mails, and letters (most of them from women) describing similar histories of earlier successes and current scorn from agents and editors based on their age and the improbability of their being available to publish subsequent books over the next two decades.

Rescue from self-destruction, for me, came now from an old friend and two new friends.

Chester Aaron, 1995 (Photograph courtesy of Chester Aaron.)

In the late nineties, Thomas Farber, that old friend (and an author of many books), introduced me to Don Ellis, owner of Creative Arts Book Company in Berkeley. Creative Arts published my novel about a Jew who tries to stop the over-radiation of African-American patients in U.S. hospitals (*Black and Blue Jew*). Unfortunately, the company went into bankruptcy before the book could be distributed.

During the period that Creative Arts was editing and preparing *Black and Blue Jew,* I had submitted a manuscript to a new publishing house (Brown Barn Books, in Weston, Connecticut) that had publicized its interest in new and innovative young-adult fiction. Nancy Hammerslough (a spirited editor intent on challenging tradition), published that novel—*Home to the Sea*—in 2004. This novel had been born of an experience many years before, in the sixties, when I had X-rayed a just-delivered fetus that exhibited symptoms of syndactyly (webbing between fingers and toes).

Tom Farber, by this time, had created his own publishing house: El Leon Literary Arts in Berkeley. Tom and his staff at El Leon published my collection of stories *Symptoms of Terminal Passion*. I have never worked with a more dedicated group (Farber, his editor Kit Duane, and his designer Andrea Young). *Symptoms of Terminal Passion* included new and previously published stories, and all three were published again, two years later, in *The Manoa Journal* (University of Hawai'i). The theme of this issue of *The Manoa Journal:* "War and Its Memories." Included: writers from around the world.

El Leon's designer, Andrea Young, had been visiting my farm for several years, in different seasons. She always had her cameras, still and video. Out of those years of recorded words and images, Andrea created a thirty-minute documentary about my life (title: *CLOVE*). The documentary won first prize at the 2008 Berkeley Film Festival.

Enter Elizabeth Burton, the hardest-working editor I have ever had and the most savvy and risk-taking publisher. Elizabeth and Zumaya Publications introduced me to so-called "e-books," so-called "P.O.D. books."

Zumaya Publications (with the expertise of Elizabeth Burton) has published four of my books and, in about two days from now (this, as I write, is the first week of September, 2009), will be publishing the fifth. Already published: an adult novel (*Whispers*) and a young-adult novel (*Willa's Poppy*). Zumaya recently published the new edition of *Garlic Kisses* and a new edition of *Gideon*. Originally published in 1982 by J.B. Lippincott, *Gideon* is about the Holocaust, more specifically the Warsaw uprising. *Willa's Poppy,* the young-adult novel, is about a troubled sixteen year old and her bloodhound. They save each other from a serial killer. The novel due out now from Zumaya: *Murder by*

Chester Aaron with Serena Enger, 2009 (Photograph courtesy of Chester Aaron.)

Metaphor. This is my first attempt to write about such an esoteric subject as poetry, meaning, here, the consequences of writing poetry on both poet and audience.

What next, meaning what now?

Though I still farm and still grow garlic, I am no longer moved to write about those activities. I write now, can not help but write now, about my past. Certain elements of my past. My childhood again in that Pennsylvania coal-mine town of my very first novel, *About Us*; my army days (only remembered in short stories); my life in Hollywood after the war, when I mingled and interacted with Hollywood luminaries (native and foreign) who were militant in their opposition to the Un-American Activities Committee; and my discovery, when I was an X-ray technician, of the over-radiation of African-American patients in U.S. hospitals and my failed efforts to convince authorities, black or white, to be concerned to the degree I think that concern was/is deserved.

Now—for the last several months (ever since I gave a lecture at Saint Mary's College of California on Holocaust Memorial Day)—when I wake up in the middle of the night to go downstairs and pick up the sentences left incomplete on my computer, I find myself going to the folder that contains those stories born of the experiences of those two days at the concentration camp of Dachau.

For relief (often a refreshing, almost giddy relief at times), I go to the folder containing stories such as "Mike's Rosie" (published in *Highlights for Children,* 1989). Twenty years ago.

That story of 1,000 words went on to win various honors and still sporadically brings me a letter of thanks from the editor (Marileta Robinson) and the editor-in-chief emeritus (Kent L. Brown, Jr.), as well as from the occasional young reader.

Recent communication with Ms. Robinson literally inspired me to begin (one more folder on my Mac's desktop) a collection of what will be very short stories for such an audience as loved "Mike's Rosie."

The pleasure that comes to me as I return to the world of *Highlights* is as satisfying as an ice cream cone on a hot summer day. Make that two ice cream cones. In succession.

Imagine this eighty-six-year-old garlic farmer sitting on his deck in the late evening, gazing out over the meadow, watching the does and their lambs gobbling up the fallen apples and pears and peaches. He is sitting there and eating the second of two ice cream cones and wondering about a third.

*   *   *

ADAMS, Georgie 1945-

Personal

Born 1945; married; husband an artist.

Addresses

Home—Cornwall, England.

Career

Writer. Has worked as an editor of children's books.

Writings

Tubby Tin and the Runaway Rainbow, illustrated by Mike Shepherd, Thurman (London, England), 1982.

Tubby Tin and the No Such Things, illustrated by Mike Shepherd, Thurman (London, England), 1982.

Tubby Tin and the Munching Moon, illustrated by Mike Shepherd, Thurman (London, England), 1982.

Tubby Tin and the Footies, illustrated by Mike Shepherd, Thurman (London, England), 1982.

Mr. Bill and the Runaway Sausages, illustrated by Margaret Chamberlain, Blackie (London, England), 1983.

Mr. Bill and the Flying Fish, illustrated by Margaret Chamberlain, Blackie (London, England), 1985.

Great Uncle Prickles and the River Boat, illustrated by Andrew Aloof, Hamlyn (London, England), 1986.

Great Uncle Prickles and the Moon Balloon, illustrated by Andrew Aloof, Hamlyn (London, England), 1986.

Word Fun, illustrated by Gill Tomblin, Beehive (London, England), 1986.

Number Fun, illustrated by Gill Tomblin, Beehive (London, England), 1986.

The Cat Sat on the Rat, illustrated by Anni Axworthy, Barron's (New York, NY), 1989.

Fish, Fish, Fish, illustrated by Brigitte Willgoss, Simon & Schuster (London, England), 1992, Dial Books for Young Readers (New York, NY), 1993.

Two Little Penguins Called Flapjack and Waddle, illustrated by Jacques Duquennoy, Orion Books (London, England), 1994.

The Bible Storybook: Ten Tales from the Old and New Testaments, illustrated by Peter Utton, Orion Books (London, England), 1994, Dial Books for Young Readers (New York, NY), 1995.

Murdoch Mole's Big Idea, illustrated by Chris Fisher, Orion (London, England), 1995.

Three Bears on Holiday, illustrated by Selina Young, Orchard Books (London, England), 1995, Gingham Dog Press (Columbus, OH), 2003.

The Drummer, the Clown, and the Dancing Doll, illustrated by Katya Mikhailovsky, Orchard Books (London, England), 1995.

The Nursery Storybook, illustrated by Peter Utton, Orion (London, England), 1996.

Highway Builders, illustrated by Peter Gregory, Mathew Price (Sherborne, England), 1996, Annick Press (New York, NY), 2001.

Nanny Fox and the Three Little Pigs, illustrated by Selina Young, Orion Books (London, England), 1996.

Nanny Fox and the Christmas Surprise, illustrated by Selina Young, Doubleday Book for Young Readers (New York, NY), 1996.

The First Christmas, illustrated by Anna C. Leplar, Orion (London, England), 1996, Broadman & Holman (Nashville, TN), 1997.

A Year Full of Stories: 366 Stories and Poems, illustrated by Selina Young, Doubleday Book for Young Readers (New York, NY), 1997.

Pumpkin Pie and Puddles: Poems for Every Day, illustrated by Selina Young, Orion (London, England), 1997.

The Real Fairy Storybook, illustrated by Sally Gardner, Orion (London, England), 1998.

Noah's Ark, illustrated by Anna C. Leplar, Broadman & Holman (Nashville, TN), 1999.

The Good Shepherd Storybook, illustrated by Peter Utton, Broadman & Holman (Nashville, TN), 1999.

Dr. Dog and Nurse Kitty, illustrated by Selina Young, Dolphin (London, England), 2000.

Flapjack and Waddle and the Polar Bear, illustrated by Jacques Duquennoy, Orion (London, England), 2001.

The Amazing Bible Storybook, illustrated by Peter Utton, Orion (London, England), 2001.

The Three Little Witches Storybook, illustrated by Emily Bolam, Hyperion Books for Children (New York, NY), 2001.

A House for Zebra and Other Stories, illustrated by Atsuko Morozumi, Mathew Price (Sherborne, England), 2005.

The Three Little Pirates, illustrated by Emily Bolam, Orion (London, England), 2006.

The Three Little Princesses, illustrated by Emily Bolam, Orion London, England), 2007.

Animal Stories for Bedtime, illustrated by Atsuko Morozumi, Mathew Price (Denton, TX), 2009.

Sidelights

A British writer, Georgie Adams is the author of dozens of books for young readers. In *Fish, Fish, Fish* the author acquaints children to a variety of aquatic creatures, focusing on their physical attributes. According to a *Publishers Weekly* critic, Adams "effectively introduces opposite qualities . . . in ways preschoolers will grasp and remember." A mild-mannered carnivore saves a trio of chicks from his hungry relatives in *Nanny Fox and the Christmas Surprise,* and here the author's "comic scenario and ever-sweet protagonist" elicited praise from a contributor in *Publishers Weekly.*

Adams presents the stories of Noah's Ark and David and Goliath, among others, in *The Bible Storybook: Ten Tales from the Old and New Testaments.* Writing in *Booklist,* Carolyn Phelan complimented the author's "fresh, appealing interpretation" of the well-known narratives. Adams teamed with illustrator Emily Bolam for *The Three Little Witches Storybook,* which relates the fantastic and often humorous adventures of Zara, Ziggy, and Zoe, the young residents of Cauldron Cottage. "Children will enjoy both the capsule adventures and the engaging art," remarked Connie Fletcher in *Booklist.* In *Animal Stories for Bedtime* Adams offers a host of tales for emerging readers, including a zebra's search for the perfect house and a puppy's encounter with a hungry fox. "All of the stories resolve in a peaceful solution for the characters," according to a contributor appraising *Animal Stories for Bedtime* for *Kirkus Reviews.*

Biographical and Critical Sources

PERIODICALS

Booklist, February 1, 1995, Carolyn Phelan, review of *The Bible Storybook: Ten Tales from the Old and New Testaments,* p. 1005; September 1, 2002, Connie Fletcher, review of *The Three Little Witches Storybook,* p. 138.

Globe & Mail (Toronto, Ontario, Canada), December 8, 2001, Susan Perren, review of *Highway Builders.*

Kirkus Reviews, April 1, 2009, review of *Animal Stories for Bedtime.*

Publishers Weekly, March 22, 1993, review of *Fish, Fish, Fish,* p. 78; September 30, 1996, review of *Nanny Fox and the Christmas Surprise,* p. 91.

School Library Journal, December, 2002, Maryann H. Owen, review of *The Three Little Witches Storybook,* p. 84; May, 2009, Maryann H. Owen, review of *Animal Stories for Bedtime,* p. 69.

Scotsman (Edinburgh, Scotland), June 30, 2001, Adéle Geras, review of *Flapjack and Waddle and the Polar Bear,* p. 16.*

*   *   *

ALLARD, Harry 1928-
(Harry G. Allard)

Personal

Born January 27, 1928, in Evanston, IL; son of Harry Grover (in sales) and Gladys Allard. *Education:* Northwestern University, B.S. (art), 1949; Middlebury College, M.A. (French), 1960; Yale University, Ph.D. (French literature), 1972. *Religion:* Russian Orthodox. *Hobbies and other interests:* Drawing, reading, listening to classical music, and learning languages.

Addresses

Home—Apdo. Postal 454, 68000 Oaxaca, Mexico.

Career

Educator and author and translator of children's books. Wabash College, Crawfordsville, IN, instructor in French, 1959-60; Trinity University, San Antonio, TX, instructor in French, 1962-65; associated with Yale University, New Haven, CT, 1965-68; Salem State College, Salem, MA, 1968-87, assistant professor, then associate professor of French; retired. Taught English at Berlitz School in Paris; worked as legal translator in Paris. *Military service:* U.S. Army Signal Corps, 1951-52; served in Korea.

Awards, Honors

New York Times Best Illustrated Children's Books selection, 1975, for *The Tutti-Frutti Case;* Children's Book Showcase selection, 1975, and *School Library Journal* Best of the Best, 1966-1978 selection, 1979, both for *The Stupids Step Out;* Edgar Allan Poe Award runner up, and Outstanding Books selection, *New York Times,* both 1977, Georgia Children's Book Award, University of Georgia, 1980, and California Young Readers Medal and Buckeye Honor designation, both 1982, all for *Miss Nelson Is Missing!;* Academy Award nomination for best animated film, Academy of Motion Picture Arts and Sciences, 1978, for movie adaptation of *It's So Nice to Have a Wolf around the House;* International Reading Association Children's Choice designation, 1979, for *The Stupids Have a Ball,* and 1982, for both *There's a Party at Mona's Tonight* and *The Stupids Die;* Best Books designation, *School Library Journal,* 1981, First Kentucky Bluegrass Award runner up, 1983, and Arizona Book Award, 1985, all for *The Stupids Die;* Parents' Choice award for literature, 1982, Golden Sower Award, 1984, and Colorado Children's Book Award, 1985, all for *Miss Nelson Is Back;* Golden Sower Award, 1987, for *Miss Nelson Has a Field Day.*

Writings

FOR CHILDREN

The Stupids Step Out, illustrated by James Marshall, Houghton (Boston, MA), 1974.

The Tutti-Frutti Case: Starring the Four Doctors of Goodge, illustrated by James Marshall, Prentice-Hall (Englewood Cliffs, NJ), 1975.

Crash Helmet, illustrated by Jean-Claude Suares, Prentice-Hall (Englewood Cliffs, NJ), 1977.

It's So Nice to Have a Wolf around the House, illustrated by James Marshall, Doubleday (New York, NY), 1977.

Miss Nelson Is Missing!, illustrated by James Marshall, Houghton (Boston, MA), 1977.

The Stupids Have a Ball, illustrated by James Marshall, Houghton (Boston, MA), 1978.

Bumps in the Night, illustrated by James Marshall, Doubleday (New York, NY), 1979, reprinted, Delacorte Press (New York, NY), 1996.

I Will Not Go to Market Today, illustrated by James Marshall, Dial (New York, NY), 1979.

The Stupids Die, illustrated by James Marshall, Houghton (Boston, MA), 1981.

There's a Party at Mona's Tonight, illustrated by James Marshall, Doubleday (New York, NY), 1981.

Miss Nelson Is Back, illustrated by James Marshall, Houghton (Boston, MA), 1982.

Miss Nelson Has a Field Day, illustrated by James Marshall, Houghton (Boston, MA), 1985.

The Stupids Take Off, illustrated by James Marshall, Houghton (Boston, MA), 1989.

The Cactus Flower Bakery, illustrated by Ned Delaney, HarperCollins (New York, NY), 1991.

The Hummingbird's Day, illustrated by Betsy Lewin, Houghton (Boston, MA), 1991.

Starlight Goes to Town, illustrated by George Booth, Farrar, Straus & Giroux (New York, NY), 2008.

TRANSLATOR

(From the German) Luis Murschetz, *A Hamster's Journey,* Prentice-Hall, 1976.

(From the German; and adapter) *May I Stay?* (fairy tale), illustrated by F.A. Fitzgerald, Prentice-Hall, 1978.

(From the German) Friedrich Karl Waechter, *Three Is Company,* illustrated by Waechter, Doubleday (New York, NY), 1980.

OTHER

(Under name Harry G. Allard) *Anna de Noailles, Nun of Passion: A Study of the Novels of Anna de Noailles,* [New Haven, CT], 1973.

Adaptations

It's So Nice to Have a Wolf around the House was adapted as a full-length television cartoon feature, Learning Corporation of America, 1978. *Miss Nelson Is Missing* was adapted for film, Learning Corporation of America, 1979. *Miss Nelson Is Back* was featured on *Reading Rainbow,* Public Broadcasting Service, 1983. *The Stupids* was adapted as a feature-length film, New Line Cinema, 1996, and adapted as the novel *The Stupids* by Clay Griffith, Bantam, 1996. *Miss Nelson Has a Field Day* and *Miss Nelson Is Back* were adapted as an animated film, Weston Woods, 1999.

Sidelights

Beginning in the 1970s, Harry Allard made a cottage industry of what Betsy Hearne typified in the *Bulletin of the Center for Children's Books* as "the folklore of noodleheads and fools' tales." Collaborating with illustrator James Marshall, he transferred such silly antics into a quartet of books illustrating the idiotic misadventures of a family led by Stanley Q. Stupid that has delighted "all those who appreciate the deep belly laugh that bypasses all logical explanation," according to a *Publishers Weekly* contributor. Equally popular have been the "Miss Nelson" books, the result of another Allard-Marshall collaboration featuring a schoolteacher whose mischievous students turn the classroom topsy turvy. In series opener *Miss Nelson Is Missing!,* beleaguered teacher attempts to regain control by disguising herself as strict substitute teacher Viola Swamp, and her battle-axe alter ego also appears in further adventures in the series, much to the delight of Allard's readers. In addition to winning praise from critics and readers alike, several Allard-Marshall stories have been adapted as feature films. The two men continued to work together until Marshall's death in 1992.

Allard was born in Evanston, Illinois, on January 27, 1928, a birthday he shares with another hugely popular children's author: Charles Ludwidge Dodgson, who wrote under the pen name Lewis Carroll. "I now look upon sharing the birthday with the creator of *Alice in Wonderland* as a good omen," Allard once told *SATA.*

Allard attended high school in Chicago, where his favorite subject was Latin, and he went on to major in art at Northwestern University, graduating in 1949. "A

Harry Allard teams up with artist James Marshall to introduce a popular character in **Miss Nelson Is Missing.** (Illustration ©1977 by James Marshall. All rights reserved. Reprinted by permission of Houghton Mifflin Harcourt Publishing Company.)

limbo of misdirected efforts followed," he later noted, "from which I was at last saved by the Korean War." Allard served in the Signal Corps in Japan and Korea, and then returned to Chicago for a time, until he grew restless. "To shake the dust of Chicago from my heels forever, I went to live in Paris for four years," he explained, describing the period in his life when he taught English and worked as a legal translator. "When I came back to the U.S.A., the only thing I could do was teach French, so I taught French. . . . To make it official I got an M.A. from Middlebury College in 1960 and a Ph.D. in French from Yale in 1973."

Allard taught at several colleges until 1968, when he found a permanent home at Salem State College in Massachusetts. Settling in nearby Charlestown, he met Marshall, an author-illustrator who was already well known for his "George and Martha" picture books. After Allard gave Marshall the text of *The Stupids Step Out,* Marshall quickly placed it at Houghton Mifflin, beginning what would prove to be a long and rewarding collaboration.

The Stupids Step Out describes a typical day in the life of Stanley Q. Stupid, wife Mrs. Stanley Stupid, children Buster and Petunia, and family dog Kitty. The Stupids get it all wrong: They wear cats on their heads instead of hats, and socks on their ears; they sleep with their feet on the pillow and revel in taking waterless baths. When they go to visit Grandpa, he asks who they are; meanwhile, Grandma stays in her closet. Finally, they go out for mashed potato sundaes before heading home. A *Publishers Weekly* critic, reviewing *The Stupids Step Out,* commented that "since most children get a charge (and an often-needed sense of superiority) from the antics of stupid folk, this dizzy book should be popular." The reviewer was prophetic: *The Stupids Step Out* has been a perennial hit among young readers.

In an interview, Allard maintained that his "Stupids" books are popular "because children are always under the thumb of somebody—adults, whether they are parents or priests or nuns or whatever—and here the children can make fun of adults and feel superior to them and know more than they do. Also because the Stupids are such a wild family . . . there's something anarchistic about them. And . . . so many books seem to be socially manipulative. They're either telling children to love children of other races or respect old people or to understand blind people and dying people. There are too many messages. With the Stupids there is no message at all. They just seem to do what they want to do."

Allard and Marshall continued their no-message fun with *The Stupids Have a Ball, The Stupids Die,* and *The Stupids Take Off.* In *The Stupids Have a Ball* the family throws a costume party to celebrate the fact that Buster and Petunia have flunked all their subjects at school. "The resulting preparations allow ample opportunity for the hearty slapstick that made *The Stupids Step Out* so popular," noted *Booklist* critic Denise M. Wilms, while

Bulletin of the Center for Children's Books contributor Zena Sutherland attempted to define the humor in the book: "It isn't just that the Stupids are stupid, but that they are so happy in their stupidity."

When their lights go off suddenly in *The Stupids Die,* everyone in the family assumes they are all dead. When the quick-witted (by comparison) dog and cat change a fuse and restore power, the Stupids believe they must have arrived in heaven. Then Grandfather stops by, and when he is welcomed to heaven he confuses it with Cleveland, Ohio. Sutherland noted of *The Stupids Die* that "the text is brisk and simple" and both text and artwork add "to the merry insanity" and "should appeal to all the fans of the confused Stupids." In *Horn Book* Ann A. Flowers concluded that the Stupids' "zany adventures . . . should elicit gleeful chuckles from young readers, who know that they themselves are not *that* stupid." In *Booklist* Wilms noted that the Stupids "are at their best—or worst, if you see it that way—in this ultrasilly string of one-liners."

The fourth "Stupids" book, *The Stupids Take Off,* carries the family on "an airborne tour of relatives as silly as they are," according to a *Kirkus Reviews* critic, the reviewer noting in particular the "genuinely ludicrous verbal and visual jokes." To avoid a visit from boring Uncle Carbuncle, the Stupids take flight, piloted by their cat Xylophone and accompanied by dog Kitty. They drop in—unannounced of course—on various relatives. They visit Little Patty who is celebrating her sixth birthday with eight candles on her cake because she cannot find six; they gather onto the narrow surface of Uncle Artichoke's new diving board, high over a green lawn without a spot of water to be seen; and they visit Farmer Joe whose pencil crop does not seem to be doing too well this year. A *Publishers Weekly* contributor wrote that "Allard and Marshall are more than ever in tune with their Stupid characters," while Julie Corsaro noted in *Booklist* that this "fourth book about the irresistible and irrepressible noodleheads is funny, very funny." In the *Bulletin of the Center for Children's Books,* Hearne concluded that *The Stupids Take Off* "is less a story than a series of gags, but they work."

Allard and Marshall also treated readers to stories dealing with kindly Miss Nelson and her adventures as a teacher at Horace B. Smedley School. *Miss Nelson Is Missing!* introduces the gentle teacher and the unruly pupils of Room 207, where chaos reigns. When her niceness prevents her from disciplining the children, Miss Nelson disguises herself as the drab Viola Swamp, a substitute from Hades who quickly gets the kids in tow. A her absence grows lengthy, the students begin to fear for Miss Nelson and report her disappearance to Detective McSmogg. The detective has no luck locating the missing teacher, but one day Miss Nelson returns to find Room 207 full of model students who are grateful to be rid of the witch-like Miss Swamp. Now McSmogg goes on the trail of the missing Miss Swamp, but this, as a *Publishers Weekly* critic pointed out, is "a case he will never solve." In *Kirkus Reviews* a critic called *Miss Nelson Is Missing!* "another slightly twisted and engaging Allard/Marshall collaboration," while *Horn Book* contributor Mary M. Burns dubbed it a "zany lesson in teacher-appreciation."

In *Miss Nelson Is Back* the kindly teacher is absent in order to have her tonsils out, and the students fear that the dreadful Miss Swamp will be the substitute once again. Relief sets in when Principal Blandsworth takes over the class, only to be followed by yawns at his effort to share his collection of ball point pens and color slides of goldfish. The kids now hatch a plot to fool the principal into believing Miss Nelson is back, disguising one of their number as the teacher, and Room 207 is in a happy uproar when . . . in walks the feared Miss Swamp. A *Kirkus Reviews* critic called *Miss Nelson Is Back* a "nifty performance, always a step or two ahead of the audience," and in *Horn Book* Flowers concluded that Marshall's "wonderfully expressive illustrations . . . and [Allard's] . . . zany story make a worthy successor to *Miss Nelson Is Missing!*"

In *Miss Nelson Has a Field Day* the kindhearted teacher sets alter ego Miss Swamp to work on the school's losing football team. The coach has quit in disgrace and now Coach Swamp sets about getting the team under control and in shape for serious competition. Readers also get a surprise when they see Miss Nelson in the classroom at the same time Coach Viola Swamp is ordering football players about on the field. Ultimately, school morale at is restored when the team wins the big game with a score of seventy-seven to three. Laura

Bacher, writing in *School Library Journal,* observed that "Allard and Marshall have combined talents once again in this crazy addition to the ever hilarious escapades . . . at the Horace B. Smedley School." A *Horn Book* reviewer concluded that "children of any age will relish the raucous carrying-on at what has to be the most gloriously awful school in the entire state of Texas," while a *Kirkus Reviews* critic summed things up nicely, calling *Miss Nelson Has a Field Day* an "A+" performance.

In addition to series fiction, Allard collaborated with Marshall on several stand-alone titles, among them *The Tutti-Frutti Case: Starring the Four Doctors of Goodge, It's So Nice to Have a Wolf around the House, I Will Not Go to Market Today, There's a Party at Mona's Tonight,* and *Bumps in the Night.* Like the "Miss Nelson" stories, *It's So Nice to Have a Wolf around the House* employs masquerade as wolf and professional bank robber Cuthbert Q. Devine quits his former life to take a position as housekeeper and companion to an old man and his three aging pets. In order to gain the confidence of his new employer, Cuthbert disguises himself in a hat and overcoat, pretending to be a dog. His true identity discovered, however, the wolf faints and has an attack of nerves. Ultimately, the old man decides to support the reformed bank robber despite his wolf-like appearance, and this "jolly, happy-ever-after ending fits just right with the prevailing nonsense," according to Wilms. Although the story contains a subtle moral—not to judge a book by its cover—*Bulletin of the Center for Children's Books* critic Sutherland predicted that *It's So Nice to Have a Wolf around the House* "is so flagrantly and engagingly silly . . . that few children will be likely to resent the message."

With *I Will Not Go to Market Today* Allard introduces a well-fed rooster named Fenimore B. Buttercrunch, whose attempts to replenish his dwindling jam supply are hindered by natural catastrophes. In *Booklist,* Wilms described this Allard-and-Marshall tale as "rife with comedic flings," while Laura Geringer wrote in *School Library Journal* that *I Will Not Go to Market Today* will provide a "good laugh for any child or adult who has ever decided to 'wait until tomorrow' to do something best done today."

In his picture-book work, Allard has worked with several other illustrators, both during Marshall's lifetime and in the years since. Joining illustrator Ned Delaney, he produced *The Cactus Flower Bakery,* the story of a snake named Sunny McFarland and an armadillo named Stewart B. Preston who open a bakery together. The book is an "offbeat fable . . . told with pleasingly dry wit, winningly extended in Delaney's cartoonlike but endearing illustrations," according to a *Kirkus Reviews* critic. A more-recent work, *Starlight Goes to Town,* features artwork by noted *New Yorker* cartoonist George Booth. Like *I Will Not Go to Market Today, Starlight Goes to Town* focuses on a farmyard fowl, but here a hen named Starlight has her wish for better things granted by a fairy godmother who looks suspiciously

The team of Allard and Marshall continue to entertain young readers with the picture book It's So Nice to Have a Wolf around the House.
(Illustration ©1977 by James Marshall. Used by permission of Dragonfly Books, an imprint of Random House Children's Books, a division of Random House, Inc.)

like a chicken. Starlight dreams of life away from the farm, and wishes are granted that involve big city lights, limousines, and a stylish prance up the fashion runway. However, when the fairy godmother takes a vacation and leaves a younger relative in charge, things go awry. When Starlight begins hatching eggs that contain odd objects—everything from egg beaters to pianos—she makes the best of things, however, and starts hosting regular (barn)yard sales. Booth's "fluid watercolors" and "straggly . . . lines" add humor to Allard's "zany tale," according to *School Library Journal* contributor Barbara Elleman, and a *Publishers Weekly* described the text as vintage Allard due to its "snarky dialogue, silly specificity and vocab gone mad."

In his writing for children, Allard lets ideas percolates for a time, and then does the initial writing "in a white heat," as he once explained to an interviewer. Revision is the key to making a good book, he added. "I keep doing it, doing it, doing it. And I think the polishing shows, because it's always obviously towards simplicity, to make the sentences as simple and almost transparent as possible. There's no way to show off in children's books. You know, you're not showing off your vocabulary. The only thing you can really work with is rhythm, as in the sense of the English Bible. The words are so simple, but very often the rhythm is mysterious and beautiful."

"I'm always writing something," Allard added. "I don't really believe in inspiration. I think you just do it, that's all. If you wait for inspiration you might wait forever."

Biographical and Critical Sources

BOOKS

Allard, Harry, interview in *Contemporary Authors,* Volume 113, Gale (Detroit, MI), 1985, pp. 20-23.

PERIODICALS

Booklist, September 1, 1977, Denise M. Wilms, review of *It's So Nice to Have a Wolf around the House,* p. 35; March 15, 1978, Denise M. Wilms, review of *The Stupids Have a Ball,* p. 1185; April 1, 1979, Denise M. Wilms, review of *I Will Not Go to Market Today,* pp. 1215-1216; March 15, 1981, Denise M. Wilms, review of *The Stupids Die,* p. 1025; October 1, 1989, Julie Corsaro, review of *The Stupids Take Off,* p. 277; September 15, 2008, Ilene Cooper, review of *Starlight Goes to Town,* p. 58.
Bulletin of the Center for Children's Books, September, 1977, Zena Sutherland, review of *It's So Nice to Have a Wolf around the House,* p. 2; October, 1978, Zena Sutherland, review of *The Stupids Have a Ball,* p. 21; June, 1981, Zena Sutherland, review of *The Stupids Die,* p. 186; October, 1989, Betsy Hearne, review of *The Stupids Take Off,* pp. 26-27.

Horn Book, June, 1977, Mary M. Burns, review of *Miss Nelson Is Missing!,* p. 296l; August, 1981, Ann A. Flowers, review of *The Stupids Die,* pp. 411-412; February, 1983, Ann A. Flowers, review of *Miss Nelson Is Back,* pp. 34-35; May-June, 1985, review of *Miss Nelson Has a Field Day,* pp. 297-298.
Kirkus Reviews, February 15, 1977, review of *Miss Nelson Is Missing!,* p. 159; September 15, 1982, review of *Miss Nelson Is Back,* p. 1055; May 15, 1985, review of *Miss Nelson Has a Field Day,* p. J24; November 1, 1989, review of *The Stupids Take Off,* p. 1600; March 1, 1991, review of *The Cactus Flower Bakery,* p. 326; August 1, 2008, review of *Starlight Goes to Town.*
Publishers Weekly, April 22, 1974, review of *The Stupids Step Out,* pp. 74-75; March 14, 1977, review of *Miss Nelson Is Missing!,* p. 95; August 20, 1982, review of *Miss Nelson Is Back,* p. 71; February 8, 1985, review of *Miss Nelson Has a Field Day,* p. 76; September 29, 1989, review of *The Stupids Take Off,* p. 67; March 29, 1991, review of *The Cactus Flower Bakery,* p. 92; August 11, 2008, review of *Starlight Goes to Town,* p. 46.
School Library Journal, March, 1979, Laura Geringer, review of *I Will Not Go to Market Today,* p. 119; August, 1985, Laura Bacher, review of *Miss Nelson Has a Field Day,* pp. 51-52; September, 2008, Barbara Elleman, review of *Starlight Goes to Town,* p. 136.

ONLINE

Macmillan Web site, http://us.macmillan.com/ (May 31, 2010), "Harry Allard."*

*   *   *

ALLARD, Harry G.
See ALLARD, Harry

*   *   *

AMORY, Jay
See LOVEGROVE, James

*   *   *

ANDERSON, Rebecca J.
See ANDERSON, R.J.

*   *   *

ANDERSON, R.J. 1970(?)-
(Rebecca J. Anderson)

Personal

Born c. 1970, in Uganda; immigrated to Canada; married; children: three sons. *Religion:* Evangelical Christian. *Hobbies and other interests:* Playing piano, singing, travel.

Addresses

Home—Stratford, Ontario, Canada. *Agent*—Adams Literary Agency, info@adamsliterary.com.

Career

Author. Presenter at conferences.

Member

Society of Children's Book Writers and Illustrators Canada.

Awards, Honors

Carnegie Medal nomination, 2009, for *Knife;* Honor Book designation, Canadian Library Association, 2010, for *Spell Hunter.*

Writings

"FAERY REBELS" MIDDLE-GRADE NOVEL SERIES

Knife, Orchard (London, England), 2008, published as *Spell Hunter,* HarperCollins (New York, NY), 2009.

Cover of R.J. Anderson's middle-grade fantasy Spellhunter, *featuring artwork by Melanie Delon.* (HarperColllins, 2009. Illustration ©2009 by Melanie Delon. Reproduced by permission.)

Rebel, Orchard (London, England), 2009, published as *Wayfarer,* HarperTeen (New York, NY), 2010.

Author's work has been translated into German and Romanian.

Adaptations

Knife was adapted as an audiobook by Oakhill Publishing, 2009.

Sidelights

Born in Uganda, fiction writer R.J. Anderson immigrated to Canada as a child and lived for a time in the United States before choosing Ontario as her permanent home. As a child she immersed herself in the rich vein of children's fantasy—books by E. Nesbit, C.S. Lewis, and J.R.R. Tolkien, continuing to follow the genre as an adult reader. Her middle-grade novels in the "Faery Rebels" series draw on this literary heritage, combining classic fantasy elements and research into British legend and lore with engaging characters designed to appeal to contemporary readers.

First published in the United Kingdom as *Knife, Spell Hunter* introduces the faery hunter Knife. A courageous creature, Knife lives in a great oak tree, the Oakenwyld, where she is part of a fragile race of tiny winged women who have lost their passion for life and magic and are slowly wasting away. Courage and compassion have not abandoned Knife, however, and she is determined to use her skills to save her people. Despite the command of the Faery Queen that faeries and humans shall never cross paths, Knife explores a human abode near the garden where the Oakenwyld stands. She realizes that humans may have the technology to find a cure, and when she is wounded by a crow while hunting Knife finds an ally in Paul, the wheelchair-bound son of the family. However, establishing a connection with the forbidden world of humans may threaten the faerie in another way, as readers soon discover in a novel that *Booklist* critic Frances Bradburn described as a "highly readable, sophisticated tale of romance and self-sacrifice." In *School Library Journal* Sue Giffard noted that Anderson enriches her "gripping and involving story" with her knowledge of numerous fairy tales and legends focusing on the interaction between mankind and sprite and producing central characters that "are vividly drawn." Calling *Spell Hunter* "a return to the old-fashioned warmth of traditional children's fiction," Amanda Craig added in her review for the London *Times* that Anderson's "magical story" melds fairy lore into "a particularly charming, well-drawn romantic thriller."

The people of the Oakenwyld are still threatened with extinction in *Wayfarer,* a "Faery Rebels" novel first published as *Rebel.* Here fourteen-year-old Linden is selected by the Faery Queen and given the last of the group's dwindling supply of magic. Tasked with the mission of finding other of the faery race, Linden reshapes herself to mix with humans and ultimately falls in with a young runaway, Timothy, who is on his way to London with the hope of becoming a musician. While Timothy is threatened due to his talent, Linden is hunted by the evil Faery Empress, and the travelers' exploits result in what Craig described as "an exciting tale, told with verve and skill."

"I'm always fascinated by questions of 'What if?,'" Anderson noted in an interview for the HarperCollins Web site. "It interests me to play around with possibilities and new ideas, and I'm also interested in the meaning behind those ideas. To me, fantasy and SF offer a chance to explore emotional, philosophical, and moral issues in a fresh and interesting way. You can talk about good and evil in a fantasy context, for instance, in a way that it's difficult to do believably in other genres. And besides, it's fun. I love seeing the ingenuity of other authors who invent new worlds and new magical systems for their stories building a really believable and consistent fantasy world is one of the purest expressions of creativity I know."

Biographical and Critical Sources

PERIODICALS

Booklist, July 1, 2009, Frances Bradburn, review of *Spell Hunter,* p. 50.
Bulletin of the Center for Children's Books, September, 2009, Kate Quealy-Gainer, review of *Spell Hunter,* p. 4.
Kirkus Reviews, April 1, 2009, review of *Spell Hunter.*
School Library Journal, August 1, 2009, Sue Giffard, review of *Spell Hunter.*
Times (London, England), January 9, 2009, Amanda Craig, review of *Knife;* January 7, 2010, Amanda Craig, review of *Rebel.*
Voice of Youth Advocates, August, 2009, Deborah L. Dubois, review of *Spell Hunter,* p. 234.

ONLINE

Harper Collins Web site, http://www.harpercollins.com/ (June 1, 2010), interview with Anderson.
R.J. Anderson Home Page, http://www.rj-anderson.com (May 30, 2010).
R.J. Anderson Web log, http:/rj-anderson.livejournal.com (June 1, 2010).*

*   *   *

ASHER, Sandra Fenichel
See ASHER, Sandy

ASHER, Sandy 1942-
(Sandra Fenichel Asher)

Personal

Born October 16, 1942, in Philadelphia, PA; daughter of Benjamin (a doctor) and Fanny Fenichel; married Harvey Asher (a professor), January 31, 1965; children: Benjamin, Emily. *Education:* Attended University of Pennsylvania, 1960-62; Indiana University, B.A., 1964; graduate study in child development at University of Connecticut, 1973; Drury College (now Drury University), elementary education certificate, 1974.

Addresses

Home—Lancaster, PA. *Agent*—Wendy Schmalz, Wendy Schmalz Agency, Box 831, Hudson, NY 12534. *E-mail*—sasher@drury.edu.

Career

Dramatist, children's author, and educator. WFIU-Radio, Bloomington, IN, scriptwriter, 1963-64; Ball Associates (advertising agency), Philadelphia, PA, copywriter, 1964; *Spectator,* Bloomington, drama critic, 1966-67; Drury University, Springfield, MO, instructor in creative writing, 1978-85, writer-in-residence, 1986-2003. Instructor, Institute of Children's Literature, 1986-92; instructor in creative writing for children's programs, including Summerscape, 1981-82, Artworks, 1982, and Step-Up, 1998-2002; cofounder and co-host *Missouri Writes for Kids!* (television program), 1997-2002; cofounder and managing director, Good Company Theatre for All Ages, 1997-2003; cofounder and director, American Writes for Kids and USA Plays for Kids, 1997—. Member of board of directors, National Association for Young Writers, 1989-91; Missouri Center for the Book, 1993-98, Writers Hall of Fame, 1994-98. Speaker at conferences, workshops, and schools.

Member

American Alliance of Theatre and Education, International Association of Theatre for Children and Young People (U.S. chapter), Authors Guild, Dramatists Guild, Association for Jewish Theatre, National Council of Teachers of English Assembly on Literature for Adolescents (member of board of directors, 1989-92), Society of Children's Book Writers and Illustrators (Missouri advisor, 1986-89; member of board of directors, 1989-97), New England Theatre Conference, Phi Beta Kappa.

Awards, Honors

Award of excellence, Festival of Missouri Women in the Arts, 1974, for *Come Join the Circus;* honorable mention, Unitarian Universalist Religious Arts Guild, 1975, for play *Afterthoughts in Eden;* creative writing fellowship grant in playwriting, National Endowment

Sandy Asher (Reproduced by permission.)

for the Arts, 1978, for *God and a Woman* (later *A Woman Called Truth*); first prize in one-act play contest, Little Theatre of Alexandria, 1983, and Street Players Theatre, 1989, for *The Grand Canyon* (later *Sunday, Sunday*); first prize, Children's Musical Theater of Mobile contest, and first prize, Dubuque Fine Arts Players contest, both 1984, both for *East of the Sun/West of the Moon;* Mark Twain Award nomination, 1984, for *Just like Jenny;* Outstanding Books for Young Adults citation, University of Iowa, and Best Books citation, Child Study Association, both 1985, both for *Missing Pieces;* best new play of the season designation, Maxwell Anderson Playwriting Series, 1985-86, and Ellis Memorial Award finalist, Theatre Americana, 1988, both for *Little Old Ladies in Tennis Shoes;* first prize, Center Stage New Horizons contest, 1986, first prize, Mercyhurst College National Playwrights Showcase, 1986-87, and first prize, Unpublished Play Project of the American Alliance for Theatre in Education, 1987-88, all for *God and a Woman;* Iowa Teen Award nomination, and Young Hoosier Award nomination, both 1986-87, both for *Things Are Seldom What They Seem;* National Children's Theatre Symposium playwriting awards, Indiana University/Purdue University at Indianapolis, 1987, for *Prince Alexis and the Silver Saucer,* 1989, for *A Woman Called Truth,* and 1995, for *The Wolf and Its Shadows;* Joseph Campbell Memorial Award, The Open Eye: New

Stagings for Youth, 1991-92, and American Alliance of Theatre and Education (AATE) Distinguished Play Award, 1994, and Outstanding Play for Young Audiences designation, U.S. Center of the International Association of Theaters for Children and Young People, 1993, all for *A Woman Called Truth;* New Play Festival Award, Actors' Guild of Lexington, 1992, for *Sunday, Sunday;* first prize, TADA! playwriting contest, 1991, and first prize, Choate Rosemary Hall Discovery playwriting contest, 1993, both for *Dancing with Strangers;* AATE Unpublished Play Project National Award, 1994, and IUPUI/Bonderman Award, 1995, both for *The Wolf and Its Shadows;* Kennedy Center New Visions/New Voices Forum selected play, 1995, and AATE Unpublished Plays Project National Award, 1996, both for *Across the Plains;* honorary life membership, Missouri Council for the Social Studies, 1998; Celebrate Literacy Award, International Reading Association, 1998-99; Pittsburgh One-Act Play Festival winner, 1999, for *Thunder Mountain;* IUPUI/Bonderman semi-finalist and AATE Unpublished Play Project National Award, both 1999, both for *Joan of ARK 5;*Jewish Library Association Pick of the Lists and National Jewish Book Award, both 1999, both for *With All My Heart, with All My Mind;,* New England Theatre Conference Aurand Harris Playwriting fellowship, Children's Theater Foundation of America, 1999; Charlotte Chorpenning Award for body of distinguished work in children's theater, AATE, 1999; IUPUI/Bonderman Award, 2001, and Aurand Harris Playwriting Award, and AATE Distinguished Play Award, both 2003, all for *In the Garden of the Selfish Giant;* North Dakota Flicker Tale Award, 2006; Florida Reading Association Children's Honor Book designation, 2006-07, and state master list nominations in NY, PA, SC, WY, MT, and GA, 2005-08, all for *Too Many Frogs!;* AATE Unpublished Play Project National Award, 2008, and Purple Crayon Players PLAYground Festival selection, 2009, both for *Jesse and Grace: A Best Friends Story.*

Writings

FOR CHILDREN

Summer Begins, Elsevier-Nelson, 1980, published as *Summer Smith Begins,* Bantam (New York, NY), 1986.

Daughters of the Law, Beaufort, 1980, published as *Friends and Sisters,* Gollancz (London, England), 1982.

Just like Jenny, Delacorte (New York, NY), 1982.

Things Are Seldom What They Seem, Delacorte (New York, NY), 1983.

Missing Pieces, Delacorte (New York, NY), 1984.

Teddy Teabury's Fabulous Fact, Dell (New York, NY), 1985.

Everything Is Not Enough, Delacorte (New York, NY), 1987.

Teddy Teabury's Peanutty Problems, Dell (New York, NY), 1987.

Princess Bee and the Royal Good-Night Story, illustrated by Cat Bowman Smith, Albert Whitman, 1990.

Stella's Dancing Days, illustrated by Kathryn Brown, Harcourt (New York, NY), 2001.

Why Rabbit's Nose Twitches, LeapFrog School House, 2004.

Too Many Frogs!, illustrated by Keith Graves, Philomel (New York, NY), 2005.

What a Party!, illustrated by Keith Graves, Philomel (New York, NY), 2007.

Here Comes Gosling!, illustrated by Keith Graves, Philomel (New York, NY), 2009.

"BALLET ONE" SERIES

Best Friends Get Better, Scholastic (New York, NY), 1989.

Mary-in-the-Middle, Scholastic (New York, NY), 1990.

Pat's Promise, Scholastic (New York, NY), 1990.

Can David Do It?, Scholastic (New York, NY), 1991.

SHORT-STORY COLLECTIONS

Out of Here: A Senior Class Yearbook, Dutton/Lodestar (New York, NY), 1993.

(Editor) *But That's Another Story: Famous Authors Introduce Popular Genres,* Walker (New York, NY), 1996.

(Editor and contributor) *With All My Heart, with All My Mind: Thirteen Stories about Growing up Jewish,* Simon & Schuster (New York, NY), 1999.

(Editor and contributor) *On Her Way: Stories and Poems about Growing up Girl,* Dutton (New York, NY), 2004.

(Editor, with David L. Harrison, and contributor) *Dude!: Stories and Stuff for Boys,* Dutton Children's Books (New York, NY), 2006.

NONFICTION

The Great American Peanut Book, illustrated by Jo Anne Metsch Bonnell, Tempo, 1977.

Where Do You Get Your Ideas?: Helping Young Writers Begin, illustrated by Susan Hellard, Walker (New York, NY), 1987.

Wild Words! How to Train Them to Tell Stories, illustrated by Dennis Kendrick, Walker (New York, NY), 1989.

Discovering Cultures: Mexico, Benchmark Books (New York, NY), 2003.

Discovering Cultures: China, Benchmark Books (New York, NY), 2003.

Writing It Right: How Successful Children's Authors Revise and Sell Their Stories, Writer's Book Store (West Redding, CT), 2009.

PLAYS; UNDER NAME SANDRA FENICHEL ASHER

Come Join the Circus (one-act), produced in Springfield, MO, 1973.

Afterthoughts in Eden (one-act), produced in Los Angeles, CA, 1975.

A Song of Sixpence (one-act), Encore Performance, 1976.

The Ballad of Two Who Flew (one-act), published in *Plays,* March, 1976.

How I Nearly Changed the World, but Didn't (one-act), produced in Springfield, MO, 1977.

Witling and the Stone Princess, published in *Plays,* 1979.

Food Is Love (one-act; produced in Springfield, MO, 1979), published in *A Grand Entrance,* Dramatic Publishing (Woodstock, IL), 2000.

The Insulting Princess (one-act; produced in Interlochen, MI, 1979), Encore Performance, 1988.

The Mermaid's Tale (one-act; produced in Interlochen, MI, 1979), Encore Performance, 1988.

Dover's Domain, Pioneer Drama Service, 1980.

The Golden Cow of Chelm (one-act; produced in Springfield, MO, 1980), published in *Plays,* 1980.

Sunday, Sunday (produced in Lafayette, IN, 1981), Dramatic Publishing (Woodstock, IL), 1994.

The Grand Canyon (one-act), produced in Alexandria, VA, 1983.

Little Old Ladies in Tennis Shoes (two-act; produced in Philadelphia, PA, 1985), Dramatic Publishing (Woodstock, IL), 1989.

East of the Sun/West of the Moon (one-act), produced at Children's Musical Theatre, Mobile, AL, 1985.

God and a Woman (two-act), produced in Erie, PA, 1987.

Prince Alexis and the Silver Saucer (one-act), produced in Springfield, MO, 1987.

A Woman Called Truth (one-act; produced in Erie, PA, as *God and a Woman,* 1987), Dramatic Publishing (Woodstock, IL), 1989, revised as a three-act, 1993.

The Wise Men of Chelm (one-act; produced in Tempe, AZ, 1991), Dramatic Publishing (Woodstock, IL), 1992.

Blind Dating (one-act), produced in New York, NY, 1992.

Perfect (one-act), produced in New York, NY, 1992.

Where Do You Get Your Ideas? (adapted from book of same title; also see below), produced in New York, NY, 1992.

All on a Saturday Morning (one-act), produced in Columbia, MO, 1992.

Dancing with Strangers (three one-acts; includes *Blind Dating, Perfect,* and *Workout!;* produced in Wallingford, CT, 1993), Dramatic Publishing (Woodstock, IL), 1994.

Once, in the Time of Trolls (one-act; produced in Lawrence, KS, 1995), Dramatic Publishing (Woodstock, IL), 1995.

The Wolf and Its Shadows (one-act; produced in Omaha, NE, 1995), Anchorage Press, 1999.

Across the Plains (produced in Kansas City, MO, 1996), Dramatic Publishing (Woodstock, IL), 1997.

Emma (two-act; produced in Springfield, MO, 1997), Dramatic Publishing (Woodstock, IL), 1997.

I Will Sing Life: Voices from the Hole in the Wall Gang Camp (one-act; produced in Springfield, MO, 1999), Dramatic Publishing (Woodstock, IL), 1999.

Little Women: Meg, Jo, Beth, and Amy (two-act; first produced in York, PA), Dramatic Publishing (Woodstock, IL), 2001.

The CASA Project: Stand up for a Child, produced in Springfield, MO, 2002.

Somebody Catch My Homework (once-act; produced in Springfield, MO, 2002), Dramatic Publishing (Woodstock, IL), 2004.

Blackbirds and Dragons, Mermaids and Mice (one-acts; includes *A Song of Sixpence, Country Mouse and the Missing Lunch Mystery, The Little Mermaid* [adapted from the story by Hans Christian Andersen], *Thunder Mountain,* and *The Insulting Princess*), Dramatic Publishing (Woodstock, IL), 2003.

(With Joseph Robinette and Kent Brown) *125 Original Audition Monologues,* Dramatic Publishing (Woodstock, IL), 2003.

Romeo and Juliet Together (and Alive!) at Last (two-act; first produced in Laguna Beach, CA, 2003), Dramatic Publishing (Woodstock, IL), 2004.

Everything Is Not Enough (one-act; based on the novel; first produced in Salt Lake City, UT, 2004), Dramatic Publishing (Woodstock, IL), 2006.

In the Garden of the Selfish Giant (one-act; first produced in Springfield, MO), Dramatic Publishing (Woodstock, IL), 2004.

We Will Remember: A Tribute to Veterans (one-act; first produced in Pittsburgh, PA), Dramatic Publishing (Woodstock, IL), 2005.

Today I Am!: Five Short Plays about Growing up Jewish, Dramatic Publishing (Woodstock, IL), 2006.

Family Matters (one-act; first produced in Salt Lake City, UT, 2006), Dramatic Publishing (Woodstock, IL), 2008.

Too Many Frogs! (based on picture book of the same title), Dramatic Publishing (Woodstock, IL), 2007.

Keeping Mr. Lincoln (one-act; produced in Lexington, KY, 2008), Dramatic Publishing (Woodstock, IL), 2009.

Jesse and Grace: A Best Friends Story, Dramatic Publishing (Woodstock, IL), 2010.

John D. Newman and Judy Matetzschk-Campbell, *Tell Your Story: The Plays and Playwriting of Sandra Fenichel Asher* (anthology; includes *A Woman Called Truth, Everything Is Not Enough, Family Matters, In the Garden of the Selfish Giant, Once, in the Time of Trolls,* and *Too Many Frogs*), Dramatic Publishing (Woodstock, IL), 2010.

Contributor of plays to anthologies, including *Center Stage,* Harper (New York, NY), 1990; *Theatre for Young Audiences: Twenty Great Plays for Children,* St. Martin's (New York, NY), 1998, *Scenes & Monologues for Young Actors,* Dramatic Publishing (Woodstock, IL), 1999, and *Theatre for Children: Fifteen Classic Plays,* St. Martin's, 2005.

OTHER

Contributor of stories and articles to books, including *Performing the Text: Reading, Writing, and Teaching the Young Adult Novel,* edited by Virginia Monseau and Gary Salvner, Heinemann-Boynton/Cook, 1992; *Authors' Perspectives: Turning Teenagers into Readers and Writers,* edited by Donald Gallo, Heinemann-Boynton/Cook, 1992; *Collins Book of Ballet and Dance,* edited by Jean Ure, HarperCollins, 1997; *Theatre for Young Audiences: Twenty Great Plays for Children,* ed-

ited by Coleman Jennings, St. Martin's Press, 1998; and *Two Decades of the ALAN Review,* edited by Patricia P. Kelly and Robert C. Small, Jr., NCTE Press, 1999. Contributor of stories and articles to magazines, including *Highlights for Children, Humpty Dumpty, Parents, ALAN Review, Journal of Reading, Spark!, Theater for Young Audiences Today, Writers Digest, Writer,* and *National Geographic World.*

Papers relating to Asher's books are housed at the de Grummond Children's Literature Collection, University of Southern Mississippi. Papers relating to Asher's plays are housed at the Child Drama Collection, Arizona State University, Tempe.

Sidelights

Sandy Asher, a playwright and children's author, is probably best known for the young-adult novels and other prose works for young readers. Drawing many of the ideas and characters for her writings from her childhood memories, Asher has earned critical praise and numerous awards for novels such as *Just like Jenny, Things Are Seldom What They Seem,* and *Everything Is Not Enough.* Asher's works "treat serious problems facing most teenagers—strains in parent-child or sibling relationships; confusions about sexuality; uncertainties about one's place in the home, the school, or the community at large; emerging perceptions of change and loss," observed Judith S. Baughman in the *Dictionary*

Asher's engaging story in **Here Comes Gosling!** *is paired with Keith Graves' quirky, stylized art.* (Philomel Books, 2009. Illustration ©2009 by Keith Graves. Reproduced by permission.)

of Literary Biography Yearbook. "Yet the dominant tone of each novel is comic, and its focus is not upon the problem addressed, the issue to be resolved, but instead upon the young person who is confronting it."

In addition to her young-adult fiction, Asher has written numerous picture books, including *Princess Bee and the Royal Good-Night Story* and *Too Many Frogs!* She has also edited works such as the award-winning *With All My Heart, with All My Mind: Thirteen Stories about Growing up Jewish* and *Dude!: Stories and Stuff for Boys,* and also supports her fellow writers with *Writing It Right: How Successful Children's Authors Revise and Sell Their Stories.* "My aim is to introduce all young readers to lots of different authors and genres," Asher told *Journal of Adolescent & Adult Literacy* interviewer James Blasingame.

Asher was raised in Philadelphia, Pennsylvania, surrounded by the members of her large, loving family. For solace, Asher often retreated to the quiet of her bedroom, where she discovered the power of imagination, remarking in the *Something about the Author Autobiography Series* (*SAAS*), "I learned early that inner space is worth exploring and that even when alone, you can find yourself in fascinating company." She continued, "I made up poems and songs, stories and plays, to fill my fantasy world and entertain myself. I read whole volumes of the *Book of Knowledge* encyclopedia and pages at a time out of the dictionary, eager to know everything about everything. Little did I know what excellent training for a writer those solitary hours up in my room would prove to be."

As Asher grew up, she developed interests in writing, drama, and dance, despite the concerns of her parents who viewed marriage and family as a young woman's most important focus. As a teen she masked her typical adolescent discomfort with a sarcastic sense of humor. "Looking back now, I suspect potentially good friends were more afraid of my sharp tongue than I realized, and their gossipy chatter probably masked insecurities much like my own," Asher wrote in *SAAS.* "This difference between surface impressions and inner vulnerability has been a rich area of exploration in all of my writing for young-adult readers. I hope those who find secondary school an unnatural habitat find comfort in my books, among people like themselves—and like me—struggling to make sense out of strange, difficult, and often painful situations."

During her teen years, Asher pursued her career interests in ballet, the theater, and writing. She credits teachers and role models from books—Jo March of Louisa May Alcott's *Little Women* in particular—for her perseverance in the things she loved. As she remarked in *SAAS,* "Until I read *Little Women,* I had no idea that people got paid to do it. Jo March succeeded in making her dream come true. And that gave me hope. Information, a dream, a plan, and hope: books can provide all of that and more."

After an eventful high school and college career that included performing in plays with La Salle College Masque and Indiana University Theatre, musicals on the traveling showboat, the *Majestic,* and ballet with the Philadelphia Civic Ballet Company, Asher graduated from Indiana University and married her husband, Harvey Asher. Within a span of several years, her parents and her grandparents died, and her husband's job necessitated a move to Missouri. During these years she worked as a scriptwriter for a radio station, an advertising copywriter, and a drama critic for an alternative newspaper before having two children and beginning graduate studies in child development.

In 1969, a year after the birth of her second child, she began to write her first novel, *Daughters of the Law,* a story about a young girl trying to understand her Jewish heritage in light of her mother's unexpressed but painful memories as a survivor of the Holocaust of World War II. As Asher became more familiar with her genre, she reworked the novel many times over the next ten years before its publication. During these years she also began to write the award-winning plays that she has seen produced throughout the United States, Canada, Mexico, and abroad.

Before she finalized *Daughters of the Law,* Asher wrote and published *Summer Begins,* a novel about an eighth-grade girl named Summer who submits an article to her school newspaper suggesting that the holiday celebrations at her school should include Buddhist and Jewish traditions along with the exclusively Christian ones currently observed. Summer finds herself the unwilling center of attention when the principal demands that she retract her article, and her teacher resigns in protest of this violation of Summer's civil rights. *Summer Begins* raises important issues of censorship and religious freedom, but many critics noted that the book's strength lies in its focus on Summer's development toward maturity, related in invitingly human and often humorous terms. A *Washington Post Book World* reviewer commented that "Summer is a winningly self-aware 13-year-old and her reluctance to take on the heroine's role is often very funny."

In her 1982 novel, *Just like Jenny,* Asher explores the friendship between Stephie and Jenny, two talented young dancers. When they are both asked to audition for a semi-professional dance group, Stephie, who is under pressure from her parents and envious of Jenny's classic skills, decides that she is not good enough to try out. The resolution of Stephie's loss of nerve, according to Judith S. Baughman in a *Dictionary of Literary Biography Yearbook: 1983* essay, entails lessons in "the nature of real friendship and the motivation underlying commitment to hard but fulfilling goals." A *Times Literary Supplement* reviewer, while criticizing *Just like Jenny* for "relying on inevitable disappointments and triumphs," commended Asher for her knowledge of teenagers, claiming that the author "knows about the dreams and aspirations of young people. . . . She understands also the stubborn crises of confidence which afflict adolescents who do not know how they compare in ability and maturity with others."

In other novels Asher has continued to raise social issues while focusing on her adolescent characters' personal development. In her award-winning 1983 book *Things Are Seldom What They Seem* she examines the effect a teacher's sexual abuse—and the silent response within the adult world to what he has done—has on some of his students. Baughman noted that the significant focus in this story is "how these complexly developed fourteen-and fifteen-year-olds deal with their discovery that things are seldom what they seem, that deceptions or misperceptions do undermine relationships."

In *Missing Pieces,* noted Virginia Marr in a *School Library Journal* review, Asher "deals with such adolescent concerns as lack of communication within families, loss, loneliness and the constant need for emotional support." Asher's 1987 novel, *Everything Is Not Enough,* the story of a seventeen-year-old boy's move toward independence, tackles the theme of violence against women in a similar manner. In this story, a supportive friendship arises between a young man and a female coworker at a restaurant when, together, they confront the fact that a friend is being beaten by her alcoholic boyfriend. And in her 1993 work *Out of Here: A Senior Class Yearbook,* Asher uses nine interconnected stories about a series of problems such as teen pregnancy, abusive parents, and alcoholism to highlight dilemmas faced by graduating seniors at a high school in a small town. "The cumulative effect," *School Library Journal* reviewer Doris A. Fong concluded, "is an accurate portrayal of high school, with concerns and activities that give Asher's work the texture of a yearbook."

Asher includes other short fiction in the fiction anthologies she has edited for pre-teen and older readers. In *With All My Heart, with All My Mind* she joins with contributors Jacqueline Dembar, Phyllis Shalant, Eric Kimmel, and Susan Beth Pfeffer to introduce Jewish teens attempting to come to terms with adulthood as well as with their Jewish heritage. Stories range in time period from Masada to World War II to the near future, but in each young men and women are presented with a conflict that involves the obligations of their faith and culture. Each story is followed by an interview with the author in which the story's message is discussed. Similarly, writers Miriam Bat Ami, Bonny Becker, Patricia Calvert, and Donna Jo Napoli join Asher in contributing tales about young, independent-minded women to *On Her Way.* Stories range in focus from the realistic to the fantastic: in one tale a girl discovers a magical make up that makes anyone who wears it popular, while in another, a new girl at school who is not as physically mature as others her age is mistaken for a boy by her new classmates.

In *School Library Journal* Janet Hilbun explained that the "entertaining and engrossing" volume "celebrates growing up female as the protagonists tackle and embrace new experiences." The critic also cited Asher's selections as editor, noting that readers of the short fiction and verse collected in *On Her Way* are introduced to "likeable characters who learn valuable lessons on their journeys to womanhood." Noting that some of the poems contain "sophisticated, challenging imagery," *Booklist* reviewer Gillian Engberg felt that most selections are accessible to teen readers, "and many girls will recognize their own challenges" in the "accessible and often inspiring" stories.

A collection of stories, plays, personal narratives, and poems concerning the challenges of male adolescence, *Dude!,* coedited by Asher and David L. Harrison, contains eighteen works by Ron Koertge, Jane Yolen, and other esteemed writers. According to Blasingame, "one thing is true of every young man in the book: All are trying to figure out their place in the world and attempting to make the most of the families they are given." *Booklist* contributor Shelle Rosenfeld observed that the selections "range from entertaining to challenging and offer an array of characters and experiences." Noting that the anthology includes works by both male and female writers, Asher told Blasingame, "My experience has been that kids are comfortable with both points of view . . . if they're left alone to make their choices. They relate to the human experience of the story, which is exactly what we authors intend."

In addition to plays and novels for older readers, Asher has also written for the early elementary grades. Her picture book *Princess Bee and the Royal Good-Night Story* takes a lighthearted look at separation anxiety, a common plight of smaller children. Princess Bee cannot go to sleep when her mom, the queen, goes out of town. When Bee's siblings attempt stories but come up short, the princess has to look within herself to solve the problem. In a review for *Booklist,* Julie Corsaro called the work a "soothing offering with potential for repeat late-night performances."

Stella's Dancing Days introduces a gray kitten named Stella, whose talent for dancing charms her human owners, as well as the family dog. However, as the kitten grows into a cat, she sets aside her dancing in favor of raising a litter of her own six kittens . . . dancers all, of course! Noting that the book will "please cat lovers and ballerinas of all ages," Shawn Brommer wrote in *School Library Journal* that in this story about maturation, "Asher's text has a natural, graceful rhythm." The "cat's-eye view reflected in the family members' names"—Tall One, Gentle One, and Littlest One with the Loudest Voice are the children's names—"is just one example of the light, precise language in this well-crafted picture book," noted *Booklist* contributor Carolyn Phelan, while a *Publishers Weekly* reviewer dubbed *Stella's Dancing Days* "a charmer."

Asher has enjoyed a successful collaboration with illustrator Keith Graves on a number of picture books, including *Too Many Frogs!* Centering on the relationship between quiet and polite Rabbit and gregarious Froggie, the tale concerns Rabbit's efforts to enjoy a quiet night at home with a favorite book, a task made more difficult by Froggie's frequent visits. Writing in *School Library Journal*, Linda M. Kenton described *Too Many Frogs!* as "a fun story that celebrates reading and standing up for oneself." In *What a Party!*, Froggie refuses to go home after participating in a fantastic celebration for his grandfather's birthday, and Rabbit devises a simple yet effective solution to the dilemma. "Parents should find the whole scenario entirely familiar," A *Kirkus Reviews* critic stated. In a third title, *Here Comes Gosling!*, the multi-talented Froggie helps to pacify a bawling baby goose. The work "effectively introduces the idea of dealing with frustrations in an amusing way," Amy Lilien-Harper noted in *School Library Journal*.

Asher has also aided the efforts of budding authors by penning the companion nonfiction books *Where Do You Get Your Ideas?: Helping Young Writers Begin* and *Wild Words! How to Train Them to Tell Stories*. These books, suited for children in grades three to eight, tackle the problems of how to begin writing and then how to edit stories to make them more effective. In *Where Do You Get Your Ideas?* chapters alternate between idea-generating activities and "stories behind the stories," with quotes from popular children's authors. *Wild Words!* gets more specific, offering advice on shaping plots and characters, then explaining the editing process that allows authors to "tame" words. "The examples," commented Martha Rosen in *School Library Journal*, "are right on target, and the original writing samples by junior-and senior-high-school students provide interest and incentive for others who are trying to hone their writing skills." Asher has also edited *But That's Another Story: Famous Authors Introduce Popular Genres*, which includes adventure, suspense, horror, and science fiction stories, creating a book useful for "language arts teachers who have dreamed of an accessible collection of genre explanations, short stories, author interviews, and story commentaries all rolled into one pleasure-reading package," according to Patti Sylvester Spencer in the *Voice of Youth Advocates*.

The role of the storyteller is essential to society, Asher believes. As she noted in *SAAS*, "Our stories define us, our place in society, and our experience of the world. They help us to reach within and without—across rooms, generations, borders, barriers, oceans and years." She concluded, "Good times, bad times, happy times, sad times, all can be woven into our life-story tapestry."

Biographical and Critical Sources

BOOKS

Asher, Sandy, *Where Do You Get Your Ideas?: Helping Young Writers Begin*, Walker (New York, NY), 1987.

Dictionary of Literary Biography Yearbook: 1983, Gale (Detroit, MI), 1984.
Something about the Author Autobiography Series, Volume 13, Gale (Detroit, MI), 1992.

PERIODICALS

Booklist, May 1, 1986, review of *Teddy Teabury's Fabulous Fact*, p. 1307; January 1, 1990, review of *Wild Words!*, p. 907; February 1, 1990, Julie Corsaro, review of *Princess Bee and the Royal Good-Night Story*, p. 1084; March 15, 2001, Carolyn Phelan, review of *Stella's Dancing Days*, p. 1402; February 14, 2004, Gillian Engberg, review of *On Her Way: Stories and Poems about Growing up Girl*, p. 1057; April 1, 2005, Todd Morning, review of *Too Many Frogs!*, p. 1364; July 1, 2006, Shelle Rosenfeld, review of *Dude!: Stories and Stuff for Boys*, p. 53; February 1, 2007, Hazel Rochman, review of *What a Party!*, p. 48.
Bulletin of the Center for Children's Books, February, 1981, review of *Daughters of the Law*, p. 106; September, 1982, review of *Just like Jenny*, p. 2; May, 1983, review of *Things Are Seldom What They See*, p. 162; June, 1984, review of *Missing Pieces*, p. 180; December, 1987, review of *Where Do You Get Your Ideas?*, p. 61; April, 2004, Karen Coats, review of *On Her Way*, p. 314; February, 2005, Timnah Card, review of *Too Many Frogs!*, p. 243.
Journal of Adolescent & Adult Literacy, April, 2008, James Blasingame, review of *Dude! Stories and Stuff for Boys*, and interview with Hopkinson and David Harrison, p. 608.
Journal of Reading, February, 1990, Robert Small and Susan Murphy, "An Interview with Sandy Asher on the Art of Writing," p. 390.
Kirkus Reviews, June 15, 1987, review of *Where Do You Get Your Ideas?*, p. 921; December 15, 2003, review of *On Her Way*, p. 1445; December 15, 2004, review of *Too Many Frogs!*, p. 1197; June 1, 2006, review of *Dude!*, p. 568; December 15, 2006, review of *What a Party!*, p. 1263; April 1, 2009, review of *Here Comes Gosling!*
Publishers Weekly, February 13, 1987, review of *Everything Is Not Enough*, p. 94; June 14, 1993, review of *Out of Here: A Senior Class Yearbook*, p. 72; November 19, 1999, review of *With All My Heart, with All My Mind*, p. 69; February 26, 2001, review of *Stella's Dancing Days*, p. 85; January 26, 2004, "On the Brink of Adulthood," p. 255.
School Library Journal, May, 1984, Virginia Marr, review of *Missing Pieces*, p. 86; August, 1987, review of *Everything Is Not Enough*, pp. 88-89; September, 1987, Cynthia Dobrez, review of *Where Do You Get Your Ideas?*, pp. 184-185; December, 1989, Cindy Darling Codell, review of *Teddy Teabury's Peanutty Problems*, p. 98; January, 1990, Martha Rosen, review of *Wild Words! How to Train Them to Tell Stories*, p. 110; March, 1990, p. 184; July, 1993, Doris A., Fong, review of *Out of Here*, p. 98; July, 1996; July, 2001, Shawn Brommer, review of *Stella's Dancing Days*, p. 72; February, 2003, Ann W. Moore, review of *Mexico*, p. 127; March, 2003, Nancy A. Gifford, review of

China, p. 214; March, 2004, Janet Hilbun, review of *On Her Way,* p. 224; March, 2005, Linda M. Kenton, review of *Too Many Frogs!,* p. 166; August, 2006, Coop Renner, review of *Dude!,* p. 113; February, 2007, Amy Lilien-Harper, review of *What a Party!,* p. 84; June, 2009, Amy Lilien-Harper, review of *Here Comes Gosling!,* p. 78.

Times Literary Supplement, September 7, 1984, review of *Just like Jenny,* p. 1006.

Voice of Youth Advocates, June, 1984, review of *Missing Pieces,* p. 94; June, 1987, review of *Everything Is Not Enough,* p. 74; December, 1993, review of *Out of Here,* p. 286; August, 1996, Patti Sylvester Spencer, review of *But That's Another Story: Famous Authors Introduce Popular Genres,* p. 176.

Washington Post Book World, July 11, 1982, review of *Summer Begins,* p. 12.

ONLINE

Dramatic Publishing Web site, http://www.dramatic publishing.com/ (May 1, 2010), "Sandra Fenichel Asher."

Sandy Asher Web site, http://usawrites4kids.drury.edu/ authors/asher (May 1, 2010).

B

BAASANSUREN, Bolormaa 1982-

Personal

Born 1982, in Ulaanbaatar, Mongolia; married Ganbaatar Ichinnorov (a painter and writer). *Education:* Institute of Fine Arts (Mongolia), degree (painting); attended art school in Moscow, Russia; University of Bunkyo, research student.

Addresses

Home—Japan.

Career

Writer and illustrator

Awards, Honors

Grand Prize, Noma Concourse, 2004, for *My Little Round House;* numerous other awards for artwork.

Writings

SELF-ILLUSTRATED

Boku No Uchi Wa Gel, Sekifu-Sha (Fukuoa, Japan), 2006, translated and adapted by Helen Mixter as *My Little Round House,* Groundwood Books (Toronto, Ontario, Canada), 2009.

Also author of books, with titles translated as *The 25th Hour,* Admon Printing Co. (Mongolia), 2003; *The Hunnu Empire Festival,* Munkhiin Useq (Mongolia), 2005; *The Legend of Wives' Hair,* Munkhiin Useq, 2005; and *The Educated Boy,* Munkhiin Useq, 2005.

ILLUSTRATOR

Jambyn Dashdondog, *Tales on Horseback* (published in Mongolian), Admon Printing Co. (Mongolia), 1999.

Contributor to periodicals, including *Puuka.*

Sidelights

Bolormaa Baasansuren in an author and artist who opens a unique window onto the world in her books for young children. Her first illustration project, Jambyn Dashdondog's picture book *Tales on Horseback,* was published when its illustrator was a sophomore in high school. Published in Japanese before being translated into English by Helen Mixter, her original, self-illustrated *My Little Round House,* captures the exotic culture of Baasansuren's native Mongolia in richly colored, stylized gouache paintings. Married to writer Ganbaatar Ichinnorov, Baanansuren now lives in Japan, where she continues to study art and share her native culture with young children.

Inspired by a story Baasansuren learned from her grandmother, *My Little Round House* focuses on an infant named Jilu. Living in a round tent, or *ger,* Jilu describes the year following his birth, as he travels with his nomadic parents during their seasonal relocations within Mongolia. His mother carries him and sings to him, and her cooking creates fragrant smells. His wrinkled grandparents also show their love, and through the seasons the family wanders with their camel as part of a greater nomadic community. Praising the "beautiful" art in *My Little Round House,* Monika Schroeder noted in *School Library Journal* that Baasansuren's images incorporate "elaborate details such as painted woodwork, embroidery, and the texture of fabrics." A *Kirkus Reviews* critic hailed the book as "a unique look at a culture unknown to most," and Carolyn Phelan noted in *Booklist* that Baaasansuren's unusual approach in *My Little Round House* allows "readers [to] see . . . through the eyes of a child discovering his world for the first time."

Although Baasansuren was raised in the city, the life of Mongolia's nomadic people has fascinated her since childhood. "I love traveling in the countryside," she told *Paper Tigers* Web site interviewer Marjorie Coughlan. "I had wanted to create a picture book about the nomadic life for a long time. In Mongolia, the no-

Bolormaa Baasansuren's unique folk-art-inspired illustrations for **My Little Round House** *introduce readers to the culture of her native Mongolia.* (Reproduced by permission of Groundwood Books Limited.)

madic people move four times a year so they are always encountering new surroundings and meeting interesting things. I have tried to express this sense of the nomadic lifestyle in *My Little Round House.*"

Biographical and Critical Sources

PERIODICALS

Booklist, May 1, 2009, Carolyn Phelan, review of *My Little Round House,* p. 78.

Bulletin of the Center for Children's Books, July-August, 2009, Hope Morrison, review of *My Little Round House,* p. 433.

Globe & Mail (Toronto, Ontario, Canada), July 18, 2009, Susan Perren, review of *My Little Round House,* p. F11.

Kirkus Reviews, April 1, 2009, review of *My Little Round House.*

School Library Journal, April, 2009, Monika Schroeder, review of *My Little Round House,* p. 99.

ONLINE

Paper Tigers Web site, http://www.papertigers.org/ (February 1, 2010), Marjorie Coughlan, interview with Baasansuren.*

*   *   *

BANCROFT, Bronwyn 1958-

Personal

Born 1958, in Tenterfield, New South Wales, Australia; daughter of Bill and Dorothy; children: Jack, Ella, Rubyrose. *Education:* Canberra School of Art, Diploma of Arts, 1980; University of Sydney, M.A. (studio practice), 2003, M.A. (painting), 2006; postgraduate work at University of Western Sydney.

Addresses

Home—Sydney, New South Wales, Australia. *Agent*—Golvan Arts Management, P.O. Box 766, Kew, Victoria 3101 Australia; golvanozemail.com.au.

Career

Painter, fabric designer, illustrator, and writer. Freelance designer, 1980-87; Palisade Restaurant, Sydney, New South Wales, Australia, restaurateur, 1982-83; Balmain Markets, Sydney, designer, 1985; Designer Aboriginals, Sydney, founder, 1985—. Speaker and lecturer at schools and conferences. *Exhibitions:* Work represented in collections, including at National Gallery of Australia, Canberra, Australian Capital Territory, Australia; Art Gallery of New South Wales, Sydney, New South Wales, Australia; Artbank, Sydney; Queensland Art Gallery, Brisbane, Queensland, Australia; University of Wollongong, Wollongong, New South Wales; Center for the Study of Political Graphics, Los Angeles, CA; and Kelton Foundation, Santa Monica, CA. Solo exhibitions staged at Framed Gallery, Darwin, Northern Territory, Australia, 1993; Coventry Gallery, Sydney, 1999; Vivien Anderson Gallery, Melbourne, Victoria, Australia, 2004; and Wilson Street Gallery, Newtown, New South Wales, 2010. Group exhibitions staged at Coo-ee Aboriginal Art Gallery, Sydney, 1991; Vivien Anderson Gallery, Melbourne, 2003-05; and Hogarth Galleries, Sydney, 2007.

Member

National Gallery of Australia (council member, 1992-97), National Indigenous Arts Advocacy Association (chair and board member, 1993-98), New South Wales Ministry of the Arts (chair of visual arts committee, 1996), Australian Council Intellectual Property Project Group, Visual Arts Copyright Collection Agency (member of board), Tranby Aboriginal College (member of board), Copyright Agency Limited (member of board), Australian Indigenous Mentoring Experience (member of board), Boomalli Aboriginal Artists Co-operative (founding member).

Awards, Honors

Australia Council Aboriginal Arts Board Arts grant, 1984, professional development grant, 1985, and creative artists fellowship, 1991-92; Australian Multicultural Children's Book Award, 1993, for *The Fat and Juicy Place;* selected as Australian candidate for UNICEF-Ezra Jack Keats International Award for Excellence in Children's Book Illustration, 1994; National Indigenous Arts Advocacy Association Incorporated Employment Award, 1995; New South Wales Premier's History Awards shortlist, and Australian Children's Picture Book of the Year shortlist, Children's Book Council of Australia, both 1997, both for *The Whalers;* May Gibbs residential fellowship, Dromkeen Centre for Children's Literature, 2000; Centenary Medal of Australia, 2003; Kate Challis RAKA Award finalist, 2003; One Hundred Titles for Reading and Sharing selection, New York Public Library, 2004, for *Sun Mother Wakes the World;* New South Wales Indigenous Art Prize finalist, 2005 and 2006; Yarramundi scholarship, University of Western Sydney.

Writings

SELF-ILLUSTRATED

Patterns of Australia, Little Hare Books (Surry Hills, New South Wales, Australia), 2005.

An Australian ABC of Animals, Little Hare Books (Surry Hills, New South Wales, Australia), 2005.

An Australian 1, 2, 3 of Animals, Little Hare Books (Surry Hills, New South Wales, Australia), 2007.

Possum and Wattle: My Big Book of Australian Words, Little Hare Books (Surry Hills, New South Wales, Australia), 2008.

W Is for Wombat: My First Australian Word Book, Little Hare Books (Surry Hills, New South Wales, Australia), 2009.

Why I Love Australia, Little Hare Books (Surry Hills, New South Wales, Australia), 2010.

ILLUSTRATOR

Diana Kidd, *The Fat and Juicy Place,* Angus & Robertson (Pymble, New South Wales, Australia), 1992.

Oodgeroo, *Stradbroke Dreamtime,* Angus & Robertson (Pymble, New South Wales, Australia), 1993, published as *Dreamtime: Aboriginal Stories,* Lothrop, Lee & Shepard Books (New York, NY), 1994.

James Cowan, *Kun-man-gur the Rainbow Serpent,* Barefoot Books (Boston, MA), 1994.

Lucy Daly and Ethan Williams, *Dirrangun,* Angus & Robertson (Pymble, New South Wales, Australia), 1994.

Percy Mumballa, *Minah: A Poem in Four Parts,* Harper-Collins (Pymble, New South Wales, Australia), 1995.

Sally Morgan, *Dan's Grandpa,* Sandcastle (South Fremantle, West Australia, Australia), 1996.

Percy Mumballa, *The Whalers,* illustrated by Bronwyn Bancroft, Angus & Robertson (Sydney, New South Wales, Australia), 1996.

Sally Morgan, *In Your Dreams,* Sandcastle Books (South Fremantle, West Australia, Australia), 1997.

Sally Morgan, *Just a Little Brown Dog,* Fremantle Arts Centre Press (South Fremantle, Western Australia, Australia), 1997.

Katrina Germein, *Big Rain Coming,* Clarion Books (New York, NY), 1999.

Katrina Germein, *Leaving,* Roland Harvey (Albert Park, Victoria, Australia), 2000.

Diane Wolkstein, adapter, *Sun Mother Wakes the World: An Australian Creation Story,* HarperCollins (New York, NY), 2004.

Annaliese Porter, *The Outback,* illustrated by Bronwyn Bancroft, Magabala Books (Broome, West Australia, Australia), 2005.

Jackie French, *Walking the Boundaries,* Angus & Robertson (Pymble, New South Wales, Australia), 2006.

Judith Morecroft, *Malu Kangaroo: How the First Children Learnt to Surf,* Little Hare Books (Surry Hills, New South Wales, Australia), 2007.

Donna Jo Napoli and Elena Furrow, *Ready to Dream,* Bloomsbury Children's Books (New York, NY), 2009.

Dawn McMillan, reteller, *A Tale of the Didgeridoo,* Oxford University Press (South Melbourne, Victoria, Australia), 2009.

Sally Morgan and Ezekiel Kwaymullina, *Sam's Bush Journey,* Little Hare Books (Surry Hills, New South Wales, Australia), 2009.

Sidelights

A native of Australia, Bronwyn Bancroft is a celebrated Aboriginal artist who has written and illustrated several highly regarded children's books, including *An Australian 1, 2, 3 of Animals.* A descendant of the Bundjalung people, Bancroft is the founder of Designer Aboriginals, which produces fabrics and jewelry and provides business training for Aboriginal women. Bancroft's work has been exhibited at more than 200 group and solo shows, and she is actively involved in a number of organizations that protect artists' rights. "The work that I do challenges people to accept Indigenous peoples as equals," Bancroft stated on her home page.

In *An Australian 1, 2, 3 of Animals,* her self-illustrated counting book, Bancroft introduces young readers to a host of creatures from her native land, including wallabies, emus, geckos, and sugar gliders, a small marsupial. "The boldly outlined animals filled with dotted designs are strikingly placed in each spread," a critic in *Kirkus Reviews* stated. In the more-recent *Why I Love Australia* Bancroft explores the wonders of the continent.

Bancroft has also provided the artwork for titles by other writers. *Stradbroke Dreamtime,* a book by fellow Australian Oodgeroo that was published in the United States as *Dreamtime: Aboriginal Stories,* contains more than twenty tales, some autobiographical, others based on Aboriginal myth. "The illustrator's background as a textile designer is reflected in the bold geometrics, silhouettes, and colors" seen in the work, observed *Booklist* contributor Janice Del Negro, and Karen Jameyson, writing in *Horn Book,* noted that Bancroft's pictures "fairly sing with the rhythms and harmonies of these people."

Set in the Australian outback, *Big Rain Coming,* a work by Katrina Germein, centers on the anticipation of a much-needed storm. *Booklist* reviewer Gillian Engberg praised "the band of swirling colors and totems that runs along the ground and across the pages," and a *Publishers Weekly* contributor noted that Bancroft "represents the earth with stylized swirls of brown and black and creates the billabong from a patchwork of limpid purples and greens. According to *School Library Journal* reviewer Doris Gebel, "Bancroft utilizes rich colors and thick black lines to good effect."

Adapted by folklorist Diane Wolkstein, *Sun Mother Wakes the World: An Australian Creation Story* recounts an Aboriginal creation myth about a supernatural being who awakens a slumbering Earth and gives birth to the human race. "Bold colors and patterns lined with thick, powerful lines draw the eye along each page and bring the story to life," Marilyn Taniguchi commented in her review of the book for *School Library Journal.* Bancroft "depicts Sun Mother as a graceful, golden form," a contributor in *Kirkus Reviews* noted, and a *Publishers Weekly* critic also praised the art in *Sun Mother Wakes the World,* stating that "dots, lines and curlicues form patterns and swirl across the pages in a kaleidoscope of saturated hues."

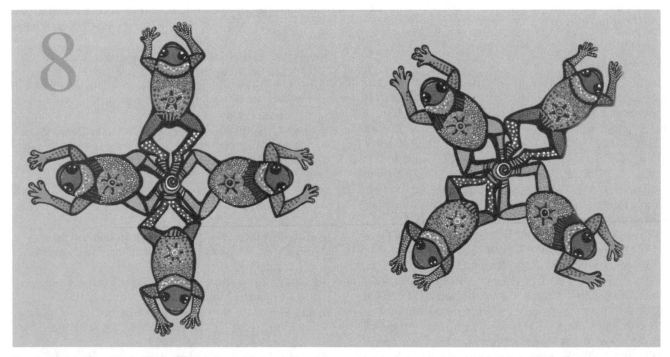

Bronwyn Bancroft's whimsical stylized drawings are a feature of her unique concept book **An Australian 1,2,3 of Animals.** (Little Hare Books, 2009. Illustration © 2007 by Bronwyn Bancroft. Reproduced by permission.)

A young artist finds inspiration during a trip to Australia in *Ready to Dream,* a picture book by Donna Jo Napoli and Elena Furrow. The work centers on Ally, an American girl who discovers a mentor in Pauline, an Aboriginal artist. "Bancroft's paintings reflect both modernity and the spirit of her ancient tradition," noted a *Kirkus Reviews* critic in reviewing *Ready to Dream,* and Ieva Bates, writing in *School Library Journal,* remarked that the "stylized images are decorated with detailed patterns that employ vibrant color combinations."

Biographical and Critical Sources

PERIODICALS

Booklist, October 1, 1994, Janice Del Negro, review of *Dreamtime: Aboriginal Stories,* p. 319; August, 2000, Gillian Engberg, review of *Big Rain Coming,* p. 2146; April 15, 2004, Gillian Engberg, review of *Sun Mother Wakes the World: An Australian Creation Story,* p. 1444; December 15, 2008, Thom Barthelmess, review of *Ready to Dream,* p. 54.

Horn Book, March-April, 1994, Karen Jameyson, review of *Stradbroke Dreamtime,* p. 242.

Kirkus Reviews, March 1, 2004, review of *Sun Mother Wakes the World,* p. 231; April 1, 2009, reviews of *An Australian 1,2,3 of Animals Ready to Dream.*

New Internationalist, April, 2008, "The Colour of Dreams: Aboriginal Art," p. 8.

New York Times Book Review, August 8, 2004, review of *Sun Mother Wakes the World,* p. 16.

Publishers Weekly, July 4, 1994, review of *Dreamtime,* p. 64; July 10, 2000, review of *Big Rain Coming,* p. 62; April 19, 2004, review of *Sun Mother Wakes the World,* p. 59; November 24, 2008, review of *Ready to Dream,* p. 57.

School Library Journal, September, 2000, Doris Gebel, review of *Big Rain Coming,* p. 198; April, 2004, Marilyn Taniguchi, review of *Sun Mother Wakes the World,* p. 144; January, 2009, Marilyn Taniguchi, review of *Malu-Kangaroo: How the First Children Learnt to Surf,* p. 81; February, 2009, Ieva Bates, review of *Ready to Dream,* p. 80.

ONLINE

Bronwyn Bancroft Home Page, http://www.bronwyn bancroft.com (June 1, 2010).

Golvan Arts Management Web site, http://www.golvanarts. com.au/ (June 1, 2010), "Bronwyn Bancroft."

Vivian Anderson Gallery Web site, http://www.vivien andersongallery.com/ (June 1, 2010), "Bronwyn Bancroft."*

* * *

BARRAGÁN, Paula 1963-

Personal

Born 1963, in Quito, Ecuador. *Education:* Pratt Institute, B.F.A. (illustration and design), 1986; studied in Paris, France, and San Francisco, CA.

Addresses

Home and office—San Ignacio 1001, Quito, Ecuador.

Career

Artist and illustrator. Designer of carpets; commercial illustrator. *Exhibitions:* Work has been exhibited at La Galería, Quito, Ecuador, beginning 1991; The Guild Gallery, KY, 1991; L'Espace Gallery, Brussels, Belgium, 1994; Portfolio Gallery, Auckland, New Zealand, 1996, and Multiple Impressions Gallery, New York, NY, beginning 1999. Paintings included in private collections of Central Bank of Ecuador and others.

Awards, Honors

First prize, Nacional Bienial (Quito, Ecuador), 1994; first prize in printmaking, Quito Salon de arte, 1994; first prize, National Design Biennial, 2002, in book category, 2004, in illustration category; NAPPA Gold Award, 2004, for *Spicy Hot Colors* by Sherry Shahan; American Library Association Notable Children's Book designation, 2006, for *Poems to Dream Together* by Francisco X. Alarcón.

Illustrator

Pat Mora, editor, *Love to Mama: A Tribute to Mothers,* Lee & Low Books (New York, NY), 2001.

Pablo Cuiv, and others, *Viva la Fiesta! Ecuador,* Dinediciones (Quito, Ecuador), 2002.

Sherry Shahan, *Spicy Hot Colors!/¡Colores Picantes!,* August House LittleFolk (Little Rock, AR), 2004.

Francisco X. Alarcón, *Poems to Dream Together/Poemas para soñar juntos,* Lee & Low (New York, NY), 2005.

Paula Barragán's illustration assignments include her work for Pat Mora's Love to Mama. (Reproduced by permission of Lee & Low Books, Inc.)

Sherry Shahan, *Cool Cats Counting,* August House Little-Folk (Little Rock, AR), 2005.

Sherry Shahan, *¡Fiesta!: A Celebration of Latino Festivals,* August House LittleFolk (Atlanta, GA), 2009.

Sidelights

Earning her bachelor's degree in fine art at New York's Pratt Institute, Ecuadorian illustrator and collage artist Paula Barragán has created artwork for several highly praised bilingual children's picture books, including texts by Sherry Shahan, Pat Mora, and noted Mexican-born poet Francisco X. Alarcón. *Poems to Dream Together/Poemas para soñar juntos* Alarcón presents seventeen short verses that feature themes of peace, community, and hope in both English and Spanish. Noting the poet's "beautifully unsophisticated imagery," Stella Clark added in her *Booklist* review that Barragán's bold and brightly colored "illustrations are a fine complement to the text," while Ann Welton wrote in *School Library Journal* that the "boldly colored, mixed-media artwork" in *Poems to Dream Together* "is varied and engaging." Employing a "cut-and-paste style" that incorporates "silhouettes, small but exaggerated details, and childishly thick figures," the artist's compelling images capture the poet's "utopian longings," concluded a *Kirkus Reviews* writer.

In *Love to Mama: A Tribute to Mothers,* a verse anthology edited by Pat Mora that includes the work of thirteen published poets, Barragán creates digitally enhanced images that capture the joy and love of family in paper, gouache, and graphite. Recalling the love of mothers from Mexico, Cuba, Venezuela, and Puerto Rico, among other places, the collected verses are chock full of "food, hugs, kisses, and endearments," according to *Booklist* critic Hazel Rochman. In art that Nell D. Beram characterized in *Horn Book* as "mural-like in scale and drenched with color," the artist transforms *Love to Mama* into "a visual feast of textures, patterns, and hues." In *School Library Journal* Ann Welton was equally enthusiastic about the collection, describing it as "that rare book that will [transcend] . . . age . . . and cultures to appeal to the common human experience."

The first of several collaborations with writer Sherry Shahan, *Spicy Hot Colors!/¡Colores Picantes!* teaches children the name of nine colors, its English/Spanish text paired with "appealing and attention grabbing" paintings that incorporate elements of well-know works of art, according to *School Library Journal* writer Rosalyn Pierini. In her text for the book Shahan uses a variety of rhyme schemes, instead focusing reader attention on participatory sounds such as tapping, clapping, and banging. Praising the author's stress on "reader/listener's participation" in *Spicy Hot Colors!,* a *Kirkus Reviews* writer added that Barragán's detailed images "echo the exuberance of the verse." "Learning a foreign language has never been so much fun," asserted Pierini, while in *Publishers Weekly* a critic dubbed *Spicy Hot Colors!* a "zingy color primer" that is brought to life in "dazzling" illustrations incorporating "collage-like layers of bold shapes and vibrantly contrasting tones." In *Booklist* Ilene Cooper characterized the picture book as "a brilliant fest of color that will entice children as it helps them learn a few Spanish words."

Other titles by Shahan and Barragán include *Cool Cats Counting,* and *¡Fiesta!: A Celebration of Latino Festivals,* the latter which introduces readers to a year's worth of holidays, one for every month of the year. From January's Fiesta de San Antonio Abad to May's Cinco de Mayo, Shahan's free-verse text pairs with warm-toned cut paper art that "dance across the pages" in "stunning" succession, according to a *Kirkus Reviews* writer. *Cool Cats Counting* treats readers to the "rhythmically jazzy beats" of Shahan's rhyming verse, and

Barragán's colorful artwork for ¡Fiesta! *reflects the high-spirited energy in Sherry Shahan's text.* (August House, 2009. Illustration ©2009 by Paul Barragan. Reproduced by permission.)

here Barragán depicts dancing animals sporting jaunty hats, fringed skirts, and high-heeled dancing shoes, according to a *Kirkus Reviews* writer.

Biographical and Critical Sources

PERIODICALS

Booklist, May 1, 2001, Hazel Rochman, review of *Love to Mama: A Tribute to Mothers,* p. 1686; September 15, 2004, Ilene Cooper, review of *Spicy Hot Colors!/ ¡Colores Picantes!,* p. 247; July, 2005, Stella Clark, review of *Poems to Dream Together/Poemas para soñar juntos,* p. 1918.

Horn Book, July, 2001, Nell D. Beram, review of *Love to Mama,* p. 468.

Kirkus Reviews, August 1, 2004, review of *Spicy Hot Colors!,* p. 749; May 1, 2005, review of *Poems to Dream Together,* p. 533; September 15, 2005, review of *Cool Cats Counting,* p. 1033; April 1, 2009, review of *¡Fiesta!: A Celebration of Latino Festivals.*

Publishers Weekly, April 30, 2001, review of *Love to Mama,* p. 80; November 15, 2004, review of *Spicy Hot Colors!,* p. 58.

School Library Journal, April, 2001, Ann Welton, review of *Love to Mama,* p. 165; November, 2004, Rosalyn Pierini, review of *Spicy Hot Colors!,* p. 130; October, 2005, Ann Welton, review of *Poems to Dream Together,* p. 148 and Maura Bresnahan, review of *Cool Cats Counting,* p 149; April, 2009, Sandra Welzenbach, review of *¡Fiesta!,* p. 126.

ONLINE

Paula Barragán Home Page, http://www.paulabarragan. com (May 31, 2010).*

*   *   *

BATEMAN, Teresa 1957-

Personal

Born December 6, 1957 in Moscow, ID; daughter of Donald S. (a financial consultant) and Peggy L. (a homemaker) Bateman. *Education:* Ricks College, Associate of Arts and Sciences, 1978; Brigham Young University, B.S., 1982; University of Washington, M.L.I.S., 1987. *Religion:* Church of Jesus Christ of Latter-day Saints (Mormon).

Addresses

Home—Tacoma, WA. *Office*—Brigadoon Elementary School, 3601 SW 336th St., Federal Way, WA 98023. *E-mail*—tbateman@fwps.org.

Teresa Bateman (Reproduced by permission.)

Career

Writer and librarian. Brigadoon Elementary School, Federal Way, WA, librarian, beginning 1987; author of books for children. Briefly taught school in Honduras and in St. Mary's, AK.

Member

Society of Children's Book Writers and Illustrators, Washington Educators Association, Washington Library Media Association.

Awards, Honors

Merit Award, *Society of Children's Book Writers and Illustrators* magazine, 1993, for "Traveling Tom and the Leprechaun"; *Highlights for Children* Fiction Contest, 1994, for "The Alien"; Paul A. Witty Short Story Award, 1997, for "Trapped in the Arctic"; Storytelling World Award, and Governor's Writers Award, both 1998, both for *The Ring of Truth;* Oppenheim Toy Portfolio Award, 2001, for *Farm Flu,* and 2004, for *The Bully Blockers Club* and *April Foolishness;* Notable Social Studies Book designation, 2002, for *Red, White, Blue, and Uncle Who?;* Notable Social Studies Trade Book for Young People designation, 2004, for *The Bully Blockers;* Arkansas Diamond Primary Book Award, 2006, for *April Foolishness;* International Reading Association

Children's Choice designation, 2003, for *The Princesses Have a Ball;* Comstock Book Award Honor Book designation, 2007, for *Keeper of Souls.*

Writings

FOR CHILDREN

The Ring of Truth: An Original Irish Tale, illustrated by Omar Rayyan, Holiday House (New York, NY), 1997.

Leprechaun Gold, illustrated by Rosanne Litzinger, Holiday House (New York, NY), 1998.

Harp o' Gold: An Original Tale, illustrated by Jill Weber, Holiday House (New York, NY), 2001.

A Plump and Perky Turkey, illustrated by Jeff Shelly, Winslow, 2001.

Farm Flu, illustrated by Nadine Bernard Westcott, Albert Whitman (Morton Grove, IL), 2001.

Red, White, Blue, and Uncle Who?: The Stories behind Some of America's Patriotic Symbols, illustrated by John O'Brien, Holiday House (New York, NY), 2001.

The Merbaby, illustrated by Patience Brewster, Holiday House (New York, NY), 2001.

Hunting the Daddyosaurus, illustrated by Benrei Huang, Albert Whitman (Morton Grove, IL), 2002.

The Princesses Have a Ball, illustrated by Lynne Cravath, Albert Whitman (Morton Grove, IL), 2002.

April Foolishness, illustrated by Nadine Bernard Westcott, Albert Whitman (Morton Grove, IL), 2004.

The Bully Blockers Club, illustrated by Jackie Urbanovic, Albert Whitman (Morton Grove, IL), 2004.

Hamster Camp: How Harry Got Fit, illustrated by Nancy Cote, Albert Whitman (Morton Grove, IL), 2005.

Fluffy, Scourge of the Sea, illustrated by Michael Chesworth, Charlesbridge (Watertown, MA), 2005.

Keeper of Soles, illustrated by Yayo, Holiday House (New York, NY), 2005.

Will You Be My Valenswine?, illustrated by Kristina Stephenson, Albert Whitman (Morton Grove, IL), 2005.

Fiona's Luck, illustrated by Kelly Murphy, Charlesbridge (Watertown, MA), 2007.

Bateman's retelling of an Irish folktale in **Harp o' Gold** *is brought to life in Jill Weber's art.* (Jacket art ©2000 by Jill Weber. Reproduced by permission of Holiday House, Inc.)

The Eyes of the Unicorn, illustrated by Greg Spalenka, Holiday House (New York, NY), 2007.

Traveling Tom and the Leprechaun, illustrated by Mélisande Potter, Holiday House (New York, NY), 2007.

Gus, the Pilgrim Turkey, illustrated by Ellen Joy Sasaki, Albert Whitman (Morton Grove, IL), 2008.

The Frog with the Big Mouth, illustrated by Will Terry, Albert Whitman (Morton Grove, IL), 2008.

Damon, Pythias, and the Test of Friendship, illustrated by Layne Johnson, Albert Whitman (Morton Grove, IL), 2009.

Regular contributor to *Cricket* and *Highlights for Children;* contributor of reviews to *Puget Sound Council* and *School Library Journal.*

Sidelights

Children's book writer Teresa Bateman has worked as a librarian for many years, inspired both in her career choice and her writing by her childhood love of stories and books. As she once told *SATA:* "I was raised in a family of ten children. My mother made a point of reading to us at every opportunity, especially on long car trips. As a result, we are all voracious readers. There are few things that delight me more than a well-written book. Perhaps that's one of the reasons why I decided to write." Among Bateman's lighthearted books for children are *Gus, the Pilgrim Turkey, The Merbaby, Fluffy, Scourge of the Sea,* and *The Frog with the Big Mouth.*

"I've always been a storyteller," Bateman explained. "When I was a teen-ager I had to share a bedroom with a younger sister who always 'ratted me out' to my parents when I stayed up past bedtime, reading. I used to tell her stories about a bear that lived in the closet and liked to eat succulent young things. I, naturally, was too old and stringy. . . .

"As the years went by I continued making up stories. Now I tell them to my many nieces and nephews. Eventually I thought it would be fun to write them down and see if they were publishable. I am now the owner of an ENORMOUS stack of rejection letters. However, I also have had many things published. I don't let rejection discourage me. I write because I love to write. I'd still write even if none of my stories ever got published. Writing is as much a part of me as breathing. I write each day, without fail. Some days I write a lot. Some days I write a little, but I write EVERY day."

Bateman's first book, *The Ring of Truth: An Original Irish Tale,* is the story of Patrick O'Kelly, a peddler who tells impressive tales as a way to keep people buying his wares. Patrick makes the mistake of bragging that he can "spout better blarney" than the king of the leprechauns, which causes the king to become upset and give Patrick a ring which will force him to tell the truth. In a twist, Patrick ends up winning a blarney contest by telling the true story of his meeting with the leprechaun king. As a *Kirkus Reviews* critic wrote, "Bateman's first book is a beautifully layered, consistently sprightly take on the notion that truth is stranger than fiction," while a *Publishers Weekly* critic noted that, "epitomizing the best of Irish storytelling, this blithe debut pokes fun at its own blustery genre." Beth Tegart, writing for *School Library Journal,* concluded that the book "is a well-crafted tale told with a storyteller's touch; the language flows, and the story satisfies."

Continuing in the Irish tradition, *Leprechaun Gold* is Bateman's story of Donald O'Dell, a kindhearted handyman who rescues a leprechaun from drowning. As a reward, the leprechaun offers Donald gold, but the man refuses, saying he does not need it. The leprechaun, who refuses to take "no" for an answer, leaves the gold in Donald's pockets, on his doorstep, and in Donald's shoes, but each time the man returns the gold. The leprechaun ends up tricking the lonely Donald into meeting a similarly lonely beautiful woman with golden hair and a golden heart, ensuring that Donald accepts this gift of gold. April Judge, in a review for *Booklist,* declared that Bateman's "well-crafted story is told in a robust, lively manner" and deemed *Leprechaun Gold* "a top-notch candidate for reading aloud." A critic for *Kirkus Reviews* noted that the story "has an Irish lilt that would certainly withstand an energetic reading out loud—and not just on St. Patrick's Day."

A touch of Ireland is also found in *Harp o' Gold: An Original Tale, Traveling Tom and the Leprechaun,* and *Fiona's Luck.* In *Harp o' Gold* a wandering minstrel named Tom happily plays his old harp but cannot seem to make a living from it. When a leprechaun offers him a new, shiny harp in exchange for his old one, Tom agrees. Although the beautiful new harp sounds tinny, people flock to listen and Tom is able to make a living as a performer, even though he realizes that getting what one wishes may not be the same as getting what one wants. Helen Foster James, writing in *School Library Journal,* called *Harp o' Gold* "a satisfying and well-crafted story."

In *Fiona's Luck* Bateman teams up with illustrator Kelly Murphy to tell another leprechaun-centered tale, this one about the efforts of the king of the leprechauns to hoard all the leprechauns' good luck and share none of it with the humans now living in Ireland. With no more "luck o' the Irish," Ireland's people now begin to suffer starvation due to the potato famine. Clever Fiona realizes what the leprechaun king has done, and she hatches a plan to return good luck to the Irish. In a *Kirkus Reviews* appraisal of the book, a critic noted that Bateman's tale "exudes Irish flair" through the action of its "cunning" heroine and its "rhythmic language," and a *Publishers Weekly* critic maintained that the "original story brims with the entertaining hallmarks of folklore and fairytales." Recommending the tale for listeners of all ages, Luella Teuton added in *School Library Journal* that *Fiona's Luck* will "delight" children through "the young woman's cleverness and quick thinking."

Bateman once commented on her decision to focus on Irish themes, telling *SATA:* "Many people ask me why I write so many Irish stories. My father says that one of our family lines goes back to Ireland. I've always loved Irish stories, and I enjoy telling them to my students. In fact, during the week of St. Patrick's Day I pick up an Irish accent that follows me around for weeks. It's usually in March that I write my best leprechaun stories."

In *The Merbaby,* Bateman tells a fantasy story about brothers Josh and Tarron, who are fishermen. Josh only fishes to make money, while Tarron appreciates the beauties of the sea as well. When the pair finds a merbaby, Josh plans to put the child on display and charge admission. Tarron knows better, however: He returns the baby to the merpeople, who reward him with treasure from the bottom of the sea. According to John Peters in *Booklist, The Merbaby* is a "well-told, elegantly illustrated original story," and a *Kirkus Reviews* critic called it "a gentle teaching story."

Bateman retells the traditional fairy tale about twelve dancing princesses in *The Princesses Have a Ball.* In her version, the "ball" referred to is a basketball, and the princesses yearn not for dancing but for playing a game of hoops. Their father will not hear of such a thing, so the princesses sneak away at night to play ball. When their worn-out shoes cause their father to grow suspicious, the cobbler suggests that the girls confess and let their father know how well they can play. A critic for *Kirkus Reviews* found that Bateman's "rhymed update of this classic tale trips cheerfully along." Bina Williams, in her review for *School Library Journal,* wrote that Bateman "offers a fresh look at the beloved story."

April Foolishness focuses on April Fool's Day, when the grandchildren visit their grandparents' farm and attempt to pull some pranks. Despite dire warnings from the children that the cows have gotten loose, the goats are stampeding, and the pigs are in the garden, Grandpa will not budge from calmly eating his breakfast. When Grandma comes in and quietly announces that April Fool's Day is tomorrow, Grandpa runs outside in panic. Her joke turns out to be the best one of all; it really is April Fool's Day and Grandpa has been tricked. Carolyn Phelan, writing in *Booklist,* found that the story contains "plenty of fun," while a critic for *Publishers Weekly* called it "a surefire giggle-inducer."

Gus, the Pilgrim Turkey is another holiday-themed offering from Bateman, this time featuring cartoon art by Ellen Joy Sasaki. Gus is a farm-grown gobbler who has a comfortable life until he hears that turkeys on the farm never live past January. In fear, he packs his bags and follows the migrating birds, albeit on foot. Everywhere he stops on his trip south Gus learns that turkeys are considered a tasty meal. Resolutely, he continues on, traveling further and further south until he arrives at the South Pole and finds safety in the chilly land of the penguins. In her story, Bateman relates the turkey's travels in a way that makes them parallel the journey of the Pilgrims from England to their ultimate home in Massachusetts. Recommending *Gus, the Pilgrim Turkey* for Thanksgiving-themed story hours, *Booklist* critic Kay Weisman added that Bateman's "witty prose works well with Sasaki's . . . colorful artwork, which fully captures Gus's exuberant innocence." The artist's colorful "palette and style" also attracted the praise of a

Bateman's imaginative riff on popular fairy-tale characters is captured in Lynne Cravath's artwork for **The Princesses Have a Ball.** (Albert Whitman &
Company, 2002. Illustration © 2002 by Lynne Cravath. Reproduced by permission.)

Kirkus Reviews writer, the critic adding that Sasaki's cartoons "suit [Bateman's] . . . silly confection to a T."

Silliness comes to South America in *The Frog with the Big Mouth,* as a boastful frog proudly announces to his rain-forest friends that he has eaten a gigantic fly. Of course, boasting to one friend is not good enough, and soon the frog has taken his tall tale on the road, repeating it to a toucan, a coati, and several other animals and then asking them what they like to eat. When the frog brags to a jungle jaguar, the large cat seems impressed, but it becomes clear that Jaguar is more interested in the teller than the tale when he tells Frog that his favorite food is . . . frog! Praising the book as "an inventive version of a long-favored tale," Gay Lynn Van Vleck added in *School Library Journal* that Will Terry's digitized illustrations "swirl with movement" and jungle colors. A *Kirkus Reviews* writer noted Bateman's inclusion of information about her story's exotic rainforest cast, adding that Terry's "exaggerated and energetic depictions" of these creatures "add to the [story's] merriment."

Bateman takes readers to Sicily in the distant past—the fourth century—in *Damon, Pythias, and the Test of Friendship,* a tale featuring paintings by Layne Johnson. In the story, Pythias is an outspoken man who speaks out against the harshness of Dionysus' rule. Condemned to death by the king, Pythias is allowed to travel to his home to say goodbye to his parents on the condition that his good friend Damon will die in his stead should Pythias not return. Pythias is delayed but returns just in time to save his loyal friend, inspiring Dionysus to cancel the execution and rethink the value of friendship. In *School Library Journal* Joy Fleishhacker dubbed *Damon, Pythias, and the Test of Friendship* a "classic tale" that features "strong dialogue" and illustrations that "evoke . . . the setting and time period with rich detail." Readers will relate to the story's themes of "rebellion, loyalty, and friendship," asserted *Booklist* critic Hazel Rochman, and "will want to talk about . . . how the tale reaches into their own lives."

"One of the things I enjoy most is doing research for nonfiction articles and books," explained Bateman in discussing the writing life. "To me, research is a blast. I love going to the University of Washington Suzzalo Library and pulling out microfilm, or prowling through stacks of old books. I find the strangest things that way—odd facts that tickle my fancy. Doing the research is often just as much fun as doing the writing! Being a librarian also helps. I'm surrounded by books and children every day. It's a great combination."

Biographical and Critical Sources

PERIODICALS

Booklist, August, 1998, April Judge, review of *Leprechaun Gold,* p. 2012; March 1, 2001, Ilene Cooper, review of *Harp o' Gold: An Original Tale,* p. 1285; April 1,

Featuring artwork by Ellen Joy Sasaki, Bateman's **Gus, the Pilgrim Turkey** *features a fun twist on an American tradition.* (Albert Whitman & Company, 2008. Illustration © 2008 by Ellen Joy Sasaki. Reproduced by permission.)

2001, Carolyn Phelan, review of *Farm Flu,* p. 1470; September 1, 2001, Ilene Cooper, review of *A Plump and Perky Turkey,* p. 119; December 15, 2001, Carolyn Phelan, review of *Red, White, Blue and Uncle Who?: The Stories behind Some of America's Patriotic Symbols,* p. 725, and Stephanie Zvirin, review of *Farm Flu,* p. 728; May 1, 2002, Carolyn Phelan, review of *Hunting the Daddyosaurus,* p. 1530; November 1, 2002, Lauren Peterson, review of *The Princesses Have a Ball,* p. 504; November 15, 2004, Carolyn Phelan, review of *April Foolishness,* p. 584; January 1, 2005, Carolyn Phelan, review of *Fluffy, Scourge of the Sea,* p. 867; May 15, 2005, Julie Cummins, review of *Hoamster Camp: How Harry Got Fit,* p. 1662; September 1, 2008, Kay Weisman, review of *Gus, the Pilgrim Turkey,* p. 57; May 1, 2009, Hazel Rochman, review of *Damon, Pythias, and the Test of Friendship,* p. 82.

Bulletin of the Center for Children's Books, May, 1997, review of *The Ring of Truth: An Original Irish Tale,* p. 313.

Children's Bookwatch, January, 2005, review of *April Foolishness.*

Horn Book, May-June, 2006, Sarah Ellis, review of *Keeper of Soles,* p. 288.

Kirkus Reviews, February 1, 1997, review of *The Ring of Truth,* p. 218; March 15, 1998, review of *Leprechaun Gold,* p. 398; August 1, 2001, review of *The Merbaby,* p. 1116; August 15, 2001, review of *A Plump and Perky Turkey,* p. 1207; September 1, 2002, review of *Red, White, Blue and Uncle Who?,* p. 1285; February 1, 2002, review of *Hunting the Daddyosaurus,* p. 176; August 15, 2002, review of *The Princesses Have a Ball,* p. 1215; October 1, 2004, review of *April Fool-*

ishness, p. 956; January 15, 2007, review of *Fiona's Luck,* p. 69; March 1, 2007, review of *Traveling Tom and the Leprechaun,* p. 216; September 1, 2007, review of *The Eyes of the Unicorn;* August 1, 2008, review of *The Frog with the Big Mouth;* August 15, 2008, review of *Gus, the Pilgrim Turkey.*

Publishers Weekly, February 24, 1997, review of *The Ring of Truth,* p. 91; September 27, 1999, review of *The Ring of Truth,* p. 107; January 29, 2001, review of *Farm Flu,* p. 88; March 5, 2001, review of *Harp o' Gold,* p. 78; September 24, 2001, review of *A Plump and Perky Turkey,* p. 46; July 15, 2002, review of *The Princesses Have a Ball,* p. 74; December 20, 2004, review of *April Foolishness,* p. 59; February 27, 2006, review of *Keeper of Soles,* p. 61; January 1, 2007, review of *Fiona's Luck,* p. 48; September 10, 2007, review of *The Eyes of the Unicorn,* p. 60.

School Library Journal, May, 1997, Beth Tegart, review of *The Ring of Truth,* p. 92; April, 2001, Kathy M. Newby, review of *Farm Flu,* p. 98; May, 2001, Helen Foster James, review of *Harp o' Gold,* p. 109; September, 2001, Gay Lynn Van Vleck, review of *A Plump and Perky Turkey,* p. 182; November, 2001, Marlene Gawron, review of *Red, White, Blue, and Uncle Who?,* p. 170; January, 2002, Miriam Lang Budin, review of *The Merbaby,* p. 89; March, 2002, Gay Lynn Van Vleck, review of *Hunting the Daddyosaurus,* p. 172; December, 2002, Bina Williams, review of *The Princesses Have a Ball,* p. 84; November, 2004, Elaine Lesh Morgan, review of *The Bully Blockers Club,* p. 90, and Mary Elam, review of *April Foolishness,* p. 90; May, 2005, Jennifer Ralston, review of *The Bully Blockers Club,* p. 49; July, 2005, Linda Staskus, review of *Hamster Camp: How Harry Got Fit,* p. 64; April, 2006, Wendy Lukehart, review of *Keeper of Soles,* p. 96; March, 2007, Mary Jean Smith, review of *Traveling Tom and the Leprechaun,* p. 151; April, 2007, Luella Teuton, review of *Fiona's Luck,* p. 94; September, 2007, Margaret Bush, review of *The Eyes of the Unicorn,* p. 157; September, 2008, Gay Lynn Van Vleck, review of *The Frog with the Big Mouth,* p. 137; June, 2009, Joy Fleishhacker, review of *Damon, Pythias, and the Test of Friendship,* p. 104; September, 2008, Lisa Egly Lehmuller, review of *Gus, the Pilgrim Turkey,* p. 137.

ONLINE

Charlesbridge Publishing Web site, http://www.charles bridge.com/ (May 31, 2010), "Teresa Bateman."

Ravenstone Press Web site, http://ravenstonepress.com/ (May 31, 2010), interview with Bateman.

*   *   *

BISHOP, Gavin 1946-

Personal

Born February 13, 1946, in Invercargill, New Zealand; son of Stanley Alan (a railway employee) and Doris Hinepau Bishop; married Vivien Carol Edwards (a

Gavin Bishop (Photograph by Martin Frielander. Reproduced by permission.)

teacher and artist), August 27, 1966; children: Cressida, Charlotte, Alexandra. *Ethnicity:* "I am of European and Māori extraction." *Education:* University of Canterbury (New Zealand), Diploma of Fine Arts (with honors), 1967; Christchurch Teachers' College, diploma (with distinction), 1968. *Politics:* Liberal. *Hobbies and other interests:* Reading, movies, gardening (in fits and starts), traveling, food.

Addresses

Home—Christchurch, New Zealand. *E-mail*—gavinbishop@netaccess.co.nz.

Career

Illustrator, author, and educator. Linwood High School, Christchurch, New Zealand, art teacher and department chair, 1969-89; Christ's College, Christchurch, New Zealand, head of art department, 1989-99. Rhode Island School of Design, Providence, RI, professor, 1996; University of Waikato, Hamilton, New Zealand, writer-in-residence, 2003. UNESCO children's literature workshop leader in China, 1992, and Indonesia, 1997; judge for Noma Concours, Tokyo, Japan, 2003. *Exhibitions:* Work included in exhibitions at Bratislava Biennial of Illustration, 1985; Premi Catalonia d'Illustracio, Barcelona, Spain, 1984; Robert McDougall Art Gallery, Christchurch, New Zealand, 1989; National Library, Wellington, New Zealand, 1992; National Library, Auckland, New Zealand, 1993; Milford House, Dunedin, New Zealand, 1993; Left Bank Gallery, Greymouth, New Zealand, 1998; Salamander Gallery, Christchurch, 2004, 2006; Bratislava Biennial of Illustration, 2005; Centre of Contemporary Art, Christchurch, 2009; and Canterbury Museum, Christchurch, 2010.

Member

New Zealand Society of Authors (PEN New Zealand Inc.), New Zealand Illustrators' Guild, Te Tai Tamariki, New Zealand Children's Literature Trust.

Awards, Honors

Russell Clark Medal for Illustration, New Zealand Library Association, 1982, for *Mrs. McGinty and the Bizarre Plant;* New Zealand Children's Picture Book of the Year, New Zealand Government Publishers and New Zealand Literary Fund, 1983, for *Mr. Fox;* Grand Prix, Noma Concours, UNESCO and Kodansha International, 1984, for illustrations in *Mr. Fox;* Russell Clark Medal for Illustration finalist, New Zealand Library Association, 1988, for *A Apple Pie,* and 1991, for *Katarina;* AIM Award for Children's Picture Book of the Year, 1994, for *Hinepau;* New Zealand Post Picture Book of the Year shortlist, 1997, for *Maui and the Sun,* 2000, for *The Video Shop Sparrow,* 2001, for *Stay Awake, Bear!,* and 2002, for *Tom Thumb; New Zealand Post* Picture Book of the Year, New Zealand Children's Book of the Year, and Spectrum Print Award, all 2000, all for *The House That Jack Built;* Margaret Mahy Lecture Award, New Zealand Book Council, 2000; *New Zealand Post* Children's Book of the Year Award, 2003, for *Weaving Earth and Sky;* Arts Council of New Zealand grant, 2004; Sylvia Ashton Warner fellow, University of Auckland, 2004; Russell Clark Medal shortlist, and Notable Book selection, Children's Literature Foundation New Zealand (CLFNZ), both 2004, both for *The Three Billy-Goats Gruff;* Notable Book selection, CLFNZ, *New Zealand Post* Children's Book of the Year Award shortlist, and White Ravens booklist inclusion, International Youth Library, all 2005, all for *The Little Tractor;* Notable Book selection, CLFNZ, New Zealand Post Children's Book of the Year Award shortlist, Russell Clark Medal shortlist, and White Ravens booklist inclusion, all 2005, all for *Taming the Sun;* Notable Book selection, CLFNZ, and Russell Clark Medal, both 2006, both for *Kiwi Moon;* Notable Book selection, CLFNZ, *New Zealand Post* Children's Book of the Year Award shortlist, and Russell Clark Medal shortlist, all 2006, all for *The Waka;* Notable Book selection, CLFNZ, *New Zealand Post* Children's Book of the Year Award shortlist, and Russell Clark Medal shortlist, all 2007, all for *Riding the Waves;* Notable Book selection, CLFNZ, *New Zealand Post* Children's Book of the Year Award shortlist, and Russell Clark Medal, all 2007, all for *Rats!; New Zealand Post* Children's Book of the Year Award shortlist, Elsie Locke Award shortlist, Notable Book selection, CLFNZ, and Design Award, Publishers Association of New Zealand, all 2009, all for *Piano Rock;* Notable Book selection, CLFNZ, White Ravens booklist inclusion, and *New Zealand Post* Children's Book of the Year Award, all 2008, all for *Snake and Lizard;* fourteen of Bishop's works have been listed as *Storylines* Notable Books, including *Tom Thumb,* 2002, *The Three Billy-Goats Gruff,* 2004, *Taming the Sun,* 2005, *Kiwi Moon* 2006, *The Waka* 2006, *Riding the Waves,* 2007, *Snake and Lizard,* 2008, *Rats!,* 2008, *Piano Rock,* 2009, *There Was a Crooked Man,* 2010, *Cowshed Christmas,* 2010, and *Counting the Stars,* 2010. The Gavin Bishop Award for Unpublished New Zealand Illustrators was established in 2009 by Random House New Zealand Ltd./Storylines New Zealand in recognition of Bishop's contribution to New Zealand children's literature.

Writings

FOR CHILDREN; SELF-ILLUSTRATED

Mrs McGinty and the Bizarre Plant, Oxford University Press (Auckland, New Zealand), 1981, reprinted, Random House (Auckland, New Zealand), 2007.

Bidibidi, Oxford University Press (Auckland, New Zealand), 1982.

(Reteller) *Mr Fox,* Oxford University Press (Auckland, New Zealand), 1982.

(Reteller) *Chicken Licken,* Oxford University Press (Auckland, New Zealand), 1984.

The Horror of Hickory Bay, Oxford University Press (Auckland, New Zealand), 1984.

(Reteller) *Mother Hubbard,* Oxford University Press (Auckland, New Zealand), 1986.

A Apple Pie, Oxford University Press (Auckland, New Zealand), 1987.

(Reteller) *The Three Little Pigs,* Ashton Scholastic (Auckland, New Zealand), 1989.

Katarina, Random House (Auckland, New Zealand), 1990, reprinted, 2008.

Hinepau, Ashton Scholastic (Auckland, New Zealand), 1993.

(Reteller) *Maui and the Sun: A Māori Tale,* North-South Books (New York, NY), 1996.

Little Rabbit and the Sea, North-South Books (New York, NY), 1997.

(Reteller) *Maui and the Goddess of Fire,* Scholastic (Auckland, New Zealand), 1997.

(Reteller) *The House That Jack Built: Being the Account of Jack Bull, Esq., Who Sailed There from These Shores to a Land Far Away to Live There and Trade with the Natives of That Said Land Twelfth Day of September 1798,* Scholastic (Auckland, New Zealand), 1999.

(Reteller) *The Wolf in Sheep's Clothing,* Shortland (Auckland, New Zealand), 1999, Shortland (Denver, CO), 2000.

Stay Awake, Bear!, Orchard Books (New York, NY), 2000.

(Reteller) *Tom Thumb: The True History of Sir Thomas Thumb,* Random House (Auckland, New Zealand), 2001.

(Reteller) *Three Billy-Goats Gruff,* Scholastic (Auckland, New Zealand), 2003.

(Reteller) *Taming the Sun: Four Māori Myths,* Random House (Auckland, New Zealand), 2004.

Kiwi Moon, Random House (Auckland, New Zealand), 2005.

(Reteller) *Riding the Waves: Four Māori Myths,* Random House (Auckland, New Zealand), 2006.

Rats!, Random House (Auckland, New Zealand), 2007.

Piano Rock: A 1950s Childhood, Random House (Auckland, New Zealand), 2008.

(Reteller) *There Was an Old Woman,* Gecko Press (Wellington, New Zealand), 2008.

(Reteller) *There Was a Crooked Man,* Gecko Press (Wellington, New Zealand), 2009.

(Reteller) *Counting the Stars: Four Māori Myths,* Random House (Auckland, New Zealand), 2009.

Cowshed Springtime, Random House (Auckland, New Zealand), 2010.

ILLUSTRATOR

Katherine O'Brien, *The Year of the Yelvertons,* Oxford University Press (Auckland, New Zealand), 1981.

Kathleen Leverich, *The Hungry Fox,* Houghton (Boston, MA), 1986.

Joy Watson, *Pets,* Department of Education (Wellington, New Zealand), 1988.

Beverley Dietz, *The Lion and the Jackal,* Simon & Schuster (New York, NY), 1991.

Jeffrey Leask, *Little Red Rocking Hood,* Ashton Scholastic (Auckland, New Zealand), 1992.

Philip Bailey, reteller, *The Wedding of Mistress Fox,* North-South (New York, NY), 1994.

Kana Riley, *A Moose Is Loose,* Brown Publishing Network (Wellesley, MA), 1994.

Joy Cowley, *The Video Shop Sparrow,* Boyds Mills Press (Honesdale, PA), 1999.

Joy Cowley, *Pip the Penguin,* Scholastic (Auckland, New Zealand), 2001.

Robert Sullivan, *Weaving Earth and Sky: Myths and Legends of Aotearoa,* Random House (Auckland, New Zealand), 2002.

Joy Cowley, *The Nice Little Tractor,* Scholastic (Auckland, New Zealand), 2004.

Jean Prior, *The Waka,* Scholastic (Auckland, New Zealand), 2005.

Bishop's colorful paintings are a highlight of his original picture book **Little Rabbit and the Sea.** (North South Books, 1997. Reproduced by permission of Gavin Bishop.)

Joy Cowley, *Snake and Lizard,* Gecko Press (Wellington, New Zealand), 2007, Kane/Miller (La Jolla, CA), 2008.

Joy Cowley, *Cowshed Christmas,* Random House (Auckland, New Zealand), 2009.

Joy Cowley, *Friends: Snake and Lizard,* Gecko Press (Wellington, New Zealand), 2009.

EARLY READERS

The Cracker Jack, illustrated by Jill Allpress, Wendy Pye (Auckland, New Zealand), 1995.

Spider, illustrated by Peter Stevenson, Wendy Pye (Auckland, New Zealand), 1995.

There Is a Planet, illustrated by Andrew Trimmer, Wendy Pye (Auckland, New Zealand), 1995.

Cabbage Caterpillar, illustrated by Jim Storey, Wendy Pye (Auckland, New Zealand), 1996.

(Self-illustrated) *Good Luck Elephant,* Wendy Pye (Auckland, New Zealand), 1996.

The Secret Lives of Mr and Mrs Smith, illustrated by Korky Paul, Wendy Pye (Auckland, New Zealand), 1996.

I Like to Find Things, illustrated by Neil Vesey, Wendy Pye (Auckland, New Zealand), 1997.

(Illustrator) Joy Cowley, *The Bears' Picnic,* Shortland (Auckland, New Zealand), 1997.

Jump into Bed, illustrated by Craig Brown, Shortland (Auckland, New Zealand), 1997.

It Makes Me Smile, illustrated by Emanuela Carletti, Wendy Pye (Auckland, New Zealand), 1998.

Mice Like Rice, illustrated by Astrid Matijasevic, Wendy Pye (Auckland, New Zealand), 1998.

(Self-illustrated) *Rhymes with Ram,* Lands End (Auckland, New Zealand), 1998.

Lucky Grub, illustrated by Jim Storey, Wendy Pye (Auckland, New Zealand), 1999.

OTHER

Author of libretto for ballets *Terrible Tom,* 1985, and *Te Maia and the Sea-Devil,* 1986, both commissioned by Royal New Zealand Ballet Company; author of scripts for TVNZ television series *Bidibidi,* broadcast 1990, and *Bidibidi to the Rescue,* 1991, both based on the book *Bidibidi.* Author of stories for Harcourt Educational Assessment, 2000-05. Creator of *Giant Jimmy Jones* (three-dimensional picture book), Human Interface Technology Laboratory New Zealand, 2003.

Adaptations

Hinepau and *Kiwi Moon* were adapted for the stage by Capital E, Wellington, New Zealand.

Sidelights

Gavin Bishop is one of the most prolific and highly honored authors and illustrators in his native New Zealand. The winner of numerous awards for his picture books and beginning readers, Bishop is noted for his attention to detail in pictures that augment, often

humorously, the stories they accompany. Among his many honors, Bishop has received the Russell Clark Award, the *New Zealand Post* Children's Book of the Year award, the Silvia Ashton Warner fellowship, and the Margaret Mahy Lecture Award. In 2009, the Storylines Gavin Bishop Award was established in recognition of his contribution to children's literature.

In addition to providing illustrations that are considered colorful and lively, Bishop has made a name for himself as an effective reteller of such traditional tales as *Mr Fox, The Three Billy-Goats Gruff,* and *There Was a Crooked Man.* Bishop's storytelling ambitions have further extended to encompass narratives that highlight the native Māori culture of his New Zealand homeland, such as *Katarina, Maui and the Sun: A Māori Tale,* and *Taming the Sun: Four Māori Myths.* Bishop has also released an autobiographical work, *Piano Rock: A 1950s Childhood,* that recounts his early years living in a small railway town.

Born in Invercargill, the southernmost city in New Zealand, Bishop lived with his parents in his grandmother's little house "with a big rhododendron in front," as he once told *SATA.* He started school when the family moved to Kingston, "a tiny collection of houses at the end of the railway line from Invercargill," where they lived until he was eight. "At the single-teacher school in Kingston, there were only eleven pupils, and I was the only one in my class. Some days I got a ride to school on the back of a huge horse with two other kids. We had to climb the school gate to get onto its back," Bishop once recollected. "I had a dog called Smudge and a cat called Calla Callutsa, which was given to us by some Greek neighbors when they shifted to Wellington."

"In Kingston, we had no electricity or telephone, and we didn't have a car," Bishop continued. "Our radio ran on a car battery, but reception was poor because of the surrounding mountains. The *Southland Times* arrived spasmodically on the freight train from Lumsden. It was the *Auckland Weekly* news, though, that excited us all, with the pictures of the young Queen Elizabeth's coronation in 1953—the pageantry and the crown jewels."

At the age of eight, Bishop returned with his family to Invercargill, where he discovered the joys of a free library system and joined the public library. He was introduced to J.R.R. Tolkien's *The Hobbit* through an extract in a magazine when he was nine years old. "I have read it several times since and still find it a source of inspiration," Bishop once noted.

"For as long as I can remember I've liked pictures and stories," Bishop told Barbara Murison in an interview reprinted on his home page. "I knew that I wanted to be an artist from a very early age, and luckily I was encouraged by my parents and teachers to hold onto this idea. Books have always been a part of my life and I was read and sung to by my mother and grandmother when I was little."

At the age of eighteen, Bishop enrolled at the Canterbury University School of Fine Arts in Christchurch to study painting. That experience "had the biggest impact on my approach to making art works," he later remarked in a *New Zealand Illustrators' Guild* interview, posted on his home page. "The most important lecturer I had there was Rudi Gopas whose approach to painting has stayed with me since that time. A general training in fine arts, rather than just in illustration, has been the foundation of all my book work." Bishop has also noted, however, that his art-school training caused a breach with a love of drawing representative objects which he has had since childhood. "When I went to art school I had to suspend that interest in drawing things—objects—animals, people, all those sorts of things, because it wasn't fashionable to draw anything in particular in art school," Bishop explained to Doreen Darnell in a *Talespinner* interview. "We had to paint abstract paintings—in fact, to paint anything that looked as though it had any sort of subject matter was called illustrative. And we were told very firmly to get rid of that from our school work, so it wasn't until some years after leaving art school that I found the courage to leave the abstract painting behind me and start painting images again. The basics are all much the same. It's just that I now allow myself to draw images."

After graduating with honors in painting in 1967, Bishop spent a year at the Christchurch Secondary Teachers' College, and for the next thirty years he earned much of his living teaching art, twenty years at a high school in Christchurch, New Zealand, and the final ten years at Christ's College in that same city. "From early in my life, I wanted to be an art teacher," Bishop once reflected. Like art, teaching has remained a constant interest throughout his life.

Bishop's first self-illustrated children's book, *Mrs McGinty and the Bizarre Plant,* won the Russell Clark Medal for Illustration from the New Zealand Library Association. In this story, the butt of the neighborhood children's jokes becomes a local hero of sorts when the plant she buys at the store grows to enormous proportions, eventually attracting the attention of a team of botanists who airlift the giant plant for their collection. Zena Sutherland, writing in the *Bulletin of the Center for Children's Books,* found the story "amusing", but offered greater praise for Bishop's illustrations, calling them "boldly designed, usually dramatically composed, nicely detailed." A critic for *Junior Bookshelf* similarly singled out Bishop's artwork for *Mrs McGinty and the Bizarre Plant,* stating that he "most effectively and subtly depicts the transformation of Mrs. McGinty's character and outlook." "I love gardening and growing things," the author once admitted. "My wife and I have times when we talk and read about nothing else. On other occasions, however, we avoid the garden for months on end."

Bishop followed this first effort with adaptations of traditional stories for children as well as original tales. His illustrations for *Mr Fox* drew comparisons to the work of Maurice Sendak from Marcus Crouch in *Junior Bookshelf,* and Margery Fisher likewise noted in *Growing Point* that Bishop's "idiosyncratic illustrations" add an element of "implied social satire" to the story that "lifts the folk-tale far away from its simple origins." *Mr Fox* is based on an old Massachusetts chain story and tells the tale of Mr. Fox who is out walking one day and finds a bumblebee which he puts in his bag. He deposits this bag, in turn, with a woman and tells her not to open it. But of course she does, and once it is opened the bumblebee flies out and is promptly eaten by a red rooster. Mr. Fox continues his walk and visits to various houses until he finally meets his match with another woman.

Bidibidi is an original tale about a high-country sheep in New Zealand who grows tired and bored with her uneventful life and diet of mountain grass. Following the rainbow in search of adventure, she has excitement galore. Similarly, according to a reviewer for the *Bulletin of the Center for Children's Books,* the "vigor and humor" of Bishop's illustrations steal the show, in the author's retelling *Chicken Licken,* the tale of a chick who thinks the sky is falling when an acorn lands on her head. "The traditional tale may be slight," wrote Ralph Lavender in *School Librarian,* "but the superbly autumnal pictures make it into something which is quite special." A review of Bishop's *Mother Hubbard* garnered the following comment from Crouch in *Junior Bookshelf:* "Bishop's distinguishing mark, apart from his brilliant technique, is his attention to detail. . . . These pictures are for reading." A *Kirkus Reviews* commentator, who began by noting that there is little need for another version of the story of *The Three Little Pigs,* concluded a review of Bishop's rendering by remarking, "Why not another version, if it's this good?"

Original tales are served up in several of Bishop's other offerings. *The Horror of Hickory Bay* takes place on a quiet summer day on Christmas in the southern hemisphere. While the grownups rest after a holiday meal, a monster emerges from the sea. Fortunately, young India Brown—modeled on Bishop's youngest daughter, Alexandra—and Uncle Atho and the dog Smudge team up to defeat the sea creature. *A Apple Pie* is a traditional English alphabet book based on an early Victorian rhyming version that follows one animal character after the other in pursuit of a slice of apple pie. With *Katarina,* Bishop tells a story closer to home. Based on the life of his great aunt, Katarina McKay, the picture book tells the story of a young Māori woman who, in the winter of 1861, leaves her tribal home in the North Island of New Zealand to travel and meet up with her Scottish husband on the South Island. A short time later, the white settlers begin to attack the Māori

Bishop's engaging animal characters take center stage in his colorful story for **Stay Awake, Bear!** *(© 2000 by Gavin Bishop. Reproduced by permission of Orchard Books, an imprint of Scholastic Inc.)*

homeland in the North Island to win more land for European settlers, cutting off the woman's contact with her family. Only when her brother arrives does Katarina learn what happened to her people.

Bishop further explores the New Zealand and Māori experience in titles such as *Hinepau, Maui and the Sun,* and *Maui and the Goddess of Fire.* "*Hinepau* is a legend-like story that I named after my mother whose family were Māori/Scots," Bishop once explained to *SATA.* The tale features a Māori woman with red hair and green eyes who is a weaver, but all of her weaving comes out backwards or inside out. Her tribe thinks she is a witch, and she is sent away to a lonely hut where she weaves all day. As if in punishment for this, the villagers are stricken by threat of death by starvation and thirst when a volcano covers all the surrounding countryside in ash. Hinepau then saves her villagers, however, making the ultimate sacrifice.

In *Maui and the Sun* and *Maui and the Goddess of Fire,* Bishop adapts Māori legends about a trickster. In *Maui and the Sun,* the trickster always plays jokes on his older brothers, but nothing could equal the time he tries to capture the sun. In *Booklist* Julie Corsaro found the tale "simple and lively." Maui makes a return in *Maui and the Goddess of Fire,* in which the mischief-maker brings fire to his people. Indeed, this playful trickster was also responsible, according to legend, for inventing the barbed fishing hook, an eel trap, and strong rope. "I would in the future like to produce more work of a bicultural nature," Bishop once told *SATA.* "New Zealand children should know and feel comfortable with their Māori heritage. Besides creating a better understanding of Māori-Pakeha values, a knowledge of Taha-Māori would provide a richer and more stimulating country in which to live."

Bishop has also found success with *Taming the Sun* and its companion volumes, *Riding the Waves: Four Māori*

Myths and *Counting the Sun: Four Māori Myths.* Aimed at young readers, the self-illustrated works contain a number of familiar legends, such as "Maui and the Big Fish," as well as less-well-known tales. Bishop, who is of English, Irish, Scots, and Māori descent, remarked in his *New Zealand Illustrators' Guild* interview that he acknowledges his cultural influences in his books. "It's something that fascinates me so intensely that I keep returning to it again and again," he stated. "I don't intellectualise it. It's intuitive."

Bishop focuses on animal characters in *Little Rabbit and the Sea,* the tale of a little bunny who has never seen the sea. All day long he thinks about the water, and at night he dreams he is sailing on a little boat in the midst of the big blue sea. Asking various relatives what the sea is like, he gets different answers from each. His curiosity grows and grows until one day a seagull takes him for a flight to see for himself. A reviewer for *Publishers Weekly* found this story to be "a poignant and affirming tribute to the powers of imagination" while Bishop's illustrations "radiate a lustrous quality reminiscent of ceramic glaze."

Bishop has traveled extensively, not only throughout New Zealand, but also to many countries overseas: England, France, Italy, Germany, Australia, Greece, Holland, Canada, and Malaysia. He has been to Japan four times, and in 1990, he and his youngest daughter took part in a cultural exchange on the island of Sakhalin in the then-Soviet Far East. In 1992, he went to Beijing and Shanghai at the invitation of UNESCO to give lectures and run workshops on children's literature. In 1997, he went to Indonesia to work again for UNESCO. He has also visited the United States several times and in the spring of 1996 taught at the Rhode Island School of Design in Providence.

It was while teaching in the United States that Bishop came up with the idea for *The House That Jack Built.*

Cover of Bishop's self-illustrated picture book **Mr Fox**, *which stars one of the classic villains of children's literature.* (Illustration courtesy of Gavin Bishop.)

Because of its distinctive New Zealand theme, however, U.S. editors felt the book would do better in New Zealand. When he returned to New Zealand from his year at the Rhode Island School of Design, Bishop showed an editor the idea and sold it immediately. One of his most popular books, *The House That Jack Built* gives this traditional rhyme a colonial flavor, by setting the action in New Zealand in 1798. Also, in Bishop's take on the tale, the tension between native Māori and the newcomers from Europe plays a central part in the action. *The House That Jack Built* went on to win several awards in New Zealand, including the *New Zealand Post* Picture Book of the Year and Book of the Year.

Bishop has also had a go at retelling the Brothers Grimm tale *Tom Thumb: The True History of Sir Thomas Thumb.* In Bishop's version, he "has added episodes of his own which appeal more to the modern child's need for action," according to Margaret Kedian, writing in *Magpies.* Kedian lauded the book, calling the artwork "stunning," and further remarking that "Bishop has . . . excelled himself with the text" in this, his "best book so far."

Working specifically for the U.S. market, Bishop created *Stay Awake, Bear!,* the story of an energetic bruin who decides not to waste all his time hibernating. To stay awake, Bear turns up the radio, makes jam tarts, and watches videos. But when summer comes, the bear is so tired that he sleeps all through the season. A reviewer for *Publishers Weekly* felt that this title "lacks the depth of imagination" of *Little Rabbit and the Sea,* but that it still "conveys a cozy mood with autumnal watercolor hues." *School Library Journal* critic Kathleen M. Kelly MacMillan, however, found the tale "lively," predicting it would appeal to children who find napping "a waste of time." MacMillan also praised Bishop's artwork for expressing the "jovial characters" and their "delight in winter camaraderie."

Bishop also contributed the illustrations to *Snake and Lizard,* a humorous chapter book by Joy Cowley. The work details the unlikely friendship between two very different creatures whose sometimes misguided antics only serve to draw them closer together. According to Joanna Rudge Long in *Horn Book,* "Bishop's art . . . enlivens almost every spread of this attractive small volume, capturing each interaction with wit and affection." A critic in *Kirkus Reviews* noted that Bishop's pen-and-ink and watercolor pictures embellish Cowley's tales, adding that the artist's "contained lines and splashes of color breathe air into the setting's dry surroundings." Kirsten Cutler, writing in *School Library Journal,* similarly noted that Bishop's "charming illustrations are suffused with warm desert colors, and the evocative landscapes enhance the brief adventures."

Bishop told Murison that the work he does for the American market is different than what he creates for the New Zealand market. In his *Talespinner* interview,

Bishop's illustration projects include introducing the reptilian stars of Joy Cowley's picture book **Snake and Lizard.** (Kane/Miller, 2008. Illustration ©Gavin Bishop. Reproduced by permission.)

he noted that publishing in the United States is important to his career. "From a financial point of view, it can make being a writer and illustrator possible, because the print runs are much bigger and the potential income from those books is much greater."

Discussing the future of picture books with Murison, Bishop stated, "I like to think that books are such an efficient and convenient unit that they will always be around. They are so simple and mobile. . . . The act of nursing a child and reading a much loved picture book seems to me to be such a natural human thing to do that something extraordinary will be needed to replace it."

Biographical and Critical Sources

BOOKS

Dunkle, Margaret, editor, *The Story Makers: A Collection of Interviews with Australian and New Zealand Authors and Illustrators for Young People,* Oxford University Press (Melbourne, Victoria, Australia), 1987.

Gaskin, Chris, *Picture Book Magic,* Reed (Auckland, New Zealand), 1996.

Marantz, Sylvia, and Kenneth Marantz, *Artists of the Page: Interviews with Children's Book Illustrators,* McFarland & Company (Jefferson, NC), 1992.

PERIODICALS

Booklist, May 1, 1996, Julie Corsaro, review of *Maui and the Sun: A Māori Tale,* p. 1508; December 1, 1999, John Peter, review of *The Video Shop Sparrow,* p. 709; August, 2000, Isabel Schon, review of *Little Rabbit and the Sea,* p. 2154.

Bulletin of the Center for Children's Books, May, 1983, Zena Sutherland, review of *Mrs McGinty and the Bizarre Plant,* p. 163; April, 1985, review of *Chicken Licken,* p. 141.

Faces: People, Places, and Cultures, January, 2001, review of *Maui and the Sun,* p. 46.

Growing Point, May, 1983, Margery Fisher, review of *Mr Fox,* p. 4080.

Horn Book, November-December, 2008, Joanna Rudge Long, review of *Snake and Lizard,* p. 699.

Junior Bookshelf, August, 1982, review of *Mrs McGinty and the Bizarre Plant,* pp. 128-129; June, 1983, Marcus Crouch, review of *Mr Fox,* p. 107; February, 1988, Marcus Crouch, review of *Mother Hubbard,* p. 18.

Kirkus Reviews, January 15, 1990, review of *The Three Little Pigs,* pp. 101-102; August 1, 2008, review of *Snake and Lizard.*

Magpies, March, 2002, Margaret Kedian, review of *Tom Thumb: The True History of Thomas Thumb,* p. 6.

Publishers Weekly, November 28, 1994, review of *The Wedding of Mistress Fox,* p. 61; October 20, 1997, review of *Little Rabbit and the Sea,* p. 74; March 20, 2000, review of *Stay Awake, Bear!,* p. 90.

School Librarian, June, 1985, Ralph Lavender, review of *Chicken Licken,* p. 133.

School Library Journal, December, 1994, Marilyn Taniguchi, review of *The Wedding of Mistress Fox,* pp. 122-123; July, 1996, Pam Gosner, review of *Maui and the Sun,* p. 77; December, 1997, Maura Bresnahan, review of *Little Rabbit and the Sea,* p. 81; December, 1999, Lisa Gangeni Kropp, review of *The Video Shop Sparrow,* p. 90; March, 2000, Kathleen M. Kelly MacMillan, review of *Stay Awake, Bear!,* p. 178; December, 2008, Kirsten Cutler, review of *Snake and Lizard,* p. 86.

Talespinner, September, 1999, Doreen Darnell, interview with Bishop, pp. 22-29.

ONLINE

Gavin Bishop Home Page, http://www.gavinbishop.com (May 15, 2010).

New Zealand Book Council Web site, http://www.bookcouncil.org.nz/ (May 1, 2010), "Gavin Bishop."

Storylines Web site, http://www.storylines.org.nz/ (May 1, 2010), "Gavin Bishop."

Te Tai Tamariki Web site, http://www.tetaitamariki.org.nz/ (May 1, 2010), "Gavin Bishop."

BREEN, M.E.
(Molly Breen)

Personal
Born in Berkeley, CA. *Education:* Yale University, B.A., M.A. (English literature).

Addresses
Home—San Francisco, CA.

Career
Writer and teacher. Carnegie Foundation, Stanford, CA, program associate and literacy advocate; lecturer at schools, including Yale University, Stanford University, Walden House, and Mission Language and Vocational School. Presenter at schools and writing workshops.

Writings

Darkwood, Bloomsbury (New York, NY), 2009.

Sidelights
In *Darkwood* M.E. Breen transports readers to a place called Howland, where the darkness of night falls like a curtain, suddenly and completely. In Howland night is not the only thing that prompts residents to bar their doors: they also fear the creatures known as kinderstalk, which are said to leave their forest home and prowl the moonlit village, hoping to make away with unattended and vulnerable children. Twelve-year-old Annie Trewitt lives in Howland, under the care of her aunt and uncle. Although she fears the forest and the dark, she fears her guardians even more, especially when she learns that they plan to sell her into slavery to work mining a valuable stone. To avoid this fate, Annie runs away into the forest, where she learns the truth about the kinderstalk, and also learns that Howland has many dark secrets of its own. Soon Annie begins a quest that will bring her to a place of amazing beauty as well as force her to face a terrible evil in a novel that draws on the sinister aspects of many traditional fairy tales.

Reviewing *Darkwood* in *Booklist,* Carolyn Phelan recommended Breen's mix of fantasy and adventure, noting that Annie's growing ability to trust belies the challenges she faces "in her grim, cruel, and perilous world." Praising the author's "finely tuned storytelling" and her respect for her reader's "intelligence," a *Kirkus Reviews* writer wrote that Breen's debut novel "shines with utterly believable strangeness," while *Bulletin of the Center for Children's Books* contributor Kate Quealy-Gainer noted that the story's "oppressively sinister atmosphere" combines with Breen's "impeccable pacing and slow revelations" to keep readers turning the pages.

Cover of M.E. Breen's debut fantasy novel Darkwood, *featuring artwork by Alexander Jansson.* (Bloomsbury, 2009. Jacket illustration ©2009 by Alexander Jansson. Reproduced by permission.)

Biographical and Critical Sources

PERIODICALS

Booklist, May 15, 2009, Carolyn Phelan, review of *Darkwood,* p. 55.
Bulletin of the Center for Children's Books, September, 2009, Kate Quealy-Gainer, review of *Darkwood,* p. 7.
Kirkus Reviews, April 1, 2009, review of *Darkwood.*
School Library Journal, June, 2009, Saleena Davidson, review of *Darkwood,* p. 116.

ONLINE

M.E. Breen Home Page, http://www.mebreen.com (May 30, 2010).*

*   *   *

BREEN, Molly
See BREEN, M.E.

BURNINGHAM, Sarah O'Leary

Personal
Female. *Hobbies and other interests:* Movies, crafts, travel.

Addresses
Home—NY. *Office*—Little Bird Publicity, 35-27 78th St., Ste. 31, Jackson Heights, NY 11372.

Career
Writer and publicist. Member of publicity departments at Workman Publishing, Miramax, Gibbs Smith, and REGAN; William Morrow, New York, NY, former associate director of publicity; HarperCollins, New York, NY, associate director of marketing for HarperStudio imprint, c. 2008; Little Bird Publicity, Jackson Heights, NY, founder and publicist.

Writings

How to Raise Your Parents: A Teen Girl's Survival Guide, illustrated by Bella Pilar, Chronicle Books (San Francisco, CA), 2008.
Boyology: A Teen Girl's Crash Course in All Things Boy, illustrated by Keri Smith, Chronicle Books (San Francisco, CA), 2009.

Advice columnist for "Dear Sarah," ABCFamily Web site.

Sidelights
Sarah O'Leary Burningham was inspired to write her first book, *How to Raise Your Parents: A Teen Girl's Survival Guide,* while recalling her own experiences as a sixteen year old butting heads with her mom and dad over house rules and punishments. "I realized they were as clueless as I was," she explained on her home page. Burningham's regular job, writing an advice column for a high-profile teen Web site, reinforced her suspicion that her parents were not that unusual; in fact, most parents are at a disadvantage when dealing with their adolescent offspring. Supporting her hypothesis with interviews with hundreds of parents and thousands of American teens, Burningham discovered the ways teens have successfully bridged their family's generation and technology gap. She shares this wealth of knowledge in *How to Raise Your Parents,* and mines her many interviews for dating advice in her second book, *Boyology: A Teen Girl's Crash Course in All Things Boy.*

How to ensure your privacy, how to get parents to understand you, what to do when you are caught lying, and techniques to acquire freedom and independence: these are among the issues addressed in *How to Raise Your Parents.* Beginning by placing one's parents in one of five categories—laid-back hippies, high-achieving yuppies, control freaks, overgrown teenagers, or perpetual teachers—readers are then guided into the most effective way to achieve communication and negotiation. Although Sarah O'Holla admitted that the author takes the (arguably correct) view that parents are the ones in charge, she added that Burningham is "a very hip adult who makes sense." A *Publishers Weekly* critic noted that *How to Raise Your Parents* "presumes a maturity on the part of readers," but added that the author's advice, if followed, will help readers "be set for life." "Is this book necessary?," asked *Kliatt* reviewer Sherri Forgesh Ginsberg. Her answer: "Absolutely."

In *Boyology* Burningham provides the lowdown on the courtship rituals of the modern adolescent male, including flirting styles, male expectations, how to handle first dates, hooking up, appropriate boundaries, dealing with "No," the art of breaking up, and how to discern boy friends from potential boyfriends. Her relaxed, upbeat prose is mixed with quizzes, quotes from celebrities, and the result of her MySpace polls, then liberally salted with pop-culture references to produce a book that Elaine Baran Black described in *School Library Jour-*

Sarah O'Leary Burningham shares a wealth of practical information with beginning daters in **Boyology.** (Used with permission of Chronicle Books LLC, San Francisco. Visit ChronicleBooks.com.)

nal as "well-written and smart." Recommending *Boyology* for teens new to the dating game, a *Publishers Weekly* critic asserted that Burningham's "humorous guide provides insight into the elusive universe of boys," and a *Kirkus Reviews* writer described it as "appealing, entertaining," and "full of useful facts and sound advice."

In addition to her writing, Burningham has become something of a public spokesman for modern teens. She has appeared on television's *Today Show, ABC News, New York 1 News,* and *CBS News.* She has also been quoted in *Newsweek,* the *Wall Street Journal,* and *Teen Vogue,* and continues to advise both teens and their parents in her column for ABCFamily.com.

Biographical and Critical Sources

PERIODICALS

Kirkus Reviews, April 1, 2009, review of *Boyology: A Teen Girl's Crash Course in All Things Boy.*
Kliatt, November, 2008, Sherri Forgash Gisnberg, review of *How to Raise Your Parents: A Teen Girl's Survival Guide,* p. 38.
Publishers Weekly, May 19, 2008, review of *How to Raise Your Parents,* p. 55; April 6, 2009, review of *Boyology,* p. 47.
School Library Journal, July, 2008, Sarah O'Holla, review of *How to Raise Your Parents,* p. 110; June, 2009, Elaine Baran Black, review of *Boyology,* p. 140.

ONLINE

Little Bird Publicity Web site, http://www.littlebirdpublicity. com (June 1, 2010), "Sarah Burningham."
Sarah O'Leary Burningham Home Page, http://sarah burningham.com (May 31, 2010).

* * *

BYRD, Tim 1964-

Personal

Born 1964; children: one son.

Addresses

Home—Dekalb County, GA.

Career

Writer. Formerly worked as a dishwasher, salesman, waiter, soldier, game designer, filmmaker, and guide.

Writings

Doc Wilde and the Frogs of Doom, G.P. Putnam's Sons (New York, NY), 2009.

Sidelights

As a child growing up in the 1960s and early 1970s, Tim Byrd collected "Doc Savage" novels, reprints of adventure yarns written by Lester Dent under the pen name Kenneth Robeson and originally serialized in the "Dog Savage" pulp magazine from 1933 to 1949. Pulp magazines were so called because they were printed on cheap rough paper; they usually featured tantalizing and sometimes suggestive cover art, ran to over one hundred pages in length, and featured stories focusing on crime detection, horror, jungle adventure, and the like. "As a father, I looked for books to share with my son that had that same sense of epic fun," Byrd explained on his home page, "but the 'Doc Savage' books were out of print and nothing else quite captured the classic spirit of the pulps. I decided to write a book for him that did. The result was *Doc Wilde and the Frogs of Doom,* a modern-day homage to the pulp greats, full of cliffhangers and gadgets and world-threatening villains being vanquished by a stalwart family of adventurers."

Geared for readers aged ten and older, *Doc Wilde and the Frogs of Doom* follows the adventures of Doc Spartacus Wilde, a martial artist, chemist, and master of disguise, as he seeks out adventures in exotic locations. Accompanying Doc Wilde are his children, ten-year-old Wren and twelve-year-old Brian, as well as two good friends whose comic banter alleviates the story's tenser moments. When Wilde's eccentric-scientist father is abducted from the Amazon rainforest by strange amphibious creatures, the adventurous group trek into danger, traversing a hidden country that turns out to be the home of a priest-led cult whose members worship a god named Frogon.

In a review of Byrd's debut novel, a *Kirkus Reviews* writer praised the author's "fast-paced, intelligent prose," which is "laced with humor and literary allusions." Noting that the story's "premise can get awfully silly," Ilene Cooper added in *Booklist* that Byrd's cliffhanger novel features non-stop adventure "and the quick pace will appeal to reluctant readers." Dubbing *Doc Wilde and the Frogs of Doom* a "genial parody," Elaine E. Knight added in her *School Library Journal* review that "the book's small format, breakneck pacing, and broad humor will appeal to middle-grade adventure fans."

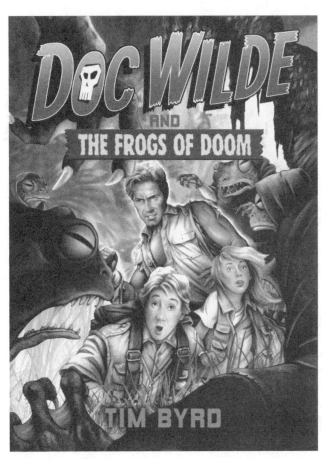

Tim Byrd recalls the action-packed pulp novels of old in his middle-grade adventure **Doc Wilde and the Frogs of Doom.** (G.P. Putnam's Sons, 2009. Jacket art ©2009 by Tim Gabor. Reproduced by permission.)

Biographical and Critical Sources

PERIODICALS

Booklist, August 1, 2009, Ilene Cooper, review of *Doc Wilde and the Frogs of Doom,* p. 69.

Kirkus Reviews, April 1, 2009, review of *Doc Wilde and the Frogs of Doom.*

School Library Journal, August, 2009, Elaine E. Knight, review of *Doc Wilde and the Frogs of Doom,* p. 99.

ONLINE

Tim Byrd Home Page, http://www.docwilde.com (May 31, 2010).*

C

CALONITA, Jen

Personal

Born on Long Island, NY; married; husband's name Mike; children: Tyler, Dylan. *Education:* College degree. *Hobbies and other interests:* Scrapbooking, watching movies.

Addresses

Home—Merrick, NY. *E-mail*—info@jencalonitaonline. com.

Career

Author, journalist, and editor. *Teen People,* former senior entertainment editor; journalist focusing on entertainment industry.

Writings

"SECRETS OF MY HOLLYWOOD LIFE" NOVEL SERIES

Secrets of My Hollywood Life, Little, Brown (New York, NY), 2006.
On Location, Little, Brown (New York, NY), 2007.
Family Affairs, Little, Brown (New York, NY), 2008.
Paparazzi Princess, Little, Brown (New York, NY), 2009.
Broadway Lights, Little, Brown (New York, NY), 2010.
There's No Place like Home, Little, Brown (New York, NY), 2011.

YOUNG-ADULT NOVEL SERIES

Sleepaway Girls, Little, Brown (New York, NY), 2009.
Reality Check, Little, Brown (New York, NY), 2010.

OTHER

Contributor to periodicals, including *Glamour, Marie Claire,* and *TV Guide.*

Sidelights

Jen Calonita turned to writing teen fiction after a career as an entertainment journalist and senior editor of a teen publisher imprint. As a reporter, she had the chance to interview a number of top Hollywood celebrities, and she has taken the best characteristics of this exclusive group in crafting the teen heroine in her popular novel series "Secrets of My Hollywood Life." Calonita "clearly knows how to appeal to Yas who . . . wonder what it would be like to be famous," observed *Kliatt* contributor Claire Rosser in appraising the series.

In the "Secrets of My Hollywood Life" books, Calonita follows Kaitlin Burke, a sixteen-year-old actress who has starred in a popular prime-time television program called *Family Affair* since she was in preschool, pretty much growing up on the set. When the stresses of being a teen celebrity and the behavior of jealous costar Sky Mackenzie get to be too much, Kaitlin hatches a plan to get some relief: she decides to hide out in the high school her best friend attends, enrolling under a fake name. In *School Library Journal* Catherine Ensley praised Kaitlin as "kind, unspoiled, and upstanding— refreshingly different" from the heroines in other teen celebrity novels.

Kaitlin's adventures continue in five other novels: *On Location, Family Affairs, Paparazzi Princess, Broadway Lights,* and *There's No Place like Home. On Location* finds the teen dating Austin Meyers and preparing to star in a feature film directed by her favorite director, even though her publicist pushes her to make public appearances with her television costar and romantic ex. The summer seems to be going well until an ex shows up and life on the film set gets complicated. Kaitlin's return to the set of her television series is the backdrop of *Family Affairs,* but an unfortunate casting decision has brought the conniving Alexis onto the set and made her determined to disrupt Kaitlin's love life. "Calonita has a knack for nailing down most teens' perception of stardom," observed *School Library Journal* critic Emily Garrett in a review of *On Location,* and Rosser dubbed the same novel "a frolic" that plays out "in a setting most YAs find fascinating."

Cover of Jen Calonita's young-adult novel Sleepaway Girls, *which finds a teen learning about life during a stint as a summer-camp counselor.* (Little, Brown & Company, 2009. Reproduced by permission.)

With *Family Affair* filming its final season in *Paparazzi Princess*, the teen finds herself in career limbo, and when a fight with good friend Liz leaves her at lose ends, she ends up in the wrong company. Late nights, shopping sprees, and tabloid photographs grouping Kaitlin with notorious party girls Lauren and Ava are the result. Fortunately, a role in a Broadway play beckons and Kaitlin travels to the East Coast for the summer, where her performance earns her rave reviews. Unfortunately, the distance mixes with a handsome costar to threaten her relationship with Austin, who languishes at a Texas lacrosse summer camp. Reviewing *Paparazzi Princess, School Library Journal* critic Kelley Siegrist dubbed the book a "quick, fun read," adding that teens will "recognize the similarities between Lauren and Ava and the party girls from today's tabloid news."

In addition to her series fiction, Calonita has produced the standalone novels *Sleepaway Girls* and *Reality Check*. *Sleepaway Girls* focuses on fifteen-year-old Samantha Montgomery, who joins a group of girls training to be summer camp counselors as a way to avoid hometown boy problems, while *Reality Check* follows a group of five friends from small-town Long Island who are chosen to star in their own reality television show.

Calling *Sleepaway Girls* "a perfect summer pick," Heather E. Miller added that "Sam and her campmates are believable characters," while *Booklist* critic Frances Bradburn recommended the novel to "fans of Ann Brashares' Traveling Pants series." Sam is "a likeable, realistically flawed heroine," concluded a *Publishers Weekly* critic, the reviewer adding that in *Sleepaway Girls* Calonita "proves that good girls can come out on top."

Biographical and Critical Sources

PERIODICALS

Booklist, May 1, 2009, Frances Bradburn, review of *Sleepaway Girls,* p. 75.
Kirkus Reviews, April 1, 2009, review of *Sleepaway Girls.*
Kliatt, May, 2006, Claire Rosser, review of *Secrets of My Hollywood Life,* p. 6; May, 2007, Claire Rosser, review of *On Location,* p. 8.
Publishers Weekly, May 25, 2009, review of *Sleepaway Girls,* p. 59.
School Library Journal, June, 2006, Catherine Ensley, review of *Secrets of My Hollywood Life,* p. 148; July, 2007, Emily Garrett, review of *On Location,* p. 97; June, 2009, Kelley Siegrist, review of *Paparazzi Princess,* p. 116 and Heather E. Miller, review of *Sleepaway Girls,* p. 118.
Voice of Youth Advocates, June, 2007, Jane Chen, review of *On Location,* p. 138; June, 2008, Rebecca White, review of *Family Affairs,* p. 138.

ONLINE

Hachette Book Group Web site, http://www.hachettebook group.com/ (June 1, 2010), "Jen Calonita."
Jen Calonita Home Page, http://www.jencaloniatonline. com (May 31, 2010).*

*　　*　　*

CANGA, C.B. 1976-
(Chris Canga)

Personal

Born 1976, in Jacksonville, FL; married; wife's name Robyn; children: Rockwell, Trinity. *Education:* Academy of Arts University (San Francisco, CA), B.F.A. (illustration), 2002.

Addresses

Home—CA.

Career

Illustrator and educator. Academy of Arts University, San Francisco, CA, instructor in drawing, beginning 2004. Freelance illustrator; creator of artwork for Forbidden Island board game, 2010; designer of interactive art for Nintendo Wii.

Illustrator

Jill Santopolo, *Alec Flint, Super Sleuth: The Nina, the Pinta, and the Vanishing Treasure,* Scholastic, Inc., (New York, NY), 2008.

Robert West, *There's a Spaceship in My Tree!,* Zonderkids (Grand Rapids, MI), 2009.

Robert West, *Attack of the Spider Bots,* Zonderkids (Grand Rapids, MI), 2009.

Robert West, *Escape from the Drooling Octopod!,* Zonderkids (Grand Rapids, MI), 2009.

Stephen Crane, *The Red Badge of Courage,* adapted by Lisa Mullarkey, Magic Wagon (Edina, MN), 2010.

Eli Stutz, *Pickle Impossible,* Bloomsbury (New York, NY), 2010.

Contributor to books, including *Fearless Flynn and Other Tales,* HarperCollins (New York, NY), 2008, and to educational materials. Contributor to periodicals, including *Highlights for Children, National Geographic, Outdoor Life,* and *Running.*

"FIELD TRIP MYSTERY" SERIES

Steve Brezenoff, *On the Bus, on the Case,* Stone Arch Books (Mankato, MN), 2010.

Steve Brezenoff, *The Painting That Wasn't There,* Stone Arch Books (Mankato, MN), 2010.

Steve Brezenoff, *The Teacher Who Forgot Too Much,* Stone Arch Books (Mankato, MN), 2010.

Steve Brezenoff, *The Village That Almost Vanished,* Stone Arch Books (Mankato, MN), 2010.

Steve Brezenoff, *The Zoo with the Empty Cage,* Stone Arch Books (Mankato, MN), 2010.

Biographical and Critical Sources

PERIODICALS

Booklist, May 1, 2008, Stephanie Zvirin, review of *Alec Flint, Super Sleuth: The Nina, the Pinta, and the Vanishing Treasure,* p. 51.

ONLINE

C.B. Canga Web log, http://www.cbcangaart.blogspot.com (May 31, 2010).

Debris Online, http://debrismagazine.com/(May 31, 2010), "C.B. Canga."*

*   *   *

CANGA, Chris
See CANGA, C.B.

CHEN, Chih-Yuan 1975-
(Chen Chih-Yuan, Zhiyuan Chen)

Personal

Born 1975, in Pingtung, Taiwan; son of Chi-Nan (a farmer) and Li-Huo (a homemaker) Chen. *Education:* Attended college.

Addresses

Home—2F, NO129. Sec 2. An-Ho Road, Taipei, Taiwan 106. *E-mail*—info@element-plus.com.

Career

Freelance children's book author and illustrator, beginning 1999.

Awards, Honors

Two-time winner of Hsin Yi Picture Book Award (Taiwan); American Library Association Notable Children's Book designation, Hsin-Yi Picture Book Award, and Virginia Reader's Choice nomination, all c. 2004, all for *Guji-Guji.*

Writings

SELF-ILLUSTRATED

Memories, Hsin Yi Publications, 2000.

On My Way to Buy Eggs, Kane/Miller Book Publishers (La Jolla, CA), 2001.

A Day Presents Are a Must, Heryin Books (Alhambra, CA), 2003.

Guji-Guji, Kane/Miller Book Publishers (La Jolla, CA), 2004.

The Best Christmas Ever, Heryin Books (Alhambra, CA), 2005.

The Featherless Chicken, Heryin Books (Alhambra, CA), 2006.

Artie and Julie, Heryin Books (Alhambra, CA), 2008.

Author's works have been translated into Spanish.

Sidelights

Taiwanese artist Chih-Yuan Chen is the author and illustrator of several books for young children, among them *On My Way to Buy Eggs, The Featherless Chicken, The Best Christmas Ever,* and *Guji-Guji,* each of which has been translated and published in the United States. In his stories, such as *The Featherless Chicken* and *Guji-Guji,* which feature his stylish ink-and-watercolor wash art, the award-winning Chen hopes to teach children to acceptance and help them open their minds to new people and new ideas.

On My Way to Buy Eggs follows a young girl named Shau-yu, as she goes on an errand for her father. Her walk quickly becomes an exciting, eye-opening experience as she views the world through a blue marble, discovers a pair of glasses that make everything appear blurry, and follows a cat's shadow. Gillian Engberg, writing in *Booklist,* praised Chen's "beautifully drawn scenes" and dubbed *On My Way to Buy Eggs* "joyful" and "understated." In *School Library Journal,* Marge Loch-Wouters predicted that the book's "universal tribute to the power of a child's imagination will strike a familiar chord with dreamers everywhere."

Chen's focus turns to an unusual friendship in *Artie and Julie,* which finds two young creatures ignoring the teachings of their parents and becoming playmates. Artie is a lion cub who is taught to hunt rabbits, while Julie is a young bunny. When a storm forces both youngsters into the same cave, they immediately become friends and spend a day playing together. When Artie and Julie return to their homes, they each tell their parents a story that challenges some family traditions. Calling *Artie and Julie* a book that will "score high on child appeal," a *Kirkus Reviews* writer noted in particular Chen's use of "soft hues and smiling, simply drawn cartoon animal" characters.

Featuring both "deft pacing and [a] spare text," in the opinion of a *Publishers Weekly* critic, *Guji-Guji* reflects several now-classic stories in its tale of a mother duck who inadvertently accepts an unusually large egg into her nest and then rears the non-duck offspring as one of her own. In this case, the hatchling is a baby crocodile that cries "gugi-gugi" instead of "quack-quack." When the creature learns that it is in fact a crocodile and is expected to eat ducks rather than live with them, young Guji-Guji devises a plan that allows both ducks and crocs to accept it. The story's "vivid characters . . . are rendered with wit and warmth," noted Jessica Bruder in her *New York Times Book Review* of *Guji-Guji,* and "careful readers will delight in the details" in the book's humorous illustrations. While the *Publishers Weekly* critic predicted that Chen's book "gives every sign of becoming a well-worn favorite," in *School Library Journal* Julie Roach praised the "compelling" artwork in *Guji-Guji* and concluded that the author/illustrator's "charming spin on the ugly duckling theme is a must-have."

Biographical and Critical Sources

PERIODICALS

Booklist, October 15, 2003, Gillian Engberg, review of *On My Way to Buy Eggs,* p. 416; December 1, 2005, Ilene Cooper, review of *The Best Christmas Ever,* p. 52.
Bulletin of the Center for Children's Books, September, 2004, Deborah Stevenson, review of *Guji-Guji,* p. 9.

Horn Book, January-February, 2004, Martha V. Parravano, review of *On My Way to Buy Eggs,* p. 68.
Kirkus Reviews, November 1, 2005, review of *The Best Christmas Ever,* p. 1191; August 15, 2006, review of *The Featherless Chicken,* p. 837; August 1, 2008, review of *Artie and Julie.*
New York Time Book Review, February 13, 2005, Jessica Bruder, review of *Guji-Guji,* p. 17.
Publishers Weekly, November 8, 2004, review of *Guji-Guji,* p. 55; September, 26, 2005, review of *The Best Christmas Ever,* p. 88; September 18, 2006, review of *The Featherless Chicken,* p. 54.
School Library Journal, October, 2003, Marge Loch-Wouters, review of *On My Way to Buy Eggs,* p. 115; November, 2004, Julie Roach, review of *Guji-Guji,* p. 94; October, 2006, Genevieve Gallagher, review of *The Featherless Chicken,* p. 103; September, 2008, Catherine Threadgill, review of *Artie and Julie,* p. 142.
Washington Post Book World, August, 2004, Elizabeth Ward, review of *Guji-Guji,* p. 12.

ONLINE

Kane/Miller Web site, http://www.kanemiller.com/ (June 15, 2010), "Chih-Yuan Chen."
Papertigers.org, http://www.papertigers.org/ (July 20, 2004), "Chih-Yuan Chen."*

*   *   *

CHEN, Zhiyuan
See CHEN, Chih-Yuan

*   *   *

CHEN CHIH-YUAN
See CHEN, Chih-Yuan

*   *   *

CLARK, David 1960-

Personal

Born 1960, in Chicago, IL; married; children: three. *Education:* Pennsylvania Academy of the Fine Arts, degree.

Addresses

Home—Luray, VA. *E-mail*—davidclark1988@gmail.com.

Career

Illustrator and cartoonist. Freelance illustrator for magazines, newspapers, and children's books, 1988—. Cartoonist for "Barney and Clyde" syndicated comic strip, 2010—.

Awards, Honors

Reuben Award, National Cartoonists Society, 1996, for newspaper illustration; Noah Bee Award for magazine illustration; Educational Press Association Award; Maryland Society of Professional Journalist Award for newspaper illustration; Virginia Press Association Award for newspaper illustration; Maryland-Delaware-DC Press Association Award for newspaper illustration.

Illustrator

Barry Louis Polisar, *Snakes and the Boy Who Was Afraid of Them,* Rainbow Morning Music (Silver Spring, MD), 1988.

Barry Louis Polisar, *The Snake Who Was Afraid of People,* Rainbow Morning Music (Silver Spring, MD), 1988.

Barry Louis Polisar, *The Trouble with Ben,* Rainbow Morning Music (Silver Spring, MD), 1992.

Barry Louis Polisar, *Peculiar Zoo,* Rainbow Morning Music (Silver Spring, MD), 1993.

Barry Louis Polisar, *Don't Do That!: A Child's Guide to Bad Manners, Ridiculous Rules, and Inadequate Etiquette,* Rainbow Morning Music (Silver Spring, MD), 1994.

Barry Louis Polisar, *The Haunted House Party,* Rainbow Morning Music (Silver Spring, MD), 1995.

Cynthia MacGregor, *"Why Do We Need Another Baby?": Helping Your Child Welcome a New Arrival—With Love and Illustrations,* Citadel Press Books (New York, NY), 1996.

Cynthia MacGregor, *"Why Do We Have to Move?": Helping Your Child Adjust—With Love and Illustrations,* Citadel Press Books (New York, NY), 1996.

Cynthia MacGregor, *"Why Do People Die?": Helping Your Child Understand—With Love and Illustrations,* Citadel Press Books (New York, NY), 1998.

Barry Louis Polisar, *Insect Soup: Bug Poems,* Rainbow Morning Music (Silver Spring, MD), 1999.

Barry Louis Polisar, *A Little Less Noise,* Rainbow Morning Music (Silver Spring, MD), 2001.

Diane Z. Shore, *Bus-a-Saurus Bop,* Bloomsbury Children's Books (New York, NY), 2003.

Bob Hartman, *Grumblebunny,* Putnam (New York, NY), 2003.

Rick Walton, *A Very Hairy Scary Story,* Putnam (New York, NY), 2004.

Micky Dolenz, *Gakky Two-Feet,* Putnam (New York, NY), 2006.

Kathryn Lasky, *Pirate Bob,* Charlesbridge (Watertown, MA), 2006.

Kim Norman, *Jack of All Tails,* Dutton Children's Books (New York, NY), 2007.

Sudipta Bardhan-Quallen, *The Mine-o-Saur,* Putnam (New York, NY), 2007.

Dave Keane, *Bobby Bramble Loses His Brain,* Clarion Books (New York, NY), 2009.

Contributor of illustrations to periodicals, including *Washington Times* and *Air & Space.*

David Clark's illustration projects include creating the stylized artwork in Barry Louis Polisar's A Little Less Noise. (© 2001 by Rainbow Morning Music. Reproduced by permission.)

Sidelights

David Clark, an award-winning cartoonist and illustrator based in Virginia, has provided the artwork for a number of highly regarded picture books, including *A Very Hairy Scary Story* and *Bobby Bramble Loses His Brain.* Early in his career, Clark enjoyed a successful collaboration with author and entertainer Barry Louis Polisar on such titles as *A Little Less Noise* and *The Trouble with Ben.* The latter work centers on the efforts of an affable but bumbling bear to fit in with his human classmates. According to a *Publishers Weekly* critic, Polisar's tale "is pepped up by Clark's droll cartoons."

Clark and Polisar have also joined forces on *Peculiar Zoo,* a volume of poems about such uncommon creatures as the dik-dik, the proboscis monkey, and the Australian numbat. In *Publishers Weekly,* a reviewer praised Clark's "witty, loosely drawn illustrations." *A Little Less Noise* collects a number of Polisar's humorous songs, including "I Lost My Pants" and "My Brother Threw Up on My Stuffed Toy Bunny." Clark again drew praise for his pictures; Jane Marino, writing in *School Library Journal,* remarked that his "illustrations are over the top and even slightly ribald with exaggerations galore," and a *Publishers Weekly* contributor observed that the artist "dishes up his trademark blend of quirky, bug-eyed cartoonlike creatures, whose exaggerated expressions heighten the humor."

Clark also contributed the illustrations to *Bus-a-Saurus Bop,* the debut work of Diane Z. Shore. In rhyming verse, Shore reimagines a vehicle familiar to many children—a yellow school bus—as a rollicking, belching creature that swallows up students and spits them out once it arrives at school. Clark's drawings, which depict a long-tailed, spiny-backed reptile with bulging eyes and a protruding tongue, "have a cartoon flavor," remarked a *Kirkus Reviews* critic. "In Clark's full-to-bursting illustrations," a *Publishers Weekly* contributor observed, ". . . the heavy creature moves so fast that pavement lifts off the ground like a loose ribbon."

A curmudgeonly rabbit helps his sweet-natured relatives escape from a hungry adversary in *Grumblebunny,* a humorous tale by Bob Hartman. After capturing Cuddle-mop, Sweetsnuffle, and Pretty, three incredibly innocent and trusting souls, Bad Wolf Peter meets his match in their sullen cousin, Grumblebunny, whose sour disposition ruins the carnivore's pot of rabbit stew. Kathy Piehl, writing in *School Library Journal,* complimented the illustrator's comedic portrayal of the title character's family members, stating, "The three bucktoothed, wide-eyed optimists have vacuous expressions that reveal their naive view of the world."

A young girl's vivid imagination gets the best of her as she walks home one night in Rick Walton's *A Very Hairy Scary Story,* which features artwork by Clark. In *School Library Journal,* Linda Staskus wrote that the "exaggerated and humorous illustrations will send tingles down readers' spines." *Gakky Two-Feet,* a prehistoric tale by Micky Dolenz, focuses on the heroic exploits of a furry, bug-eyed creature that discovers the advantages of walking upright. Clark's "vibrant, earth-toned watercolor-and-ink illustrations add just the right comic edge," observed *Booklist* reviewer Julie Cummins.

Clark teamed up with award-winning author Kathryn Lasky on *Pirate Bob,* a tale of friendship and jealousy among a group of roguish characters. "Clark's google-eyed buccaneers appear to be a fun-loving bunch, if slightly deranged," wrote Kara Schaff Dean in *School Library Journal.* A youngster finds it difficult to concentrate on even the simplest of things when his mind literally wanders off in *Bobby Bramble Loses His Brain,* a work by Dave Keane. The title character "makes a suitably daffy center for Clark's comic cartoons," a contributor stated in *Kirkus Reviews.*

Biographical and Critical Sources

PERIODICALS

Booklist, June 1, 2006, Julie Cummins, review of *Gakky Two-Feet,* p. 80; July 1, 2006, Gillian Engberg, review of *Pirate Bob,* p. 65; April 15, 2009, Daniel Kraus, review of *Bobby Bramble Loses His Brain,* p. 46.

Clark's art takes a surreal slant in bringing to life David Keane's story for **Bobby Bramble Loses His Brain.** (Illustration ©2009 by David Clark. Reprinted by permission of Clarion Books, an imprint of Houghton Mifflin Harcourt Publishing Company. All rights reserved.)

Kirkus Reviews, June 15, 2003, review of *Bus-a-Saurus Bop,* p. 864; July 1, 2004, review of *A Very Hairy Scary Story,* p. 639; April 1, 2009, review of *Bobby Bramble Loses His Brain.*

Publishers Weekly, June 8, 1992, review of *The Trouble with Ben,* p. 62; August 2, 1993, review of *Peculiar Zoo,* p. 81; April 16, 2001, review of *A Little Less Noise,* p. 64; May 5, 2003, review of *Grumblebunny,* p. 220; July 21, 2003, review of *Bus-a-Saurus Bop,* p. 194; April 3, 2006, review of *Gakky Two-Feet,* p. 73.

School Library Journal, May, 2001, Jane Marino, review of *A Little Less Noise,* p. 145; July, 2003, Kathy Piehl, review of *Grumblebunny,* p. 98; August, 2004, Linda Staskus, review of *A Very Hairy Scary Story,* p. 103; July, 2006, Kara Schaff Dean, review of *Pirate Bob,* p. 82; November, 2007, Marian Drabkin, review of *The Mine-o-Saur,* p. 86; June, 2009, Madigan McGillicuddy, review of *Bobby Bramble Loses His Brain,* p. 92.

ONLINE

Creativeshake Web site, http://www.creativeshake.com/ (May 1, 2010), "David Clark."

FPO Web site, http://www.fpomagazine.com/ (May 1, 2010), "David Clark."*

*   *   *

CLEMENS, James
See ROLLINS, James

*   *   *

CONAHAN, Carolyn
See CONAHAN, Carolyn Digby

*   *   *

CONAHAN, Carolyn Digby 1961-
(Carolyn Conahan)

Personal

Born 1961; married; husband's name Mark; children: Gillian, Kathleen. *Education:* Attended Reed College and Pacific Northwest College of Art.

Addresses

Home—Portland, OR. *Agent*—Laura Rennert, Andrea Brown Literary Agency, ljrennertmac.com. *E-mail*—carolyn@carolyndigbyconahan.com.

Career

Author and artist. Carus Publishing Company, Peterborough, NH, staff illustrator of *Cricket* magazine, 2002—.

Member

Society of Children's Book Writers and Illustrators.

Awards, Honors

Gold Medal for Distinctive Illustration, Mom's Choice Awards, 2009, for *The Prairie-dog Prince.*

Writings

SELF-ILLUSTRATED

(As Carolyn Conahan) *The Twelve Days of Christmas Dogs,* Dutton Children's Books (New York, NY), 2005.

ILLUSTRATOR

Anne E. Kitch, *Bless This Way,* Morehouse Publishing (Harrisburg, PA), 2003.

Deb Lund, *Me and God: A Book of Partner Prayers,* Morehouse Publishing (Harrisburg, PA), 2003.

Deb Lund, *All Day Long: A Book of Partner Prayers,* Morehouse Publishing (Harrisburg, PA), 2004.

L. Frank Baum, *The Discontented Gopher,* South Dakota State Historical Society Press (Pierre, SD), 2006.

Eva Katharine Gibson, *The Prairie-dog Prince,* South Dakota State Historical Society Press (Pierre, SD), 2008.

(As Carolyn Conahan) Fiona Bayrock, *Bubble Homes and Fish Farts,* Charlesbridge (Watertown, MA), 2009.

Sidelights

Carolyn Digby Conahan, who serves as the staff artist for *Cricket,* the popular magazine for children, has illustrated a number of well-received children's books, including *Bubble Homes and Fish Farts,* a work by Fiona Bayrock. In addition, Conahan has produced *The Twelve Days of Christmas Dogs,* a humorous visioning of the traditional holiday carol.

In *Bubble Homes and Fish Farts* Bayrock examines the varied and often amazing ways that animals use bubbles to live. The violet sea snail, for example, sails along the surface of the water on a raft of bubbles, and the humpback whale creates a "net" of bubbles to trap prey. "Conahan's whimsical watercolor illustrations, complete with conversational bubbles, add humor and interest," remarked a critic in *Kirkus Reviews.* As the illustrator noted in a *Seven Impossible Things before Breakfast* online interview, she was surprised by the assignment. "I am not widely known for my grasp of facts," Conahan admitted. "I elaborate. I exaggerate. I twist and tweak and fabricate. I wouldn't have thought these qualities qualified me to illustrate a non-fiction picture book." Nonetheless, she found the experience rewarding. "There was a lot of research, which I enjoyed to excess. I learned all kinds of things about all kinds of things—and their habits and habitats."

In *The Twelve Days of Christmas Dogs* Conahan offers a canine-centric version of the familiar and beloved tune, in which two friends exchange such gifts as a pug puppy, French poodles, and Chihuahuas. According to a *Kirkus Reviews* critic, the ever-growing menagerie is "illustrated with flair in watercolor and ink." "Canine cavorting is the game," Julie Cummins noted in her *Booklist* review of *The Twelve Days of Christmas Dogs,* "and it's great fun."

Biographical and Critical Sources

PERIODICALS

Booklist, October 15, 2005, Julie Cummins, review of *The Twelve Days of Christmas Dogs,* p. 55; June 1, 2009, Carolyn Phelan, review of *Bubble Homes and Fish Farts,* p. 53.

Kirkus Reviews, November 1, 2005, review of *The Twelve Days of Christmas Dogs,* p. 1191; January 15, 2009, review of *Bubble Homes and Fish Farts.*

School Library Journal, March, 2009, Frances E. Millhouser, review of *Bubble Homes and Fish Farts,* p. 131.

ONLINE

Carolyn Digby Conahan Home Page, http://www.carolyn digbyconahan.com (June 1, 2010).

Cricket Online, http://www.cricketmagkids.com/ (June 1, 2010), "Carolyn Digby Conahan."

Seven Impossible Things before Breakfast Web log, http://blaine.org/sevenimpossiblethings/ (May 17, 2009), interview with Fiona Bayrock and Conahan.*

*   *   *

COSSI, Olga 1921-

Personal

Name pronounced "all-ga cah-see"; born January 28, 1921, in St. Helena, CA; daughter of Orlando (an olive oil manufacturer) and Filomena (a homemaker) Della Maggiora; married Don Cossi (in construction); children: Tamara Frishberg, Caren Franci, Donald. *Education:* Palmer School of Authorship, degree. *Hobbies and other interests:* Travel, whitewater rafting, backpacking, tennis, most sports.

Addresses

Home—Santa Cruz, CA.

Career

Author and journalist. *Santa Rosa Press Democrat,* Santa Rosa, CA, staff correspondent; *Mendocino Beacon,* Mendocino, CA, staff member and author of col-

Olga Cossi (Reproduced by permission.)

umn, "Barnacles around the Bay"; freelance writer and photographer. Affiliated with "Meet the Author" program, San Diego County Schools, Authors' Fair, California Reading Association, and "Year of the Lifetime Reader" speakers' forum; teacher of writing workshops. KUSP, Santa Cruz, CA, broadcaster on "First Person Singular" series. Vice president, then president of Gualala Community Center.

Member

Society of Children's Book Writers and Illustrators, National Women's History Project.

Awards, Honors

California Media and Library Educators Association Authors Breakfast honors, 1990; Books for the Teen Age citation, New York Public Library, 1991, for *The Magic Box,* and c. 1994, for *Water Wars;* Outstanding Children's Science Trade Book designation, National Science Teachers Association/Children's Book Council, for *Harp Seals;* Assembly on Literature for Adolescents (ALAN) honors inclusion, for *Adventure on the Graveyard of the Wrecks, The Magic Box, Water Wars,* and *Edna Hibel: Her Life and Art.*

Writings

FICTION

Robin Deer, Naturegraph, 1967.

Fire Mate, photographs by John McLaughlin, Independence Press (Independence, MO), 1977, new edition published as part of "Council for Indian Education" series, illustrated by Paulette Livers Lambert, Roberts Rinehart (Lanham, MD), 1995.

Gus the Bus, illustrated by Howie Schneider, Scholastic, Inc. (New York, NY), 1989.

Orlanda and the Contest of Thieves, illustrated by Tom Sarmo, Bookmakers Guild (Lakewood, CO), 1989.

The Wonderful Wonder-full Donkey, illustrated by Sharon Hill Porter, Windswept House (Mount Desert, ME), 1989.

The Magic Box, Pelican Publishing (Gretna, LA), 1990.

The Great Getaway, illustrated by Ellen Anderson, Gareth Stevens (Milwaukee, WI), 1990.

Adventure on the Graveyard of the Wrecks, Pelican Publishing (Gretna, LA), 1991.

Think Pink, illustrated by Lea Anne Clarke, Pelican Publishing (Gretna, LA), 1994.

Pemba Sherpa, illustrated by Gary Bernard, Odyssey Books (Longmont, CO), 2009.

Pony Summer, illustrated by Cathy Morrison, Odyssey Books (Longmont, CO), 2010.

NONFICTION

Harp Seals, Carolrhoda Books (Minnepolis, MN), 1991.

Cover of Cossi's nonfiction picture book Harp Seals, *featuring photography by Kit M. Kovacs.* (Carolrhoda Books, Inc., 1991. Reproduced by permission of the photographer.)

Water Wars: The Fight to Control and Conserve Nature's Most Precious Resource, Discovery Books (New York, NY), 1993.

Edna Hibel: Her Life and Art, Discovery Enterprises (Lowell, MA), 1994.

Contributor to periodicals, including *Christian Science Monitor, Club House, Cricket, Highlights for Children, Humpty Dumpty,* and *Young American.* Works included in anthologies *Voices of the Wineland,* Alta Napa Press, 1979, *Having Choices,* Pegasus, *Chicken Soup for the Girl's Soul,* Health Communications, Inc., and *Stories from Where We Live: The California Coast,* Milkweed Editions.

Adaptations

Water Wars was selected by the Library of Congress for their Books for the Blind Cassette list, 1997.

Sidelights

Focusing her stories on independent-minded young people makes writing especially exciting for children's author Olga Cossi. She draws on her interest in travel and the environment, as well as on her Italian heritage and her California upbringing, to produce nonfiction as well as picture books that include *Orlanda and the Contest of Thieves* and juvenile novels such as *The Magic Box.* Cossi's empathy for young people—from preschoolers to high schoolers—is reflected in such issue-oriented books as *The Magic Box,* which addresses the moral issue of smoking and teen sports, and *Pemba Sherpa,* an exposition of cultural expectations and gender roles.

Cossi grew up in the small town of St. Helena, in the heart of California's Napa Valley. "I always felt that I was different and that my independence was worth a price," she once told *SATA.* "I have been swimming upstream ever since." Cossi cannot recall a time when she was not working on a written project. "When I was in elementary school, my older sister talked me into reading all the books and doing all the book reports for her high-school English class. One day she came home and told me I had to write a book. I tried to argue, but she was my big sister. So I went to work, choosing poetry as the form. My sister not only got an 'A' on the assignment, but the text was so well received it was made into a book, with her name as author, of course. She got the credit, but I got a solid background in good literature that turned out to be a wonderful gift. Even today, this sister continues to be a strong and important influence in my writing career."

While Cossi was in school she worked for the local newspaper, building on her experience working with words. After she got married and started a family, she was able to continue her journalistic work while devoting a good portion of her time to her family, a combination that provided Cossi with what she considers "a rich collection of story ideas." Eventually she completed her first book for children, which was published in 1967 as *Robin Deer.*

During this same time, Cossi began a five-year study that she called "linguistic archeology." "For this study," she once recalled, "I delved into the roots of words, especially key words on which great religions and nations were founded and great wars and civilizations carried forth. I literally dug through ancient Hebrew and Greek texts, using phonics as my basis, seeking the connection between the oral root or idea behind the work and the meaning that evolved. This study turned out to be a most exciting adventure. Sometimes I would work all night tracing a word to discover what it might have meant in the beginning."

As her study of words wound to an end, Cossi felt she was ready to write her second book for children. "*Fire Mate* was written on the beach at Mazatlan, using what I had learned about the poetical connection of words to give the text a deeper meaning. I would carry my thesaurus, binders, and a stack of dictionaries with me and pile them on a towel spread on the sand. Within a few minutes I was surrounded by native children as fascinated with me as I was with them. They taught me Spanish and I taught them English. Their eyes lit up when I showed them Spanish words in the unabridged dictionary that I took everywhere with me, especially when I let them touch the printed pages. How they loved and respected those books! So did I."

Published in 1989, *Gus the Bus* is the story of a school bus that, with a brand-new set of heavy-duty radial tires, decides to follow in the tread of larger-tired vehicles—outspeeding fire trucks and even attempting to take off from an airport runway like a plane. Finally, Gus's driver discovers the problem—too much air in the tires—and deflates Gus's ego back down to school-bus size. "The idea came to me when we had our huge converted bus parked beside our house," Cossi once told *SATA,* describing the camper she and her family took on trips around the United States. "The children who saw it couldn't get over the size of the tires. So Gus was born." Noting that the "secret life" of cars and trucks fascinates young children, a *Publishers Weekly* critic praises *Gus the Bus* as "confirm[ing] their craziest imaginings."

Cossi's picture book *Orlanda and the Contest of Thieves,* was inspired by an Italian folktale told by her father. A spunky young pickpocket named Orlanda must test her skills as a thief against all the pickpockets in Naples when the wife of the mayor devises a contest designed to rid the city of crime—all but the winner will be forced to leave the city and never return. *Adventure on the Graveyard of the Wrecks* is based on the actual exploits of some California teens as they explore a deserted beach where boats are carried by the tide after being loosened from their moorings by a large storm. Another picture book by Cossi, *The Great Getaway,* tells of the adventures of two runaway sisters as they venture a whole block from home before discovering that home is the best place to be when you are too young to cross the street by yourself.

Written for young-adult readers, Cossi's *The Magic Box* focuses on the sport of girls' basketball as it affects the teens who play it, their relationships with friends and family members, and their efforts to deal with the pressure to win. High-school senior and basketball star Mara Benetti's intention to qualify for a sports scholarship to college is thwarted when she is caught smoking and kicked off the team. Mara does not buy the "no smoking rule" enforced by the school board, and resents her mother's efforts to enforce it, until she realizes that her mother, a former smoker, has been diagnosed with throat cancer. While *School Library Journal* reviewer Susan Schuller complained that the novel verges on melodrama, she added that "the plot of this first-person narrative moves swiftly, and Mara's addiction to cigarettes is clearly shown." In her review for *Booklist,* contributor Sue-Ellen Beauregard noted that "despite its faults," *The Magic Box* "will hold teenage interest, especially among readers who can relate to the mother-daughter conflict."

A glimpse of a beautiful sunrise changes the life of a pampered duck in *Think Pink,* a humorous picture book inspired by a decades-old tradition. The work centers on Debbie Duck, a member of the famed Peabody Ducks, a group of five mallards that descends each day from a penthouse apartment in the Peabody Orlando hotel, march through the building's elegant halls, and hop into a luxurious fountain. When Debbie views a gorgeous pink sky one morning, she becomes obsessed with any object of that color, forcing her Duck Master to take drastic measures to keep her on task. In *Pemba Sherpa,* Cossi tells the story of Yang Ki, a Nepalese youth who longs to become a guide for explorers in the Himalayas, even though her culture forbids girls from

Cossi's biographical picture book Pemba Sherpa *features artwork by illustrator Gary Bernard.* (Illustration ©2009 Gary Bernard. Reproduced by permission.)

accepting this position. While trailing her older brother, Pemba, through the mountains on his way to gather firewood, Yang Ki witnesses a devastating landslide, and she must act quickly to save her sibling's life.

In addition to fiction, Cossi has written several works of nonfiction. Her first, *Harp Seals,* examines the white-coated seals that live on the ice fields of the Arctic. Explaining the life cycle of the species of seal sometimes called a "saddleback," she also discusses efforts by environmentalists and other nature lovers to protect these unique mammals. Praising the book's "high standard of information [and] organization," Betsy Hearne cited *Harp Seals* as "a logical springboard for discussion of environmental checks and balances" in her *Bulletin of the Center for Children's Books* critique. According to *Booklist* reviewer Kay Weisman, Cossi's work serves as "an informative introduction for report writers" and "an attractive choice for browsers." Another nonfiction work, *Water Wars: The Fight to Control and Conserve Nature's Most Precious Resource,* places even more focus on the efforts of environmentalists in what *Booklist* contributor Mary Romano Marks characterized as a "thought-provoking discussion."

Cossi's book *Pemba Sherpa* reflects her concern over a part of the world where human rights are at issue. "It really is an important story in today's world," she told *SATA.* "Tibet must not be forgotten. This book will remind the next generation that there are children who are not free to live at home in peace." Illustrated by with charcoal and watercolor by artist Gary Bernard, *Pemba Sherpa* recounts the story of Nepalese two siblings who hope to eventually work as guides like other children in their native Himalayan village. While Pemba is confident in his future, younger sister Yang Ki is ridiculed for her dream and she must learn the skills of a guide in secret. When Pemba is injured in a landslide while gathering firewood on a rocky mountain slope, Yang Ki has followed and her efforts to rescue her older brother proves to everyone her ability to become a Sherpa guide. In *Booklist* online, Gillian Engberg wrote that Cossi's "dramatic story gracefully embeds specifics of Tibetan culture as it captures a child's universal feelings of frustration."

In addition to researching and writing, Cossi spent eleven years traveling full time, living in a motor home while crossing the United States five times, visiting Alaska and most of Mexico and Canada, and also taking side trips to Europe. On her trips she has visited schools and libraries, meeting her young fans. and teaching writing workshops. "Remaining a child at heart is the key to becoming a worthwhile adult," she once remarked to *SATA.* "It is the spark of life that responds to others. It makes living fun, no matter what. I am fortunate that the child in me continues to imagine stories and to write."

Biographical and Critical Sources

PERIODICALS

Booklist, October 15, 1990, Sue-Ellen Beauregard, review of *The Magic Box,* pp. 435-436; May 1, 1991, Kay Weisman, review of *Harp Seals,* p. 1707; November 1, 1993, Mary Romano Marks, review of *Water Wars: The Fight to Control and Conserve Nature's Most Precious Resource,* p. 510.
Bulletin of the Center for Children's Books, April, 1988, Betsy Hearne, review of *Harp Seals,* p. 188.
Publishers Weekly, December 9, 1988, Sue-Ellen Beauregard, review of *Gus the Bus,* p. 64; June 13, 1994, review of *Think Pink,* p. 64.
School Library Journal, August, 1990, Susan Schuller, review of *The Magic Box,* p. 163; February, 1994, Gloria Amann, review of *Water Wars,* p. 123.

ONLINE

Booklist Online, http://bookends.booklistonline.com/ (October 7, 2009), Gillian Engberg, review of *Pemba Sherpa.*
Pelican Publishing Web site, http://pelicanpub.com/ (June 1, 2010), "Olga Cossi."

*　　*　　*

COVILLE, Bruce 1950-
(Robyn Tallis)

Personal

Born May 16, 1950, in Syracuse, NY; son of Arthur J. (a sales engineer) and Jean (an executive secretary) Coville; married Katherine Dietz (an illustrator), October 11, 1969; children: Orion Sean, Cara Joy, Adam Benjamin. *Education:* Attended Duke University and State University of New York at Binghamton; State University of New York at Oswego, B.A., 1974. *Politics:* "Eclectic." *Religion:* Unitarian.

Addresses

Office—Oddly Enough, P.O. Box 6110, Syracuse, NY 13217. *Agent*—Ashley Grayson, 1342 18th St., San Pedro, CA 90732.

Career

Author. Wetzel Road Elementary, Liverpool, NY, teacher, 1974-81; Full Cast Audio, Syracuse, NY, founder, president, and publisher, 2002—. Co-host and co-producer of *Upstage,* a cable program promoting local theater, 1983. Has also worked as a camp counselor, grave digger, assembly line worker, and toy maker.

Member

Society of Children's Book Writers and Illustrators, Science Fiction and Fantasy Writers of America, Authors Guild, Dramatists Guild.

Bruce Coville (Reproduced by permission.)

Awards, Honors

California Young Reader Medal, 1996-97, for *Jennifer Murdley's Toad;* Knickerbocker Award, New York State Library Association, for body of work, 1997; Children's Choice selection, International Reading Association/ Children's Book Council, for *The Monster's Ring;* Best Book for Young Adults selection and Quick Picks for Reluctant Readers selection, both American Library Association, both for *Oddly Enough;* Children's Choice awards from various states, including Arizona, Hawai'i, Maryland, and Nevada.

Writings

PICTURE BOOKS

The Foolish Giant, illustrated by wife, Katherine Coville, Lippincott (Philadelphia, PA), 1978.

Sarah's Unicorn, illustrated by Katherine Coville, Lippincott (Philadelphia, PA), 1979.

Sarah and the Dragon, illustrated by Beth Peck, Harper (New York, NY), 1984.

My Grandfather's House, illustrated by Henri Sorensen, BridgeWater (Mahwah, NJ), 1996.

The Lapsnatcher, illustrated by Marissa Moss, BridgeWater (Mahwah, NJ), 1997.

The Prince of Butterflies, illustrated by John Clapp, Harcourt (San Diego, CA), 2000.

Hans Brinker, illustrated by Laurel Long, Dial Books for Young Readers (New York, NY), 2007.

JUVENILE FICTION

Space Station Ice-3, Scholastic (New York, NY), 1987, revised, Archway (New York, NY), 1996.

Monster of the Year, illustrated by Harvey Kurtzman, Pocket (New York, NY), 1989.

Goblins in the Castle, illustrated by Katherine Coville, Pocket (New York, NY), 1992.

The Dragonslayers, illustrated by Katherine Coville, Pocket (New York, NY), 1994.

The World's Worst Fairy Godmother, illustrated by Katherine Coville, Pocket (New York, NY), 1996.

The Monsters of Morley Manor, Harcourt (San Diego, CA), 2001.

Thor's Wedding Day, Harcourt (Orlando, FL), 2005.

"I WAS A SIXTH-GRADE ALIEN" SERIES; ILLUSTRATED BY TONY SANSEVERO

I Was a Sixth-Grade Alien, Pocket (New York, NY), 1999.

The Attack of the Two-Inch Teacher, Pocket (New York, NY), 1999.

I Lost My Grandfather's Brain, Pocket (New York, NY), 1999.

Peanut Butter Lover Boy, Pocket (New York, NY), 2000.

Zombies of the Science Fair, Pocket (New York, NY), 2000.

Don't Fry My Veeblax!, Pocket (New York, NY), 2000.

Too Many Aliens, Pocket (New York, NY), 2000.

Snatched from Earth, Pocket (New York, NY), 2000.

There's an Alien in My Backpack, Pocket (New York, NY), 2000.

Revolt of the Miniature Mutants, Pocket (New York, NY), 2001.

There's an Alien in My Underwear, Pocket (New York, NY), 2001.

Farewell to Earth, Pocket (New York, NY), 2001.

YOUNG-ADULT NOVELS

Fortune's Journey, BridgeWater (Mahwah, NJ), 1995.

(With Jane Yolen) *Armageddon Summer,* Harcourt (San Diego, CA), 1998.

SHORT STORY COLLECTIONS; FOR YOUNG-ADULTS

Oddly Enough, illustrated by Michael Hussar, Harcourt (San Diego, CA), 1994.

Odder than Ever, Harcourt (San Diego, CA), 1999.

Odds Are Good (omnibus; contains *Oddly Enough* and *Odder than Ever*), Harcourt (Orlando, FL), 2006.

Oddest of All, Harcourt (Orlando, FL), 2008.

"CHAMBER OF HORROR" YOUNG-ADULT NOVEL SERIES

Spirits and Spells, Dell (New York, NY), 1983, revised edition published as *Bruce Coville's Chamber of Horror: Spirits and Spells,* Archway (New York, NY), 1996.

The Eyes of the Tarot, Dell (New York, NY), 1983, revised edition published as *Bruce Coville's Chamber of Horror: The Eyes of the Tarot,* Archway (New York, NY), 1996.

Waiting Spirits, Dell (New York, NY), 1984, revised edition published as *Bruce Coville's Chamber of Horror: Waiting Spirits,* Archway (New York, NY), 1986.

Amulet of Doom, Dell (New York, NY), 1985, revised edition published as *Bruce Coville's Chamber of Horror: Amulet of Doom,* Archway (New York, NY), 1996.

"A.I. GANG" SERIES

Operation Sherlock, NAL (New York, NY), 1986, revised edition, Minstrel (New York, NY), 1995.

Robot Trouble, NAL (New York, NY), 1986, revised edition, Minstrel (New York, NY), 1995.

Forever Begins Tomorrow, NAL (New York, NY), 1986, revised edition, Minstrel (New York, NY), 1995.

"CAMP HAUNTED HILLS" SERIES

How I Survived My Summer Vacation, illustrated by Tom Newsom, Pocket Books (New York, NY), 1988.

Some of My Best Friends Are Monsters, illustrated by Tom Newsom, Pocket Books (New York, NY), 1989.

The Dinosaur That Followed Me Home, illustrated by John Pierard, Pocket Books (New York, NY), 1990.

"MY TEACHER" SERIES

My Teacher Is an Alien, illustrated by Mike Wimmer, Pocket Books (New York, NY), 1989.

My Teacher Fried My Brains, illustrated by J. Pierard, Pocket Books (New York, NY), 1991.

My Teacher Glows in the Dark, illustrated by J. Pierard, Pocket Books (New York, NY), 1991.

My Teacher Flunked the Planet, illustrated by J. Pierard, Pocket Books (New York, NY), 1992.

"MAGIC SHOP" SERIES

The Monster's Ring, illustrated by Katherine Coville, Knopf (New York, NY), 1982.

Jeremy Thatcher, Dragon Hatcher, illustrated by Gary A. Lippincott, Harcourt (New York, NY), 1991.

Jennifer Murdley's Toad, illustrated by Gary A. Lippincott, Harcourt (New York, NY), 1992.

The Skull of Truth, illustrated by Gary A. Lippincott, Harcourt (New York, NY), 1997.

Juliet Dove, Queen of Love, Harcourt (Orlando, FL), 2003.

"NINA TANLEVEN" SERIES

The Ghost in the Third Row, Bantam (New York, NY), 1987.

The Ghost Wore Gray, Bantam (New York, NY), 1988.

Ghost in the Big Brass Bed, Bantam (New York, NY), 1991.

"SPACE BRAT" SERIES; CHAPTER BOOKS; ILLUSTRATED BY KATHERINE COVILLE

Space Brat, Pocket Books (New York, NY), 1992.

Blork's Evil Twin, Pocket Books (New York, NY), 1993.

The Wrath of Squat, Pocket Books (New York, NY), 1994.

Planet of the Dips, Pocket Books (New York, NY), 1995.

The Saber-toothed Poodnoobie, Pocket Books (New York, NY), 1997.

"ALIEN ADVENTURES" SERIES; ILLUSTRATED BY KATHERINE COVILLE

Aliens Ate My Homework, Pocket Books (New York, NY), 1993.

I Left My Sneakers in Dimension X, Pocket Books (New York, NY), 1994.

The Search for Snout, Pocket Books (New York, NY), 1995.

Aliens Stole My Body, Pocket Books (New York, NY), 1998.

"UNICORN CHRONICLES" SERIES

Into the Land of the Unicorns, Scholastic, Inc. (New York, NY), 1994.

The Song of the Wanderer, Scholastic, Inc. (New York, NY), 1999.

Dark Whispers, Scholastic Press (New York, NY), 2008.

The Last Hunt, Scholastic Press (New York, NY), 2010.

"MOONGOBBLE AND ME" SERIES; ILLUSTRATED BY KATHERINE COVILLE

The Dragon of Doom, Simon & Schuster (New York, NY), 2003.

The Weeping Werewolf, Simon & Schuster (New York, NY), 2004.

The Evil Elves, Simon & Schuster (New York, NY), 2004.

The Mischief Monster, Simon & Schuster (New York, NY), 2007.

The Naughty Nork, Simon & Schuster (New York, NY), 2008.

COMPILER AND EDITOR

The Unicorn Treasury, illustrated by Tim Hildebrandt, Doubleday (New York, NY), 1987.

Herds of Thunder, Manes of Gold: A Collection of Horse Stories and Poems, illustrated by Ted Lewin, Doubleday (New York, NY), 1991.

Bruce Coville's Book of Monsters, Scholastic, Inc. (New York, NY), 1993.

Bruce Coville's Book of Aliens, Scholastic, Inc. (New York, NY), 1994.

Bruce Coville's Book of Ghosts, illustrated by J. Pierard, Scholastic, Inc. (New York, NY), 1994.

Bruce Coville's Book of Nightmares, Scholastic, Inc. (New York, NY), 1995.

Bruce Coville's Book of Spine Tinglers, Scholastic, Inc. (New York, NY), 1996.

Bruce Coville's Book of Magic, Scholastic, Inc. (New York, NY), 1996.

Bruce Coville's Book of Monsters II, illustrated by J. Pierard, Scholastic, Inc. (New York, NY), 1996.

Bruce Coville's Book of Aliens II, Scholastic, Inc. (New York, NY), 1996.

Bruce Coville's Book of Ghosts II, illustrated by J. Pierard, Scholastic, Inc. (New York, NY), 1997.

Bruce Coville's Book of Nightmares II, illustrated by J. Pierard, Scholastic, Inc. (New York, NY), 1997.

Bruce Coville's Book of Spine Tinglers II, Scholastic, Inc. (New York, NY), 1997.

Bruce Coville's Book of Magic II, Scholastic, Inc. (New York, NY), 1997.

(Compiler) *A Glory of Unicorns,* illustrated by Alix Berenzy, Scholastic, Inc. (New York, NY), 1998.

(With Elizabeth Skurnick) *Bruce Coville's Alien Visitors,* illustrated by Alex Sunder and John Nyberg, Avon (New York, NY), 1999.

(With Steve Roman) *Bruce Coville's Shapeshifters,* illustrated by Ernie Colon and John Nyberg, Avon (New York, NY), 1999.

(With Steve Roman) *Bruce Coville's UFO's,* illustrated by Ernie Colon and John Nyberg, Avon (New York, NY), 2000.

(With Steve Roman) *Bruce Coville's Strange Worlds,* illustrated by Ernie Colon and John Nyberg, Avon (New York, NY), 2000.

Half-Human (short story anthology), illustrated by Marc Tauss, Scholastic, Inc. (New York, NY), 2001.

RETELLER; PICTURE BOOKS

William Shakespeare's The Tempest, illustrated by Ruth Sanderson, Bantam (New York, NY), 1993.

William Shakespeare's A Midsummer Night's Dream, illustrated by Dennis Nolan, Dial (New York, NY), 1996.

William Shakespeare's Macbeth, illustrated by Gary Kelley, Dial (New York, NY), 1997.

William Shakespeare's Romeo and Juliet, illustrated by Dennis Nolan, Dial (New York, NY), 1999.

William Shakespeare's Twelfth Night, illustrated by Tim Raglin, Dial (New York, NY), 2003.

William Shakespeare's Hamlet, illustrated by Leonid Gore, Dial (New York, NY), 2004.

William Shakespeare's The Winter's Tale, illustrated by LeUyen Pham, Dial Books for Young Readers (New York, NY), 2007.

OTHER

(Author of book and lyrics) *The Dragonslayers,* music by Angela Peterson, produced in Syracuse, NY, 1981.

(Author of book and lyrics) *Out of the Blue,* music by Angela Peterson, produced in Syracuse, NY, 1982.

(Author of book and lyrics with Barbara Russell) *It's Midnight: Do You Know Where Your Toys Are?,* music by Angela Peterson, produced in Syracuse, NY, 1983.

(With others) *Seniority Travel Directory,* Schueler Communications, 1986.

(With others) *The Sophisticated Leisure Travel Directory,* Schueler Communications, 1986.

(Author of lyrics) *Faculty Room* (adult musical), music by Angela Peterson, produced, 1989.

The Dark Abyss (adult novel), Bantam (New York, NY), 1989.

Prehistoric People (nonfiction), illustrated by Michael McDermott, Doubleday (New York, NY), 1990.

Contributor to anthologies, including *Dragons and Dreams,* 1986, and *Am I Blue?,* 1994. Contributor to periodicals, including *Harper's Bookletter, Sesame Street Parent's Newsletter, Cricket,* and *Wilson Library Bulletin.* Associate editor, *Syracuse Business* and *Syracuse* magazine, both 1982-83; editor and columnist, *Seniority,* 1983-84. Author, under pseudonym Robyn Tallis, of two books in the "Planet Builder" series, *Night of Two New Moons,* 1985, and *Mountain of Stolen Dreams,* 1988.

Adaptations

Adaptations include: *The Monster's Ring* (cassette), Recorded Books, 1992; *The Ghost Wore Gray* (cassette), Recorded Books, 1993; *Jennifer Murdley's Toad* (cassette), Listening Library, 1996; *Jeremy Thatcher, Dragon Hatcher* (cassette), Listening Library, 1996; *The Ghost in the Big Brass Bed* (cassette), Recorded Books, 1996; *The Ghost in the Third Row* (cassette), 1996; *Aliens Ate My Homework* (cassette), Listening Library, 1998; *Into the Land of the Unicorns* (cassette), Listening Library, 1998; *The Skull of Truth,* (cassette), Listening Library, 1998; *My Teacher Is an Alien* (cassette), Listening Library, 1998; *The Attack of the Two-Inch Teacher* (cassette), Listening Library; *Bruce Coville's Book of Monsters* (cassette), Listening Library; *The Dragonslayers* (cassette), Listening Library; *I Lost My Grandfather's Brain* (cassette), Listening Library; *Fortune's Journey* (cassette), Recorded Books, 1998; *Armageddon Summer* (cassette), Recorded Books, 1999; *I Was a Sixth-Grade Alien* (cassette), Recorded Books, 2000; *Shakespeare's Greatest Hits, Vol. 1* (cassette), Full Cast Audio, 2003; *William Shakespeare's A Midsummer Night's Dream* (cassette), Recorded Books; *The Dragon of Doom* (cassette), Full Cast Audio; *Juliet Dove, Queen of Love* (cassette), Full Cast Audio; *The Monsters of Morley Manor* (cassette), Full Cast Audio; *Song of the Wanderer* (cassette), Full Cast Audio; and *The Weeping Werewolf* (cassette), Full Cast Audio. *The Monster's Ring* was broadcast on CBS Storybreak, Columbia Broadcasting System, Inc. (CBS); *I Was a Sixth-Grade Alien* was adapted as a television series, Fox Family TV, 1999-2000, Fox Family/YTV (Canada), 2000—.

Sidelights

Bruce Coville is a popular and prolific author of bestselling novels for children and young adults. His works draw heavily on fantastic creatures, such as unicorns and dragons and science-fiction traditions such as aliens and space stations, often with a humorous twist. Coville is well known for the books in his "I Was a Sixth-Grade Alien" series, including *I Lost My Grandfather's Brain,* as well as for the crowd-pleasing "Magic Shop" titles such as *Jeremy Thatcher, Dragon Hatcher.* He has also contributed to and edited volumes of short stories, retold a number of Shakespearean dramas, and completed several musical plays for younger audiences. "I feel like a very lucky person," Coville stated on his home page. "From the time I was young, I had a dream of becoming a writer. Now that dream has come true, and I am able to make my living doing something that I really love."

Coville cherishes memories of his childhood, noting that his early surroundings nurtured his vivid imagination. "I was raised in Phoenix, a small town in central New York," he once remarked to *SATA.* "Actually, I lived well outside the town, around the corner from my grandparents' dairy farm, which was the site

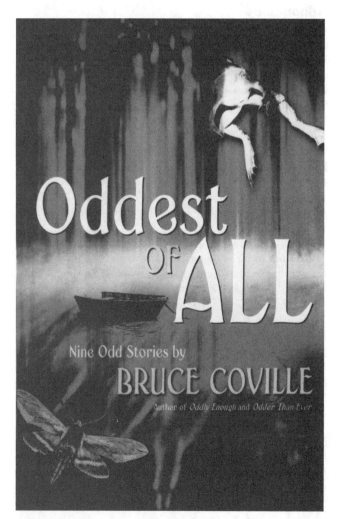

Cover of Coville's short-story collection **Oddest of All,** *which takes readers on a series of sometimes funny, sometimes frightening adventures.* (Harcourt, 2008. Jacket photographs (background)copyright image100/ Corbis (background) American Images, Inc/Getty Images. Reproduced by permission of Houghton Mifflin Harcourt Publishing Company. This material may not be reproduced in any form or by any means without the prior written permission of the publisher.)

of my happiest childhood times. I still have fond memories of the huge barns with their mows and lofts, mysterious relics, and jostling cattle. It was a wonderful place for a child to grow up. In addition to the farm, there was a swamp behind the house, and a rambling wood beyond that, both of which were conducive to all kinds of imaginative games." It was during this period that Coville began to develop the heightened sensibility often possessed by writers of fantasy.

Coville's father, not bookish himself, was instrumental in exposing his son to the delights of literature. As Coville once recounted in *SATA:* "Despite this wonderful setting, much of what went on at that time went on in my head, when I was reading, or thinking and dreaming about what I had read. I was an absolute bookaholic. My father had something to do with this." Coville went on to explain: "He was a traveling salesman, a gruff but loving man, who never displayed an overwhelming interest in books. But if anyone was to ask me what was the best thing he ever did for me I could reply without hesitation that he read me *Tom Swift in the City of Gold.* Why he happened to read this to me I was never quite certain, but it changed my life. One night after supper he took me into the living room, had me sit in his lap, and opened a thick, ugly brown book (this was the original *Tom Swift*) and proceeded to open a whole new world for me. I was enthralled, listened raptly, waited anxiously for the next night and the next, resented any intrusion, and reread the book several times later on my own. It was the only book I can ever remember him reading to me, but it changed my life. I was hooked on books."

Coville may have loved books, but like many other authors, the realization that he wanted to be a writer came very abruptly. He once told *SATA:* "I think it was sixth grade when I first realized that writing was something that I could do, and wanted to do very much. As it happened, I had spent most of that year making life miserable for my teacher by steadfastly failing to respond to the many creative devices she had to stimulate us to write. Then one day she simply (finally!) just let us write—told us that we had a certain amount of time to produce a short story of substance. Freed from writing topics imposed from without, I cut loose, and over several days found that I loved what I was doing. This may not be the first time that I knew I wanted to write, but it's the time that I remember." In addition to writing, Coville went on to be a teacher. He held a full-time position at Wetzel Road Elementary School, in Liverpool, New York, for seven years starting in 1974.

Coville was introduced to the possibilities of writing for children by the woman who later became his mother-in-law. He once explained in *SATA* that she "gave me a copy of *Winnie the Pooh* to read, and I suddenly knew that what I really wanted to write was children's books—to give to other children the joy that I got from books when I was young. This is the key to what I write now. I try with greater or lesser success, to make

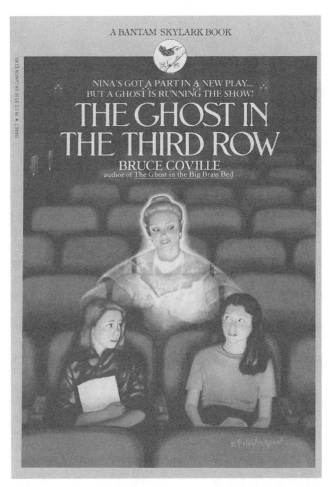

Cover of Coville's middle-grade novel **The Ghost in the Third Row,** *featuring artwork by D.F. Henderson.* (Cover illustration © 1987 by Yearling Books. Used by permission of Yearling, an imprint of Random House Children's Books, a division of Random House, Inc.)

turistic creatures lurking at the outer edge of the known universe. He once discussed this characteristic of his work in *SATA:* "Myth is very important to me. My picture books have firm roots in basic mythic patterns. Hopefully, the patterns do not intrude, but provide a structure and depth that enhances my work." *Oddest of All,* a collection of nine stories, includes such works as "The Boy with Silver Eyes," about a youngster's encounter with a unicorn; "The Hardest, Kindest Gift," a tragic tale of a half-human; and "The Mask of Eamonn Tiyado," a haunting Halloween tale. "All of the stories are well paced," Todd Morning commented in *Booklist,* "and most furnish a surprise at the end."

Coville often combines imaginary creatures with present-day situations to create tales of mystery and adventure. In *The Ghost in the Third Row,* for instance, Nina discovers an actual ghost haunts the theater where she is acting in a murder drama. Nina returns with her friend Chris in *The Ghost Wore Gray,* where the two try to discover the story behind the spirit of a Confederate soldier who appears in a New York hotel. "Despite the fantasy element of a ghost, this is a mystery," said

my stories the kinds of things that I would have enjoyed myself when I was young; to write the books I wanted to read, but never found. My writing works best when I remember the bookish child who adored reading and gear the work toward him. It falters when I forget him."

As he developed into an experienced writer, Coville worked in different genres. He also created musical plays such as *The Dragonslayers,* which was produced at the Syracuse Musical Theater. He contributed to anthologies of fantasy stories, such as *Dragons and Dreams.* Ultimately, however, it was in the area of picture books, beginning with the publication of *The Foolish Giant* in 1978, that Coville made a significant mark. Illustrated by his wife, Katherine, this story for younger readers tells of a mild-mannered and clumsy giant who has difficulty being accepted by the ordinary people of his village until he saves them from an evil wizard. In the years since that first book, Coville has published numerous other tales for children, culminating in several appearances on children's best-seller lists.

Many of Coville's books are jam-packed with the trappings of traditional mythic imagery: supernatural spirits, tarot cards, unicorns, prehistoric monsters, and fu-

Cover of Coville's middle-grade novel **Song of the Wanderer,** *featuring artwork by Rebecca Guay.* (Scholastic, 1999. Jacket painting © 1999 by Rebecca Guay. Reproduced by permission of the illustrator.)

School Library Journal contributor Carolyn Caywood, who added that the tale "evokes real feeling."

Some of Coville's most popular books have been those that involve Mr. Elive's Magic Shop. In *Jeremy Thatcher, Dragon Hatcher,* for example, young Jeremy escapes his tormenter Mary Lou only to find himself in a strange shop where he buys an unusual egg. When the egg hatches a baby dragon—that no one else but Mary Lou can see—Jeremy finds himself in the midst of adventure. "The book is filled with scenes that will bring laughter and near tears to readers," noted Kenneth E. Kowen in *School Library Journal.* Reviewer Kathleen Redmond wrote in *Voice of Youth Advocates* that the story is a good combination of real and fantasy worlds and "is right on target." Coville returns readers to the magic shop in *Jennifer Murdley's Toad,* in which Jennifer purchases a lonely toad that is hatched from a witch's mouth. In aiding her pet, Bufo, who seeks his lost love, Jennifer herself is turned into a toad and learns to appreciate her inner strengths. *School Library Journal* contributor Margaret C. Howell praised the theme as "particularly well handled," adding that "the story moves well, with realistic characterizations." In *Juliet Dove, Queen of Love,* a shy girl grabs the attention of all the boys at school after she finds a magic charm at Mr. Elive's shop. The cast of likeable characters, according to Candace Smith in *Booklist,* includes "snippy girls, love-struck boys, Greek gods, and talking rats" that will have readers "caught up in the fun."

Coville believes that a knowledge of mythic patterns and imagery can facilitate children's growth and social understanding. He once argued in *SATA:* "This 'making sense' is a process that generally takes a lifetime and yet, sadly, it is all too often never even begun. To utilize myth as a guide in this quest one must be familiar with its patterns and structures, a familiarity that is best gained from reading or hearing myth and its reconstructions from earliest childhood on." Coville thinks that the literature he writes plays a part in exposing young people to the realm of the mythological. "I do not expect a child to read my picture books and suddenly discover the secret of the universe,'" he explained in *SATA.* "I do hope that something from my works will tuck itself away in the child's mind, ready to present itself as a piece of a puzzle on some future day when he or she is busy constructing a view of the world that will provide at least a modicum of hope and dignity."

Beyond his grounding in classic fantasy, Coville has filled many of his books with humor aimed squarely at his young audience. In reviewing *Planet of the Dips,* *School Library Journal* critic Anne Connor referred to the book as "literary junk food" appealing to "beginning readers with a passion for weird words, stupid jokes and odd behavior." For his part, Coville defends the outrageous extremes of his stories. "There are those who want to keep children's books 'tasteful,' and ten-year-old boys are not tasteful," he once told *SATA.* "One of the reasons we have this problem of reluctant read-

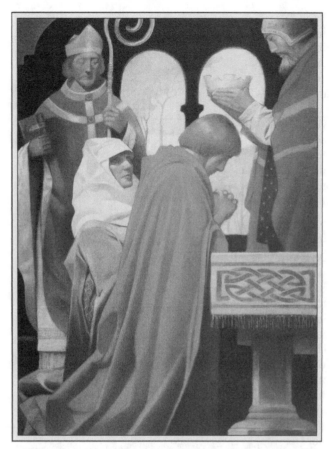

Coville retells a famous tale of Scottish kings and murder in his adaptation of Shakespeare's **Macbeth,** *featuring artwork by Garry Kelley.* (Illustration ©1997 by Gary Kelley. Reproduced by permission of Dial Books, a division of Penguin Putnam Books for Young Readers.)

ers, especially among boys, is that we're not writing to who and what we are. If you write a book that's a brilliant character study and is wonderfully tasteful and no kid ever reads it, you've failed. . . . There's another problem, where you publish to only the lowest common denominator, where you start with that and don't go anywhere else. If you do that, you've failed, too. To me, there's a sweet spot in between, where you start with boisterous energy that will engage, and then you take the reader somewhere else."

Coville acknowledged that he has a knack for fast-paced comedic storytelling, a talent borne out by the success of his four books in the "My Teacher" series, each of which sold over one million copies. He also diversified into other types of books, including a series of retellings of Shakespeare's plays. Coville found the task of adapting *The Tempest, A Midsummer Night's Dream, Macbeth,* and other works to be a satisfying challenge. "I've learned little ways to squeeze in more and more of the language, but keep it accessible," he told *SATA.* "Both my editor and I are aware of the chutzpah of what we are doing. We want to be respectful of the source and of the audience. We work really hard on these books." Reviewing *William Shakespeare's Hamlet* in *School Library Journal,* Nancy Menaldi-Scanlan called it "incredibly faithful to the original" and added that Coville's "carefully chosen words suit the mood of the haunting tragedy," while *Booklist* reviewer Carolyn Phelan observed that he retells the drama "with grace and style." *William Shakespeare's The Winter's Tale,* a story of palace intrigue, "includes poetic lines quoted appropriately within the story to introduce the Bard's language and style, and the tale is easy to follow," as Menaldi-Scanlan remarked. Coville also offers his version of the popular romantic comedy *William Shakespeare's Twelfth Night,* a classic story of mistaken identity. "Prospective audiences or cast members will get a clear sense of the play's tangled plot" from Coville's retelling, a contributor in *Kirkus Reviews* stated.

Coville has retold a number of other works, including *Hans Brinker,* a nineteenth-century tale by Mary Mapes Dodge in which a Dutch boy selflessly allows his friend to win a pair of prized silver skates. "This striking work is an ideal way to introduce a classic story to a new generation of readers," Shawn Brommer remarked in *School Library Journal.* In *Thor's Wedding Day,* a story based on the Norse poem *Thrymskvitha,* the mighty Thor must disguise himself as Freya, the goddess of love, to retrieve his powerful hammer from the clutches of a giant named Thrym. "The animated banter among this diverse cast gives this parody a spirited pace," according to a *Publishers Weekly* contributor, and Morning, writing in *Booklist,* noted that Coville "injects a modern sensibility while keeping the feel of the original myth."

Expanding further, Coville has published several novels for young adults. *Fortune's Journey* combines action and romance in its tale of a resourceful teenage actress leading a theater troupe across the American West during the Gold Rush era. The book received mixed reviews, with some critics praising the work and others faulting the author for less-than-believable characters. "Part of it was, people complained that it was warped by a kind of contemporary mindset taking on these historical characters," Coville once told *SATA.* "But I'd done the research, and I knew there was a lot more that young women were doing back then than people now think." Co-written with author Jane Yolen, *Armageddon Summer* follows the story of two teenagers caught up in a religious cult with their parents. Writing in *Booklist,* Roger Leslie praised Coville and Yolen for "explor[ing] their rich, thought-provoking theme with the perfect balance of gripping adventure and understated pathos, leavened by a dollop of humor."

Coville's "Moongobble and Me" series offers early readers a taste of magic through the adventures of Edward, a boy who befriends his new neighbor, the would-be magician Moongobble, in the small town of Pigbone. In the series' first book, *The Dragon of Doom,* Edward serves as Moongobble's assistant on the quest to obtain three golden acorns from the dreaded dragon of doom, a task that will hopefully get Moongobble accepted into the Society of Magicians. Moongobble's talking pet toad injects humor into the story, which is full of "unexpected and fantastic adventures" according to Anna Rich in *Booklist.* Calling *The Dragon of Doom* "fast paced," Kristina Aaronson added in *School Library Journal* that its "cliffhanger endings will keep youngsters turning the pages."

Coville turned his love for theater into a business when he launched Full Cast Audio in 2002. The company produces audiobooks with actors reading the parts of each character, rather than a single narrator reading the whole story. Coville himself produces each reading, working with actors in the recording studio to bring the stories to life. In *Kliatt,* Coville explained that "it was probably a fairly daffy career move," but he did it because "I love the sound of great books being read by terrific actors." Full Cast Audio released Coville's Shakespearean retellings as the audiobook *Shakespeare's Greatest Hits, Vol. 1,* with his versions of *A Midsummer Night's Dream, Macbeth, Romeo and Juliet,* and *Twelfth Night* each condensed to a half-hour performance. The format works, according to Melody Moxley in *Kliatt,* the critic noting that "the spirit and essentials of the story and characters are well conveyed."

Personal motivation and social idealism both fuel Coville's commitment to children's literature. "There are two reasons that people go into writing for children," he told *SATA.* "It's either to heal a wounded childhood, or to celebrate a happy one. It's about nine to one (in favor of) the healing to the happy. But I had a happy childhood, and I love children's books. They're delicious . . . the writing is better, the stories are more interesting. I do it out of a sense of joy and excitement. But it's also a political choice. I feel that one of the ways I can have real impact is working for kids."

With more than ninety books to his credit, Coville shows no signs of slowing down. In fact, he revels in the imaginative and entertaining aspects of his profession. "I'm a parent and I'm a citizen but there's nothing to say that you can't have the adult part and have the kid part still there," he remarked on a *Houghton Mifflin Harcourt* interview. "I've worked very hard to keep the celebrating, having a good time, isn't the world wonderful, part of me alive too."

Biographical and Critical Sources

BOOKS

Coville, Bruce, autobiographical essay in *Something about the Author,* Volume 155, Gale (Detroit, MI), 2005.

PERIODICALS

Booklist, November 1, 1997, Hazel Rochman, review of *William Shakespeare's Macbeth,* p. 464; August, 1998, Roger Leslie, review of *Armageddon Summer,* p. 272;

December 1, 1999, Michael Cart, review of *William Shakespeare's Romeo and Juliet,* p. 700; September 1, 2001, Grace Anne A. DeCandido, review of *The Monsters of Morley Manor,* p. 103; December 15, 2001, Frances Bradburn, review of *Half-Human,* p. 723; January 1, 2003, Carolyn Phelan, review of *William Shakespeare's Twelfth Night,* p. 878; April 15, 2003, Candace Smith, interview with Coville, p. 1485; January 1, 2004, Louise Brueggemann, review of *Juliet Dove, Queen of Love,* p. 854; May 15, 2004, Carolyn Phelan, review of *William Shakespeare's Hamlet,* p. 1616; June 1, 2004, Candace Smith, review of *Juliet Dove, Queen of Love,* p. 1768; October 15, 2004, Anna Rich, review of *The Dragon of Doom,* p. 433; August, 2005, Todd Morning, review of *Thor's Wedding Day,* p. 2026; November 1, 2007, Carolyn Phelan, review of *William Shakespeare's The Winter's Tale,* p. 45; September 15, 2008, Todd Morning, review of *Oddest of All,* p. 51.

Kirkus Reviews, August 1, 2001, review of *The Monsters of Morley Manor,* p. 1119; March 1, 2002, review of *The Prince of Butterflies,* p. 332; January 1, 2003, review of *William Shakespeare's Twelfth Night,* p. 59; December 15, 2003, review of *The Dragon of Doom,* p. 1448; August 1, 2005, review of *Thor's Wedding Day,* p. 846; September 15, 2007, review of *William Shakespeare's The Winter's Tale.*

Kliatt, May, 2004, Bruce Coville, "The Sound of Story," p. 3, and Melody Moxley, review of *Shakespeare's Greatest Hits, Vol. 1,* p. 59.

Publishers Weekly, March 18, 2002, review of *The Prince of Butterflies,* p. 104; May 6, 2002, Shannon Maugham, "Coville's Full Cast Audio," p. 20; December 15, 2003, review of *The Dragon of Doom,* p. 73; December 5, 2005, review of *Thor's Wedding Day,* p. 55; November 12, 2007, review of *Silver Skates,* p. 58.

School Library Journal, May, 1991, Kenneth E. Kowen, review of *Jeremy Thatcher, Dragon Hatcher,* p. 91; September, 1992, Margaret C. Howell, review of *Jennifer Murdley's Toad,* p. 250; December, 1995, Anne Connor, review of *Planet of the Dips,* p. 79; December, 2003, B. Allison Gray, review of *Juliet Dove, Queen of Love,* p. 148; January, 2004, Kristina Aaronson, review of *The Dragon of Doom,* p. 96; February, 2004, Nancy Menaldi-Scanlan, review of *William Shakespeare's Hamlet,* p. 160; December, 2007, Nancy Menaldi-Scanlan, review of *William Shakespeare's The Winter's Tale,* p. 149; February, 2008, Shawn Brommer, review of *Hans Brinker,* p. 112.

Voice of Youth Advocates, June, 1991, Kathleen Redmond, review of *Jeremy Thatcher, Dragon Hatcher,* p. 106.

ONLINE

Bruce Coville Home Page, http://www.brucecoville.com (June 1, 2010).

Houghton Mifflin Harcourt Web site, http://www.hmh books.com/ (June 1, 2010), interview with Coville.

Random House Web site, http://www.randomhouse.com/ (June 1, 2010), "Bruce Coville."

Scholastic Web site, http://www2.scholastic.com/ (June 1, 2010), interview with Coville.*

*   *   *

CROSS, Sarah

Personal

Born in OH; married. *Education:* Attended college.

Addresses

Home—NY. *E-mail*—dullboybook@gmail.com.

Career

Writer.

Writings

Dull Boy, Dutton (New York, NY), 2009.

Sidelights

Ohio-based novelist Sarah Cross loves superheroes as much as she loves writing, and she melds the two in her middle-grade novel *Dull Boy.* Energized by Cross's effervescent prose, the story follows Avery Pirzwick, who pretends to be a normal teen but is actually a superhero. Even Avery's parents are unaware that their son possesses amazing physical strength and the power of flight, and they would be surprised to learn that the nerdy boy roams his hometown at night, catching ne'er-do-wells and performing other superhero responsibilities. Inevitably, Avery is caught in situations that bring his own character into question, and his distraught parents trundle him off to a school for troubled teens where he meets up with super-smart Darla, super-sticky Sophie, and super-heated Nicholas. While the young people are learning to master their super powers for good, a woman named Cherchette attempts to seduce them to the dark side, hoping to augment her own superpowers and bring her evil schemes to fruition.

Praising Cross's ability to create an engaging first-person narrative, Connie Tyrell Burns wrote in her *School Library Journal* review of *Dull Boy* that Avery's narrative voice "is hip, witty, funny, and sarcastic." Avery's perspective "is a highlight" of the novel, a *Kirkus Reviews* noted, citing the "normal, goofy interactions" of the teen characters in *Dull Boy,* and predicting that readers will be entertained through to Cross's "page-turning finale." Classing Cross's fiction debut among "the best superhero stories," a *Publishers Weekly* contributor cited "crisp action . . . and a good sense of humor" and added that the author gives *Dull Boy* added resonance by spotlighting "the fears and struggles of teenagers who simply don't fit in."

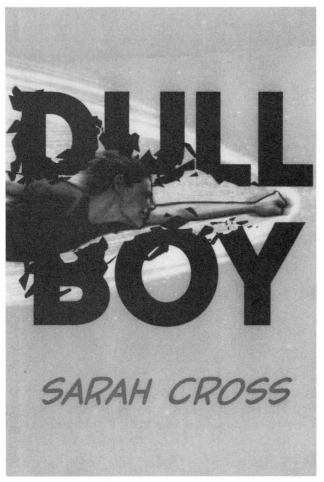

Cover of Sarah Cross's middle-grade novel Dull Boy, *featuring artwork by Jackie Baldus.* (Jacket art © 2009 by Zachary Baldus. Reproduced by permission.)

Biographical and Critical Sources

PERIODICALS

Kirkus Reviews, April 1, 200, review of *Dull Boy.*
Publishers Weekly, May 11, 2009, review of *Dull Boy,* p. 53.
School Library Journal, August, 2009, Connie Tyrrell Burns, review of *Dull Boy,* p. 100.

ONLINE

Sarah Cross Home Page, http://www.sarahcross.com (May 31, 2010).
Sarah Cross Web log, http://sarahcross.livejournal.com (May 31, 2010).*

*   *   *

CUMMINGS, John Michael 1963(?)-

Personal

Born c. 1963, in Harpers Ferry, WV; married; wife's name Susan.

Addresses

Home—NY. *E-mail*—john@johnmichaelcummings.com.

Career

Writer, novelist, and short-story writer.

Awards, Honors

Pushcart Prize nomination, 1998, for "Strangers," and 2006, for "The Scratchboard Project"; honorable mention in *Best American Short Stories 2007,* for "The Scratchboard Project."

Writings

The Night I Freed John Brown (young adult novel), Philomel Books (New York, NY), 2008.

Contributor of short stories and to periodicals, including *North American Review, Kenyon Review, Iowa Review, Providence* magazine, *Portland Monthly* magazine, *Wisconsin Review, Colorado North Review, Catalyst, Maryland Review, Alaska Quarterly Review, Southeast Review, Flipside, Painted Bride Quarterly, Hudson Valley Echoes, Pearl, Buffalo Spree, Oregon East, Oregon English Journal, Skylark, Blue Mesa Review, Westview, Baltimore Review, Eureka Literary* magazine, *Pangolin Papers, Spindrift, Louisiana Literature, Rosebuds, GW Review, Northwords Journal, North Dakota Quarterly, Old Red Kimono, Talking River Review, Concho River Review, Distillery, Chattahoochee Review, Snake Nation Review, Oyez Review, Natural Bridge,* and *North Atlantic Review.*

Sidelights

John Michael Cummings is a novelist and prolific short-story writer with some seventy-five story publications to his credit. He is a two-time Pushcart Prize nominee, and his short story "The Scratchboard Project" received an honorable mention in the *Best American Short Stories 2007.*

A native of Harpers Ferry, West Virginia, Cummings has long been steeped in the history of the region, particularly its importance as a place where slavery in America was challenged and fought. U.S. president Thomas Jefferson and Frederick Douglass, the latter a towering figure in African-American and abolitionist history, were both major players in the area. One particularly important historical figure in Harpers Ferry's past is John Brown, a white abolitionist zealot who advocated armed force as a means of eliminating slavery. On October 16, 1859, Brown led a raid on the federal armory at Harpers Ferry, seizing the large cache of government weapons with the intent of arming slaves to fight against slavery. The attack was ultimately unsuccessful and Brown was wounded and captured. Eventually, he was convicted of treason and hanged in December 1959, for his role in the raid.

In *The Night I Freed John Brown*, Cummings's debut novel and a work for young-adult readers, the author uses the emotionally charged history of Brown and his cause as the backdrop for the modern-day story of Josh Connors, a thirteen year old who is trapped in an oppressive household with an abusive father and unassuming mother. For Josh's father, being a resident of the notorious Harpers Ferry causes shame and anger. Living in the shadow of one of the town's historic houses, Josh's father lets the weeds and brush grow wild in order to hide his family's rundown and shabby home. Josh does not understand why his father is perpetually angry, but he endures the intense family stress as best he can.

Life changes for Josh when a new family, the Richmonds, moves into the historical home next door. The father of the family is an employee of the local national park. To Josh, the Richmonds are everything that his family is not. The family is intellectual and worldly. The elder Richmond is kind and supportive of his family, while the younger Richmond brothers are bright and genial. Josh is particularly envious of Luke Richmond, a boy about his age, who gets to enjoy a pleasant family life in a beautiful home. His contact with the Richmonds shows Josh that there is much more to the world than the stifling and restrictive life he knows, and he finds himself eager to leave his miserable existence behind and find a better life elsewhere. Soon, however, revelations begin to surface about Josh's father's past. The Richmonds' home, he discovers, is a near-duplicate of the house his father grew up in. Events from the past hint at the source of his father's virulent anger and resentment. When the years of pent-up emotions finally reach a bursting point, the world that Josh has known is altered forever. Even amidst the turmoil, however, with the historical specter of John Brown looming large in the background, hope for a transcendent change seems possible.

Although John Brown reacted violently to the profound wrongs of American slavery and history has painted him an overzealous radical, Cummings argued out in the first part of an interview with *Newsvine* contributor Scott Butki that the man's actions cannot be automatically categorized and labeled those of a radical or murderer, nor can Brown be condemned for what he did in the context of his times. He is "certainly not a 'cold-blooded' killer—Brown was nothing but hot blood—but a killer, yes. He was also a hero against a barbaric wrong. The problem is, Brown can't be captured by any one word, because our language is not set up to easily name people of his deeds. Behavior like his is simply too uncharacteristic."

A *Kirkus Reviews* contributor called *The Night I Freed John Brown* "a highly original meditation on how the past can haunt the present." Cummings offers a "story where things are not always as they seem, with burning emotions begging to be freed and lonely souls desperate for healing," commented *Teenreads.com* reviewer Chris Shanley-Dillman. The novel stands as a "historically rich story with colorful characters and a family secret that will draw readers in and keep the pages turning," the critic added.

Biographical and Critical Sources

PERIODICALS

Kirkus Reviews, April 1, 2008, review of *The Night I Freed John Brown.*

School Library Journal, July, 2008, Lynn Rashid, review of *The Night I Freed John Brown,* p. 95.

Voice of Youth Advocates, June, 2008, Kimberly Paone, review of *The Night I Freed John Brown,* p. 138.

ONLINE

Cynsations Web log, http://cunthialeitichsmith.blogspot.com/ (November 12, 2008), Cynthia Leitich Smith, interview with Cummings.

John Michael Cummings Home Page, http://www.johnmichaelcummings.com (December 29, 2008).

Newsvine, http://www.newsvine.com/ (September 12, 2008), Scott Butki, interview with Cummings.

Teenreads.com, http://www.teenreads.com/ (December 29, 2008), Chris Shanley-Dillman, review of *The Night I Freed John Brown.**

*   *   *

CZAJKOWSKI, James
See ROLLINS, James

D

DAVENIER, Christine 1961-

Personal

Born October 9, 1961, in Tours, France; daughter of Pierre (a teacher) and Michèle (a teacher) Davenier; companion of Philippe Harel (a film director); children: Joséphine.

Addresses

Home and office—30 rue de la Clef, Paris 75005, France. *Agent*—Judy Sue Goodwin-Sturges, 166 W. Newton St., Boston, MA 02118.

Career

Artist, author, and educator. School teacher in Paris, France, 1986-89; author and illustrator of children's books.

Awards, Honors

Charlotte Zolotow Award Honor Book designation, 2003, for *The First Thing My Mama Told Me* by Susan Marie Swanson.

Writings

SELF-ILLUSTRATED

León et Albertine, Kaleidoscope (Paris, France), 1997, translation by Dominic Barth published as *Leon and Albertine,* Orchard Books (New York, NY), 1998, published as *Frankie and Albertine,* Walker Books (London, England), 1999.
Sleepy Sophie, Walker Books (London, England), 1999.

ILLUSTRATOR

Paul B. Janeczko, editor, *Very Best (Almost) Friends: Poems of Friendship,* Candlewick Press (Cambridge, MA), 1999.

C.M. Millen, *The Low-Down Laundry Line Blues,* Houghton Mifflin (Boston, MA), 1999.
Amy Hest, *Mabel Dancing,* Candlewick Press (Cambridge, MA), 2000.
Madeleine L'Engle, *The Other Dog,* SeaStar Books (New York, NY), 2000.
Steve Kroll, *That Makes Me Mad!,* SeaStar Books (New York, NY), 2002.
Susan Marie Swanson, *The First Thing My Mama Told Me,* Harcourt (San Diego, CA), 2002.
Carole Lexa Schaefer, *Full Moon Barnyard Dance,* Candlewick Press (Cambridge, MA), 2003.
Margaret Park Bridges, *I Love the Rain,* Chronicle Books (San Francisco, CA), 2005.
Juanita Havill, *I Heard It from Alice Zucchini: Poems about the Garden,* Chronicle Books (San Francisco, CA), 2006.
Cari Best, *Sally Jean, the Bicycle Queen,* Farrar, Straus & Giroux (New York, NY), 2006.
Norma Fox Mazer, *Has Anyone Seen My Emily Green?,* Candlewick Press (Cambridge, MA), 2007.
Jack Prelutsky, *Me I Am!,* new edition, Farrar, Straus & Giroux (New York, NY), 2007.
Judith Viorst, *Nobody Here but Me,* Farrar, Straus & Giroux (New York, NY), 2008.
Hallie Durand, *Dessert First,* Atheneum Books for Young Readers (New York, NY), 2009.
Juanita Havill, *Just like a Baby,* Chronicle Books (San Francisco, CA), 2009.
Sandra Jordan, *Mr. and Mrs. Portly and Their Little Dog Snack,* Farrar Straus & Giroux (New York, NY), 2009.
Hallie Durand, *Just Desserts,* Atheneum Books for Young Readers (New York, NY), 2010.
Grace Maccarone, *Miss Lina's Ballerinas,* Feiwel & Friends (New York, NY), 2010.
Julie Andrews and Emma Walton, *The Very Fairy Princess,* Little, Brown Books for Young Readers (New York, NY), 2010.
Hallie Durand, *No Room for Dessert,* Atheneum Books for Young Readers (New York, NY), 2011.

Contributor to *In Every Tiny Grain of Sand: A Child's Book of Prayers and Praise,* edited by Reeve Lindbergh, Candlewick Press (Cambridge, MA), 2000.

ILLUSTRATOR; "IRIS AND WALTER" PICTURE-BOOK SERIES BY ELISSA HADEN GUEST

Iris and Walter, Harcourt (San Diego, CA), 2000.

Iris and Walter: Riding Rain, Harcourt (San Diego, CA), 2001.

Iris and Walter and Baby Rose, Harcourt (San Diego, CA), 2002.

Iris and Walter: The Sleepover, Harcourt (San Diego, CA), 2002.

Iris and Walter: The School Play, Harcourt (San Diego, CA), 2003.

Iris and Walter and Cousin Howie, Harcourt (San Diego, CA), 2003.

Iris and Walter: Lost and Found, Harcourt (San Diego, CA), 2004.

Iris and Walter and the Substitute Teacher, Harcourt (San Diego, CA), 2004.

Iris and Walter and the Field Trip, Harcourt (San Diego, CA), 2005.

Iris and Walter and the Birthday Party, Harcourt (San Diego, CA), 2006.

ILLUSTRATOR; "PIPER REED" SERIES BY KIMBERLY WILLIS HOLT

Piper Reed, Navy Brat, Henry Holt (New York, NY), 2007.

Piper Reed, the Great Gypsy, Henry Holt (New York, NY), 2008.

Piper Reed Gets a Job, Henry Holt (New York, NY), 2009.

Piper Reed: Into the Wild, Henry Holt (New York, NY), 2010.

***Christine Davenier's illustrations projects include Elissa Haden Guest's beginning reader* Iris and Walter.** (Illustration ©2000 by Christine Davenier. Reproduced by permission of Harcourt, Inc.)

Sidelights

Based in Paris, where she once worked as a school teacher, Christine Davenier is a French illustrator whose pen-and-ink and watercolor drawings have been consistently cited by critics as both charming and humorous. "Like that of Rosemary Wells, Davenier's art evokes more emotion than seems possible," remarked Lisa Falk in a *School Library Journal* review of Davenier's self-illustrated picture-book debut, *Leon and Albertine.* While she has since narrowed her focus to illustration, creating artwork for texts by Jack Prelutsky, Amy Hest, Steve Kroll, Norma Fox Mazer, Juanita Havill, Judith Viorst, and Kimberly Willis Holt, among others, Davenier continues to gain a positive response from both readers and reviewers. Reviewing Holt's *Piper Reed Gets a Job,* part of her "Piper Reed" chapter-book series, *Booklist* contributor Carolyn Phelan credited Davenier's "lively drawings" for "bring[ing] the characters to life," while her "clever illustrations" in Hallie Durand's chapter book *Dessert First* "add to the charm" of Durand's story about an eight-year-old free spirit, according to *School Library Journal* critic Jessica Marie.

Davenier's "large, loosely rendered line and watercolor illustrations are expressive and packed with action," noted a *Kirkus Reviews* writer in appraising her early work, while in a *Booklist* review of *Iris and Walter and the Birthday Party* Hazel Rochman deemed Davenier's collaboration with author Elissa Haden Guest on the popular "Iris and Walter" series "both joyful and touching." In the *Times Educational Supplement,* fellow illustrator Ted Dewan also focused on the success of Davenier's illustrations, noting in his critique of *Leon and Albertine* that "Davenier's style is quite special; her stylish watercolours have an invigorating spontaneity. Eschewing painstaking craft in favour of scribbly economy is a daring decision for a picture book illustrator to take."

Leon and Albertine was first published in Davenier's native France, then released in translation in the United States as well as in England, where it was published as *Frankie and Albertine.* In the picture book Leon the pig falls in love with Albertine the hen, and the lovelorn swine seeks advice from the other farm animals on how to catch the eye of his beloved. After the rooster's advice on singing, the rabbit's advice on dancing, and the bull's advice on being strong all fail to impress the imperious Albertine, Leon gives up and goes off to play in the mud with a friend. The two pigs have such a good time that everyone in the barnyard soon decides to join in, even Albertine, who admires her muddy suitor for knowing how to have fun. In her authorial debut, Davenier was praised for creating a universal story with a simple text.

Davenier brings the same breezy, expressive style she showcases in *Leon and Albertine* to the illustrations she creates for texts by other authors. In C.M. Millen's *The Low-Down Laundry Line Blues,* a younger sister tries to cajole her older sister out of a bad mood with a session

Davenier's artwork for Madeleine L'Engle's picture book The Other Dog *shows an unusual side of the well-known fantasy writer.* (Illustration © 2001 by Christine Davenier. Used with permission of Chronicle Books LLC, San Francisco. Visit ChronicleBooks.com.)

of jumping rope. "The rhyme and the fluid watercolor illustrations, executed with real verve, successfully capture" the personalities of the sisters, noted Kate McClelland in appraising Davenier's contribution to the book for *School Library Journal.* In Paul B. Janeczko's *Very Best (Almost) Friends: Poems of Friendship* the artist's pen-and-ink-and-watercolor art reflects the variety of feelings evoked by friendship, from joyous to angry and everything in between. "Clear blues and reds dominate the artist's palette, adding richness to the ink lines that sweep across the pages," observed Jane Marino in a review of *Very Best (Almost) Friends* for *School Library Journal.*

Praising Davenier's "spontaneous, ebullient watercolors" for Cari Best's *Sally Jean, the Bicycle Queen* as "reminiscent of the work of Marc Simont," *Booklist* contributor Jennifer Mattson concluded that the artist "capture[s] the irresistible qualities of a little girl who knows how to make things happen." The portraits of busy children she creates to decorate the pages of Prelutsky's *Me I Am!,* Davenier's "delicate use of watercolors and . . . sketchy line create the feeling of gaiety and movement, yet elegantly convey personality and emotion," according to *School Library Journal* contributor Carole Phillips. The artist's "playful watercolors" also entertain readers of Mazer's upbeat picture book *Has Anyone Seen My Emily Greene?,* in which a

father searches for the playful toddler hidden in places that are quickly discovered in Davenier's engaging art. "Very young children . . . will applaud Emily's mischievous ingenuity" in this "utterly endearing" book, concluded a *Publishers Weekly* critic,

In addition to capturing high spirits, Davenier's illustrations can also emphasize the softer side of human relations, as they do in Amy Hest's picture book *Mabel Dancing,* about a little girl who feels left out during her parents' dance party until the music floats her down the stairs and into her parents' accepting arms. Writing in the *New York Times Book Review,* Betsy Groban called this story "a dreamy, evocative portrait of parental love as it's supposed to be: all encompassing and unconditional." The artist takes a similarly lyrical approach in her work for Juanita Havill's *I Heard It from Alice Zucchini: Poems about the Garden,* and her "pencil, ink, and pastel illustrations lend a timeless quality" to Susan Marie Swanson's picture book *The First Thing My Mama Told Me,* in the opinion of *School Library Journal* contributor Martha Link. Calling Davenier's ink-and-watercolor drawings for Sandra Jordan's *Mr. and Mrs. Portly and Their Little Dog, Snack* "stylish," Kathleen Finn added in *School Library Journal* that Jordan's "witty, urbane story . . . is well matched by the illustrations' energy, flair, and ebullient use of color."

Davenier once told *SATA:* "I don't feel really familiar with words and that's why I work with images. It is very hard for me to speak about my work. Each time I start to create a new story for a book, even if there is a chronology in what I have done and what I am doing at the moment, there is something I can't explain, something that escapes me. I will understand it or discover it through the children who will read or listen to my story. Maybe I create a story to share it with an audience and expect to understand why I did it from their reaction."

Biographical and Critical Sources

PERIODICALS

Booklist, July, 2002, Lauren Peterson, review of *The First Thing My Mama Told Me,* p. 1861; February 1, 2006, Hazel Rochman, review of *Iris and Walter and the Birthday Party,* p. 54; May 1, 2006, Jennifer Mattson, review of *Sally Jean, the Bicycle Queen,* p. 88; July 1, 2008, Carolyn Phelan, review of *Piper Reed, the Great Gypsy,* p. 67; September 15, 2008, Randall Enos, review of *Nobody Here but Me,* p. 58; August 1, 2009, Carolyn Phelan, review of *Piper Reed Gets a Job,* p. 60; September 15, 2009, Ilene Cooper, review of *Mr. and Mrs. Portly and Their Little Dog, Snack,* p. 58.

Books for Keeps, September, 1999, George Hunt, review of *Frankie and Albertine,* p. 22.

Horn Book, May-June, 2005, Betty Carter, review of *Iris and Walter and the Field Trip,* p. 325; September-October, 2007, Robin Smith, review of *Piper Reed, Navy Brat,* p. 578; September-October, 2008, Robin L. Smith, review of *Piper Reed, the Great Gypsy,* p. 588; September-October, 2009, Martha V. Parravano, review of *Piper Reed Gets a Job,* p. 564.

Kirkus Reviews, January 1, 1998, review of *Leon and Albertine,* p. 56; September 1, 2003, review of *Full*

Davenier's colorful illustrations team with Amy Hest's story in the engaging picture book **Mabel Dancing.** (Illustration © 2000 by Christine Davenier. Reproduced by permission of the publisher Candlewick Press.)

Sandra Jordan's story about a doting family and their beloved pup are captured by Davenier's artwork for **Mr. and Mrs. Portly and Their Little Dog, Snack.** (Illustration © 2009 by Christine Davenier. Used by permission of Farrar, Straus & Giroux, LLC.)

Moon Barnyard Dance, p. 1130; April 1, 2009, review of *Dessert First;* August 15, 2009, review of *Mr. and Mrs. Portly and Their Little Dog, Snack.*

New York Times Book Review, March 11, 2001, Betsy Groban, "Mabel, the Night and the Music," p. 27; October 20, 2002, Abby McGanney Nolan, review of *The First Thing My Mama Told Me,* p. 23.

Publishers Weekly, June 10, 2002, review of *That Makes Me Mad!,* p. 60; June 26, 2006, review of *Sally Jean, the Bicycle Queen,* p. 51; March 5, 2007, review of *I Am Me!,* p. 59; June 25, 2007, review of *Has Anyone Seen My Emily Greene?,* p. 59; July 30, 2007, review of *Piper Reed: Navy Brat,* p. 82; June 23, 2008, review of *Nobody Here but Me,* p. 53; August 24, 2008, review of *Mr. and Mrs. Portly and Their Little Dog, Snack,* p. 59; March 9, 2009, review of *Just like a Baby,* p. 46; May 4, 2009, review of *Dessert First,* p. 50.

School Library Journal, March, 1998, Lisa Falk, review of *Leon and Albertine,* p. 168; January, 1999, Jane Marino, review of *Very Best (Almost) Friends: Poems of Friendship,* p. 143; May, 1999, Kate McClelland, review of *The Low-Down Laundry Line Blues,* p. 93; August, 2002, Martha Link, review of *The First Thing My Mama Told Me,* p. 170; November, 2003, Maryann H. Owen, review of *Full Moon Barnyard Dance,* p. 115; April, 2006, Teresa Pfeifer, review of *I Heard It from Alice Zucchini: Poems about the Garden,* p. 126; May, 2007, Carole Phillips, review of *I Am Me!,* p. 106; June, 2007, Mary Jean Smith, review of *Has Anyone Seen My Emily Greene?,* p. 115; August, 2007, Terrie Dorio, review of *Piper Reed: Navy Brat,* p. 81; August, 2008, Mary Jean Smith, review of *Nobody Here but Me,* p. 104; June, 2009, Rachel Kamin, re-

view of *Just like a Baby,* p. 90; July, 2009, Jessica Marie, review of *Dessert First,* p. 62; August, 2009, Elizabeth Swistock, review of *Piper Reed Gets a Job,* p. 77; September, 2009, Kathleen Finn, review of *Mr. and Mrs. Portly and Their Little Dog, Snack,* p. 126.

Times Educational Supplement, August 27, 1999, Ted Dewan, review of *Frankie and Albertine,* p. 21.

ONLINE

Bulletin of the Center for Children's Books Online, http://www.bbcb.lis.uiuc.edu/ (March 1, 2001), Deborah Stevenson, "Christine Davenier."

Chronicle Books Web site, http://www.chroniclebooks.com/ (June 1, 2010), "Christine Davenier."

Macmillan Web site, http://us.macmillan.com/ (June 1, 2010), "Christine Davenier."*

*　　*　　*

DESIMINI, Lisa 1964-

Personal

Born March 21, 1964, in Brooklyn, NY; daughter of Pat (a money broker) and Vera (a medical assistant) Desimini; married Matt Mahurin (an artist and filmmaker). *Education:* School of Visual Arts (New York, NY), B.F.A., 1986.

Addresses

Home—New York, NY; Northport, NY. *E-mail*—desimini@earthlink.net.

Career

Children's book illustrator and writer. Taught illustration at the School of Visual Arts, New York, NY.

Awards, Honors

Critici in Erba Honor Book, Bologna Book Fair, for *I Am Running Away Today;* National Parenting Publications Award, 1992, for *How the Stars Fell into the Sky: A Navajo Legend* by Jerrie Oughton; *New York Times* Best Illustrated and American Booksellers Association Pick of the List citations, 1994, both for *My House;* Best Picture Book of the Year, *Publishers Weekly,* Blue Ribbon citation, *Bulletin of the Center for Children's Books,* and Best Book of the Year selection, *School Library Journal,* all 1997, all for *Love Letters* written by Arnold Adoff.

Writings

SELF-ILLUSTRATED

I Am Running Away Today, Hyperion (New York, NY), 1992.

Moon Soup, Hyperion (New York, NY), 1993.

Lisa Desimini (Photograph by Matt Mahurin. Reproduced by permission.)

My House, Holt (New York, NY), 1994.
Sun and Moon: A Giant Love Story, Scholastic, Inc. (New York, NY), 1999.
Dot the Fire Dog, Scholastic, Inc. (New York, NY), 2001.
Policeman Lou and Policewoman Sue, Scholastic, Inc. (New York, NY), 2003.
Trick-or-Treat, Smell My Feet!, Blue Sky Press (New York, NY), 2005.

ILLUSTRATOR

Ann Turner, *Heron Street,* HarperCollins (New York, NY), 1989.
Liz Rosenberg, *Adelaide and the Night Train,* HarperCollins (New York, NY), 1989.
Christine Widman, *Housekeeper of the Wind,* HarperCollins (New York, NY), 1990.
Nancy White Carlstrom, *Moose in the Garden,* HarperCollins (New York, NY), 1990.
Nancy White Carlstrom, *Light: Stories of a Small Kindness,* Little, Brown (Boston, MA), 1990.
Dennis Haseley, *The Thieves' Market,* HarperCollins (New York, NY), 1991.
Jerrie Oughton, *How the Stars Fell into the Sky: A Navajo Legend,* Houghton (Boston, MA), 1993.
Liliane Atlan, *The Passersby,* translated from the French by Rochelle Owens, Holt (New York, NY), 1993.
Holly Near, *The Great Peace March,* Holt (New York, NY), 1993.

Nancy White Carlstrom, *Fish and Flamingo,* Little, Brown (Boston, MA), 1993.
Jerrie Oughton, *The Magic Weaver of Rugs: A Tale of the Navajo,* Houghton (Boston, MA), 1994.
Tree De Gerez, *When Bear Came Down from the Sky,* Viking (New York, NY), 1994.
Nancy Van Laan, *In a Circle Long Ago,* Knopf (New York, NY), 1995.
Douglas Wood, *Northwoods Cradle Song: From a Menominee Lullaby,* Simon & Schuster (New York, NY), 1996.
Verna Aardema, *Anansi Does the Impossible: An Ashanti Tale,* Simon & Schuster (New York, NY), 1997.
Arnold Adoff, *Love Letters,* Scholastic, Inc. (New York, NY), 1997.
Cynthia Rylant, *Tulip Sees America,* Scholastic, Inc. (New York, NY), 1998.
J. Patrick Lewis, *Doodle Dandies: Poems That Take Shape,* Atheneum (New York, NY), 1998.
Arnold Adoff, *Touch the Poem,* Scholastic, Inc. (New York, NY), 2000.
Nancy Van Laan, *The Laughing Man,* Atheneum (New York, NY), 2000.
J. Patrick Lewis, *Good Mousekeeping, and Other Animal Home Poems,* Atheneum (New York, NY), 2001.
Marcia K. Vaughan, *Night Dancer: Mythical Piper of the Native American Southwest,* Orchard (New York, NY), 2002.
J. Patrick Lewis, *The Snowflake Sisters,* Atheneum (New York, NY), 2003.
Arlene Alda, *Iris Has a Virus,* Tundra Books of Northern New York (Plattsburgh, NY), 2008.
Jan Godown Annino, *She Sang Promise: The Story of Betty Mae Jumper, Seminole Tribal Leader,* National Geographic Society (Washington, DC), 2010.

OTHER

My Beautiful Child, illustrated by Matt Mahurin, Scholastic, Inc. (New York, NY), 2004.

Contributor of poem and illustrations to *All Year Round: A Book to Benefit Children in Need,* Scholastic, Inc. (New York, NY), 1997.

Adaptations

Dot the Fire Dog was adapted for video, Weston Woods.

Sidelights

An award-winning author and illustrator, Lisa Desimini has gained notice for her unusual and provocative narratives as well as her richly colored, visually stunning artwork. "Desimini's paintings and stories describe dream worlds in which everyday essentials—umbrellas, for instance, or footprints, or houses—are recognizable, but somehow different," wrote *Print* magazine critic Carol Stevens. Such common objects take on uniqueness at the hands of Desimini, changing color or shape and even function. "Desimini, herself," Stevens further commented, "seems to be motivated, if not by magic, then by some extra-conscious perception." In her self-illustrated titles, as well as the artwork she does for the work of other authors, Desimini creates a distinctive, sometimes surreal, look that has become her trademark.

Born in Brooklyn, New York, Desimini moved often as a child, and her family lived in Florida and New Jersey for a time. "Drawing helped me through the adjustment time in each new place," she remarked in *Talking with Artists, Volume 3.* "It made me very happy and comfortable to be alone." Desimini's skills and creativity were evident at a young age. "My mother, father, teachers, relatives, and friends all told me I should be an artist. Now, this was a lot of support. So I thought, 'I am good. I will be an artist.' After that if anyone told me I couldn't or shouldn't I only tried harder."

Desimini came to children's-book illustration almost by accident. After graduating from New York's School of Visual Arts in 1986, she expected to go to work illustrating for magazines and newspapers. She told Janet Schnol of *Publishers Weekly* that even after she was referred to a Harper Junior Books editor and then given the opportunity to produce sample illustrations for Ann Turner's *Heron Street,* she still was not certain she was interested in working with children's books. She quickly found the work highly satisfying, however, and even proclaimed herself "addicted." "What I love about children's books," Desimini told Schnol, "is that I'm involved with so much—decisions about end pages, color, and type. I have a great deal of freedom, especially in the layout."

Desimini creates unique artwork for Arnold Adoff's whimsical picture book **Love Letters.** (Illustration © 1997 by Lisa Desimini. Reproduced by permission of Scholastic Inc.)

Desimini's illustrations have been described as surreal and seemingly naïve, and have invited comparisons to the work of artist Henri Rousseau. In *Adelaide and the Night Train* by Liz Rosenberg, Desimini's illustrations of a night ride on a train heading toward the land of sleep echo the author's evocative language, according to critics. Stephen Dobyns remarked in the *New York Times Book Review* that Desimini's illustrations possess "a slightly primitive cast, a magical weirdness that bears close examination. . . . At my house these days, when the youngest child has trouble settling down, *Adelaide and the Night Train* is the book we try first. It's as good as a glass of warm milk, and half the bother."

Desimini has had many profitable repeat collaborative efforts. Working with writer Jerrie Oughton, she produced artwork for both the award-winning *How the Stars Fell into the Sky: A Navajo Legend* and *The Magic Weaver of Rugs: A Tale of the Navajo.* In the latter story, author and illustrator "bring to life . . . the origins of weaving and the famous Navajo rug," according to a reviewer for *Publishers Weekly.* Spider Woman, so legend has it, erected a huge loom and left instructions for the Navajo women how to use it. A *Publishers Weekly* critic wrote that Oughton's "poetic" text is "mirrored" by Desimini's illustrations, which "gleam with an otherworldliness." Similarly, *Booklist* critic Elizabeth Bush suggested that "Desimini's surreal paintings underscore the otherworldly nature" of the meeting between Spider Woman and the Navajo women.

Other Native-American themes are explored in books such as *In a Circle Long Ago* by Nancy Van Laan, *Northwoods Cradle Song: From a Menominee Lullaby* by Douglas Wood, and *Night Dancer: Mythical Piper of the Native American Southwest* by Marcia K. Vaughan. Van Laan's book is a collection of twenty-five verses and myths of North American indigenous people. *Horn Book* critic Maeve Visser Knoth praised Desimini's artwork for this book, noting that "each illustration suits the tone of the story it accompanies." Knoth pointed out that even the image borders echo the content: in the section of Northwest Indians, for example, Desimini includes totem poles of regional tribes such as the Haida. A reviewer for *Publishers Weekly* also commended Desimini's "especially effective" artwork, citing her us of "dazzling oils" in a number of different styles. For Wood's lullaby, Desimini "paints with a tranquil, velvety softness," according to a reviewer for *Publishers Weekly,* while Margaret A. Bush, reviewing *Northwoods Cradle Song* in *Horn Book,* commented that the picture's "deep tones of rust, green, and gold glow in soft light." In *Night Dancer* the illustrator "tackles several tough assignments" in her artwork, according to Sally Bates Goodroe in *School Library Journal.* First, she had to transform the usual stick figure of Kokopelli into a more human form; next, she needed to show the animation of the dancers; and lastly, all this needed to be done in the soft, dark tones of moonlight. A critic for *Publishers Weekly* praised the result, noting that "Desimini's keen use of color and light effects a dreamlike, movie stills quality."

Desimini's illustration projects include creating art for her original picture book My House. (Illustration courtesy of Lisa Desimini.)

Further successful collaborative efforts include working with writer and poet Arnold Adoff on *Love Letters* and *Touch the Poem,* and with J. Patrick Lewis on both *Doodle Dandies: Poems That Take Shape* and *Good Mousekeeping, and Other Animal Home Poems.* Valentine's Day is celebrated in the twenty poems of Adoff's *Love Letters.* Reviewing that title, a contributor for *Publishers Weekly* thought that "Desimini's artwork, like Adoff's poetry, suggests secrecy and shyness." In *Booklist* Ilene Cooper had high praise for Desimini's illustrations in that same title, noting that her "wondrous artwork is a constant delight." Working with Adoff again on *Touch the Poem,* Desimini contributes "striking mixed-media collages," according to a reviewer for *Publishers Weekly.*

Desimini serves up more mixed-media illustrations to accompany the poems of Lewis in *Doodle Dandies,* a "mix of clever language and visual delights [that] makes a dandy treat for all ages," as a contributor for *Publishers Weekly* noted. The text itself takes concrete shape on the pages, often representing visually what the text describes. For example, verses about a skyscraper are actually laid out on the page in skyscraper form. *Horn Book* critic Lauren Adams wrote that "Desimini's mixed-media collage provides a wide variety of backdrops for the poems" in this collection. Adams further commented that *Doodle Dandies* represents a "true collaboration of text and art." GraceAnne A. DeCandido,

writing in *Booklist,* remarked that Desimini's "art is full of textures and dark, rich colors that repay close examination," and in *School Library Journal* Kathleen Whalin had further praise for Desimini's "brilliant" collage artwork in *Doodle Dandies.* Lewis and Desimini work together again on *Good Mousekeeping, and Other Animal Home Poems,* once more blending verse and image. Through computer-enhanced collages, Desimini's pictures for this book "lift" Lewis's "rhymes into dazzling visual images," according to Whalin, writing in *School Library Journal.* Likewise, a reviewer for *Publishers Weekly* found that Desimini's "inventive" illustrations for *Good Mousekeeping, and Other Animal Home Poems* "yield the greater wit and humor."

Desimini has also garnered praise for her illustrations in *The Snowflake Sisters,* a work by J. Patrick Lewis. The story, told in verse, centers on Crystal and Ivory, two snowflakes who drift through a variety of amazing experiences that include alighting on Santa's sleigh, arriving in Times Square on New Year's Eve, and coming to rest on a snowman in Central Park. According to a *Kirkus Reviews* contributor, "Desimini matches Lewis's sprightly verse with equally exuberant collages" composed of cotton, lace, rice paper, maps, newsprint, and other materials. In *School Library Journal,* Susan Patron complimented the "witty collage illustrations," and Ilene Cooper, writing in *Booklist,* remarked that the artwork "delightfully catches the wordplay."

In addition to her work as an illustrator, Desimini has also produced self-illustrated titles of poetry and stories for young readers. "I like writing books that have a touch of magic," she once told *SATA.* "I illustrated many books for other authors before I started writing my own. I feel like I can truly express myself this way." Desimini's first solo effort, *I Am Running Away Today,* presents a lighthearted treatment of the theme of running away. At the book's opening, a cat decides to leave his home since his best friend next door is moving away. The simple text is accompanied by illustrations critics have cited for their innovation, style, and dramatic qualities. Although Zack Rogow wrote in the *New York Times Book Review* that *I Am Running Away Today* "reads like a book written by someone whose training and experience have been largely in the visual arts," he praised the "playful, colorful and stylized" illustrations. Similarly, a reviewer for *Publishers Weekly* maintained that Desmini's illustrative style almost overwhelms her "fun and fanciful" story.

Desimini's illustrations for her story *Moon Soup* likewise captured much of the critical attention bestowed upon the book. In this story, she offers a fanciful recipe for soup that concludes with the main character flying off to the moon to stir and serve it. Although Ruth Semrau wrote in *School Library Journal* that *Moon Soup* has a weak story line, she added that "shapes, lines, and colors combine to create an exciting visual experience." Ilene Cooper concluded in *Booklist* that while "Desimini's fanciful art may be over the top for some, . . . it's hard to tear your eyes away."

Desimini's "brief text serves mainly as a springboard for stunning illustrations," remarked a reviewer in *Publishers Weekly* about *My House.* Here the artist uses collage with paintings, photographs, and other media to depict a house in different kinds of light and weather conditions. "For all the showiness" of the art, the review continued, "the book is reassuring" because it emphasizes the friendliness and security of the home. Reviewing the same book, Hanna B. Zeiger wrote in *Horn Book* that Desimini takes a basic theme and employs an "innovative combination of paint, collage, and photographs" to create "uniquely crafted" and "dramatic portrayals" of the house in question. In *Booklist* Janice M. Del Negro also commended the work, noting that while "the text is essentially a vehicle for the pictures," *My House* is "a successful whole."

In *Sun and Moon: A Giant Love Story,* Desimini creates "surreal mixed-media images [that] light up a larger-than-life romance," according to a reviewer for *Publishers Weekly.* In her text she tells the tale of a lonely giant and giantess who live on opposite sides of the earth and wander about looking for someone the right size who they can love. The two outsized persons continually miss one another because she searches by night, . . . he searches by day. Finally the two are brought together by an eclipse. The *Publishers Weekly* reviewer felt that Desimini's "haunting" illustrations "bespeak an original artistic vision." Del Negro, while less impressed, wrote in her *Bulletin of the Center for Children's Books* review that the artwork demonstrates Desimini's "touch of mad elegance." DeCandido was more positive, however, calling *Sun and Moon* an "enchanting fable" with "fabulous" computer-enhanced, mixed-media artwork.

With *Dot the Fire Dog* and *Policeman Lou and Policewoman Sue* Desimini presents companion profiles about public servants. In the first title, she looks at the work of firefighters through the eyes of the firehouse dog who helps to rescue a kitten while the firemen save an old man. Connie Fletcher, writing in *Booklist,* commented favorably on the "interesting details" in the text and the "richly hued and appealing" companion illustrations, while *Horn Book* critic Lauren Adams noted that "Desimini provides a bold, engaging outlet for preschoolers' perennial fascination with firefighters." Lisa Dennis, reviewing *Dot the Fire Dog* for *School Library Journal,* commended Desimini's oil painting illustrations, which "offer quirky perspectives and unusual angles."

A self-illustrated holiday tale, *Trick-or-Treat, Smell My Feet!* concerns twin sisters Delia and Ophelia and their efforts to ruin Halloween for their neighbors. Creating a potent brew from a pair of stinky socks, the wicked witches cast a spell that makes it impossible for children to ask for candy; instead, all anyone can utter is the phrase "smell my feet." When Delia and Ophelia accidentally toss a baby booty into their potion, however, their spell backfires in a most unpredictable fashion. Gillian Engberg, writing in *Booklist,* commented that "Desimini's lively cut-paper collages provide plenty of humor," and *Horn Book* reviewer Kitty Flynn asserted that the pictures "conjure up just the right amount of child-friendly fright in this lighthearted Halloween treat."

A youngster's bout with a nasty illness is the focus of Arlene Alda's *Iris Has a Virus,* featuring illustrations by Desimini. After a visit to the doctor, who informs Iris that she has contracted a "bug," the girl begins having wild, fantastic dreams about the colorful creatures that are the cause of all her problems. Fortunately, Iris recovers just in time to celebrate her grandfather's birthday, while her germs have found another target: her brother. "Desimini's cut-paper collage and digital art is full of emotion," Kristine M. Casper wrote in *School Library Journal,* and Shelle Rosenfeld noted in *Booklist* that the pictures "incorporate whimsical perspectives and scenarios."

With *Policeman Lou and Policewoman Sue* Desimini does the same job for police officers, offering young readers a view into their working lives. This involves activities both mundane and exciting, from ticketing a car parked by a fire hydrant to chasing down a purse-snatcher. A *Publishers Weekly* critic noted that the "calm and low-key" text in the book is filled with more information than drama, and also had praise for "the easy friendship and professionalism" demonstrated by Lou and Sue.

For her picture book *My Beautiful Child,* Desimini teams with her husband and fellow artist Matt Mahurin, who provides the book's illustrations. An ode to parental love, the work offers scenes of adults and children engaged in a host of shared activities, from tasting fruit to launching paper airplanes to making hand shadows. "Like many of Desimini's titles," observed Lauralyn Persson in *School Library Journal,* "this volume lends itself to imaginative contemplation in its sense of joy and wonder."

Biographical and Critical Sources

PERIODICALS

Cummings, Pat, editor, *Talking with Artists, Volume 3,* Clarion (New York, NY), 1999.

PERIODICALS

Booklist, November 1, 1993, Ilene Cooper, review of *Moon Soup,* p. 528; March 1, 1994, Elizabeth Bush, review of *The Magic Weaver of Rugs: A Tale of the Navajo,* pp. 1265-1266; November 15, 1994, Janice M. Del Negro, review of *My House,* p. 610; December 1, 1996, Linda Perkins, review of *Anansi Does the Impossible: An Ashanti Tale,* p. 638; January 1, 1997, Ilene Cooper, review of *Love Letters,* p. 863; December 15, 1997, Julie Corsaro, review of *All Year Round: A Book to Benefit Children in Need,* p. 702; March 15, 1998, GraceAnne A. DeCandido, review of *Tulip Sees America,* p. 1252; July, 1998, GraceAnne A. DeCandido, review of *Doodle Dandies: Poems That Take Shape,* p. 1876; January 1, 1999, GraceAnne A. DeCandido, review of *Sun and Moon: A Giant Love Story,* p. 886; March 15, 2000, Ilene Cooper, review of *Touch the Poem,* p. 1378; October 1, 2001, Connie Fletcher, review of *Dot the Fire Dog,* p. 324; May 15, 2003, Julie Cummins, review of *Policeman Lou and Policewoman Sue,* p. 1670; November 15, 2003, Ilene Cooper, review of *The Snowflake Sisters,* p. 601; September 15, 2004, Ilene Cooper, review of *My Beautiful Child,* p. 247; September 15, 2005, Gillian Engberg, review of *Trick-or-Treat, Smell My Feet!,* p. 71; October 15, 2008, Shelle Rosenfeld, review of *Iris Has a Virus,* p. 46.

Bulletin of the Center for Children's Books, January, 1999, Janice M. Del Negro, review of *Sun and Moon,* p. 165.

Horn Book, November-December, 1994, Hanna B. Zeiger, review of *My House,* p. 71; January-February, 1996, Maeve Visser Knoth, review of *In a Circle Long Ago,* p. 84; May-June, 1996, Margaret A. Bush, review of *Northwoods Cradle Song: From a Menominee Lullaby,* p. 331; July-August, 1998, Lauren Adams, review of *Doodle Dandies,* pp. 505-506; November-December, 2001, Lauren Adams, review of *Dot the Fire Dog,* pp. 734-735; September-October, 2005, Kitty Flynn, review of *Trick-or-Treat, Smell My Feet!,* p. 560.

Kirkus Reviews, December 15, 1998, review of *Sun and Moon,* p. 1795; September 1, 2001, review of *Dot the Fire Dog,* p. 1288; June 1, 2003, review of *Policeman Lou and Policewoman Sue,* p. 802; September 15, 2003, review of *The Snowflake Sisters,* p. 1177; August 1, 2008, review of *Iris Has a Virus.*

New York Times Book Review, April 1, 1990, Stephen Dobyns, review of *Adelaide and the Night Train,* p. 26; March 17, 1992, Zack Rogow, review of *I Am Running Away Today,* p. 31.

Print, May-June, 1995, Carol Stevens, "Lisa Desimini," pp. 106-108.

Publishers Weekly, December 22, 1989, Janet Schnol, "Flying Starts: New Faces of 1989," pp. 28-29; March 16, 1992, review of *I Am Running Away Today,* p. 79; February 21, 1994, review of *The Magic Weaver of Rugs,* p. 253; September 5, 1994, review of *My House,* p. 110; November 6, 1995, review of *In a Circle Long Ago,* pp. 93-94; April 15, 1996, review of *Northwoods Cradle Song,* p. 67; December 2, 1996, review of *Love Letters,* pp. 59-61; October 13, 1997, review of *All Year Round,* p. 73; April 20, 1998, review of *Tulip Sees America,* p. 66; June 29, 1998, review of *Doodle Dandies,* p. 57; December 21, 1998, review of *Sun and Moon,* p. 67; April 17, 2000, review of *Touch the Poem,* p. 80; April 30, 2001, review of *Good Mousekeeping, and Other Animal Home Poems,* p. 77; October 15, 2001, review of *Dot the Fire Dog,* p. 70; October 14, 2002, review of *Night Dancer: Mythical Piper of the Native American Southwest,* p. 82; May

26, 2003, review of *Policeman Lou and Policewoman Sue,* p. 68; August 1, 2005, review of *Trick-or-Treat, Smell My Feet!,* p. 64.

School Library Journal, January, 1994, Ruth Semrau, review of *Moon Soup,* p. 88; May, 1996, Ruth K. McDonald, review of *Northwoods Cradle Song,* p. 109; September, 1997, Donna S. Scanlon, review of *Anansi Does the Impossible,* pp. 198-199; April, 1998, Karen Jones, review of *Tulip Sees America,* p. 109; August, 1998, Kathleen Whalin, review of *Doodle Dandies,* p. 153; March, 1999, Steven Engelfried, review of *Sun and Moon,* p. 173; June, 2000, Jane Marino, review of *Touch the Poem,* p. 128; June, 2001, Kathleen Whalin, review of *Good Mousekeeping,* p. 138; December, 2001, Lisa Dennis, review of *Dot the Fire Dog,* pp. 98-99; October, 2002, Sally Bates Goodroe, review of *Night Dancer,* pp. 132-133; October, 2003, Susan Patron, review of *The Snowflake Sisters,* p. 65; June, 2004, Lauralyn Persson, review of *My Beautiful Child,* p. 106; August, 2005, Kara Schaff Dean, review of *Trick-or-Treat, Smell My Feet!,* p. 93; November, 2008, Kristine M. Casper, review of *Iris Has a Virus,* p. 84.

ONLINE

Houghton Mifflin Harcourt Web site, http://www.eduplace.com/ (May 1, 2010), "Meet the Author: Lisa Desimini."

Lisa Desimini Home Page, http://www.lisadesimini.com (May 1, 2010).

Scholastic Web site, http://www2.scholastic.com/ (May 1, 2010), "Lisa Desimini."

* * *

DOKAS, Dara 1968-

Personal

Born 1968; married; children: one daughter. *Education:* M.A. (education). *Hobbies and other interests:* Animals.

Addresses

Home—St. Paul, MN. *E-mail*—dara@cs.umn.edu; Dara@daradokas.com.

Career

Author and bookseller. Has worked for children's theatre, on a science-themed television program, and in a museum; teacher of English and drama. Presenter at schools, teacher workshops, and writing conferences.

Writings

Remembering Mama, illustrated by Angela L. Chostner, Augsburg Fortress (Minneapolis, MN), 2002.

Muriel's Red Sweater, illustrated by Bernadette Pons, Dutton Children's Books (New York, NY), 2009.

Saving Shadow, illustrated by Evelyne Duverne, Picture Window Books (Minneapolis, MN), 2009.

Biographical and Critical Sources

PERIODICALS

Kirkus Reviews, January 15, 2009, review of *Muriel's Red Sweater.*

School Library Journal, February, 2009, Ieva Bates, review of *Muriel's Red Sweater,* p. 74.

ONLINE

Dara Dokas Home Page, http://www.daradokas.com (May 15, 2010).*

*   *   *

DURAND, Hallie 1964(?)-
(Holly M. McGhee)

Personal

Born c. 1964, in NY; married Michael Steiner; children: two daughters, one son. *Education:* College degree. *Hobbies and other interests:* Cooking for family.

Addresses

Home—Maplewood, NJ. *Office*—Pippin Properties, 155 E. 38th St., Ste. 2H, New York, NY 10016.

Career

Literary agent and writer. Worked in publishing for twelve years, including as advertising director and executive editor; HarperCollins Publishers, New York, NY, associate publisher for Michael di Capua imprint, beginning 1991; Pippin Properties (literary agency), New York, NY, founder, c. 1998. Presenter at conferences.

Writings

Dessert First, Atheneum Books for Young Readers (New York, NY), 2009.

Just Desserts, illustrated by Christine Davenier, Atheneum Books for Young Readers (New York, NY), 2010.

No Room for Dessert, illustrated by Christine Davenier, Atheneum Books for Young Readers (New York, NY), 2011.

Mitchell's License, illustrated by Tony Fucile, Atheneum Books for Young Readers (New York, NY), 2011.

Sidelights

Hallie Durand is the pen name of Holly McGhee, the literary agent who heads Pippin Properties in New York City. With fond memories of family gatherings and the way home-cooked meals can make a home feel cozier and create loving bonds with friends, McGhee acknowledges that her love affair with food has helped define much of her life, from her friendships to her pastimes to a slew of memorable moments. While sharing dessert with a close friend one day, the suggestion was made that, since her job brings her into contact with many children's authors, McGhee might try her hand at writing a story of her own. On the way home from that visit, the character Dessert Schneider was born.

Readers meet Dessert in *Dessert First,* as the eight year old becomes tantalized by a plate of double-decker chocolate bars that are destined to be served at a family celebration. Encouraged by her teacher to cultivate her unique spirit, Dessert decides that since her tummy craves sweets, she should by rights indulge it, and over several excursions to the kitchen she eats every last chocolaty treat. When dinner comes, the girl's indulgence is discovered, and Dessert's scheme to repair her mistake by helping out at her family's restaurants also runs into a snag. *Dessert First* closes with a special treat: McGhee's home-tested recipe for double-decker chocolate bars.

Calling *Dessert First* a "refreshing debut," a *Publishers Weekly* critic dubbed McGhee's young protagonist "endearing" and noted that the author "displays a knack for comedic timing." Christine Davenier's "clever illustrations . . . add to the charm" of the "delectable story," in the view of *School Library Journal* critic Jessica Marie, the reviewer calling Dessert "a plucky young heroine." In *Kirkus Reviews* a contributor noted that the chapter book "nimbly balances" the girl's school and home life and predicted that young readers will "benefit from a second helping of lovable Dessert's adventures." In fact, McGhee generously accommodates such wishes in two humorous sequels to *Dessert First: Just Desserts* and *No Room for Dessert.*

In writing her book, McGhee based many of her characters on friends, her family, and her Maplewood, New Jersey, neighbors. She also found inspiration and ideas at Marshall Elementary, a school in nearby South Orange that was the inspiration for Lambert Elementary, Dessert's alma mater. Her character's sweet tooth did not need outside research, however; a passion for sweets is something McGhee can relate to one hundred percent.

Biographical and Critical Sources

PERIODICALS

Bulletin of the Center for Children's Books, September, 2009, Hope Morrison, review of *Dessert First,* p. 16.

Kirkus Reviews, April 1, 2009, review of *Dessert First.*

Publishers Weekly, May 4, 2009, review of *Dessert First,* p. 50.

School Library Journal, July, 2009, Jessica Marie, review of *Dessert First,* p. 62.

ONLINE

Hope Is the Word Web log, http://hopeistheword.wordpress.com/ (May 22, 2009), interview with Durand.

Hunger Mountain Online, http://www.hungermtn.org/ (February 2, 2010), interview with Holly M. McGhee and Emily Van Beek.

Simon & Schuster Web site, http://authors.simonandschuster.com/ (June 1, 2010), "Hallie Durand."*

E-F

ECHEVERRIA GYORKOS, Charmaine
(Charmaine Echeverria Gyorkos)

Personal

Born in East Los Angeles, CA; married (divorced); children: one son. *Education:* East Lost Angeles College, degree (advertising design); B.A. (graphic design).

Addresses

Home—West Point, CA.

Career

Artist and illustrator. Formerly worked as an engineering aide, draftsperson, and graphic designer. Textile artist. Volunteer at Indian Grinding Rock State Park and Native American Museum.

Illustrator

Olivia Echevveria-Bis, *The EGGbees: A Story about Family,* Arte Publico Press/Piñata Books (Houston, TX), 2009.

Biographical and Critical Sources

PERIODICALS

Kirkus Reviews, April 1, 2009, review of *The EGGbees: A Story about Family.*
School Library Journal, April, 2009, Mary Elam, review of *The EGGbees,* p. 102.

ONLINE

Charmaine Echeverria Gyorkos Home Page, http://litaville.com (June 1, 2010).*

ELLERY, Amanda

Personal

Married Tom Ellery (a director and animator/artist); children: Thomas, Jr., John, Katie.

Addresses

Home—Santa Clarita, CA. *E-mail*—amandae@canyons.org.

Career

Writer.

Writings

If I Had a Dragon, illustrated by husband, Tom Ellery, Simon & Schuster Books for Young Readers (New York, NY), 2006.
If I Were a Jungle Animal, illustrated by Tom Ellery, Simon & Schuster Books for Young Readers (New York, NY), 2009.
Close the Door, Morton, illustrated by Tom Ellery, Simon & Schuster Books for Young Readers (New York, NY), 2010.

Author's work has been translated into Spanish.

Sidelights

Collaborating with her husband, artist Tom Ellery, West Coast writer Amanda Ellery established her career as an author of children's books with *If I Had a Dragon.* Featuring engaging pen-and-ink, charcoal, and watercolor cartoon art by Tom Ellery, the picture book focuses on an imaginative young boy named Morton as he imagines that his toddler brother is actually something far more interesting than a human child. While spending time with a giant, lumbering dragon can be interesting,

Morton eventually realizes that there are some things that dragons just cannot do, like playing catch, swimming, or making sand castles. Ellery's minimal text "captures the boy's voice . . . while leaving . . . room for listeners to interpret," according to *Booklist* critic Carolyn Phelan, and in *School Library Journal* Marge Loch-Wouters recommended *If I Had a Dragon* as "a great choice for newly independent readers as well as for sharing aloud." In *Kirkus Reviews* a critic also had praise for the book's illustrations, calling them "simply drawn, but with expressive faces and postures."

The young hero of *If I Had a Dragon* returns in *If I Were a Jungle Animal,* which finds the red-haired boy once again indulging in a colorful daydream. Bored while standing in the right outfield and waiting for a base ball that never comes, little-leaguer Morton decides that being an animal wandering through the jungle would be far more interesting. As readers follow, Morton's imagination transports him to the land of lions in a story that Loch Wouters dubbed "an exuberant paean to imagination and daydreaming." "Ellery's tale is simple but delicious, and accessible to very young readers," according to a *Kirkus Reviews* writer, and Tom Ellery's illustrations for *If I Were a Jungle Animal* are "funny, original and . . . lively."

Biographical and Critical Sources

PERIODICALS

Booklist, July 1, 2006, Carolyn Phelan, review of *If I Had a Dragon,* p. 64.
Kirkus Reviews, May 1, 2006, review of *If I Had a Dragon,* p. 456; April 1, 2009, review of *If I Were a Jungle Animal.*
School Library Journal, July, 2006, Marge Loch-Wouters, review of *If I Had a Dragon,* p. 77; April, 2009, Marge Loch-Wouters, review of *If I Were a Jungle Animal,* p. 102.

ONLINE

Simon & Schuster Web site, http://authore.simonand schuster.com/ (May 31, 2010), "Amanda Ellery."*

*　　*　　*

FIELDS, Lisa 1984(?)-

Personal

Born c. 1984. *Education:* Ringling School of Art and Design, B.F.A.; attended Illustration Academy.

Addresses

Home—Katonah, NY. *E-mail*—LisaAFields@gmail. com.

Career

Illustrator.

Illustrator

Lucha Corpi, *The Triple Banana Split Boy/El niño goloso,* Piñata Books (Houston, TX), 2009.
Trudy Ludwig, *Too Perfect,* Tricycle Press (Berkeley, CA), 2009.

Also illustrator of *Jake's Lemonade Stand,* Kaeden Books. Contributor to periodicals, including *Boy's Life, Cobblestone, Highlights for Children, Las Olas, Living Real Miami, Rhode Island Monthly,* and *Westchester Magazine.*

Biographical and Critical Sources

PERIODICALS

Kirkus Reviews, April 1, 2009, review of *Too Perfect.*
School Library Journal, April, 2009, Meg Smith, review of *Too Perfect,* p. 112; July, 2009, Irania Macias Patterson, review of *The Triple Banana Split Boy/El niño goloso,* p. 75.

ONLINE

Lisa Fields Home Page, http://www.lisafields.com (May 15, 2010).
Lisa Fields Web log, http://www.lisafields.blogspot.com (May 15, 2010).*

*　　*　　*

FOREMAN, Michael 1938-

Personal

Born March 21, 1938, in Pakefield, Suffolk, England; son of Walter Thomas (a crane operator) and Gladys Foreman; married Janet Charters, September 26, 1959 (divorced 1966); married Louise Phillips, December 22, 1980; children: (first marriage) Mark; (second marriage) Ben Shahn, Jack. *Education:* Lowestoft School of Art, national diploma in design (painting), 1958; Royal College of Art, A.R.C.A. (with first-class honours), 1963.

Addresses

Home and office—5 Church Gate, London SW6, England. *Agent*—John Locke, 15 E. 76th St., New York, NY 10021. *E-mail*—michaelforemanbooks@yahoo.co. uk.

Career

Graphic artist and author of children's books. Lecturer in graphics at St. Martin's School of Art, London, England, 1963-66, London College of Printing, 1966-

Michael Foreman (Photograph by Mark Gerson. Reproduced by permission.)

68, Royal College of Art, London, 1968-70, and Central School of Art, London, 1971-72. Art director of *Ambit,* beginning 1960, *Playboy,* 1965, and *King,* 1966-67. Elected Royal Designer to Industry, 1985. *Exhibitions:* Work exhibited in solo show at Royal Festival Hall, London, England, 1985, and in Europe, North America, and Japan.

Member

Chelsea Arts.

Awards, Honors

Festival International du Livre Silver Eagle Award, France, 1972; Francis Williams Memorial awards, Victoria & Albert Museum, 1972, and 1977, for *Monkey and the Three Wizards;* Kate Greenaway Commended Book designation, British Library Association (BLA), 1978, for *The Brothers Grimm: Popular Folk Tales;* Carnegie Medal, BLA, and Kate Greenaway Highly Commended Book designation, both 1980, and Graphics Prize, International Children's Book Fair (Bologna, Italy), 1982, all for *City of Gold, and Other Stories from the Old Testament;* Kate Greenaway Medal, and Kurt Maschler (Emil) Award, British Book Trust, both 1982, both for *Sleeping Beauty, and Other Favourite Fairy Tales;* Kate Greenaway Medal, 1982, for *Longneck and Thunderfoot;* Federation of Children's Book Groups award (England), 1983, for *The Saga of Erik the Viking;* Kate Greenaway Commended Book desig-

nation, and *New York Times* Notable Book designation, both 1985, both for *Seasons of Splendour; Signal* Poetry award, 1987, for *Early in the Morning;* named honorary fellow, Royal College of Arts, 1989; Kate Greenaway Medal, and W.H. Smith/Books in Canada Award, both 1990, both for *War Boy;* Nestlé Smarties' Book Prize Gold Award, 1993, for *War Game,* and Silver Award, 1997, for *The Little Reindeer;* honorary degree from Plymouth University, 1998.

Writings

SELF-ILLUSTRATED

The Perfect Present, Coward (New York, NY), 1967.

The Two Giants, Pantheon (New York, NY), 1967.

The Great Sleigh Robbery, Hamish Hamilton (London, England), 1968, Pantheon (New York, NY), 1969.

Horatio, Hamish Hamilton (London, England), 1970, published as *The Travels of Horatio,* Pantheon (New York, NY), 1970.

Moose, Hamish Hamilton (London, England), 1971, Pantheon (New York, NY), 1972.

Dinosaurs and All That Rubbish, Hamish Hamilton (London, England), 1972, Crowell (New York, NY), 1973.

War and Peas, Crowell (New York, NY), 1974.

All the King's Horses, Hamish Hamilton (London, England), 1976, Bradbury Press (Scarsdale, NY), 1977.

Panda's Puzzle, and His Voyage of Discovery (also see below), Hamish Hamilton (London, England), 1977, Bradbury Press (Scarsdale, NY), 1978.

Panda and the Odd Lion (also see below), Hamish Hamilton (London, England), 1979.

Trick a Tracker, Philomel (New York, NY), 1981.

Land of Dreams, Holt (New York, NY), 1982.

Panda and the Bunyips, Hamish Hamilton (London, England), 1984, Schocken (New York, NY), 1988.

Cat and Canary, Andersen (London, England), 1984, Dial (New York, NY), 1985.

Panda and the Bushfire, Prentice-Hall (Englewood Cliffs, NJ), 1986.

Ben's Box (pop-up book), Hodder & Stoughton (London, England), 1986, Piggy Toes Press (Kansas City, MO), 1997.

Ben's Baby, Andersen (London, England), 1987, Harper (New York, NY), 1988.

The Angel and the Wild Animal, Andersen (London, England), 1988, Atheneum (New York, NY), 1989.

War Boy: A Country Childhood, Pavilion (London, England), 1989.

One World, Andersen (London, England), 1990.

(Editor) *Michael Foreman's World of Fairy Tales,* Pavilion (London, England), 1990, Arcade (New York, NY), 1991.

(Editor) *Michael Foreman's Mother Goose,* Harcourt (New York, NY), 1991.

(With Richard Seaver) *The Boy Who Sailed with Columbus,* Arcade (New York, NY), 1992.

Jack's Fantastic Voyage, Harcourt (San Diego, CA), 1992.

Grandfather's Pencil and the Room Full of Stories, Andersen (London, England), 1993, Harcourt (San Diego, CA), 1994.

War Game, Arcade (New York, NY), 1993.

Dad! I Can't Sleep!, Andersen (London, England), 1994, Harcourt (San Diego, CA), 1995.

After the War Was Over (sequel to *War Boy*), Pavilion (London, England), 1995, Arcade (New York, NY), 1996.

Surprise! Surprise!, Harcourt (San Diego, CA), 1995.

Seal Surfer, Andersen (London, England), 1996, Harcourt (San Diego, CA), 1997.

The Little Reindeer, Dial (New York, NY), 1996.

Look! Look!, Andersen (London, England), 1997.

Angel and the Box of Time, Andersen (London, England), 1997.

Jack's Big Race, Andersen (London, England), 1997.

Chicken Licken, Andersen (London, England), 1998.

Panda (includes *Panda's Puzzle* and *Panda and the Odd Lion*), Pavilion (London, England), 1999.

Little Red Hen, Andersen (London, England), 1999.

Rock-a-Doodle-Do!, Andersen (London, England), 2000.

Michael Foreman's Christmas Treasury, Pavilion (London, England), 2000.

Cat in the Manger, Andersen (London, England), 2000, Holt (New York, NY), 2001.

Saving Sinbad, Andersen (London, England), 2001, Kane/Miller (La Jolla, CA), 2002.

Michael Foreman's Playtime Rhymes, Candlewick Press (Cambridge, MA), 2002.

Wonder Goal, Andersen (London, England), 2002, Farrar, Straus & Giroux (New York, NY), 2003.

Evie and the Man Who Helped God, Andersen (London, England), 2002.

Dinosaur Time, Andersen (London, England), 2002, published as *A Trip to Dinosaur Time,* Candlewick Press (Cambridge, MA), 2003.

The Little Reindeer, Red Fox (London, England), 2003.

Hello, World, Candlewick (Cambridge, MA), 2003.

Cat on the Hill, Andersen (London, England), 2003.

Cat in the Manger, Red Fox (London, England), 2004.

Can't Catch Me!, Andersen (London, England), 2005.

(Reteller) *Classic Fairy Tales,* Sterling (New York, NY), 2005.

Mia's Story, Walker (London, England), 2006, published as *Mia's Story: A Sketchbook of Hopes and Dreams,* Candlewick (Cambridge, MA), 2006.

Noah's Ark, Tiger Tales (Wilton, CT), 2006.

The Littlest Dinosaur, Walker & Company (New York, NY), 2008.

The Littlest Dinosaur's Big Adventure, Walker (New York, NY), 2009.

ILLUSTRATOR

Janet Charters, *The General,* Dutton (New York, NY), 1961.

Cledwyn Hughes, *The King Who Lived on Jelly,* Routledge & Kegan Paul (London, England), 1963.

Eric Partridge, *Comic Alphabets,* Routledge & Kegan Paul (London, England), 1964.

Derek Cooper, *The Bad Food Guide,* Routledge & Kegan Paul (London, England), 1966.

Gwen Clemens, *Making Music,* 1966.

Leonore Klein, *Huit enfants et un bébé,* Abelard (London, England), 1966.

Mabel Watts, *I'm for You, You're for Me,* Abelard (London, England), 1967.

Sergei Vladimirovich Mikalkov, *Let's Fight!, and Other Russian Fables,* Pantheon (New York, NY), 1968.

Donald Davie, *Essex Poems,* 1969.

Jane Elliott, *The Birthday Unicorn,* 1970.

William Ivan Martin, *Adam's Balm,* Bowmar (Los Angeles, CA), 1970.

C.O. Alexander, *Fisher v. Spassky,* Penguin (London, England), 1972.

William Fagg, editor, *The Living Arts of Nigeria,* Studio Vista (Eastbourne, England), 1972.

Barbara Adachi, *The Living Treasures of Japan,* Wildwood House (Aldershot, England), 1973.

Janice Elliott, *Alexander in the Land of Mog,* Brockhampton Press (Leicester, England), 1973.

Janice Elliott, *The Birthday Unicorn,* Penguin (London, England), 1973.

Sheila Burnford, *Noah and the Second Flood,* Gollancz (London, England), 1973.

Jane H. Yolen, *Rainbow Rider,* Crowell (New York, NY), 1974.

Georgess McHargue, *Private Zoo,* Viking (New York, NY), 1975.

Barbara K. Walker, *Teeny-Tiny and the Witch-Woman,* Pantheon (New York, NY), 1975.

Cheng-en Wu, *Monkey and the Three Wizards,* translated by Peter Harris, Collins & World (London, England), 1976.

Alan Garner, *The Stone Book,* Collins & World (London, England), 1976.

Alan Garner, *Tom Fobble's Day,* Collins & World (London, England), 1976.

Alan Garner, *Granny Reardun,* Collins & World (London, England), 1977.

Hans Christian Andersen, *Hans Christian Andersen: His Classic Fairy Tales,* translated by Erik Haugaard, Gollancz (London, England), 1977.

K. Bauman, *Kitchen Stories,* Nord Sud, 1977, published as *Mickey's Kitchen Contest,* Andersen (London, England), 1978.

Alan Garner, *The Aimer Gate,* Collins & World (London, England), 1978.

Bryna Stevens, reteller, *Borrowed Feathers, and Other Fables,* Random House (New York, NY), 1978.

Brian Alderson, translator, *The Brothers Grimm: Popular Folk Tales,* Gollancz (London, England), 1978.

Oscar Wilde, *The Selfish Giant,* Kaye & Ward (London, England), 1978.

Seven in One Blow, Random House (New York, NY), 1978.

Alan Garner, *Fairy Tales of Gold,* Volume 1: *The Golden Brothers,* Volume 2: *The Girl of the Golden Gate,* Volume 3: *The Three Golden Heads of the Well,* Volume 4: *The Princess and the Golden Mane,* Collins & World (London, England), 1979.

Bill Martin, *How to Catch a Ghost,* Holt (New York, NY), 1979.

Anthony Paul, *The Tiger Who Lost His Stripes,* Andersen (London, England), 1980, 2nd edition, Harcourt (San Diego, CA), 1995.

Ernest Hemingway, *The Faithful Bull,* Emme Italia, 1980.

Aldous Huxley, *After Many a Summer,* Folio Society (London, England), 1980.

Allen Andrews, *The Pig Plantagenet,* Hutchinson (London, England), 1980.

Peter Dickenson, *City of Gold, and Other Tales from the Old Testament,* Gollancz (London, England), 1980.

Terry Jones, *Terry Jones' Fairy Tales,* Pavilion (London, England), 1981, excerpts published separately as *The Beast with a Thousand Teeth, A Fisherman of the World, The Sea Tiger,* and *The Fly-by-Night,* P. Bedrick (New York, NY), 1994.

Oscar Wilde, *The Nightingale and the Rose,* Kaye & Ward, 1981.

John Loveday, editor, *Over the Bridge,* Penguin (London, England), 1981.

Robert McCrum, *The Magic Mouse and the Millionaire,* Hamish Hamilton (London, England), 1981.

Rudyard Kipling, *The Crab That Played with the Sea: A Just So Story,* Macmillan (London, England), 1982.

Angela Carter, selector and translator, *Sleeping Beauty and Other Favourite Fairy Tales,* Gollancz (London, England), 1982, Schocken (New York, NY), 1984.

Helen Piers, *Longneck and Thunderfoot,* Kestrel (London, England), 1982.

Robert McCrum, *The Brontosaurus Birthday Cake,* Hamish Hamilton (London, England), 1982.

Terry Jones, *The Saga of Erik the Viking,* Pavilion (London, England), 1983.

Charles Dickens, *A Christmas Carol,* Dial (New York, NY), 1983.

Nanette Newman, *A Cat and Mouse Love Story,* Heinemann (London, England), 1983.

Robert Louis Stevenson, *Treasure Island,* Penguin (London, England), 1983.

Kit Wright, editor, *Poems for Nine Year Olds and Under,* Puffin (London, England), 1984.

Helen Nicoll, editor, *Poems for Seven Year Olds and Under,* Puffin (London, England), 1984.

Kit Wright, editor, *Poems for Ten Year Olds and Over,* Puffin (London, England), 1985.

Roald Dahl, *Charlie and the Chocolate Factory,* Puffin (London, England), 1985.

Madhur Jaffrey, *Seasons of Splendour: Tales, Myths, and Legends of India,* Pavilion (London, England), 1985.

Robert McCrum, *Brontosaurus Superstar,* Hamish Hamilton (London, England), 1985.

Leon Garfield, adaptor, *Shakespeare Stories,* Gollancz (London, England), 1985, Houghton (Boston, MA), 1991.

William McGonagall, *Poetic Gems,* Folio Society (London, England), 1985.

Robert Louis Stevenson, *A Child's Garden of Verses,* Delacorte (New York, NY), 1985.

Nigel Gray, *I'll Take You to Mrs. Cole!,* Bergh, 1986, Kane/Miller (New York, NY), 1992.

Edna O'Brien, *Tales for the Telling: Irish Folk and Fairy Tales,* Pavilion (London, England), 1986.

Eric Quayle, *The Magic Ointment, and Other Cornish Legends,* Andersen (London, England), 1986.

Terry Jones, *Nicobobinus,* Pavilion (London, England), 1986.

Michael Moorcock, *Letters from Hollywood,* Harrap (London, England), 1986.

Charles Causley, *Early in the Morning,* Kestrel (London, England), 1986, Viking (New York, NY), 1987.

Rudyard Kipling, *Just So Stories,* Kestrel (London, England), 1987.

Rudyard Kipling, *The Jungle Book,* Kestrel (London, England), 1987.

Jan Mark, *Fun,* Gollancz (London, England), 1987, Viking (New York, NY), 1988.

Daphne du Maurier, *Classics of the Macabre,* Gollancz (London, England), 1987.

Clement C. Moore, *The Night before Christmas,* Viking (New York, NY), 1988.

Terry Jones, *The Curse of the Vampire's Socks,* Pavilion (London, England), 1988.

J.M. Barrie, *Peter Pan and Wendy,* Pavilion (London, England), 1988.

Martin Bax, *Edmond Went Far Away,* Harcourt (New York, NY), 1989.

David Pelham, *Worms Wiggle,* Simon & Schuster (New York, NY), 1989.

Eric Quayle, editor, *The Shining Princess, and Other Japanese Legends,* Arcade (New York, NY), 1989.

Ann Turnbull, *The Sand Horse,* Macmillan (New York, NY), 1989.

Christina Martinez, *Once upon a Planet,* Puffin (London, England), 1989.

Roald Dahl, *The Complete Adventures of Charlie and Mr. Willy Wonka,* Puffin (New York, NY), 1990.

Kiri Te Kanawa, *Land of the Long White Cloud,* Arcade (New York, NY), 1990.

Charles Causley, *The Young Man of Cury, and Other Poems,* Macmillan (London, England), 1991.

Brian Alderson, reteller, *The Arabian Nights; or, Tales Told by Sheherezade during a Thousand and One Nights,* Gollancz (London, England), 1992, Morrow (New York, NY), 1995.

Stacie Strong, adaptor, *Over in the Meadow* (pop-up book), Simon & Schuster (New York, NY), 1992.

Mary Rayner, *The Echoing Green,* Viking (New York, NY), 1992.

Terry Jones, *Fantastic Stories,* Viking (New York, NY), 1993.

Roald Dahl, *Charlie and the Great Glass Elevator,* Puffin (New York, NY), 1993.

Troon Harrison, *The Long Weekend,* Andersen (London, England), 1993, Harcourt (San Diego, CA), 1994.

Kit Wright, *Funnybunch: A New Puffin Book of Funny Verse,* Puffin (London, England) 1993.

Toby Forward, *Wyvern Spring,* Anderson (London, England), 1993.

Nanette Newman, *Spider the Horrible Cat,* Harcourt (San Diego, CA), 1993.

In his self-illustrated **War Boy** *Foreman shares his memories of growing up in England during World War II.* (Arcade Publishing, 1990. © 1989 by Michael Foreman. Reprinted by permission of the author.)

Nanette Newman, *There's a Bear in the Bath!,* Pavilion (London, England), 1993, Harcourt (San Diego, CA), 1994.

Toby Forward, *Wyvern Summer,* Anderson (London, England), 1994.

Toby Forward, *Wyvern Fall,* Anderson (London, England), 1994.

Michael Morpurgo, *Arthur, High King of Britain,* Pavilion (London, England), 1994, Harcourt (San Diego, CA), 1995.

Andrew Baynes, *Sarah and the Sandhorse,* Anderson (London, England), 1994.

Sally Grindley, *Peter's Place,* Andersen (London, England), 1995, Harcourt (San Diego, CA), 1996.

Leon Garfield, adaptor, *Shakespeare Stories II,* Houghton (Boston, MA), 1995.

Antoine de Saint-Exupéry, *The Little Prince,* new edition, Pavilion (London, England) 1995.

Michael Morpurgo, editor, *Beyond the Rainbow Warrior: A Collection of Stories to Celebrate Twenty-five Years of Greenpeace,* Pavilion (London, England), 1996.

Michael Morpurgo, *Robin of Sherwood,* Harcourt (San Diego, CA), 1996.

James Riordan, *The Songs My Paddle Sings: Native-American Legends,* Pavilion (London, England), 1996.

Michael Morpurgo, *Farm Boy,* Pavilion (London, England), 1997.

Louise Borden, *The Little Ships: The Heroic Rescue at Dunkirk in World War II,* Margaret McElderry Books (New York, NY), 1997.

Ann Pilling, reteller, *Creation: Read-aloud Stories from Many Lands,* Candlewick Press (Cambridge, MA), 1997.

Michael Morpurgo, *Joan of Arc of Domrémy,* Harcourt (San Diego, CA), 1999.

Terry Jones, *The Lady and the Squire,* Pavilion (London, England), 2001.

Kenneth Grahame, *The Wind in the Willows,* new edition, Harcourt (San Diego, CA), 2002.

Sophie Smiley, *Bobby, Charlton, and the Mountain,* Andersen (London, England), 2003.

Michael Morpurgo, reteller, *Sir Gawain and the Green Knight,* Candlewick Press (Cambridge, MA), 2004.

L. Frank Baum, *The Wonderful Wizard of Oz,* Sterling (New York, NY), 2005.

Michael Morpurgo, *Kensuke's Kingdom,* Egmont (London, England), 2005.

Michael Morpurgo, reteller, *Beowulf,* Candlewick Press (Cambridge, MA), 2006.

Nicola Davies, *White Owl, Barn Owl,* Candlewick Press (Cambridge, MA), 2007.

Terry Jones, *Fairy Tales and Fantastic Stories,* Anova Children's (London, England), 2007.

Michael Morpurgo, *The Mozart Question,* Candlewick Press (Cambridge, MA), 2008.

Jack Foreman, *Say Hello,* Candlewick Press (Cambridge, MA), 2008.

Janet Charters, *The General,* Templar Books (Somerville, MA), 2010.

Books featuring Foreman's illustrations have been translated into Spanish.

OTHER

Winter's Tales, illustrated by Freire Wright, Doubleday (New York, NY), 1979.

Also creator of animated films for television in England and Scandinavia.

Sidelights

British children's author and graphic artist Michael Foreman has drawn upon his real-life experiences as well as his imagination when writing and illustrating his many books for young children. While best known for creating artwork for the texts of such beloved authors as Rudyard Kipling, Oscar Wilde, Michael Morpurgo, and Terry Jones, Foreman has also produced a number of original self-illustrated works, including *Seal Surfer, Jack's Fantastic Voyage, Michael Foreman's Mother Goose,* and the award-winning *War Boy: A Country Childhood.* His artwork, whether rendered in expressive watercolor or more detailed pen and ink,

was described by *Booklist* contributor Shelley Townsend-Hudson as possessing "a special peaceful, cozy elegance." Calling Foreman's writing "in turn serious, whimsical, and poetic," an essayist in the *St. James Guide to Children's Writers* also hailed the author/illustrator's art, dubbing it "outstanding." "He combines a distinctive style of flowing watercolour with a genius for conveying atmosphere," the essayist commented, "and the visual richness of his work is always a feast for the eye."

Foreman was born in Pakefield, a fishing village on England's east coast, in 1938, "and grew up there during [World War II]," as he once recalled. Pakefield is the British Isles' closest town to Germany, and as Foreman once wrote, "The memory of those who passed

Foreman's watercolor art captures the fantasy in Brian Alderson's retelling of a beloved tale in **The Arabian Nights.** (Morrow Junior Books, 1995. Illustration ©1992 by Michael Foreman. Reproduced by permission.)

Foreman demonstrates his art for creating evocative picture books in the pages of A Child's Garden. (©2009 by Michael Foreman. Reproduced by permission of Candlewick Press, on behalf of Walker Books, London.)

through our village on the way to war will remain forever with the ghosts of us children in the fields and woods of long ago." His book *War Boy,* as well as its sequel, *After the War Was Over,* is a memoir of growing up in England during the war years, as Nazi bombers flew over the Suffolk coast, goods were rationed, fathers and older brothers were called to arms, and British children played in the wreckage of bombed-out

buildings. Commented reviewer Christopher Lehmann-Haupt in his *New York Times* review of *War Boy:* "Though his memories are haunted by enemy bombers and V1 and V2 rockets, the author recalls in delicate watercolors the many joys of being a shopkeeper's child under siege: the licorice comforts that left your teeth stained black, or the millions of flower seeds that were exploded out of gardens and showered around the district so that 'the following spring and summer, piles of rubble burst into bloom.'" As *School Library Journal* critic Phyllis G. Sidorsky wrote, "Foreman's recollections are sharp and graphic as he poignantly recalls the servicemen who crowded into his mother's shop, grateful for her welcoming cup of tea and a place to chat." Because his mother ran the village shop, he also grew up delivering newspapers. "I used to read all the comics," he admitted on the British Council's Magic Pencil Web site.

A sequel to *War Boy*, *After the War Was Over* begins during the summer of 1945, and focuses on Foreman's years growing up in the aftermath of World War II. The story features moments such as playing on the beach, now cleared of mines, and using wrecked landing crafts as pirate ships. Foreman was also able to use these memories of war in illustrations for books such as Michael Morpurgo's *Toro! Toro!*

After graduating from the Lowestoft School of Art in the late 1950s, Foreman got his first illustration job, providing pictures for Jane Charters' text in *The General*. This story, published in 1961, is set in Pakefield, "and the local people recognised the church, the ice cream hut, and other scenes in the pictures," Foreman later explained. By the time *The General* reached bookstore shelves, however, the artist had left Pakefield and was living in London, studying toward the advanced design degree he ultimately received from the Royal College of Art in 1963. *The Perfect Present,* Foreman's first self-illustrated title, contains many scenes from London, where he has continued to make his home.

Although he worked as an art director for magazines and also taught at several schools in the United Kingdom, Foreman has devoted most of his career as a graphic artist to book illustration. Well traveled, he has been inspired by the diversity of culture and surroundings he has seen; "the sketches I bring back become the backgrounds for new books," he explained. For example, a trip to New Mexico and the state of Arizona inspired Foreman's artwork for Jane Yolen's 1974 picture book *Rainbow Rider,* while his own *Panda and the Odd Lion* contains illustrations based on his travels throughout Africa and in the city of Venice, Italy. *Mia's Story: A Sketchbook of Hopes and Dreams,* written and illustrated by Foreman, is based on people he met near Santiago, Chile. The fictional Mia lives in a shanty town; when she discovers a beautiful white flower and starts to cultivate the species at her home, she begins to make money for her family by selling the blossoms. "Foreman already has a distinguished reputation as an illustrator, but this is his finest work to date," wrote Nicolette Jones in the London *Sunday Times*. A *Kirkus Reviews* contributor noted that the tale has an "underlying tone of respect rather than outrage or pity" for Mia's family.

"Occasionally, I get the idea for a story while traveling, but usually it takes a long time to get the right place, the right story, and the right character to meet," Fore-

man once explained. "Much of my time I am illustrating the work of other writers, and the subject matter varies from the Bible to Shakespeare to stories set in contemporary Britain or the future. My own books are never really about a place or country, but about an idea which is hopefully common to the dreams of everyone, one which works best, however, against a particular background."

One of these common dreams is the focus of *Wonder Goal,* Foreman's story of a new boy on the soccer team who comes through for his team mates at the last moment in a pivotal game. From that golden goal, the story follows the boy as he grows up to play in the World Cup. The story's "language is appealingly simple," Todd Morning noted in *Booklist,* while Peter D. Sieruta wrote in *Horn Book* that Foreman's watercolor art "emphasizes dramatic sports action yet contains subtle touches." An earlier, more universal experience is the theme of *Hello World,* wherein a young child wakes up and ventures out into the world, tugging his teddy bear along. As he depicts the child discovering frogs, puppies, rocks and trees, and other wonders of the natural world, Foreman "taps into a child's sense of wonder and discovery," according to a *Publishers Weekly* contributor. The universal longing for peace is at the core of *A Child's Garden: A Story of Hope,* in

A frisky monkey on the run is captured in Foreman's whimsical self-illustrated story in **Can't Catch Me!** (Andersen Press, 2006. ©Michael Foreman, 2005. Reproduced by permission.)

which a young boy nurtures a young sprout that grows into a thriving vine in contrast to the militaristic confines that prohibit the boy's actions. "Foreman's expertly shaded pencil-and-watercolor illustrations deepen the story's heavy messages of war and peace," noted Gillian Engberg in *Booklist,* and *School Library Journal* critic Grace Oliff wrote that the book's images "make effective use of color."

Many of Foreman's works as author/illustrator feature engaging animal characters. In *Dad, I Can't Sleep,* Little Panda's father helps him to fall asleep by counting other animals. *Can't Catch Me!* follows the adventures of a spunky monkey, and *Seal Surfer* focuses on a handicapped boy living in Cornwall, England, who bonds with the seal he has watched being born on the rocky coast. While building a dramatic storyline—in one scene the boy is almost drowned, while in another the coastal seals are threatened by a particularly harsh winter— Foreman "keeps the tension loose" in *Seal Surfer,* noted a *Publishers Weekly* contributor, "thereby emphasizing the preeminence of the life cycles that shape his story."

Foreman features an unusual animal character in his self-illustrated picture books *The Littlest Dinosaur* and *The Littlest Dinosaur's Big Adventure.* A young triceratops, Littlest Dinosaur hatches from his egg later than his siblings and remains the smallest creature in the family. Although his small size often presents the creature with challenges, when the other dinosaurs become stuck in the mud due to their weight, Littlest calls another lonely dinosaur, a long-necked diplodocus, to the rescue. A trip into a shadowy forest makes Littlest Dinosaur unsure, but he fights his fears to help a baby pteranodon find its nest in the young dino's second outing. The titular hero of *The Littlest Dinosaur* will appeal to "children who are often left out of the fun," predicted *School Library Journal* critic Marianne Saccardi,

One of several Christmas stories written and illustrated by Foreman, *The Little Reindeer* follows what happens when a city boy is accidentally given a young reindeer for a present. "Foreman's touching tale sparkles like a Christmas ornament," noted a *Publishers Weekly* contributor who also praised the book's "lyrical watercolors." Two dogs are the main characters of *Saving Sinbad,* in which an unnamed canine hero saves a little girl's terrier from drowning. The tale is set in a fishing village, much like the one where the author/illustrator grew up. "Foreman's watercolors give a dog's-eye view of both the heroics and of the aftermath," wrote Connie Fletcher in *Booklist.*

While many of Foreman's books are inspired by people and places he has seen, some have a more personal basis. *War Game* is a picture-book tribute to four of his uncles who perished in World War I. In this unusual book Foreman presents the many sides of war—the excitement, the daily grind, the horror—through a combination of original watercolors, archived material, and

stark text. The main portion of *War Game* focuses a hopeful moment where English and German soldiers joined in a game of soccer on Christmas Day, 1914, before the realities of war intruded once again. As *Junior Bookshelf* reviewer Marcus Crouch noted, *War Game* "is a story to be retold to each generation, and it could hardly have been told to deeper effect." Writing in *Publishers Weekly,* a reviewer commented that Foreman "transmutes the personal experiences of his uncles into a universal story," and "history springs to life in this admirable work." Equally appreciative of the value of Foreman's book, *Bulletin of the Center for Children's Books* contributor Deborah Stevenson called *War Game* "an unusual war story [that] would certainly help to humanize a faraway but significant event for young readers."

In *Say Hello* Foreman joins his son, Jack Foreman, to create a story about loneliness that is brought to life in what *School Library Journal* critic Amy Rowland described as Michael Foreman's "spare charcoal, pastel, and colored pencil drawings." In the story, a lonely dog asks to join a group of children playing ball, and when he is rewarded with a joyful "Yes!," the pup shares his good fortune with a lonely young boy who watches the game from the sidelines. In *Kirkus Reviews* a writer praised *Say Hello* as a "poignant" and "beautiful pairing of son's sparse rhyming text with father's simple drawings," and in *Booklist* Carolyn Phelan recommended the "beautifully designed" book as "short and simple enough for beginning readers."

Among his book projects, Foreman has also illustrated numerous anthologies of activities, rhymes, and stories, many of which he has also edited. About *Michael Foreman's Playtime Rhymes,* a *Kirkus Reviews* contributor wrote: "Foreman's legions of fans will turn to this one to prompt their memories of long-forgotten poems or to learn new ones."

"My books are not intended for any particular age group," Foreman once commented, "but the type is large and inviting for young readers who like to explore the pages after the story has been read to them. In addition I want the story to have some relevance for the adult reader. Less a question of age—more a state of mind." Foreman added on the *British Council Magic Pencil Web site,* "It's a question of creating another world, believable in its own right. . . . I keep trying to make things more real . . . in an emotional sense, telling a story by capturing the essence of the situation, giving it some meaning."

Biographical and Critical Sources

BOOKS

Children's Literature Review, Volume 32, Gale (Detroit, MI), 1994.

Something about the Author Autobiography Series, Volume 21, Gale (Detroit, MI), 1996.

St. James Guide to Children's Writers, 5th edition, St. James Press (Detroit, MI), 1999.

PERIODICALS

Booklist, March 15, 1998, Karen Hutt, review of *The Songs My Paddle Sings: Native-American Legends*, p. 1242; December 1, 2000, Shelley Townsend-Hudson, review of *Michael Foreman's Christmas Treasury*, p. 702; February 15, 2001, John Peters, review of *The Lady and the Squire*, p. 1137; December 15, 2002, Connie Fletcher, review of *Saving Sinbad*, p. 766; April 15, 2003, Todd Morning, review of *Wonder Goal*, p. 1477; February 15, 2004, Todd Morning, review of *Toro! Toro!*, p. 1060, Julie Cummins, review of *Hello World*, p. 1062; April 15, 2004, Connie Fletcher, review of *Gentle Giant*, p. 1447; November 1, 2004, Carolyn Phelan, review of *Sir Gawain and the Green Knight*, p. 480; August 1, 2006, Carolyn Phelan, review of *Mia's Story*, p. 86; March 1, 2007, Linda Perkins, review of *Beowulf*, p. 74; May 15, 2007, Gillian Engberg, review of *White Owl, Barn Owl*, p. 53; March 15, 2008, Hazel Rochman, review of *The Mozart Question*, p. 48; August 1, 2008, Carolyn Phelan, review of *Say Hello*, p. 69; May 1, 2009, Gillian Engberg, review of *A Child's Garden: A Story of Hope*, p. 84.

Bookseller, February 18, 2005, Caroline Horn, "Brand Status for Foreman," p. 27; May 12, 2006, "Tips for Time at the Top," p. 19.

Bulletin of the Center for Children's Books, October, 1994, Deborah Stevenson, review of *War Game*, p. 43; November, 2006, Karen Coats, review of *Mia's Story*, p. 122; March, 2007, Karen Coats, review of *Beowulf*, p. 303.

Horn Book, May-June, 1996, Elizabeth S. Watson, review of *Peter's Place*, p. 323; May-June, 1997, Ann A. Flowers, review of *The Little Ships: The Heroic Rescue at Dunkirk in World War II*, p. 302; March-April, 2003, Peter D. Sieruta, review of *Wonder Goal*, p. 202.

Junior Bookshelf, February, 1994, Marcus Crouch, review of *War Game*, p. 31.

Kirkus Reviews, September 1, 2002, review of *Michael Foreman's Playtime Rhymes*, p. 1308; October 1, 2002, review of *Saving Sinbad*, p. 1469; March 15, 2003, review of *Wonder Goal*, p. 466; October 15, 2003, review of *Hello World*, p. 1271; January 15, 2004, review of *Toro! Toro!*, p. 86; July 1, 2004, review of *Cat on the Hill*, p. 629; October 15, 2004, review of *Sir Gawain and the Green Knight*, p. 1011; January 1, 2005, review of *Dolphin Boy*, p. 55; July 1, 2006, review of *Mia's Story*, p. 677; October 15, 2006, review of *Beowulf*, p. 1075; December 1, 2006, review of *Can't Catch Me*, p. 1219; April 1, 2008, review of *The Littlest Dinosaur;* May 15, 2008, review of *Say Hello;* April 1, 2009, review of *The Littlest Dinosaur's Big Adventure*.

New York Times, December 3, 1990, Christopher Lehmann-Haupt, "Presents of Words, Pictures, and Imagination."

Publishers Weekly, April 25, 1994, review of *War Game*, p. 78; August 12, 1996, review of *Robin of Sherwood*, p. 84; March 24, 1997, review of *Seal Surfer*, p. 83; October 6, 1997, review of *The Little Reindeer*, p. 55; February 22, 1999, review of *Joan of Arc of Domrémy*, p. 95; September 24, 2001, review of *Cat in the Manger*, p. 52; December 22, 2003, review of *Hello World*, p. 59; April 26, 2004, review of *Gentle Giant*, p. 64; February 11, 2008, review of *The Mozart Question*, p. 70; May 5, 2008, review of *The Littlest Dinosaur*, p. 61.

Resource Links, December, 2003, Kathryn McNaughton, review of *Evie's Garden*, p. 4.

School Librarian, winter, 2005, review of *Dolphin Boy*, p. 187; winter, 2006, Trevor Dickinson, review of *Mia's Story*, p. 187.

School Library Journal, May, 1990, Phyllis G. Sidorsky, review of *War Boy: A Country Childhood*, p. 116; October, 2000, review of *Michael Foreman's Christmas Treasury*, p. 59; March, 2001, Lisa Prolman, review of *The Lady and the Squire*, p. 250; April, 2003, Blair Christolon, review of *Wonder Goal*, p. 118; December, 2003, Kathleen Simonetta, review of *A Trip to Dinosaur Time*, p. 113; January, 2004, Judith Constantinides, review of *Hello World*, p. 97; May, 2004, Kathy Krasniewicz, review of *Gentle Giant*, p. 120, Shawn Brommer, review of *Toro! Toro!*, p. 154; October, 2004, Connie C. Rockman, review of *Sir Gawain and the Green Knight*, p. 172; April, 2006, Miriam Lang Budin, review of *Classic Fairy Tales*, p. 124; August, 2006, Marianne Saccardi, review of *Mia's Story*, p. 87; December, 2006, Susan Scheps, review of *Beowulf*, p. 166; July, 2007, Margaret Bush, review of *White Owl, Barn Owl*, p. 89; May, 2008, Marianne Saccardi, review of *The Littlest Dinosaur*, p. 98; July, 2008, Amy Rowland, review of *Say Hello*, p. 72; May, 2009, Sara Paulson-Yarovoy, review of *The Littlest Dinosaur's Big Adventure*, p. 76; June, 2009, Grace Oliff, review of *A Child's Garden: A Story of Hope*, p. 86.

Sunday Times (London, England), June 18, 2006, Nicolette Jones, review of *Mia's Story*, p. 48.

Times Educational Supplement, November 5, 2004, Geraldine Brennan, "Dear Mr Morpingo: Inside the World of Michael Morpurgo," p. 19.

ONLINE

Andersen Press Web site, http://www.andersenpress.co.uk/ (June 1, 2010), "Michael Foreman."

British Council Contemporary Writers Web site, http://www.contemporarywriters.com/ (June 1, 2010), "Michael Foreman."

British Council Magic Pencil Web site, http://magicpencil.britishcouncil.org/ (November 19, 2007), "Michael Foreman."

Eduplace Web site, http://www.eduplace.com/ (November 19, 2007), "Michael Foreman."

Walker Books Web site, http://www.walkerbooks.co.uk/ (June 1, 2010), "Michael Foreman."*

FRENCH, S. Terrell

Personal

Born in MD; married; children: two sons, one daughter. *Education:* Harvard College, degree; University of California, J.D.

Addresses

Home—San Francisco, CA. *Agent*—Kate Schafer Testerman, KT Literary, Highlands Ranch, CO 80129; contactktliterary.com. *E-mail*—sterrellfrench@gmail. com.

Career

Attorney and author. Works as an environmental lawyer in San Francisco, CA. U.S. Forest Service volunteer in Alaska.

Awards, Honors

100 Titles for Reading and Sharing inclusion, New York Public Library, and National Outdoor Book Awards honorable mention, both 2009, and John and Patricia Beatty Award, California Library Association, and Green Earth Book Award for Children's Fiction, both 2010 all for *Operation Redwood.*

Writings

Operation Redwood (novel), Amulet Books (New York, NY), 2009

Sidelights

An environmental lawyer based in San Francisco, California, S. Terrell French made her literary debut in 2009 with *Operation Redwood,* an award-winning ecological adventure tale. The work centers on the efforts of a twelve-year-old boy to prevent the destruction of an old-growth redwood forest. French told Susane Fine on the *Class of 2K9* Web log that her novel was inspired in part by the struggle to establish the Headwaters Forest Reserve. "The story of the battle over the Headwaters Forest in California during the 1990s—the last major stand of ancient redwoods on private land—was a fascinating story of greed and protest and divisions within a community," the author noted. "I thought it suggested a great adventure story that would tap into kids' real interest in the environment."

French, who grew up in Maryland, has always enjoyed the outdoors: she often played near the creek that ran behind her subdivision and also went swimming and sailing in the Chesapeake Bay. Her mother worked at a day camp in rural Maryland, so French and her sister spent their summers kayaking, swimming, and riding horses. "I remember the distress we felt at the thought of going back to school and having to wear shoes," she recalled to Fine. "We were always envious of the kids whose family ran the camp who got to live there all year—their feet were so tough they could run on gravel!"

French also developed a love of literature as a child, and she read such classic works as *20,000 Leagues under the Sea* by Jules Verne, *Little Women* by Louisa May Alcott, and *The Swiss Family Robinson* by Johann D. Wyss. "While *Operation Redwood,* is a contemporary book, . . . there is an innocence to the children—and a kind of good-natured camaraderie—that I associate with my childhood reading," she told *Cynsations* online interviewer Cynthia Leitich Smith. "Also, many of these books have a rather romantic view of the wholesomeness of nature, which I seem to have incorporated into . . . *Operation Redwood.*"

After graduating from Harvard College, French moved to California, where she began working for an environmental organization. She later attended law school at the University of California, Berkeley and then landed a job with a land-use firm in San Francisco that repre-

S. Terrell French creates the illustrations for Greg Swearingen's middle-grade novel **Operation Redwood**. (Amulet Books, 2009. Jacket illustration © 2009 by Greg Swearingen. Reproduced by permission.)

sents public agencies and environmental groups. French also married and had three children, with whom she has shared her love of literature. As she remarked on her home page, "I read so many stories over so many years that it made me want to write a story of my own—one that would be exciting, would reflect my children's love of nature, and would include kids that you might find in the wonderful multi-cultural city of San Francisco."

Operation Redwood centers on Julian Carter-Li, who lives with his wealthy Uncle Sibley while his mother travels abroad. When Julian stumbles upon an e-mail disclosing his uncle's plans to harvest a redwood grove, he joins forces with the e-mail's sender, Robin Elder, to protect the land. "Fast paced and full of fun, the story captures the excitement and satisfaction of defeating a large corporation," observed *School Library Journal* reviewer Chris Shoemaker, and *Horn Book* critic Susan Dove Lempke praised French's well-developed characters, remarking that *Operation Redwood* "has a modern multicultural feel that balances the pastoral nature scenes." Elizabeth Bird, writing on the *Fuse #8 Production* blog, called *Operation Redwood* "a true emotional journey full of adventure, friendship, complex morality, trust, lies, and discovery. You believe in this book and you believe in the characters."

Biographical and Critical Sources

PERIODICALS

Horn Book, July-August, 2009, Susan Dove Lempke, review of *Operation Redwood,* p. 423.
Kirkus Reviews, April 1, 2009, review of *Operation Redwood.*
School Library Journal, July, 2009, Chris Shoemaker, review of *Operation Redwood,* p. 82.

ONLINE

Class of 2K9 Web log, http://community.livejournal.com/classof2k9/ (April 23, 2009), Susane Fine, interview with French.
Cynsations Web log, http://cynthialeitichsmith.blogspot.com/ (November 2, 2009), Cynthia Leitich Smith, interview with French.
Examiner.com, http://www.examiner.com/ (February 21, 2010), Laure Latham, "Meet S. Terrell French, Award-winning author of *Operation Redwood.*"
Fuse #8 Production Web log, http://www.schoollibraryjournal.com/blog/ (September 1, 2009), Elizabeth Bird, review of *Operation Redwood.*
S. Terrell French Home Page, http://www.operationredwood.com (May 1, 2010).

G-H

GYORKOS, Charmaine Echeverria
See ECHEVERRIA GYORKOS, Charmaine

* * *

HINMAN, Bonnie 1950-

Personal
Born 1950, in MO; married; children: one daughter, one son. *Education:* Missouri State University, B.A.

Addresses
Home—Joplin, MO.

Career
Author of juvenile nonfiction. Presenter at schools.

Writings

FOR CHILDREN

Benjamin Banneker: American Mathematician and Astronomer, Chelsea House (Philadelphia, PA), 2000.
John F. Kennedy, Jr., Chelsea House (Philadelphia, PA), 2001.
Faith Hill, Chelsea House (Philadelphia, PA), 2001.
General Thomas Gage: British General, Chelsea House (Philadelphia, PA), 2002.
Tony Blair, Chelsea House (Philadelphia, PA), 2003, revised edition, 2007.
Florence Nightingale and the Advancement of Nursing, Mitchell Lane Publishers (Hockessin, DE), 2004.
A Stranger in My Own House: The Story of W.E.B. Du Bois, Morgan Reynolds Pub. (Greensboro, NC), 2005.
Jennie's War: The Home Front in World War II, Barbour (Uhrichsville, OH), 2005.

Franklin Delano Roosevelt: The Great Depression and World War II: 1929-1945, McGraw Hill, 2006.
Extreme Cycling with Dale Holmes, Mitchell Lane Publishers (Hockessin, DE), 2007.
Pennsylvania: William Penn and the City of Brotherly Love, Mitchell Lane (Hockessin, DE), 2007.
William Penn, Mitchell Lane Publishers (Hockessin, DE), 2007.
The Massachusetts Bay Colony: The Puritans Arrive from England, Mitchell Lane Publishers (Hockessin, DE), 2007.
Threat to the Leatherback Turtle, Mitchell Lane Publishers (Hockessin, DE), 2008.
Xtreme Athletes: Danica Patrick, Morgan Reynolds Pub. (Greensboro, NC), 2009.
John Legend, Mitchell Lane Publishers (Hockessin, DE), 2009.
Thanksgiving/Acción de gracias, Mitchell Lane Publishers (Hockessin, DE), 2010.
Christmas/Navidad, Mitchell Lane Publishers (Hockessin, DE), 2010.
We Visit Perú, Mitchell Lane Publishers (Hockessin, DE), 2010.
We Visit Panama, Mitchell Lane Publishers (Hockessin, DE), 2010.
Eternal Vigilance: The Story of Ida B. Bells-Barnett, Morgan Reynolds Pub. (Greensboro, NC), 2010.

Contributor to periodicals, including *Child Life.*

FOR CHILDREN; "AMERICAN ADVENTURE" SERIES

Earthquake in Cincinnati, Barbour Pub. (Uhrichsville, OH), 1997.
Riot in the Night, Barbour Pub. (Uhrichsville, OH), 1998.
The Bootlegger Menace, Barbour Pub. (Uhrichsville, OH), 1998.
The San Francisco Earthquake, Barbour Pub. (Uhrichsville, OH), 1998.
The Home Front, Barbour Pub. (Uhrichsville, OH), 1999.

Biographical and Critical Sources

PERIODICALS

Booklist, March 15, 2005, Carolyn Phelan, review of *A Stranger in My Own House: The Story of W.E.B. Du Bois,* p. 1283; October 15, 2006, Gillian Engberg, review of *Extreme Cycling with Dale Holmes,* p. 78; January 1, 2007, Jennifer Mattson, review of *Tony Blair,* p. 86.

School Library Journal, April, 2002, Tim Widham, review of *Faith Hill,* p. 162; July, 2005, Gerry Larson, review of *A Stranger in My Own House,* p. 118; January, 2007, Andrew Medlar, review of *The Life and Times of William Penn,* p. 148; February, 2007, Lucinda Snyder Whitehurst, review of *Pennsylvania: William Penn and the City of Brothery Love,* p. 138; September, 2008, Marilyn Taniguchi, review of *Xtreme Athletes: Danica Patrick,* p. 204.

ONLINE

Bonnie Hinman Home Page, http://www.bonniehinman. com (May 15, 2010).*

*   *   *

HOLLAND, Richard 1976-

Personal

Born 1976, in Maldon, England. *Education:* Loughborough University, degree (illustration).

Addresses

Home—Essex, England.

Career

Illustrator.

Illustrator

Enebor Attard, reteller, *Ali Baba and the Forty Thieves,* Mantra Lingua (London, England), 2004.

Jan Mark, *The Museum Book: A Guide to Strange and Wonderful Collections,* Candlewick Press (Cambridge, MA), 2007.

Martin Jenkins, *The Time Book: A Brief History from Lunar Calendars to Atomic Clocks,* Candlewick Press (Somerville MA), 2009.

Tanya Landman, *Mary's Penny,* Candlewick Press (Somerville, MA), 2010.

Work featuring Holland's illustrations has been translated into Albanian, Chinese, Croatian, French, Italian, Polish, Portuguese, Romanian, Russian, Shona, Somali, Spanish, Swahili, and Turkish.

Sidelights

Richard Holland grew up in a small town in England, where reading and art took a back seat to playing cricket. Because art was his favorite subject in school,

he went on to attend art school, where he developed the mixed-media technique he uses in illustrating Jan Mark's *The Museum Book: A Guide to Strange and Wonderful Collections,* which *School Library Journal* critic Mary Elam described as an "information-packed" profile of museums that "highlights the need to investigate, collect, and respect history through scientific study."

In his collage artwork for *The Museum Book* Holland captures the visual excitement of a trip to a museum, where collections of everything from ocean shells to dinosaur bones to works of art are housed. Beginning with a description of what a museum is and when it originated, Mark's text ranges over history, describing such authoritative assemblages as Russian king Peter the Great's collection of teeth, the Alexandrian museum in ancient Egypt, and Medieval caches of holy relics before turning to modern museums such as the Ashmolean Museum on the campus of Oxford University. Holland's "stylish" collages, which mix ink drawings with engravings and photographs, "play with perspective, type and design," noted a *Publishers Weekly* critic, and their "intricate details . . . invite close perusal." In

Jan Mark's cultural guide **The Museum Book** *is enlivened by Richard Holland's engaging modernist art.* (Illustration ©2007 by Richard Holland. Reproduced by permission of Candlewick Press, on behalf of Walker Books, London.)

Booklist Hazel Rochman praised *The Museum Book* as "informal and never reverential," noting that Mark's "brisk, chatty" text pairs well with Holland's multimedia images, studded as they are with "small, rich particulars."

Like *The Museum Book, The Time Book: A Brief History from Lunar Calendars to Atomic Clocks* focuses on man's need to organize; it also features Holland's unique collage art. With a text by Martin Jenkins, *The Time Book* prompts young readers to think outside what they know about measuring time by explaining the way time was measured in different cultures. Jenkins also shows how man's need for exact measurements veered from nature's seasonal clock to produce "corrections" such as the leap year. In *Booklist* Ian Chipman dubbed *The Time Book* a "diverting" volume that tackles "a pretty heady subject" in a "succinct" text and engaging art. "The inventiveness of Holland's [surreal] illustrations is more than a match for the quirky journey on which Jenkins takes his readers," wrote Susan Perren in her *Globe & Mail* review of the work, the critic adding that the author's "well-written, thoughtful book about time and timekeeping" exemplifies "the new normal in science books for the young, which favours a multitude of bytes of information embedded in cartoon illustrations and accompanied by sidebars of related trivia."

Biographical and Critical Sources

PERIODICALS

Booklist, November 1, 2007, Hazel Rochman, review of *The Museum Book: A Guide to Strange and Wonderful Collections,* p. 45; May 1, 2009, Ian Chipman, review of *The Time Book: A Brief History from Lunar Calendars to Atomic Clocks,* p. 76.

Globe & Mail (Toronto, Ontario, Canada), July 4, 2009, Susan Perren, review of *The Time Book,* p. F14.

Horn Book, January-February, 2008, Martha V. Parravano, review of *The Museum Book,* p. 114.

Observer (London, England), April 8, 2007, Kate Kellaway, review of *The Museum Book,* p. 23.

Publishers Weekly, November 19, 2007, review of *The Museum Book,* p. 57.

School Library Journal, January, 2008, Mary Elam, review of *The Museum Book,* p. 144.

ONLINE

Walker Books Web site, http://www.walker.co.uk/ (June 1, 2010).*

*   *   *

HOPKINSON, Deborah 1952-

Personal

Born February 4, 1952, in Lowell, MA; daughter of Russell W. (a machinist) and Gloria D. Hopkinson; mar-

Deborah Hopkinson (Photograph by Deborah Wiles. Reproduced by permission.)

ried Andrew D. Thomas (a winemaker); children: Rebekah, Dimitri. *Education:* University of Massachusetts—Amherst, B.A. (English), 1973; University of Hawai'i, M.A. (Asian studies), 1978. *Hobbies and other interests:* Reading, hiking, gardening, history.

Addresses

Home—West Linn, OR. *Office*—Pacific Northwest College of Art, 1241 NW Johnson St., Portland, OR 97209. *E-mail*—deborahhopkinson@yahoo.com.

Career

Author and administrator. American Red Cross, Honolulu, HI, staff writer; Manoa Valley Theater, Honolulu, marketing director, 1981-84; University of Hawai'i Foundation, Honolulu, development director, 1985-89; East-West Center, Honolulu, development director, 1989-94; Whitman College, Walla Walla, WA, director of grants and advancement services, 1994-2004; Oregon State University Foundation, Corvallis, director of foundation relations, 2004-08; Pacific Northwest College of Art, Portland, OR, currently vice president for college advancement.

Member

Society of Children's Book Writers and Illustrators, Association of Fundraising Professionals.

Awards, Honors

Merit award, Society of Children's Book Writers and Illustrators, 1991; work-in-progress grant, Society of Children's Book Writers and Illustrators, 1993; International Reading Association Award for Young People, 1994, for *Sweet Clara and the Freedom Quilt;* Golden Kite Award for Picture-Book Text, 1999, and Notable Children's Books designation, American Library Association (ALA), 2000, both for *A Band of Angels;* Golden Kite Honor award for picture-book text, 2002, for *Bluebird Summer;* National Council of Teachers of English/Orbis Pictus Award Honor Book designation, and Jane Addams Children's Book Award Honor Book designation, both 2004, both for *Shutting out the Sky;* Golden Kite Award for Picture-Book Text, 2004, and Notable Children's Books designation, ALA, 2005, and Time of Wonder Children's Book Award, and Oregon Reads selection, both 2009, all for *Apples to Oregon;* Notable Children's Books designation, ALA, and *Boston Globe/Horn Book* Award Honor Book designation, both 2006, both for *Sky Boys;* Notable Children's Books designation, ALA, and Carter G. Woodson Honor Book, National Council for the Social Studies, both 2007, both for *Up before Daybreak;* Teachers' Choices Booklist, International Reading Association, for *Sweet Land of Liberty;* Notable Children's Books designation, ALA, and Comstock Book Award, Minnesota State University, Moorhead, 2009, both for *Abe Lincoln Crosses a Creek;* Eloise Jarvis McGraw Award for Children's Literature, 2009, and Notable Social Studies Trade Book, National Council for the Social Studies/Children's Book Council, 2010, both for *Keep On!*

Writings

Bluebird Summer, illustrated by Bethanne Andersen, Greenwillow (New York, NY), 2001.
Deborah Hopkinson and You (autobiography), Libraries Unlimited (Westport, CT), 2007.

Contributor of short stories to periodicals, including *Cricket, Ladybug,* and *Storyworks.*

NONFICTION FOR CHILDREN

Pearl Harbor, Dillon Press/Macmillan (New York, NY), 1991.
Shutting out the Sky: Life in the Tenements of New York, 1880-1915, Orchard Books (New York, NY), 2003.
Up before Daybreak: Cotton and People in America, Scholastic, Inc. (New York, NY), 2006.
First Family, illustrated by A.G. Ford, Katherine Tegen Books (New York, NY), 2010.

HISTORICAL FICTION FOR CHILDREN

Sweet Clara and the Freedom Quilt, illustrated by James E. Ransome, Knopf (New York, NY), 1993.
Birdie's Lighthouse, illustrated by Kimberly Bulcken Root, Atheneum (New York, NY), 1996.
A Band of Angels: A Story Inspired by the Jubilee Singers, illustrated by Raul Colón, Atheneum (New York, NY), 1999.

Maria's Comet, illustrated by Deborah Lanino, Atheneum (New York, NY), 1999.
Fannie in the Kitchen: The Whole Story from Soup to Nuts of How Fannie Farmer Invented Recipes with Precise Measurements, illustrated by Nancy Carpenter, Atheneum (New York, NY), 2001.
Under the Quilt of Night, illustrated by James E. Ransome, Atheneum (New York, NY), 2002.
Girl Wonder: A Baseball Story in Nine Innings, illustrated by Terry Widener, Atheneum (New York, NY), 2003.
Apples to Oregon: Being the (Slightly) True Narrative of How a Brave Pioneer Father Brought Apples, Peaches, Plums, Grapes, and Cherries (and Children) across the Plains, illustrated by Nancy Carpenter, Atheneum (New York, NY), 2003.
A Packet of Seeds, illustrated by Bethanne Anderson, Greenwillow (New York, NY), 2004.
Hear My Sorrow: The Diary of Angela Denoto, a Shirtwaist Worker, Scholastic, Inc. (New York, NY), 2004.
Billy and the Rebel: Based on a True Civil War Story, illustrated by Brian Floca, Atheneum (New York, NY), 2005.
Saving Strawberry Farm, illustrated by Rachel Isadora, Greenwillow (New York, NY), 2005.
From Slave to Soldier: Based on a True Civil War Story, illustrated by Brian Floca, Atheneum (New York, NY), 2005.
Sky Boys: How They Built the Empire State Building, illustrated by James E. Ransome, Schwartz & Wade (New York, NY), 2006.
Into the Firestorm: A Novel of San Francisco, 1906, Knopf (New York, NY), 2006.
Sweet Land of Liberty, illustrated by Leonard Jenkins, Peachtree Publishers (Atlanta, GA), 2007.
Abe Lincoln Crosses a Creek: A Tall, Thin Tale (introducing His Forgotten Frontier Friend), illustrated by John Hendrix, Schwartz & Wade (New York, NY), 2008.
Stagecoach Sal: Inspired by a True Tale, illustrated by Carson Ellis, Disney/Hyperion Books (New York, NY), 2009.
The Humblebee Hunter, illustrated by Jen Corace, Disney/Hyperion Books (New York, NY), 2010.

"PRAIRIE SKIES" SERIES; CHAPTER BOOKS

Pioneer Summer, illustrated by Patrick Faricy, Aladdin (New York, NY), 2002.
Cabin in the Snow, illustrated by Patrick Faricy, Aladdin (New York, NY), 2002.
Our Kansas Home, illustrated by Patrick Faricy, Aladdin (New York, NY), 2003.

"KLONDIKE KID" SERIES; CHAPTER BOOKS

Sailing for Gold, illustrated by Bill Farnsworth, Aladdin (New York, NY), 2004.
Adventure in Gold Town, illustrated by Bill Farnsworth, Aladdin (New York, NY), 2004.
The Long Trail, illustrated by Bill Farnsworth, Aladdin (New York, NY), 2004.

BIOGRAPHIES; FOR CHILDREN

Susan B. Anthony: Fighter for Women's Rights, illustrated by Amy Bates, Aladdin (New York, NY), 2005.

Who Was Charles Darwin?, illustrated by Nancy Harrison, Grosset & Dunlap (New York, NY), 2005.

John Adams Speaks for Freedom, illustrated by Craig Orback, Aladdin (New York, NY), 2005.

Home on the Range: John A. Lomax and His Cowboy Songs, illustrated by S.D. Schindler, Putnam (New York, NY), 2009.

Keep On!: The Story of Matthew Henson, Co-discoverer of the North Pole, illustrated by Stephen Alcorn, Peachtree Publishers (Atlanta, GA), 2009.

Michelle, illustrated by A.G. Ford, Katherine Tegen Books (New York, NY), 2009.

Sidelights

Deborah Hopkinson is an award-winning author of historical fiction, picture-book biographies, and works of nonfiction, including *Up before Daybreak: Cotton and People in America* and *Sky Boys: How They Built the Empire State Building.* Frequently narrated from the point-of-view of both real-life and imagined characters, Hopkinson's texts engage young readers by drawing parallels between past and present social issues. Her books have earned praise for their historical accuracy and creative approach.

Hopkinson was born and raised in Lowell, Massachusetts, where she developed an early interest in literature. "Sometime during elementary school, I decided I wanted to be a writer when I grew up," she wrote in an autobiographical essay for *SATA.* "Now, I didn't really know what I wanted to write, or what being a writer actually meant. I only knew one thing: I loved to read. I loved how stories let me slip off into other worlds. I liked reading about real-life adventures or mysteries that made me keep turning the page. I especially loved staying up late to find out how the story ended."

After graduating from high school, Hopkinson attended the University of Massachusetts—Amherst, earning a bachelor's degree in English, and the University of Hawai'i, where she completed a master's degree in Asian studies. She then began a long career in philanthropy and fundraising, serving as a development director for nonprofit organizations and colleges and universities in Hawai'i, Washington, and Oregon. While living in Hawai'i, she began writing short stories and eventually became a regular contributor to *Cricket, Ladybug,* and other periodicals.

Hopkinson's first book, *Pearl Harbor,* was published in 1991 as part of Dillon Press's "Places in American History" series. Aimed at older children, the book tells the story of the surprise Japanese bombing of Pearl Harbor during World War II and includes photographs showing the Hawaiian harbor both during and after the war. For her second book, Hopkinson decided to try her hand at

fiction. *Sweet Clara and the Freedom Quilt* is about a slave girl who is separated from her mother and sent to work in the fields. While living with an elderly woman named Aunt Rachel, who teaches her to sew, Clara becomes a seamstress. Preoccupied with thoughts of her mother and freedom, Clara overhears other slaves discussing the "underground railroad," and decides to use her sewing skills to help herself and other slaves escape. In her spare time, she sews a quilt; but instead of patchwork, Clara quilts a map detailing an escape route. When she finally does escape the plantation, she leaves the quilt behind to help other slaves. The story "brings power and substance to this noteworthy picture book," according to a reviewer for *Publishers Weekly,* the critic concluding of *Sweet Clara and the Freedom Quilt* that Hopkinson's "first-rate book is a triumph of the heart."

Several of Hopkinson's picture books revisit the issues discussed in *Sweet Clara and the Freedom Quilt.* In *A Band of Angels: A Story Inspired by the Jubilee Singers,* the author tells a tale based on pianist Ella Sheppard's experience at the Fisk School, which took freed slaves on a performance tour to raise money. When singing classical music, they could not draw a crowd, but when they started to sing spirituals, audiences flocked to hear them perform. Hopkinson's "lilting text interweaves subtle details about racial tensions . . . emphasizing the importance of education and of being true to oneself," wrote a *Publishers Weekly* contributor of the title. *Under the Quilt of Night,* which is considered to be a companion to *Sweet Clara and the Freedom Quilt,* follows an unnamed girl and her companions as they escape from slavery, watching for the message, through a quilt, that they have reached a safe house. "Hopkinson captures the fear of the escaping slaves, but tempers their fear with the bravery and hope that spurred them on," wrote a contributor to *Kirkus Reviews.* According to Marianne Saccardi in *School Library Journal,* "the narrative is told in a series of poems . . . and the language is lovely."

Hopkinson shares with readers another exciting story about a brave young girl in *Birdie's Lighthouse.* Set in the mid-nineteenth century, the book takes the form of a ten-year-old girl's diary. Bertha "Birdie" Holland, the main character, moves to a lighthouse island in Maine with her father after he gives up life as a sailor. Birdie's brother is more interested in fishing than in the workings of the beacon light, but Birdie herself becomes fascinated with the job. Eventually, she learns enough about the lighthouse to man it herself when her father falls gravely ill. Although Birdie is a fictional character, she is closely based on real-life girls whose heroic lighthouse adventures are well documented. A *Kirkus Reviews* contributor enthused that "period details and a spirited heroine with a clear voice make this book a genuine delight." A *Publishers Weekly* reviewer found *Birdie's Lighthouse* to be "atmospheric" and Birdie herself "brave and likable." While noting that the narrative "is unlikely to be mistaken for the voice of an actual young girl," the critic went on to praise Hopkinson's "careful attention to period and setting," concluding that the "nuances of feeling and historical detail shine through" in the novel. Anne Parker, writing in *School Library Journal,* called *Birdie's Lighthouse* "a shining bit of historical fiction."

Told through the eyes of young Marcia Shaw, *Fannie in the Kitchen: The Whole Story from Soup to Nuts of How Fannie Farmer Invented Recipes with Precise Measurements* introduces young readers to an important woman in history. "Hopkinson fashions her clever narrative after her subtitle, presenting the book as seven courses-cum-chapters," explained a *Horn Book* critic. Although Marcia at first resents Fannie's invasion of the kitchen, she soon becomes mystified by the magic of the young woman's cooking. It's not magic, Fannie explains, but science. A *Publishers Weekly* contributor called *Fannie in the Kitchen* "prepared to perfection and served up with style," while Genevieve Ceraldi commented in *School Library Journal* that, "in a time of celebrity chefs on television, this is a whimsical look back to when it all began."

Though less famous that Fannie Farmer, Alta Weiss also serves as an historical role model for young women in Hopkinson's retelling of her story in *Girl Wonder: A Baseball Story in Nine Innings.* A young woman during the early years of baseball, Weiss manages to convince

Hopkinson turns back the clock to focus on Fannie Farmer, author of the first cookbook, in **Fannie in the Kitchen,** *featuring artwork by Nancy Carpenter.* (Illustration ©2001 Nancy Carpenter. Reprinted with the permission of Atheneum Books for Young Readers, an imprint of Simon & Schuster Children's Publishing Division.)

a coach of a semi-professional team to let her play with the men, because watching the spectacle of a girl playing baseball is sure to sell tickets. "Cleverly organized into nine brief 'innings,' this graphically rich, rewarding tale will inspire readers," a *Publishers Weekly* critic wrote of the book. In order to help readers understand the actual history behind the story, "Hopkinson enriches her burnished prose with an author's note about the real Alta Weiss," according to GraceAnne A. DeCandido in *Booklist.*

Hopkinson has also approached historical fiction through chapter books for beginning readers. Her "Prairie Skies" trilogy follows Charlie and Ida Jane Keller's move to Kansas from Massachusetts in the 1850s. In *Pioneer Summer,* the Keller family makes the long journey west, leaving behind Charlie's grandfather, who comforts the boy by explaining that they will both still be under the same sky. Several adventures, including a fall through a frozen pond and a battle with a prairie wildfire, mark the Kellers' journey. "Distinguished by taut sentences well tailored to the audience, this informative tale rolls at a promising clip," according to a *Publishers Weekly* contributor.

In the second entry in the series, *Cabin in the Snow,* Charlie must decide whether to sympathize with the Morgans, a family they once traveled with who support slavery, or stand with his family, who are abolitionists. The final book in the trilogy, *Our Kansas Home,* deals with the Underground Railroad, and the dangers that the Keller family must face in order to stay true to their abolitionist beliefs. "Hopkinson tells a good story, steeped in rich history and research," concluded a *Kirkus Reviews* contributor of *Cabin in the Snow.* A *Kirkus Reviews* contributor wrote of *Our Kansas Home* that "dramatic cliffhanging chapters, brisk action, and exciting historical situations mesh together into a memorable, exciting tale." Susan Shaver, writing in *School Library Journal,* noted that the trilogy "brings an era of history alive, and will pique children's interest." Hopkinson used the same trilogy format in her "Klondike Kids" series, recounting the adventures of Davey Hill, the Klondike Kid, as he travels Alaska during the early 1800s.

Apples to Oregon: Being the (Slightly) True Narrative of How a Brave Pioneer Father Brought Apples, Peaches, Plums, Grapes, and Cherries (and Children) across the Plains sets the pioneer journey in picture-book format. Based on the true story of Henderson Luelling, a family travels from Iowa to Oregon, keeping Daddy's fruit trees from being damaged on the journey. "The flavor is in the folksy telling of this clever tall tale," wrote a *Kirkus Reviews* critic. *Booklist* contributor Kay Weisman found the tale to be "rich in language that begs to be read out loud."

In *Saving Strawberry Farm* Hopkinson tells the story of how young Davy got a whole community together during the Great Depression to help Miss Elsie save her

Hopkinson describes one of the most adventurous construction projects in U.S. history in her picture book Sky Boys, *featuring artwork by James E. Ransome.* (Illustration ©2006 by James E. Ransome. Used by permission of Schwartz & Wade Books, an imprint of Random House Children's Books, a division of Random House.)

strawberry farm. "Hopkinson's graceful text [is] filled with colloquial dialogue," wrote Gillian Engberg in *Booklist.* Kristine M. Casper, reviewing the book for *School Library Journal,* considered the picture book "an excellent introduction to this time period." *Sky Boys* shows another aspect of the Great Depression: how the construction of the tallest building in the world gave hope to the people of New York. Engberg complimented Hopkinson's "crisp, lyrical free verse" and suggested that the "unique, memorable title" will "enhance poetry and history units." According to a critic for *Publishers Weekly,* "the drama of the building's rise makes for a literally riveting account."

Along with her historical fiction, Hopkinson has also written contemporary picture books. *Bluebird Summer* is the story of how two young children help bluebirds return to their grandfather's yard after their grandmother dies. "Hopkinson's prose expresses the tightly knit love of the family," wrote a contributor to *Publishers Weekly.* Noting that the book has an open conclusion, John Peters predicted in *Booklist* that "youngsters will understand that the work, and the feelings behind it, are more important than the ostensible goal."

Two of Hopkinson's tales, *Billy and the Rebel* and *From Slave to Soldier,* invite readers to imagine life during the U.S. Civil War. The latter follows Johnny, a young African American who, when released from slavery, quickly joins the Union army. Unlike many slaves who became soldiers, Johnny is welcomed by the unit he joins, and, in a dire situation, he manages to save the entire company. "Young Civil War buffs will welcome something they can read themselves," wrote a *Kirkus Reviews* contributor, and Peters maintained that Hopkinson's chapter book "will bring the era and people to life for modern young readers."

Into the Firestorm: A Novel of San Francisco, 1906 is the story of Nick Dray, a Texas farm boy who moves to San Francisco to make his way in the world. When the 1906 earthquake and subsequent great fire strikes, Nick's quick thinking helps save his employer's business as well as the lives of two of his neighbors. "Characterization and action are strong in this memorable tale," commented a *Kirkus Reviews* contributor, while Kristen Oravec wrote in *School Library Journal* that "the terror of the 1906 disaster is brought powerfully alive" by Hopkinson.

Inspired by the research she gathered for her "Dear America" title, *Hear My Sorrow: The Diary of Angela Denoto, a Shirtwaist Worker,* Hopkinson's *Shutting out the Sky: Life in the Tenements of New York* helps young readers imagine what life was like for young immigrants in America near the turn of the twentieth century. "Hopkinson's enthusiasm for research, primary sources, and individual stories that make history come alive is evident," noted a contributor to *Kirkus Reviews.* A *Publishers Weekly* critic found the book to be "a highly readable discussion of change and reform with a look at the culture, joy and play" of the era. Another nonfiction title, *Up before Daybreak,* helps young readers understand how the economics of the cotton trade helped shape the culture of the Americas. "The prose is clear, the documentation excellent . . . the voices of the children vivid and personal," noted a *Kirkus Reviews* contributor. Jennifer Mattson, writing in *Booklist,* felt that the complexity of America's cotton industry is "skillfully distilled for this audience," and *School Library Journal* critic Ann Welton recommended *Up before Daybreak* as "a first-rate report and research source."

In *Sweet Land of Liberty,* Hopkinson examines the life of Oscar Chapman, the government official who battled racism and helped celebrated African-American contralto Marian Anderson perform a free concert on the steps of the Lincoln Memorial in Washington, DC, in 1939. According to *School Library Journal* contributor Miriam Lang Budin, "the book could provoke meaningful discussion about character formation and civic responsibility." To celebrate the 200th anniversary of the birth of the sixteenth president of the United States, Hopkinson wrote *Abe Lincoln Crosses a Creek: A Tall,*

Thin Tale (introducing His Forgotten Frontier Friend). This work of historical fiction concerns the misguided efforts of seven-year-old Abe and his friend, Austin Gollaher, to cross the swollen waters of Kentucky's Knob Creek. Here Hopkinson earned praise for her ability to fuse her humorous narrative with John Hendrix's artwork. "In dialogic asides and exclamations, the author addresses the illustrator and brings him (or, rather, his pencil-wielding hand) onstage to collaborate and correct," noted Kathy Krasniewicz in *School Library Journal.*

A pioneering folklorist and musicologist is the focus of *Home on the Range: John A. Lomax and His Cowboy Songs.* A college professor and administrator, Lomax traveled the nation collecting and recording frontier ballads and work songs, including "Sweet Betsy from Pike" and "Poor Lonesome Cowboy." Betty Carter, writing in *Horn Book,* described the tale as "pitch perfect in its scope for younger readers." Hopkinson's *Keep On!: The Story of Matthew Henson, Co-discoverer of the North Pole* recounts the story of the African-American explorer who joined Robert E. Peary on his famed 1909 Arctic voyage. Noting that the author concentrates on Henson's strengths as a navigator and translator, a critic in *Kirkus Reviews* stated that the work offers readers "a portrait of a singularly determined yet ever-affable man."

Stagecoach Sal: Inspired by a True Tale is based on the life of Delia Haskett Rawson, the first girl stage driver ever to carry the U.S. mail in California. The fictional tale finds the spunky youngster using her wits to save her cargo during an encounter with Poetic Pete, a smooth-talking outlaw. "Sal is an engaging, adventuresome character [who is] sure to delight readers with her gutsiness and determination," predicted C.J. Connor in *School Library Journal.* In *The Humblebee Hunter* Hopkinson looks at Charles Darwin, the father of evolutionary theory, recounting an experiment Darwin conducted with the help of his children. *School Library Journal* critic Barbara Auerbach remarked that the story "offers readers an introduction to both the renowned naturalist and scientific inquiry."

As for her goal as an author, Hopkinson told Sharon L. McElmeel of *Talk* that she hopes "to write stories good

Artist John Hendrix teams with Hopkinson to produce the imaginative biographical picture book **Abe Lincoln Crosses a Creek.** (Illustration ©2008 by John Hendrix. Used by permission of Schwartz & Wade Books, an imprint of Random House Children's Books, a division of Random House, Inc.)

enough, important enough, that if a library didn't have much money, they would still want to have them."

Biographical and Critical Sources

BOOKS

Children's Literature Review, Volume 118, Gale (Detroit, MI), 2006.
Hopkinson, Deborah, *Deborah Hopkinson and You* (autobiography), Libraries Unlimited (Westport, CT), 2007.
Hopkinson, Deborah, autobiographical essay in *Something about the Author,* Volume 180, Gale (Detroit, MI), 2008.

PERIODICALS

Black Issues Book Review, May-June, 2003, Adrienne Ingrum, review of *Sweet Clara and the Freedom Quilt,* p. 58; January-February, 2004, Kitty Flynn, review of *Shutting out the Sky: Life in the Tenements of New York, 1880-1915,* p. 101.
Booklist, April 15, 1999, Ilene Cooper, review of *A Band of Angels: A Story Inspired by the Jubilee Singers,* p. 1529; September 15, 1999, Carolyn Phelan, review of *Maria's Comet,* p. 268; April 15, 2001, John Peters, review of *Bluebird Summer,* p. 1564; May 15, 2001, Shelle Rosenfeld, review of *Fannie in the Kitchen: The Whole Story from Soup to Nuts of How Fannie Farmer Invented Recipes with Precise Measurements,* p. 1751; February 15, 2002, Cynthia Turnquest, review of *Under the Quilt of Night,* p. 1034; May 1, 2002, Susan Dove Lempke, review of *Pioneer Summer,* p. 1526; December 15, 2002, Susan Dove Lempke, review of *Cabin in the Snow,* p. 759; January 1, 2003, GraceAnne A. DeCandido, review of *Girl Wonder: A Baseball Story in Nine Innings,* p. 880; March 1, 2003, Susan Dove Lempke, review of *Our Kansas Home,* p. 1197; November 1, 2003, Hazel Rochman, review of *Shutting out the Sky,* p. 492; January 1, 2004, Hazel Rochman, review of *Sailing for Gold,* p. 856; May 15, 2004, Gillian Engberg, review of *A Packet of Seeds,* p. 1625; September 1, 2004, Kay Weisman, review of *Apples to Oregon: Being the (Slightly) True Narrative of How a Brave Pioneer Father Brought Apples, Peaches, Plums, Grapes, and Cherries (and Children) across the Plains,* p. 132; February 1, 2005, Hazel Rochman, review of *Billy and the Rebel,* p. 965; May 1, 2005, Gillian Engberg, review of *Saving Strawberry Farm,* p. 1590; December 1, 2005, Gillian Engberg, review of *Sky Boys: How They Built the Empire State Building,* p. 66; January 1, 2006, John Peters, review of *From Slave to Soldier,* p. 116; February 1, 2006, Ilene Cooper, review of *Susan B. Anthony: Fighter for Women's Rights,* p. 52; April 15, 2006, Jennifer Mattson, review of *Up before Daybreak: Cotton and People in America,* p. 46; September 1, 2006, John Peters, review of *Into the Firestorm: A Novel of San Francisco, 1906,* p. 129; April 15, 2007, Hazel Rochman, review of *Sweet Land of Liberty,* p. 40; February 15, 2009, Carolyn

Phelan, review of *Keep On! The Story of Matthew Henson, Co-Discoverer of the North Pole,* p. 77; November 1, 2009, Hazel Rochman, review of *Michelle,* p. 50.
Children's Bookwatch, April, 2006, review of *Sky Boys.*
Horn Book, March, 1999, Joanna Rudge Long, review of *A Band of Angels,* p. 190; May, 2001, review of *Fannie in the Kitchen,* p. 312; July-August, 2002, Susan P. Bloom, review of *Under the Quilt of Night,* p. 447; November-December, 2002, Deborah Hopkinson, "The Missing Parts," p. 812; March-April, 2003, Martha V. Parravano, review of *Girl Wonder,* p. 204; March-April, 2006, Susan Dove Lempke, review of *Sky Boys,* p. 172; May-June, 2006, Kathleen Isaacs, review of *Up before Daybreak,* p. 343; September-October, 2008, Betty Carter, review of *Abe Lincoln Crosses a Creek: A Tall, Thin Tale (introducing His Forgotten Frontier Friend),* p. 569; January-February, 2009, Betty Carter, review of *Home on the Range: John A. Lomax and His Cowboy Songs,* p. 116.
Kirkus Reviews, November 1, 2001, review of *Under the Quilt of Night,* p. 1550; April 15, 2002, review of *Pioneer Summer,* p. 570; August 1, 2002, review of *Cabin in the Snow,* p. 1133; December 15, 2002, review of *Our Kansas Home,* p. 1850; February 1, 2003, review of *Girl Wonder,* p. 232; September 15, 2003, review of *Shutting out the Sky,* p. 1175; February 1, 2004, review of *Sailing for Gold,* p. 134; March 1, 2004, review of *A Packet of Seeds,* p. 223; August 15, 2004, review of *Apples to Oregon,* p. 807; June 15, 2004, review of *The Long Trail,* p. 577; January 15, 2005, review of *Billy and the Rebel,* p. 121; April 15, 2005, review of *Saving Strawberry Farm,* p. 475; September 1, 2005, review of *From Slave to Soldier,* p. 974; January 15, 2006, review of *Sky Boys,* p. 85; March 1, 2006, review of *Up before Daybreak,* p. 231; August 15, 2006, review of *Into the Firestorm,* p. 2006; January 15, 2009, review of *Keep On!;* July 15, 2009, review of *Stagecoach Sal.*
New York Times Book Review, June 17, 2001, Alida Becker, review of *Fannie in the Kitchen,* p. 25; December 21, 2003, review of *Shutting out the Sky,* p. 16; January 16, 2005, Stephanie Deutsch, review of *Apples to Oregon,* p. 14.
Publishers Weekly, February 8, 1993, review of *Sweet Clara and the Freedom Quilt,* p. 87; April 14, 1997, review of *Birdie's Lighthouse,* p. 74; January 4, 1999, review of *A Band of Angels,* p. 90; October 11, 1999, review of *Maria's Comet,* p. 75; April 23, 2001, reviews of *Fannie in the Kitchen,* p. 77, and *Bluebird Summer,* p. 78; November 26, 2001, review of *Under the Freedom Quilt,* p. 61; April 15, 2002, review of *Pioneer Summer,* p. 65; December 23, 2002, review of *Girl Wonder,* p. 71; December 1, 2003, review of *Shutting out the Sky,* p. 58; August 30, 2004, review of *Apples to Oregon,* p. 54; January 9, 2006, review of *Sky Boys,* p. 52; December 15, 2008, review of *Home on the Range,* p. 54; October 12, 2009, review of *Michelle,* p. 48.
School Library Journal, May, 2001, Karen Land, review of *Bluebird Summer,* p. 123; May, 2001, Genevieve Ceraldi, review of *Fannie in the Kitchen,* p. 143; January, 2002, Marianne Saccardi, review of *Under the Quilt of Night,* p. 102; October, 2002, Kristen Oravec,

review of *Pioneer Summer,* p. 112; January, 2003, Be Astengo, review of *Cabin in the Snow,* p. 97; March, 2003, Susan Shaver, review of *Our Kansas Home,* p. 196; March, 2003, Blair Christolon, review of *Girl Wonder,* p. 193; December, 2003, Carol Fazioli, review of *Shutting out the Sky,* p. 169; April, 2004, Marian Creamer, review of *A Packet of Seeds,* p. 114; July, 2004, Anne Knickerbocker, review of *Sailing for Gold,* p. 77; September, 2004, Roxanee Burg, review of *Apples to Oranges,* p. 162; November, 2004, Anne Knickerbocker, review of *The Long Trail,* p. 107; February, 2005, Joyce Adams Burner, review of *Fannie in the Kitchen,* p. 57; April, 2005, Sharon R. Pearce, review of *Adventure in Gold Town,* and Bethany L.W. Hankinson, review of *Billy and the Rebel,* both p. 98; August, 2005, Kristine M. Casper, review of *Saving Strawberry Farm,* p. 97; October, 2005, Anne Knickerbocker, review of *From Slave to Soldier,* p. 116; February, 2006, Grace Oliff, review of *Sky Boys,* p. 120; March, 2006, John Peters, review of *Girl Wonder,* p. 88; May, 2006, Julie R. Ranelli, review of *Susan B. Anthony,* p. 112; June, 2006, Ann Welton, review of *Up before Daybreak,* p. 178; December, 2006, Kristen Oravec, review of *Into the Firestorm,* p. 146; May, 2007, Miriam Lang Budin, review of *Sweet Land of Liberty,* p. 118; September, 2008, Kathy Krasniewicz, review of *Abe Lincoln Crosses a Creek,* p. 149; September, 2009, C.J. Connor, review of *Stagecoach Sal,* p. 125; April, 2010, Barbara Auerbach, review of *The Humblebee Hunter,* p. 128.

Talk, November-December, 1998, "Author Profile: Deborah Hopkinson."

Teacher Librarian, December, 2005, GraceAnne A. DeCandido, "Food, Glorious Food," p. 13.

USA Today, February 4, 2010, review of *First Family,* p. 6D.

ONLINE

BookPage.com, http://www.bookpage.com/ (May 1, 2010), Deborah Hopkinson, "Behind the Book: Learning from History—and Experimenting Outdoors."

Deborah Hopkinson Home Page, http://www.deborah hopkinson.com (May 1, 2010).

Deborah Hopkinson Web log, http://deborahhopkinson. blogspot.com/ (May 1, 2010).

OregonLive.com, http://www.oregonlive.com/ (September 23, 2009), Jeff Baker, "Oregon Book Awards Prizewinner Skips the Suspense"; (October 29, 2009) Bill Graves, "Share Your Secrets: Deborah Hopkinson."

Rutgers University Web site, http://www.scils.rutgers.edu/ (January, 1999), "Words from Deborah Hopkinson."

Scholastic Web site, http://www2.scholastic.com/ (May 1, 2010), "Deborah Hopkinson."

*   *   *

HUGHES, Susan 1960-

Personal

Born 1960, in Canada; partner's name Ken; has children. *Education:* Attended Queen's University; University of Toronto, B.A. (English literature).

Addresses

E-mail—susanhughes@sympatico.ca.

Career

Writer of books for children. Crabtree Publishing Co., Toronto, Ontario, Canada, editor researcher and writer for one year; freelance writer and editor of educational materials.

Writings

JUVENILE NONFICTION

(With Bobbie Kalman) *I Live in a City,* Crabtree Pub. Co. (Toronto, Ontario, Canada), 1986.

The Environmental Detective Kit (with equipment), Somerville House (Toronto, Ontario, Canada), 1991, revised, 1998.

(With Stephen Cumbaa) *Megalodon: The Prehistoric Shark,* illustrated by Ron Berg, Penguin Putnam Books for Young Readers (New York, NY), 1998.

The Titanic Book and Submersible Model, illustrated by Steve Santini, Somerville House (Toronto, Ontario, Canada), 1999.

Canada Invents, illustrated by Paul McCusker, Owl Books (Toronto, Ontario, Canada), 2002.

When Beep-Beep Came to Earth, Nelson Thomson Learning (Toronto, Ontario, Canada), 2002.

Let's Call It Canada: Amazing Stories of Canadian Place Names, illustrated by Clive Dobson and Jolie Dobson, Firefly Books (New York, NY), 2003.

Lester B. Pearson, Fitzhenry & Whiteside (Markham, Ontario, Canada), 2003.

Coming to Canada: Building a Life in a New Land, Maple Tree Press (Toronto, Ontario, Canada), 2005.

(Reteller) *The Promise,* illustrated by June Bradford, Scholastic Canada (Markham, Ontario, Canada), 2005.

Buses, Cars, and Trucks, illustrated by Chris Jackson, Scholastic Canada (Markham, Ontario, Canada), 2005.

Where Are the Bears?, illustrated by Dimitri Kostic, Scholastic Canada (Markham, Ontario, Canada), 2005.

(Reteller) *The Frog Prince,* illustrated by June Bradford, Scholastic Canada (Markham, Ontario, Canada), 2005.

True or False: Finding out about Newfoundland Dogs, Scholastic Canada (Markham, Ontario, Canada), 2005.

Raise Your Voice, Lend a Hand, Change the World, Scholastic Canada (Toronto, Ontario, Canada), 2006.

Canadian Festivals, Scholastic Canada (Toronto, Ontario, Canada), 2007.

No Girls Allowed: Tales of Daring Women Dressed as Men for Love, Freedom, and Adventure, illustrated by Willow Dawson, Kids Can Press (Toronto, Ontario, Canada), 2008.

Canadian Sports, Scholastic Canada (Toronto, Ontario, Canada), 2009.

Canada's Birds, Scholastic Canada (Toronto, Ontario, Canada), 2010.

Case Closed?: Nine Mysteries Unlocked by Modern Science, illustrated by Michael Wandelmaier, Kids Can Press (Toronto, Ontario, Canada), 2010.

Contributor to educational science-book series published by Nelson Thomson Learning.

Author's work has been translated into French.

FICTION; FOR CHILDREN

Anything Can Happen (middle-grade novel), Doubleday Canada (Toronto, Ontario, Canada), 1992.

The Not-quite World Famous Scientist, illustrated by Stephen Taylor, Fitzhenry & Whiteside (Markham, Ontario, Canada), 2002.

Earth to Audrey (picture book), illustrated by Stéphane Poulin, Kids Can Press (Toronto, Ontario, Canada), 2005.

Virginia (young-adult novel), KCP Fiction (Toronto, Ontario, Canada), 2010.

"IN MY WORLD" SERIES; FOR CHILDREN

Animal Worlds, Crabtree Pub. Co. (Toronto, Ontario, Canada), 1986.

Time and the Seasons, Crabtree Pub. Co. (Toronto, Ontario, Canada), 1986.

The Food We Eat, Crabtree Pub. Co. (Toronto, Ontario, Canada), 1986.

People at Play, Crabtree Pub. Co. (Toronto, Ontario, Canada), 1986.

People at Work, Crabtree Pub. Co. (Toronto, Ontario, Canada), 1986.

"HOLIDAYS AND FESTIVALS" SERIES; FOR CHILDREN

(With Bobbie Kalman) *We Celebrate Family Days,* illustrated by Karen Harrison, Crabtree Pub. Co. (Toronto, Ontario, Canada), 1986, Crabtree Pub. Co. (New York, NY), 1993.

(With Bobbie Kalman) *We Celebrate Valentine's Day,* illustrated by Allen and Deborah Drew-Brook-Cormack, Crabtree Pub. Co. (Toronto, Ontario, Canada), 1986, Crabtree Pub. Co. (New York, NY), 1994.

We Celebrate Hanukkah, illustrated by Cecilia Ohm-Ericksen, Crabtree Pub. Co. (Toronto, Ontario, Canada), 1986, Crabtree Pub. Co. (New York, NY), 1993.

(With Bobbie Kalman) *We Celebrate the Harvest,* illustrated by Janet Wilson and Greg Ruhl, Crabtree Pub. Co. (New York, NY), 1993.

(With Bobbie Kalman) *We Celebrate Winter,* illustrated by Brenda Clark and Elaine Macpherson, Crabtree Pub. Co. (Toronto, Ontario, Canada), 1986, Crabtree Pub. Co. (New York, NY), 1994.

"WILD PAWS" CHAPTER-BOOK SERIES; FOR CHILDREN

Bobcat Rescue, illustrated by Heather Graham, Scholastic Canada (Toronto, Ontario, Canada), 2003.

Lonely Wolf Pup, illustrated by Heather Graham, Scholastic Canada (Toronto, Ontario, Canada), 2003.

Bunnies in Trouble, illustrated by Heather Graham, Scholastic Canada (Toronto, Ontario, Canada), 2004.

Orphaned Beluga, illustrated by Heather Graham, Scholastic Canada (Toronto, Ontario, Canada), 2004.

Cubs All Alone, illustrated by Heather Graham, Scholastic Canada (Toronto, Ontario, Canada), 2004.

"LANDS, PEOPLES, AND CULTURES" SERIES; FOR CHILDREN

(With April Fast) *Cuba: The Culture,* photographs by Marc Crabtree, Crabtree Pub. Co. (New York, NY), 2004.

(With April Fast) *Cuba: The Land,* photographs by Marc Crabtree, Crabtree Pub. Co. (New York, NY), 2004.

(With April Fast) *Cuba: The People,* photographs by Marc Crabtree, Crabtree Pub. Co. (New York, NY), 2004.

Adaptations

Anything Can Happen was adapted as a sound recording by Vancouver, British Columbia, Library Services Branch, 1994.

Sidelights

A prolific author of children's books who has produced both fiction and nonfiction, Susan Hughes began her writing career in her mid-twenties, after working as part of a team researching, editing, and writing a nonfiction series for a Toronto-based publisher. As a Canadian, Hughes gears her books such as *Canada Invents, Let's Call It Canada: Amazing Stories of Canadian Place Names,* and *Canadian Sports* to Canadian children. Her ability to explain complex scientific concepts has also served her well in books such as *Case Closed?: Nine Mysteries Unlocked by Modern Science, Megalodon: The Prehistoric Shark,* and the books in the "In My World" series. According to Heather Myers in *Resource Links,* Hughes' "breezy" text in the "substantial" *Canada Invents* "highlights Canadian resourcefulness" through stories about creative problem-solvers that exhibit "substance and lots of style."

Hughes' interest in history inspired *No Girls Allowed: Tales of Daring Women Dressed as Men for Love, Freedom, and Adventure,* a graphic novel illustrated by artist Willow Dawson. In *School Library Journal* Benjamin Russell praised the seven "quietly charming" profiles in the book, which introduces women from history who pass as men in order fulfill a goal in their lives. Another book that focuses on human history, *Coming to Canada: Building a Life in a New Land,* spotlights stories from among the 263 different nationalities and ethnicities that have assimilated into the population of Canada over time. Highlighting the country's immigrant roots, *Coming to Canada* features what *Resource Links* critic Victoria Pennell described as a "very readable" text that contains "lots of information without being overwhelming." "Upbeat and patriotic about the brave, hardworking, proud newcomers," the book also deals candidly with discrimination, observed Hazel Rochman in her review of *Coming to Canada* for *Booklist,* and in *School*

Susan Hughes teams up with comic artist Willow Dawson to produce the illustrated history book **No Girls Allowed.** (Illustration © 2008 Willow Dawson. Used by permission of Kids Can Press Ltd., Toronto.)

Library Journal Robyn Walker recommended Hughes' "comprehensive and informative" book as "a must-buy for all Canadian libraries."

In addition to nonfiction, Hughes showcases her storytelling skills in novels such as *The Not-Quite World Famous Scientist, Anything Can Happen,* and *Virginia,* as well as in the picture book *Earth to Audrey* and the animal-centered stories in her "Wild Paws" series. In *The Not-Quite World Famous Scientist* fourth grader Alex lives and breathes science, but when she is teamed up with the new boy in class during her school's science fair Alex learns a lot about social relationships and the value of friends with all kinds of interests. Calling the novel "funny and fast-paced with lots of scientific interest and information," Ann Abel added in *Resource Links* that *The Not-Quite World Famous Scientist* "pictures students enjoying and having fun with science."

Illustrated in oil paintings by Stéphane Poulin, *Earth to Audrey* focuses on a friendship between an upbeat little girl and a lonely little boy. Over the summer, Audrey's happiness and love of the natural world first startles, then inspires Roy. Hughes' story "examines the simple concept of observing Earth . . . with lots of gentle humour," according to *Resource Links* critic Isobel Lang, and in *School Library Journal* Linda Ludke dubbed *Earth to Audrey* "a cleverly written look at the powers of friendship and creative thinking."

Illustrated by Heather Graham, the "Wild Paws" books—which include *Bobcat Rescue, Lonely Wolf Pup, Bunnies in Trouble, Orphaned Beluga,* and *Cubs All Alone*—are geared for beginning readers and taps children's natural interest in animals. *Bobcat Rescue* finds Max and her younger brother and grandmother hiking when they discover an orphaned and stranded baby bobcat. Named Tuffy, the young cat is taken to the Wild Paws animal rehabilitation center where Max helps with mustering public support for rehabilitation efforts while also visiting her new wild friend. In *Bunnies in Trouble* two children rescue a snowshoe hare and work with Wild Paws to cure the creature and return it to its babies, while a pair of orphaned bear cubs are rescued by Max and friend Sarah in *Cubs All Alone.* While noting that the plot of *Bobcat Rescue* develops slowly, Grace Sheppard added in *Resource Links* that "Hughes keeps the language clear and simple," and her "appealing" story is well researched. In another *Resource Links* review, Judy Cottrell recommended *Bunnies in Trouble* as "a good, easy-to-read short story which could be used to nudge students into research."

Hughes told *SATA:* "I am a writer and editor, and I have been writing children's books and articles for nearly twenty years. I've always loved writing. When I was in grade five, several friends and I started a writing club. We'd gather with our most recent poems and stories and read them aloud to one another. We always tried to say one thing that was positive, along with a more critical but constructive comment. Also, because I was so crazy about horses, my good friend, Barb, and I began writing and 'publishing' a magazine about horses and horse-back riding. We sold *The Saddle and Bridle Club* magazine to our friends for five cents an issue!

"After finishing high school, I studied English literature at Queen's University and then at the University of Toronto. Before my final year of university, I was fortunate to get a summer job working for a children's publishing company, Crabtree. There, along with other students, I wrote, researched, proofread, and edited manuscripts—and loved it. I learned so much! Upon graduation, I worked for a year with Crabtree and then began a career as a freelancer, which I am still enjoying.

"Now I do lots of editing work, mainly for educational publishers, and I also write articles for several magazines, such as *Canadian Living* and *More.* But my true love is writing fiction and nonfiction for the educational and trade markets. I really enjoy doing the research for my books. I get to learn so many new things!

"I live in Toronto in a tall house with a red door. I work at home in my living room, sitting on the couch with my laptop in front of me. When the weather is warm, I open the windows wide and sit where I can see the trees and enjoy the sunlight. One of the favourite parts of my day is when my kids come home after school and I get to visit with them and hear about their day."

Biographical and Critical Sources

PERIODICALS

Booklist, August, 2005, Hazel Rochman, review of *Coming to Canada: Building a Life in a New Land,* p. 1964.

Globe & Mail, September 9, 2005, review of *Earth to Audrey.*

Kirkus Reviews, September, 15, 2005, review of *Earth to Audrey,* p. 1028; August 1, 2008, review of *No Girls Allowed: Tales of Daring Women Dressed as Men for Love, Freedom, and Adventure.*

Kliatt, September, 2008, Claire Rosser, review of *No Girls Allowed,* p. 37.

Resource Links, June, 2002, Heather Myers, review of *Canada Invents,* p. 21; December, 2002, Ann Abel, review of *The Not-quite World Famous Scientist,* p. 22; June, 2003, Victoria Pennell, review of *Let's Call It Canada,* p. 20; February, 2004, Adriane Pettit, review of *Lonely Wolf Pup,* p. 14; April, 2004, Grace Sheppard, review of *Bobcat Rescue,* Judy Cottrell, review of *Bunnies in Trouble,* and Carroll Chapman, review of *Orphaned Beluga,* all pp. 13-14; June, 2004, Evette Berry, reviews of *Cuba: The Land, Cuba: The People,* and *Cuba: The Culture,* all p. 13; February, 2005, Susan Miller, review of *Cubs All Alone,* p. 18; February, 2006, Isobel Lang, review of *Earth to Audrey,* p. 5, and Victoria Pennell, review of *Coming to Canada,* p. 35; December, 2007, Heather Empey, review of *Canadian Festivals,* p. 27.

School Library Journal, July, 2003, Laura Reed, review of *Let's Call It Canada: Amazing Stories of Canadian Place Names,* p. 142; November, 2005, Robyn Walker, review of *Coming to Canada,* p. 162; January, 2006, Linda Ludke, review of *Earth to Audrey,* p. 103; September, 2008, Benjamin Russell, review of *No Girls Allowed,* p. 215.

ONLINE

Susan Hughes Home Page, http://www.susanhughes.ca (May 15, 2010).

J

JAGO 1979-
(Jago Silver)

Personal

Born Jago Silver, November 12, 1979; married; wife's name Alex; children: Lily Peach. *Education:* Attended Truro College; Falmouth College of Arts, B.A., 2003.

Addresses

Home—St. Maybn, Cornwall, England. *Agent*—Ronnie Ann Herman, Herman Agency, 350 Central Park W., New York, NY 10025; RonnieHermanAgencyInc.com. *E-mail*—jago@earthling.net.

Career

Illustrator and educator. Illustrator of children's books, 2003—. Truro College, Cornwall, England, lecturer, 2007—.

Awards, Honors

Further Education Funding Council Calendar Prize, 2000; Highly Commended award, Macmillan Prize for Children's Illustration, 2003; Association of Illustrators Silver Award, Student Section, 2004; International Youth Library White Ravens Book List selection, 2005, for *Myron's Magic Cow;* Wow! Award, National Literacy Association, 2006, for *The Little Red Hen and the Grains of Wheat;* Holyer an Gof Award for Best Children's Book, 2006, for "Brave Tales" series; Gold Medal, Moonbeam Children's Book Awards, 2007, for *The Jesus Storybook Bible.*

Illustrator

Marlene Newman, *Myron's Magic Cow,* Barefoot Books (Cambridge, MA), 2005.

Geraldine McCaughrean, *Fig's Giant,* Oxford University Press (Oxford, England), 2005.

Manju Gregory, *Hansel and Gretel,* Mantra Lingua (London, England), 2005.

Henriette Barkow, *Little Red Hen and the Grains of Wheat,* Mantra Lingua (London, England), 2005.

Sally Lloyd-Jones, *The Jesus Storybook Bible: Every Story Whispers His Name,* Zonderkidz (Grand Rapids, MI), 2007.

Henriette Barkow, *The Elves and the Shoemaker,* Mantra Lingua (London, England), 2007.

Deborah Bodin Cohen, *Nachshon, Who Was Afraid to Swim: A Passover Story,* Kar-Ben Publishing (Minneapolis, MN), 2009.

Contributor of illustrations to "Brave Tales" series of books, 2004. Contributor to anthologies published by Houghton Mifflin, McGraw-Hill, and Macmillan.

Sidelights

British illustrator Jago has provided the artwork for a number of books for young readers, including *Myron's Magic Cow* by Marlene Newman and *Nachshon, Who Was Afraid to Swim: A Passover Story* by Deborah Bodin Cohen. "I enjoy working on children's books and am drawn to stories with a hint of eccentricity," Jago noted on his home page.

In *Myron's Magic Cow,* a fractured fairy tale, an inner-city youth takes possession of a bovine with fantastic abilities. On his way to the store to buy milk, Myron meets a fast-talking blonde who convinces the youngster to part with his mother's hard-earned cash in exchange for a huge cow. As Newman's tale continues, Myron soon learns that his new "pet" not only gives milk (including skim) but also talks and grants wishes. *School Library Journal* critic Angela J. Reynolds praised Jago's "folklike, digitally prepared, mixed-media illustrations," noting that the artist "deftly employs shadow and perspective to bring the story to life." A contributor in *Kirkus Reviews* complimented the tale's urban setting, remarking that Jago places Newman's characters in "a neighborhood of well-spaced walkups, all overlaid with an arty-looking smudge that looks like old varnish."

Nachshon, Who Was Afraid to Swim, concerns the youngster who is believed to be the first Israelite to enter the Sea of Reeds during the Jews' historic exodus

Jago's illustration assignments include creating the unique artwork for Deborah Bodin Cohen's **Nachson, Who Was Afraid to Swim.** (Illustration ©2009 by Lerner Publishing Group, Inc. Reprinted with the permission of Kar-Ben Publishing, a division of Lerner Publishing Group, Inc. All rights reserved. No part of this excerpt may be used or reproduced in any manner whatsoever without the prior written permission of Lerner Publishing Group, Inc.)

from Egypt. Inspired by the wisdom of Moses, Nachshon overcomes his fear of the water to lead his people to safety as Pharoah's army approaches. "Jago's highly stylized digital pictures are handsome and heartfelt," a *Publishers Weekly* critic observed in a review of Cohen's story. According to Rachel Kamin in *School Library Journal*, the artist uses an earth-toned palette "to depict the sweltering heat of the desert and bright blue and green tones to illustrate the celebration of freedom."

Biographical and Critical Sources

PERIODICALS

Bulletin of the Center for Children's Books, January, 2006, Maggie Hommel, review of *Myron's Magic Cow,* p. 244.

Kirkus Reviews, September 1, 2005, review of *Myron's Magic Cow,* p. 979; January 15, 2009, review of *Nachshon, Who Was Afraid to Swim: A Passover Story.*

Publishers Weekly, December 22, 2008, review of *Nachshon, Who Was Afraid to Swim,* p. 51.

School Library Journal, January, 2006, Angela J. Reynolds, review of *Myron's Magic Cow,* p. 110; March, 2009, Rachel Kamin, review of *Nachshon, Who Was Afraid to Swim,* p. 108.

ONLINE

Jago Home Page, http://www.jagoillustration.com (May 1, 2010).

Jago Web log, jagoillustration.blogspot.com/ (May 1, 2010).*

JENKINS, Martin 1959-
(M.D. Jenkins)

Personal

Born 1959, in Surrey, England. *Education:* Cambridge University, degree.

Addresses

Home—Cambridge and London, England.

Career

Conservation biologist and author. World Conservation Monitoring Centre, member of staff; freelance consultant and conservationist, beginning 1990.

Awards, Honors

London *Times* Junior Information Book of the Year shortlist, 1996, for *Fly Traps!* and Award, 1999, for *The Emperor's Egg;* Kate Greenaway Medal, 2004, for *Gulliver's Travels* illustrated by Chris Riddell.

Writings

FOR CHILDREN

Deserts, Cherytree Books (Bath, England), 1995.
Fly Traps!: Plants That Bite Back, illustrated by David Parkins, Candlewick Press (Cambridge, MA), 1996.
Wings, Stings, and Wriggly Things, Candlewick Press (Cambridge, MA), 1996.
Chameleons Are Cool, illustrated by Sue Shields, Walker (London, England), 1997, Candlewick Press (Cambridge, MA), 1998.
Vampires, Candlewick Press (Cambridge, MA), 1998.
(With Jay Young) *The Art of Science: A Pop-up Adventure in Art,* Candlewick Press (Cambridge, MA), 1999.
The Emperor's Egg, illustrated by Jane Chapman, Candlewick Press (Cambridge, MA), 1999.
Grandma Elephant's in Charge, illustrated by Ivan Bates, Candlewick Press (Cambridge, MA), 2003.
(Reteller) *Jonathan Swift's Gulliver's Travels,* illustrated by Chris Riddell, Walker (London, England), 2004, Candlewick Press (Cambridge, MA), 2005.
Ape, illustrated by Vicky White, Candlewick Press (Cambridge, MA), 2007.
Titanic, illustrated by Brian Sanders, Walker (London, England), 2007.
(Reteller) *Don Quixote,* illustrated by Chris Riddell, Candlewick Press (Somerville, MA), 2009.
The Time Book: A Brief History from Lunar Calendars to Atomic Clocks, illustrated by Richard Holland, Candlewick Press (Somerville MA), 2009.

OTHER

(Compiler, with Jane Thornback) *The IUCN Mammal Red Data Book,* IUCN (Gland, Switzerland), 1982.

(Editor, as M.D. Jenkins) *Madagascar: An Environmental Profile,* IUCN (Gland, Switzerland), 1987.
The Diversity of the Seas: A Regional Approach, World Conservation Press (Cambridge, England), 1996.
Global Biodiversity: Earth's Living Resources in the 21st Century, Hoechst Foundation (Cambridge, England), 2000.
(With Brian Groombridge) *World Atlas of Biodiversity: Earth's Living Resources in the 21st Century,* University of California Press (Berkeley, CA), 2002.
(Editor with Stuart Chape and Mark Spalding) *The World's Protected Areas: Status, Values, and Prospects in the 21st Century,* foreword by Achim Steiner and Julia Marton-Lefévre, University of California Press (Berkeley, CA), 2008.

Also author of environmental reports.

Sidelights

A scientist and writer, Martin Jenkins shares his wide-ranging knowledge in nonfiction books that have been praised for inspiring young readers with an interest in many scientific subjects. Born in England, Jenkins moved with his family to Spain and Ireland while growing up. After attending Cambridge University, where he studied biology, he worked for the World Conservation Monitoring Centre, where he wrote on conservation issues. When Walker Books asked him to serve as a consultant for their "Animals at Risk" series, it provided Jenkins with a welcome break from the highly technical writing he was used to. In addition to continu-

Martin Jenkins' picture book The Emperor's Egg *features acrylic paintings by Jane Chapman.* (Illustration ©1999 by Jane Chapman. All rights reserved. Reproduced by permission of Candlewick Press, on behalf of Walker Books, London.)

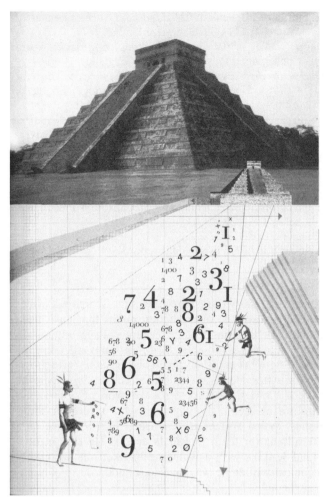

Featuring artwork by Richard Holland, Jenkins' compelling The Time Book *presents a history of the measurement that defines man's history.*
(Illustration ©2009 by Richard Holland. Reproduced by permission of Candlewick Press, on behalf of Walker Books, London.)

ing his consulting work in environmental science, since the mid-1990 he has also produced a steady stream of nonfiction books for younger readers, among them the award-winning picture books *Fly Traps!: Plants That Bite Back* and *The Emperor's Egg*. Praising *Fly Traps!* in *Horn Book*, Margaret A. Bush wrote that Jenkins' combination of an "intriguing subject" and "goofy humor" results in an "inviting introduction to the [flytrap] species."

In *Ape* Jenkins joins with former zookeeper Vicky White to introduce children to the five species of ape that live on earth: chimpanzees, bonobos, gorillas, orangutans, . . . and man. In contrast to White's "stunning" paintings, Jenkins' "economical, conservation-oriented text ably sets each scene," according to a *Publishers Weekly* writer, while Roger Sutton noted in *Horn Book* that *Ape* features a "concise, respectful text." Another book chock full of fun science facts, *Wings, Stings, and Wriggly Things* focuses on insects of all sorts, from snails and slugs to grasshoppers and dragonflies, while *Chameleons Are Cool* introduces readers to the small Madagascarean reptiles that are known for their ability

to shift colors to blend with their environment. "No scholarly solemnity here," noted *Booklist* contributor Hazel Rochman in a review of *Wings, Stings, and Wriggly Things*, "but a lot of facts and fun."

Featuring acrylic paintings by illustrator Jane Chapman, *The Emperor's Egg* uses a picture-book format to introduce children to an unusual bird, the emperor penguin of Antarctica. While mother penguins lay the egg, it is the father penguin that incubates and protects his young offspring, resting it on top of his feet and blanketing it with the downy feathers of his belly. Although *Booklist* contributor Linda Perkins found Jenkins' "conversational narrative" to be overly informal, the art in *The Emperor's Egg* "captures the penguins' dignity and stolidity," the critic added. Also praising Chapman's use of "realistic details" in her illustrations, a reviewer for *Publishers Weekly* concluded that "Jenkins's lively text" and his inclusion of "abundant penguin facts" will "attract many readers."

In *The Time Book: A Brief History from Lunar Calendars to Atomic Clocks* Jenkins encourages young readers to explore the abstract concept that guides most human life on earth. The book discusses how time has been measured by a variety of different cultures and how man's need for exact measurements has veered from nature's seasonal clock to produce calendrical "corrections" such as the leap year. In *Booklist* Ian Chipman dubbed *The Time Book* a "diverting" volume that tackles "a pretty heady subject" in a "succinct" text and engaging art. "The inventiveness of [Richard] Holland's illustrations is more than a match for the quirky journey on which Jenkins takes his readers," wrote Susan Perren in her *Globe & Mail* review of the work, the critic adding that the author's "well-written, thoughtful book about time and timekeeping" exemplifies "the new normal in science books for the young, which favours a multitude of bytes of information embedded in cartoon illustrations and accompanied by sidebars of related trivia."

In addition to his science-based books, Jenkins has also retold Jonathan Swift's classic novel *Gulliver's Travels* for a new generation of readers, his text brought to life in Chris Riddell's award-winning art. By simplifying some of the language in the eighteenth-century novel, as well as by editing down the text, Jenkins preserves the satire of Swift's preposterous story about a man who finds himself in the land of the Lilliputians. He produces what *School Library Journal* contributor Heide Piehler described as a "streamlined story" featuring "a lively adventure filled with bizarre and entertaining characters," while in *Booklist* Michael Cart called Jenkins' retelling of *Gulliver's Travels* "nicely realized" and "beautifully illustrated."

Biographical and Critical Sources

PERIODICALS

Booklist, December 1, 1996, Hazel Rochman, review of *Wings, Stings, and Wriggly Things,* p. 658; January 1,

2000, Linda Perkins, review of *The Emperor's Egg,* p. 932; March 15, 2005, Michael Cart, review of *Gulliver's Travels,* p. 1293; May 1, 2009, Ian Chipman, review of *The Time Book: A Brief History from Lunar Calendars to Atomic Clocks,* p. 76.

Horn Book, September-October, 2003, Danielle J. Ford, review of *Grandma Elephant's in Charge,* p. 630; January-February, 2008, Roger Sutton, review of *Ape,* p. 113.

Kirkus Reviews, April 1, 2009, review of *The Time Book.*

Publishers Weekly, January 26, 1998, review of *Chameleons Are Cool,* p. 91; November 15, 1999, review of *The Emperor's Egg,* p. 65; July 14, 2003, review of *Grandma Elephant's in Charge,* p. 76; December 17, 2007, review of *Ape,* p. 50.

School Arts, May, 2000, Ken Marantz, review of *The Art of Science: A Pop-up Adventure in Art,* p. 62.

School Library Journal, April, 2000, Carolyn Angus, review of *The Art of Science,* p. 157; December, 2003, Jody McCoy, review of *Grandma Elephant's in Charge,* p. 135; March, 2005, Heide Piehler, review of *Gulliver's Travels,* p. 213; October, 2007, John Peters, review of *Titanic,* p. 178; September, 2009, Joy Fleishhacker, review of *The Time Book,* p. 182.

ONLINE

Walker Books Web site, http://www.walker.co.uk/ (May 31, 2010), "Martin Jenkins."

JENKINS, M.D.
See JENKINS, Martin

*   *   *

JOHNSTON, Lynn 1947-

Personal

Born May 28, 1947, in Collingwood, Ontario, Canada; daughter of Mervyn (a jeweler) and Ursula (an artisan) Ridgway; married (husband a cameraman), c. 1975 (divorced); married John Roderick Johnston (a dentist and pilot), February 15, 1977 (divorced, c. 2008); children: (first marriage) Aaron Michael; (second marriage) Katherine Elizabeth. *Education:* Attended Vancouver School of Arts, 1964-67. *Religion:* Unitarian-Universalist. *Hobbies and other interests:* Travel, doll collecting, playing the accordion, co-piloting and navigating aircraft.

Addresses

Home—North of North Bay, Ontario.

Career

Cartoonist, writer, and illustrator. McMaster University, Hamilton, Ontario, Canada, medical artist, 1968-73;

Lynn Johnston (Reproduced by permission.)

freelance commercial artist and writer, beginning 1973; author and illustrator of "For Better or for Worse" cartoon strip syndicated by Universal Press Syndicate, 1979-97, United Features Syndicate, 1997—. President, Lynn Johnston Productions, Inc.

Member

National Cartoonist Society (former president).

Awards, Honors

Reuben Award, National Cartoonists Society, 1986, for outstanding cartoonist of the year; named member, Order of Canada, 1992; National Cartoonists Society Category Award for best comic strip; Quill Award, National Association of Writing Instrument Distributors; Inkpot Award, San Diego Comics Convention; EDI Award; Pulitzer Prize nomination, 1994; inducted into International Museum of Cartoon Art Hall of Fame, 1997; Media Award, American Speech-Language-Hearing Association, 2007; named member, Order of Manitoba, 2007; named to Giants of the North roster, Doug Wright Awards, 2008; inducted into Canadian Cartoonists' Hall of Fame, 2008; two honorary degrees.

Writings

SELF-ILLUSTRATED CARTOON BOOKS

David! We're Pregnant!, Potlatch Publications, 1973, published as *David! We're Pregnant!: 101 Cartoons for Expecting Parents,* Meadowbrook, 1977, revised edition, 1992.

Hi, Mom! Hi, Dad!: The First Twelve Months of Parenthood, P.M.A. Books, 1975, revised edition, Meadowbrook, 1977.

Do They Ever Grow Up?, Meadowbrook, 1978, published as *Do They Ever Grow Up?: 101 Cartoons about the Terrible Twos and Beyond,* 1983.

Graduation, a Time for Change, Andrews McMeel (Kansas City, MO), 2001.

Wags and Kisses, Andrews McMeel (Kansas City, MO), 2001.

Graduation: Just the Beginning!, Andrews McMeel (Kansas City, MO), 2003.

Leaving Home: Survival of the Hippest, Andrews McMeel (Kansas City, MO), 2003.

So You're Going to Be a Grandma!, Andrews McMeel (Kansas City, MO), 2005.

"FOR BETTER OR FOR WORSE" CARTOON COLLECTIONS

I've Got the One-More-Washload Blues, Andrews McMeel (Kansas City, MO), 1981.

Is This "One of Those Days," Daddy?, Andrews McMeel (Kansas City, MO), 1982.

It Must Be Nice to Be Little, Andrews McMeel (Kansas City, MO), 1983.

More than a Month of Sundays, Andrews McMeel (Kansas City, MO), 1983.

Our Sunday Best, Andrews McMeel (Kansas City, MO), 1984.

Just One More Hug, Andrews McMeel (Kansas City, MO), 1984.

The Last Straw, Andrews McMeel (Kansas City, MO), 1985.

Keep the Home Fries Burning, Andrews McMeel (Kansas City, MO), 1986.

It's All Downhill from Here, Andrews McMeel (Kansas City, MO), 1987.

Pushing 40, Andrews McMeel (Kansas City, MO), 1988.

A Look Inside—For Better or for Worse: The Tenth Anniversary Collection, Andrews McMeel (Kansas City, MO), 1989.

It All Comes Out in the Wash (omnibus), Tor Books (New York, NY), 1990.

If This Is a Lecture, How Long Will It Be?, Andrews McMeel (Kansas City, MO), 1990.

Another Day, Another Lecture (omnibus), Tor Books (New York, NY), 1991.

What, Me Pregnant?, Andrews McMeel (Kansas City, MO), 1991.

You Can Play in the Barn, but You Can't Get Dirty (omnibus), Tor Books (New York, NY), 1992.

You Never Know What's around the Corner (omnibus), Tor Books (New York, NY), 1992.

Things Are Looking Up, Andrews McMeel (Kansas City, MO), 1992.

It's a Pig-Eat-Chicken World (omnibus), Tor Books (New York, NY), 1993.

Shhh—Mom's Working! (omnibus), Tor Books (New York, NY), 1993.

But, I Read the Destructions!, Tor Books (New York, NY), 1993.

"There Goes My Baby!," Andrews McMeel (Kansas City, MO), 1993.

It's the Thought That Counts: For Better or for Worse Fifteenth-Anniversary Collection, Andrews McMeel (Kansas City, MO), 1994.

Starting from Scratch, Andrews McMeel (Kansas City, MO), 1995.

Love Just Screws Everything Up, Andrews McMeel (Kansas City, MO), 1996.

Remembering Farley: A Tribute to the Life of Our Favorite Cartoon Dog, Andrews McMeel (Kansas City, MO), 1996.

Growing like a Weed, Andrews McMeel (Kansas City, MO), 1997.

Middle Age Spread, Andrews McMeel (Kansas City, MO), 1998.

The Lives behind the Lines: Twenty Years of For Better or for Worse, Andrews McMeel (Kansas City, MO), 1999.

Sunshine and Shadow, Andrews McMeel (Kansas City, MO), 1999.

Isn't He Beautiful?, Andrews McMeel (Kansas City, MO), 2000.

Isn't She Beautiful?, Andrews McMeel (Kansas City, MO), 2000.

The Big 5-0, Andrews McMeel (Kansas City, MO), 2000.

A Perfect Christmas, Andrews McMeel (Kansas City, MO), 2001.

All About April: Our Little Girl Grows Up!, Andrews McMeel (Kansas City, MO), 2001.

Family Business, Andrews McMeel (Kansas City, MO), 2002.

Reality Check, Andrews McMeel (Kansas City, MO), 2003.

With This Ring, Andrews McMeel (Kansas City, MO), 2003.

Laugh 'n' Learn Spanish, McGraw-Hill (New York, NY), 2004.

Suddenly Silver: Celebrating Twenty-five Years of For Better or for Worse, Andrews McMeel (Kansas City, MO), 2004.

Never Wink at a Worried Woman, Andrews McMeel (Kansas City, MO), 2005.

Striking a Chord, Andrews McMeel (Kansas City, MO), 2005.

I Love My Grandpa!, Andrews McMeel (Kansas City, MO), 2006.

She's Turning into One of Them!, Andrews McMeel (Kansas City, MO), 2006.

Seniors' Discount, Andrews McMeel (Kansas City, MO), 2007.

Teaching . . . Is a Learning Experience!, Andrews McMeel (Kansas City, MO), 2007.

Home Sweat Home, Andrews McMeel (Kansas City, MO), 2008.

OTHER

(With Beth Cruikshank; and illustrator) *Farley Follows His Nose,* Bowen Press (New York, NY), 2009.

Contributor to *Canadian Children's Annual.*

Johnston's quirky comic-book series "For Better or for Worse" is collected in books such as **Middle Age Spread.** (©1998 by Lynn Johnston Productions, Inc. For Better or For Worse © Universal Press Syndicate. Reproduced by permission.)

More of Johnston's "For Better or for Worse" comics are collected in **What, Me Pregnant?** (Andrews McMeel, 1991. For Better or for Worse © 1991 Lynn Johnston Productions. Dist. By Universal Press Syndicate. Reprinted with permission. All rights reserved.)

ILLUSTRATOR

Bruce Lansky, editor, *The Best Baby Name Book in the Whole Wide World,* Meadowbrook Press, 1979.

Vicki Lansky, *The Taming of the C.A.N.D.Y. Monster,* revised edition, Book Peddlers, 1988.

Vicki Lansky, *Practical Parenting Tips for the First Five Years,* revised and enlarged edition, Meadowbrook Press, 1992.

Sidelights

When it comes to chronicling the problems and phobias of the typical North American family, no one does it like Lynn Johnston, creator of the "For Better or for Worse" comic strip. In 1986, Johnston won the prestigious Reuben Award for outstanding cartoonist of the year from the National Cartoonists Society, making her the first female and the youngest person ever to win, and by 2010 her drawings of the fictional—but believable—Patterson family appeared in over 2,000 newspapers throughout the United States and Canada, as well as in dozens of entertaining cartoon collections. A frequent winner of newspaper reader polls, "For Better or For Worse" ranks near the likes of the megapopular "Doonesbury" and "Calvin and Hobbes" strips, remaining popular due to its combination of warmth, creativity, and humor.

Populated by the Patterson family—two parents, two children, and a family dog—"For Better or for Worse" developed out of many of Johnston's real-life situations and concerns. For example, harried mother Elly Patterson, who feels motivated to try to fix everyone and everything in her family, was named after Johnston's friend who died in high school from a tumor. Like the Johnstons, the Pattersons are Canadian. Johnston's then-husband, like his fictional counterpart, Elly's nice but slightly bumbling husband John, was a tall, affable dentist who was also a pilot. Patterson children Michael and Elizabeth, are near in age to Johnston's children, Aaron and Katie, and the Johnston family once had an English sheep dog named Farley, just like the comic-strip family does. Finally, Elly's brother Phil is a wayward trumpet player, just like Johnston's brother Alan Philip Ridgway.

The suburban and slightly idyllic life of the Patterson family is somewhat removed from Johnston's own beginnings. The child of a watchmaker and a self-taught calligrapher and illustrator, Johnston was a self-described angry child who used drawing and art as an outlet for her emotions. "I drew lots when I was mad," she recalled to Ned Geeslin in *People* magazine. "It helped me vent my anger. I was really an angry girl, even in elementary school. I wanted to be grown up. I'd fantasize and draw a picture of what I'd look like when I was old and what my husband would look like."

Her parents' artistic sensibilities greatly influenced Johnston in her later career. "My mother had tremendous talent when it came to painting and craft work.

She was always making hooked rugs and all that sort of thing, but she was a calligrapher for my grandfather who had a stamp dealership." Johnston spent a lot of time with her father and she considers him to be one of the greatest influences on her artistic talent. "My dad was a closet cartoonist," she asserted. "More than drawing cartoons, he appreciated cartoons. We would pour over these illustrations one at a time and he would point out the drawings and what made them funny. He just loved comics; he just loved cartoons."

More than simply appreciating cartoons and movies, Johnston's father encouraged her to analyze the humor they contain and study role of timing and setting in the humor of a piece. This proved to be great training for the work Johnston would later do as a cartoonist, where timing is essential. "He wouldn't just take you to a movie. He would talk about the comedy as it was timed and as it was set up and how difficult it was to set up these pratfalls. So comedy for me was not just a matter of sitting down and enjoying it, it was a matter of analyzing it as well. That went for both cartoons in the paper and cartoon behavior on live film."

For a short while, Johnston was enrolled in the Vancouver School of Art. She quit, however, and took jobs in animation and illustration. Marrying a cameraman named Doug, she moved to Ontario because of the better job opportunities. Johnston found herself missing the mountains of British Columbia. Still, the move proved to be the right decision when she found a job in the city of Hamilton. "I got a wonderful job as a medical artist for McMaster University. . . . They trained me to do medical illustration. I did first year medical school and went to all the anatomy courses and did dissection and everything with the medical students," she once said. "It was a great time of learning and a whole new career and I loved it." Soon, her son Aaron was born. Unfortunately, Johnston and her husband soon separated and Doug moved back to Vancouver.

After her divorce, Johnston started to do freelance work out of her home and soon found her business booming. Oddly enough, it was her obstetrician who started the chain of events that would eventually lead to her being offered a contract for a comic strip. Knowing that she was a comic artist, the man challenged Johnston to come up with some cartoons to be put on the ceiling above his examining tables. "I was the type of person that liked a challenge, and if somebody I admired gave me a challenge, I went through that open door. That challenge was enough to make me do eighty drawings for him." With her friend's help, she found a publisher for the illustrations, eventually completing enough material for three books.

Submissions editors at Universal Press Syndicate had seen Johnston's first book, *David! We're Pregnant!,* and they were impressed with the quality and humor in her drawings. They were searching for a comic strip that could compete with the family-oriented "Blondie" and

"Hi and Lois" and thought Johnston might be a shoo-in for that position. She sent them samples of a strip she had developed based loosely on her own family life. To her surprise, they accepted her submissions and offered her a daily, syndicated strip. Over 150 papers signed on to carry "For Better or for Worse," even before the strip began to officially run.

As Johnston's comic career was developing, another story had been brewing as well. A few years before, while driving along with her young son, she happened to spot a small plane flying overhead. She loved flying and small aircraft, so on a whim she drove to the airport to see the plane land. "This nice young fellow jumped out of the plane and walked over and we had a conversation. He invited me to fly with him to the next airport for a hamburger," she told an *Authors and Artists for Young Adults* interviewer. Shortly afterward, the two realized that they were pretty compatible, except for one thing. He wanted to move north, and she wanted to stay in southern Canada. Overlooking this slight obstacle she and Rod Johnston were married in 1976. He adopted her son and they had a daughter of their own shortly afterward. Rod's graduation from dental school and their move to the north coincided with Johnston's proposal for Universal Press Syndicate. Shortly afterward, they moved to northern Manitoba, where Rod became a flying dentist.

Johnston's early comics were very simple sketches of the Pattersons, a family with two young children and a small sheepdog puppy who would grow into the massive Farley and eventually star in his own children's book, *Farley Follows His Nose*. Her strips also dealt with the normal grind of a family growing up together: parents and kids fighting, exhaustion and mess, and so on. But as the Patterson family has grown and grown up, Johnston has tackled more complex and controversial issues in her strip.

At one point, Elly has to deal with the problem of her friend, who gave birth to a baby with six fingers on both hands. Later on, the Pattersons discover their own feelings on race relations as an Asian family moves into the house across the street. In a 1992 story line, which was taken from an incident that had happened to a friend of Johnston's daughter, Mike Patterson finds out that his friend, Gordon, is being abused by his father, and in 1995 Johnston killed off the Patterson's family dog, Farley. The character of Grandfather was also afflicted with aphasia, which results from damage to the brain's language center, and the storylines involving his struggles to recover the power of speech after a debilitating stroke earned Johnston plaudits from social service agencies.

In another point in the strip, family friend Lawrence Poirier admits to his family that he is gay. Unfortunately, his parents react badly, denying the news and eventually kicking Lawrence out of the house. This topic choice was partly inspired by Johnston's brother-in-law, Ralph, who is gay, and by writing a series of strips about a gay character, the cartoonist hoped to share with readers the information and support she learned from Ralph's experience. However, the controversial topic prompted nineteen newspapers to cancel the strip. Johnston received more than 3,000 letters after the strips were published, two thirds of which praised her for having the courage to address the issue in "For Better or for Worse."

In general, Johnston has received positive feedback from her more-controversial strips. "If I do something of a serious nature, I'll get one letter against and 20 letters for," she told *Las Vegas Review-Journal* interviewer John Przybys. "People are really comfortable reading about (serious) stuff as long as I'm careful to treat it with dignity and in a light way, because it *is* an entertainment medium and people do read comics for fun." The problem with confronting a controversial issue is that certain special interest groups have sometimes requested that Johnston give equal time to their causes: A "lot of people want me to go further: 'Oh gosh, if she's willing to talk about child abuse, let's have her champion the abortion issue.' It's dangerous, when you do realistic things, turning the strip into a soapbox and people wanting you to champion their cause. You can't do that."

In 2006 Johnston began transforming "For Better or for Worse" into a "hybrid" version by updating the older strips with newer texts and drawings. Now the Pattersons no longer age: they are frozen in time in 1979 and character history, such as the courtship of Elly and John, are woven into Johnston's ongoing storyline through the use of flashbacks, reflections, and daydreams. Since 2006 Johnston's drawing style has also reverted to the looser style of her earlier years. Although rumors had circulated that Johnston would be ending the strip, circumstances in her life—namely, a divorce from her husband, Rod—prompted a change of heart, and "For Better or for Worse" is still going strong, although its hold on Johnston's time has relaxed substantially.

Johnston works almost every day, and it takes up to two days to write the dialogue for just one week's worth of her comic strip. After the writing process, she finally sets to work creating the art. "I waste almost no paper. I draw it in pencil, then I go over it with India ink pens, and then I put on the Lettra film, with the little dots that gives you the gray tones," she told *St. Petersburg Times Floridian* correspondent Jeanne Malmgren. "You have to be the characters as you are drawing." Johnston told Janice Dineen of the *Toronto Star.* "You have to feel what the character is feeling. Even Farley the dog: as he stretches, I feel that." In this way, her feelings of being a frustrated actor have benefited her drawing. In her career, Johnston has drawn close to 5,000 "For Better or for Worse" sketches. "It's like writing little sitcoms all the time and I'm playing all the roles and controlling all the camera angles," she told Dineen. When asked about the reasons for the popularity of her strips,

As her strip has matured, Johnston began to revisit her early "For Better or for Worse" comics and updated her humorous storylines. (For Better or for Worse © 2004 Lynn Johnston Productions. Distributed by Universal Press Syndicate. Reprinted with permission. All rights reserved.)

Johnston replied, "I think because people can identify with it, and I try to be very true to life. I enjoy what I do and I think it shows. The letters I get tend to tell me that people trust me and want to confide in me. They feel that I'm talking about their family and that it's the truth."

Biographical and Critical Sources

PERIODICALS

Detroit Free Press, March 17, 1993, John Tanasychuk, "Gay Teen Comes out in 'For Better or for Worse.'"

Editor & Publisher, November 26, 2001, Dave Astor, "'Better' Is Best of the Family Comics," p. 14; January 8, 2007, Dave Astor, "Popular Cartoon Will Stay on . . . as Old/New Hybrid"; January 22, 2008, Dave Astor, "Lynn Johnston Says 'For Better' Comic Will Still Have New Content."

Horn Book, July-August, 2009, Susan Dove Lempke, review of *Farley Follows His Nose,* p. 408.

Las Vegas Review-Journal, May 31, 1992, John Przybys, "Getting Serious."

Maclean's, September 8, 2008, Anne Kingston, interview with Johnston, p. 18.

People, September 15, 1986, Ned Geeslin, "For Better or Worse, Canadian Cartoonist Lynn Johnston Draws Her Inspiration from Reality."

Publishers Weekly, March 23, 2009, review of *Farley Follows His Nose,* p. 59.

St. Petersburg Times Floridian, February 1, 1989, Jeanne Malmgren, "It's Getting 'Better.'"

School Library Journal, May, 2009, Marge Loch-Wouters, review of *Farley Follows His Nose,* p. 82.

Toronto Star, October 9, 1992. Janice Dineen, "Better than Ever."*

K

KEANE, Dave 1965-

Personal

Born 1965, in San Jose, CA; married; wife's name Christine; children: two daughters, one son. *Education:* San Diego State University, B.A. *Hobbies and other interests:* Watching movies, drawing, lifting weights, reading books and newspapers.

Addresses

Home—CA. *Agent*—Linda Pratt, Sheldon Fogelman Agency, 10 E. 40th St., New York, NY 10011. *E-mail*—dave@mrdavekeane.com; linda.pratt@sheldonfogelman agency.com (agent).

Career

Advertising director, author, and illustrator. P3M, Los Gatos, CA, creative director, 1989-90; Keane Advertising, San Jose, CA, founder, 1996-2008; TiVo, Inc., San Jose, manager of marketing communications, 2009—. Writer and illustrator, 1995—.

Awards, Honors

Five Summit Creative Awards, 2002.

Writings

Bobby Bramble Loses His Brain, illustrated by David Clark, Clarion Books (New York, NY), 2009.
Sloppy Joe, illustrated by Denise Brunkus, HarperCollins (New York, NY), 2009.

"JOE SHERLOCK, KID DETECTIVE" SERIES; SELF-ILLUSTRATED

The Haunted Toolshed, HarperCollins (New York, NY), 2006.

The Neighborhood Stink, HarperCollins (New York, NY), 2006.
The Missing Monkey-eye Diamond, HarperCollins (New York, NY), 2006.
The Headless Mummy, HarperCollins (New York, NY), 2007.
The Art Teacher's Vanishing Masterpiece, HarperCollins (New York, NY), 2007.

Adaptations

The Haunted Toolshed, The Neighborhood Stink, and *The Missing Monkey-eye Diamond* were adapted as audio books.

Sidelights

Dave Keane, an award-winning creative director, is also the author of *The Haunted Toolshed, The Neighborhood Stink,* and other works in his self-illustrated "Joe Sherlock, Kid Detective" series of humorous mysteries. Additionally, Keane has a pair of critically acclaimed picture books to his credit: *Bobby Bramble Loses His Brain* and *Sloppy Joe.* Keane notes that the inspiration for his comedic tales come from a variety of sources, remarking on his home page: "Sometimes things in my own life provide good material for the stories I'm writing. Sometimes it's things that interested me when I was a kid. Often I get ideas from funny things that my kids say or do. Sometimes ideas come from books, magazines, newspapers, or movies. The best ideas seem to come from just watching what's going on around you."

In *The Haunted Toolshed* Keane introduces his enthusiastic young sleuth, Joe Sherlock, a student at Baskerville Elementary School. In the work, Joe investigates the strange goings-on at his neighbor's home, including the mysterious disappearance of a bundt cake, a mailbox, and a glass eye. A *Publishers Weekly* critic noted that the "slapstick-laced story of his first case reveals some of Sherlock's bumbling moves, many of which are certainly chuckle-worthy." Joe must track down the canine that befouls a beautiful lawn in *The Neighbor-*

hood Stink, the second work in the series. "The gross-out factor is high in these easy chapter books," Kathleen Meulen reported in *School Library Journal.*

In *Bobby Bramble Loses His Brain,* a young risk-taker notices his mind wandering—literally—after he takes a hard fall and breaks open his skull. Soon, Bobby's friends and neighbors begin a riotous pursuit of his gray matter, which has plans of its own. "Keane's mischievous mind comes out through his demented asides," remarked Daniel Kraus in *Booklist,* and a *Kirkus Reviews* critic noted that the author "keeps the pacing as quick as the wit." An incredibly messy tyke cleans up his act when his family members fall ill with the flu in *Sloppy Joe.* "From start to finish," wrote a contributor in *Publishers Weekly,* "this is good, not-so-clean fun."

Biographical and Critical Sources

PERIODICALS

Booklist, April 15, 2009, Daniel Kraus, review of *Bobby Bramble Loses His Brain,* p. 46.
Kirkus Reviews, April 1, 2009, review of *Bobby Bramble Loses His Brain.*
Publishers Weekly, August 14, 2006, review of *The Haunted Toolshed,* p. 205; June 22, 2009, review of *Sloppy Joe,* p. 43.
School Library Journal, July, 2006, Kathleen Meulen, review of *The Haunted Toolshed* and *The Neigborhood Stink,* both p. 80; June, 2009, Madigan McGillicuddy, review of *Bobby Bramble Loses His Brain,* p. 92; September, 2009, Mary Hazelton, review of *Sloppy Joe,* p. 126.

ONLINE

Dave Keane Home Page, http://www.mrdavekeane.com (May 1, 2010).
Dean Keane Web log, http://www.davekeane.blogspot.com/ (May 1, 2010).*

*   *   *

KELLER, Holly 1942-

Personal

Born February 11, 1942, in New York, NY; married Barry Keller (a pediatrician), June, 1963; children: Corey (daughter), Jesse (son). *Education:* Sarah Lawrence College, A.B., 1963; Columbia University, M.A., 1964; studied printmaking at Manhattanville College; studied illustration at Parsons School of Design. *Hobbies and other interests:* Tennis, travel.

Addresses

Home—New Haven, CT.

Holly Keller (Photograph by Corey Keller. Reproduced by permission.)

Career

Writer. Redding Board of Education, Redding, CT, member and vice chair, 1975-85.

Awards, Honors

Children's Book of the Year designation, Library of Congress, 1983, for *Ten Sleepy Sheep;* Best Book designation, *School Library Journal,* 1984, for *Geraldine's Blanket;* Children's Choice selection, and Child Study Association Children's Book of the Year, both 1987, both for *Goodbye, Max;* Notable Children's Trade Book in the Field of Social Studies selection, National Council for the Social Studies/Children's Book Council (NCSS/CBC), 1989, for *The Best Present;* Fanfare Honor Book designation, *Horn Book,* 1991, for *Horace;* Pick of the Lists, American Booksellers Association, 1991, for *The New Boy,* 1992, for *Island Baby,* and 1994, for *Geraldine's Baby Brother;* Notable Children's Trade Book in the Field of Social Studies selection, NCSS/CBC, 1994, for *Grandfather's Dream.*

Writings

FOR CHILDREN; SELF-ILLUSTRATED

Cromwell's Glasses, Greenwillow (New York, NY), 1982.
Ten Sleepy Sheep, Greenwillow (New York, NY), 1983.
Too Big, Greenwillow (New York, NY), 1983.

Geraldine's Blanket, Greenwillow (New York, NY), 1984.

Will It Rain?, Greenwillow (New York, NY), 1984.

Henry's Fourth of July, Greenwillow (New York, NY), 1984.

When Francie Was Sick, Greenwillow (New York, NY), 1985.

A Bear for Christmas, Greenwillow (New York, NY), 1986.

Lizzie's Invitation, Greenwillow (New York, NY), 1987.

Goodbye, Max, Greenwillow (New York, NY), 1987.

Geraldine's Big Snow, Greenwillow (New York, NY), 1988.

Maxine in the Middle, Greenwillow (New York, NY), 1989.

The Best Present, Greenwillow (New York, NY), 1989.

Henry's Happy Birthday, Greenwillow (New York, NY), 1990.

What Alvin Wanted, Greenwillow (New York, NY), 1990.

Horace, Greenwillow (New York, NY), 1991.

The New Boy, Greenwillow (New York, NY), 1991.

Furry, Greenwillow (New York, NY), 1992.

Island Baby, Greenwillow (New York, NY), 1992.

Harry and Tuck, Greenwillow (New York, NY), 1993.

Grandfather's Dream, Greenwillow (New York, NY), 1994.

Geraldine's Baby Brother, Greenwillow (New York, NY), 1994.

Rosata, Greenwillow (New York, NY), 1995.

Geraldine First, Greenwillow (New York, NY), 1996.

I Am Angela, Greenwillow (New York, NY), 1997.

Merry Christmas, Geraldine, Greenwillow (New York, NY), 1997.

Angela's Top-Secret Computer Club, Greenwillow (New York, NY), 1998.

Brave Horace, Greenwillow (New York, NY), 1998.

Jacob's Tree, Greenwillow (New York, NY), 1999.

What I See, Harcourt Brace (New York, NY), 1999.

A Bed Full of Cats, Harcourt Brace (New York, NY), 1999.

That's Mine, Horace, Greenwillow (New York, NY), 2000.

Geraldine and Mrs. Duffy, Greenwillow (New York, NY), 2000.

Cecil's Garden, Greenwillow (New York, NY), 2002.

Farfallina and Marcel, Greenwillow (New York, NY), 2002.

What a Hat!, Greenwillow (New York, NY), 2003.

The Hat, Harcourt (Orlando, FL), 2005.

Pearl's New Skates, Greenwillow (New York, NY), 2005.

Sophie's Window, Greenwillow (New York, NY), 2005.

Nosy Rosie, Greenwillow (New York, NY), 2006.

Help!: A Story of Friendship, Greenwillow (New York, NY), 2007.

The Van, Harcourt (Orlando, FL), 2008.

Miranda's Beach Day, Greenwillow (New York, NY), 2009.

ILLUSTRATOR

Jane Thayer, *Clever Raccoon,* Morrow (New York, NY), 1981.

Melvin Berger, *Why I Cough, Sneeze, Shiver, Hiccup, and Yawn,* Crowell (New York, NY), 1983.

Roma Gans, *Rock Collecting,* Crowell (New York, NY), 1984.

Franklyn Mansfield Branley, *Snow Is Falling,* Crowell (New York, NY), 1986.

Franklyn Mansfield Branley, *Air Is All around You,* Crowell (New York, NY), 1986.

Patricia Lauber, *Snakes Are Hunters,* Crowell (New York, NY), 1988.

Franklyn Mansfield Branley, *Shooting Stars,* Crowell (New York, NY), 1989.

Patricia Lauber, *An Octopus Is Amazing,* Crowell (New York, NY), 1990.

Paul Showers, *Ears Are for Hearing,* Crowell (New York, NY), 1990.

Barbara Juster Ebensen, *Sponges Are Skeletons,* Harper-Collins (New York, NY), 1993.

Patricia Lauber, *Be a Friend to Trees,* HarperCollins (New York, NY), 1994.

Wendy Pfeffer, *From Tadpole to Frog,* HarperCollins (New York, NY), 1994.

Patricia Lauber, *Who Eats What?: Food Chains and Food Webs,* HarperCollins (New York, NY), 1995.

Patricia Lauber, *You're Aboard Spaceship Earth,* Harper-Collins (New York, NY), 1996.

Wendy Pfeffer, *What's It Like to Be a Fish?,* HarperCollins (New York, NY), 1996.

Stuart J. Murphy, *The Best Bug Parade,* HarperCollins (New York, NY), 1996.

Roma Gans, *Let's Go Rock Collecting,* HarperCollins (New York, NY), 1997.

Nola Buck, *Morning in the Meadow,* HarperCollins (New York, NY), 1997.

Wendy Pfeffer, *Sounds All Around,* HarperCollins (New York, NY), 1999.

Franklyn Mansfield Branley, *Snow Is Falling,* revised edition, HarperCollins (New York, NY), 1999.

Anne Rockwell, *Growing like Me,* Silver Whistle (San Diego, CA), 2001.

Paul Showers, *Hear Your Heart,* HarperCollins (New York, NY), 2001.

Sidelights

Author/illustrator Holly Keller is noted for her penchant for creating animal protagonists, which she draws in a minimalist, flat, cartoon style. While her picture books are entertaining to read, they also have a message, dealing with issues ranging from adoption to fitting in, from sibling relationships to saying farewell to a beloved pet. Keller's endearing characters include Geraldine, the plucky piglet stars of books such as *Geraldine's Blanket, Geraldine First,* and *Geraldine and Mrs. Duffy.* Horace, a whimsical young leopard, is adopted into a family of tigers and his adventures play out in *Horace, Brave Horace,* and *That's Mine, Horace,* while a rambunctious possum named Henry takes center stage in *Too Big, Henry's Fourth of July,* and *Henry's Happy Birthday.* Other popular self-illustrated picture-books by Keller include *Ten Sleepy Sheep, Goodbye, Max, What a Hat!,* and *Sophie's Window.* She has also expanded her writing repertoire to include chapter books featuring a young girl named Angela, who stars in *I Am Angela* and *Angela's Top-Secret Computer Club.*

Keller was born in 1942, in New York City, and was a fan of reading from an early age. Drawing also quickly became an early form of self-entertainment; one of Keller's early projects was copying all the bird illustrations from a book by noted American naturalist illustrator John James Audubon. A school project, translating *Little Red Riding Hood* into Latin and illustrating it, also served as a sort of preview of things to come for Keller, however, when she attended Sarah Lawrence College, she ultimately traded the study of art for a degree in history. At Columbia University, she continued her history studies by earning a master's degree, even though she retained her love of drawing and painting. Married in 1963, Keller soon became the mother of two children and found herself living in rural Connecticut.

When Keller began taking classes in printmaking, she was encouraged to try her hand at children's book illustration. After taking a course in illustration at Parsons School of Design, she put together a portfolio of her works and submitted it to an editor at Greenwillow Press in 1981. For her first assignment, Keller took a week to write her first picture book, *Cromwell's Glasses,* the tale of a young rabbit's anxiety at receiving his first pair of spectacles. Carolyn Noah, reviewing Keller's debut for the *School Library Journal,* noted that "this brief tale thoughtfully treats the difficulties that glasses present to a young child," and concluded that the book would make "a serviceable addition to storytime collections." In *Cromwell's Glasses* Keller exhibits her now-characteristic cartoon-style black ink drawings filled in with watercolor and takes a positive approach to a difficult childhood issue.

Another early work, *Ten Sleepy Sheep,* features a little boy who cannot fall asleep; when he tries counting sheep things get worse because the animals throw a giant party in his room. A critic for *Kirkus Reviews* called the book "neatly done" and "lightly whimsical," while Margery Fisher, writing in *Growing Point,* dubbed it an "elegantly produced picture-book." *Ten Sleepy Sheep* was voted a Library of Congress Children's Book of the Year and firmly established Keller in her new career as a picture-book author and illustrator.

In *Too Big* Henry the possum encounters new-brother problems when baby Jake comes home from the hospital. Each time he tries to join in with Jake's activities—from sucking on a bottle to putting on a diaper—Henry is told that he is too big. Finally the possum begins to realize that he really is too big for babyish things, and a new bike christens his role as official older brother. *Too Big* is "both touching and funny," according to Sarah Wintle in the *Times Literary Supplement.*

In *Henry's Fourth of July* the possum has a great time at a Fourth of July picnic, running a sack race and watching the fireworks. He reappears in *Henry's Happy Birthday,* this time fearing that his fifth birthday is going to be a disaster, especially when his mother insists he wear a shirt and tie to his own party. *Booklist* re-

viewer Ilene Cooper called *Henry's Fourth of July* a "happy introduction" to the national holiday, and *Horn Book* critic Elizabeth S. Watson deemed *Henry's Happy Birthday* an "appealing and refreshingly honest approach to the traditional birthday party story."

Keller introduces readers to a likeable young piglet in *Geraldine's Blanket.* Now old enough to be self-assured, Geraldine realizes that her security blanket needs to be reworked into a more socially acceptable product: like new dresses for her dolls. *Geraldine's Big Snow* finds the piglet bursting with anticipation while awaiting for the first snow of the season. "Geraldine may be a pig," commented Janet Hickman in a review of the book for *Language Arts,* "but her experience with waiting out a weather forecast will be familiar to young children wherever snow falls." Writing in *School Library Journal,* Trev Jones described *Geraldine's Big Snow* as "fresh, appealing, and perfectly delightful."

Geraldine finds herself with a new baby brother named Willie in tow in *Geraldine's Baby Brother,* which explores sibling rivalry. Willie also makes an appearance in *Geraldine First,* doing his best to live up to his responsibility as an annoying little brother by mimicking everything Geraldine says and does. Reviewing *Geraldine's Baby Brother,* Harriett Fargnoli observed in *School Library Journal* that the "expressive pig's appeal remains timeless," while a *Kirkus* reviewer noted that the "whimsical line drawings add to the overall charm" of Keller's "wise, funny, accepting little book." *School Library Journal* contributor Virginia Opocensky

Many of Keller's self-illustrated picture books, such as **Geraldine's Blanket,** *feature her cartoon animal characters.* (Greenwillow Books, 1988. ©1984 by Holly Keller. Reproduced by permission of Greenwillow Books, a division of William Morrow & Company, Inc.)

commented that in *Geraldine First* Keller successfully captures a familiar sibling problem with "understated humor and a satisfying denouement," and also noted that the author's "marvelously minimalist pen-and-watercolor drawings [extend] the story beyond the words."

Her own experience meeting a child troubled by the knowledge that she was adopted inspired Keller to create the award-winning picture book *Horace*. A spotted leopard-cub adoptee, Horace feels out of place with his new family—striped tigers all—especially when all his striped cousins arrive at Horace's first birthday party. Cooper wrote in *Booklist* that while adopted children can identify with Keller's "gentle story," *Horace* also has appeal for children "who simply feel like the odd one out." Anna Biagioni Hart, writing in *School Library Journal,* called "Keller's use of appealing animal characters in a fictional tale . . . a welcome approach" to the difficult issue of adoption.

In *Brave Horace* the leopard cub comes unglued in anticipation of going to his friend's monster-movie party, and in *That's Mine, Horace* he lays claim to a toy truck he "found" on the playground even after his good friend Walter claims to have lost just such a toy. "This sensitive and entertaining picture book is just right for young children," noted Phelan in her *Booklist* review of *Brave Horace,* while *School Library Journal* contributor Jody McCoy called the book a "boon for timid youngsters." Noting that "Keller raises ethical issues that will be easily grasped by young readers," a *Horn Book* contributor praised *That's Mine, Horace* as a picture book containing a "perfectly paced, dramatic story with appealing illustrations and a satisfying resolution."

In addition to her books featuring Henry, Horace, and the irrepressible Geraldine, Keller has also produced a number of standalone picture books. *Goodbye, Max* deals with the death of a pet, and *What a Hat!* illustrates that true tolerance means respecting the harmless quirks of others. In *Cecil's Garden* Keller focuses on the squabbles of three rabbits that are unsure about what seeds to plant in their garden plot until Cecil the rabbit realizes that small disagreements are usually resolved using simple solutions. *Booklist* contributor Gillian Engberg called *Cecil's Garden* a "sunny story about cooperation," while a *Publishers Weekly* reviewer noted that Keller's illustrations for the book "possess a sophisticated color sensibility even as they play up the . . . comedy" in a succession of silly arguments.

Also featuring animal characters, *Farfallina and Marcel* finds a caterpillar and a gosling becoming fast friends, even after they both transform into a more mature phase of life. Calling the book a "deceptively simple story of friendship," a *Publishers Weekly* reviewer deemed Keller's work to be "perfectly paced," while in *Christian Century* a critic praised *Farfallina and Marcel* as a "quietly dramatic and beautifully illustrated" story in which Keller effectively intertwines the rhythms of nature with the strong bonds of true friendship.

More animal friends are the focus of *Help!: A Story of Friendship* and *Nosy Rosie,* while a timid young pigeon who is afraid to fly is the star of *Sophie's Window.* In *Help!* Mouse reacts to a rumor that friend Snake actually prefers to feast on mice by worrying and hiding. When the young rodent tumbles into a deep hole, Snake proves his friendship by rescuing Mouse in a story that features what a *Publishers Weekly* contributor dubbed "an irresistibly insouciant spirit." Caruso the pigeon is blown of his city rooftop and into an open apartment window where he meets a dog named Sophie. Returned to his mother's coop, Caruso musters the strength to return to Sophie's window sill under his own wing power in a story that "will reinforce . . . the wisdom of waiting for the right time to take a new step," according to *Horn Book* contributor Susan Dove Lempke. Rosie the fox uses her strong sense of smell to aid her animal friends, earning the titular nickname in *Nosy Rosy.* Ultimately, the fox's nose leads her to a lost child, and her heroic rescue is brought to life in "simple words and . . . clear line-and-watercolor pictures," according to *Booklist* contributor Hazel Rochman. In *School Library Journal* Kirsten Cutler dubbed the picture book "gentle, simple, and compassionate," while a *Kirkus Reviews* writer dubbed the work a "lovely story" and "a sure pick to share with any youngster struggling with peer issues."

A human child is the main character of *Miranda's Beach Day,* another standalone title both written and illustrated by Keller. Weaving science facts into a gentle story about a girl's event-filled day at the seashore, *Miranda's Beach Day* finds Miranda upset when the rising tide washes away her sand castle. Fortunately, the girl's mother is wise, and she shows how all creatures and things—from little girls and sand shovels to sea birds to crabs, to sea tides to sand castles and sunny days—work together in the engine of life. In *Kirkus Reviews* a writer praised Keller's "reassuring and simple message" and added that her watercolor-and-collage images for *Miranda's Beach Day* feature "breezy patterns" and contrasts that "add movement and depth." In *School Library Journal* Sally R. Dow dubbed the picture book a "disarmingly simple and reassuring" choice for toddler story hours.

In addition to writing and illustrating her own picture books, Keller has also created artwork for stories by other writers, such as Paul Showers, Wendy Pfeffer, and Anne Rockwood. While she initially limited her own writing to short picture-book texts, Keller has expanded into the easy-reader chapter-book format with *I Am Angela* and *Angela's Top-Secret Computer Club.* The first book details five episodes in the life of feisty Angela, including playing softball at camp, visiting the zoo with her Scout troop, creating a class exhibit, and becoming a dog walker. *Booklist* contributor Stephanie Zvirin noted that in *I Am Angela* "there's always some goofy complication in the goings-on to ensure laughs." In *Angela's Top-Secret Computer Club,* after someone breaks in to the school's computer system and misprints all the student report cards, Angela and her computer-whiz friends are called on to solve the mystery before total chaos ensues. In her *Booklist* review, Kay Weisman called *Angela's Top-Secret Computer Club* an "upbeat mystery" and wrote that Keller's entertaining illustrations combine with her creation of an "intrepid heroine" in a book that "hits just the right note" with novice readers.

Biographical and Critical Sources

BOOKS

Authors of Books for Young People, 3rd edition, Scarecrow Press (Metuchen, NJ), 1990.
Children's Books and Their Creators, Houghton Mifflin (Boston, MA), 1995, pp. 363-364.
Children's Literature Review, Volume 45, Gale (Detroit, MI), 1997, pp. 43-61.

PERIODICALS

Booklist, June 15, 1984, Ilene Cooper, review of *Geraldine's Blanket,* p. 1484; April 1, 1985, Ilene Cooper, review of *Henry's Fourth of July,* p. 1120; February 11, 1991, Ilene Cooper, review of *Horace,* p. 1130; May 15, 1997, Stephanie Zvirin, review of *I Am Angela,* p. 1575; September 1, 1997, Carolyn Phelan, review of *Merry Christmas, Geraldine,* p. 139; March 1, 1998, Carolyn Phelan, review of *Brave Horace,* p. 1140; August 19, 1998, Kay Weisman, review of *Angela's Top-Secret Computer Club,* p. 1140; February 15, 2000, Gillian Engberg, review of *Snow Is Falling,* p. 1115; August, 2000, Gillian Engberg, review of *That's Mine, Horace,* p. 2147; March 1, 2001, Hazel Rochman, review of *Growing like Me,* p. 1284; February 1, 2002, Gillian Engberg, review of *Cecil's Garden,* p. 947; September 15, 2002, Hazel Rochman, review of *Farfallina and Marcel,* p. 240; September 15, 2003, Ilene Cooper, review of *What a Hat!,* p. 246; January 1, 2005, Gillian Engberg, review of *Pearl's New Skates,* p. 870; July 1, 2006, Hazel Rochman, review of *Nosy Rosie,* p. 66; April 1, 2009, Randall Enos, review of *Miranda's Beach Day,* p. 44.
Christian Century, December 13, 2003, review of *Farfallina and Marcel,* p. 25.
Growing Point, March, 1984, Margery Fisher, review of *Ten Sleepy Sheep,* p. 4220.
Horn Book, November-December, 1990, Elizabeth S. Watson, review of *Henry's Happy Birthday,* p. 729; July, 2000, review of *That's Mine, Horace,* p. 437; September, 2001, review of *Growing like Me,* p. 615; November-December, 2003, Susan Dove Lempke, review of *What a Hat!,* p. 731; November-December, 2005, Susan Dove Lempke, review of *Sophie's Window,* p. 707; January-February, 2008, Susan Dove Lempke, review of *Help!: A Story of Friendship,* p. 73.
Kirkus Reviews, September 1, 1983, review of *Ten Sleepy Sheep,* p. J150; March 1, 1984, review of *Geraldine's Blanket,* pp. J5-J6; August 15, 1994, review of *Geraldine's Baby Brother,* p. 1131; December 15, 2001, review of *Cecil's Garden,* p. 1759; August 1, 2003, review of *What a Hat!,* p. 1019; August 15, 2006, review of *Nosy Rosie,* p. 844; April 1, 2009, review of *Miranda's Beach Day.*
Language Arts, January, 1989, Janet Hickman, review of *Geraldine's Big Snow,* pp. 65-66.
Publishers Weekly, March 12, 2001, review of *Growing like Me,* p. 88; December 24, 2001, review of *Cecil's Garden,* p. 64; July 29, 2002, review of *Farfallina and Marcel,* p. 71; October 6, 2003, review of *What a Hat!,* p. 84; December 20, 2004, review of *Pearl's New Skates,* p. 58; July 18, 2005, review of *Sophie's Window,* p. 205; September 3, 2007, review of *Help!,* p. 57.
School Library Journal, March, 1982, Carolyn Noah, review of *Cromwell's Glasses,* p. 136; February, 1989, Trev Jones, review of *Geraldine's Big Snow,* p. 72; April, 1991, Anna Biagioni Hart, review of *Horace,* p. 97; August, 1994, Harriett Fargnoli, review of *Geraldine's Baby Brother,* p. 133; May, 1996, Virginia Opocensky, review of *Geraldine First,* p. 93; April, 1998, Jody McCoy, review of *Brave Horace,* p. 102; May, 2000, Kay Bowles, review of *Snow Is Falling,* p. 160; June, 2000, Marianne Saccardi, review of *That's Mine, Horace,* p. 116; April, 2001, Judith Constantinides, review of *Growing like Me,* p. 134; March, 2002, Karen Scott, review of *Cecil's Garden,* p. 190; October, 2002, Maryann H. Owen, review of *Farfallina and Marcel,* p. 114; October, 2003, Leanna Manna, review of *What a Hat!,* p. 128; February, 2005, Blair Christolon, review of *Pearl's New Skates,* p. 104; August, 2005, Maryann H. Owen, review of *Sophie's Window,* p. 98; September, 2006, Kirsten Cutler, review of *Nosy Rosie,* p. 176; September, 2007, Mary Jean Smith review of *Help!,* p. 166; April, 2009, Sally R. Dow, review of *Miranda's Beach Day,* p. 108.
Times Literary Supplement, September 30, 1983, Sarah Wintle, review of *Too Big,* p. 1050.

ONLINE

HarperCollins Web site, http://www.harpercollins.com/ (June 13, 2010), "Holly Keller."*

* * *

KELLY, Jacqueline

Personal

Born in New Zealand; immigrated to Canada, then United States; daughter of Brian and Noeline Kelly; married Robert Duncan. *Education:* M.D.; University of Texas, J.D.

Addresses

Home and office—P.O. Box 301300, Austin, TX 78703. *Agent*—Marcy Posner, Folio Literary Management, 505 8th Ave., New York, NY 10018. *E-mail*—jackie.callie@sbcglobal.net.

Career

Physician, attorney, and author. Works as a physician. Presenter at schools.

Member

Society of Children's Book Writers and Illustrators, Authors Guild, Writers' League of Texas.

Awards, Honors

Newbury Honor Book designation, International Reading Association Award, Virginia Law Award, Daughters of the Republic of Texas, and Judy Lopez Memorial Award, National Women's Book Association, all 2009, and Josette Frank Award, Bank Street College of Education, 2010, all for *The Evolution of Calpurnia Tate*.

Writings

The Evolution of Calpurnia Tate, Henry Holt (New York, NY), 2009.

Contributor of short fiction to *Mississippi Review*.

Sidelights

Jacqueline Kelly worked as a doctor and a lawyer before following her dream and becoming a fiction writer. Born in New Zealand, Kelly and her family immigrated to Vancouver Island off the coast of British Columbia, Canada when she was young. Several years later, a second family move landed her in El Paso, Texas, where she completed high school and then went on to attend college. After graduating from medical school, Kelly worked as a physician, and then earned her law degree at the University of Texas. Work as an attorney was challenging, but ultimately unfulfilling, however. Kelly eventually transformed her love of writing fiction into a profession when she published her first short story in the *Mississippi Review* in 2001, eight years before *The Evolution of Calpurnia Tate* became her first published book.

In her young-adult novel *The Evolution of Calpurnia Tate* Kelly introduces readers to a bright and energetic eleven year old who lives in the small town of Fentress, Texas. The year is 1899 and Calpurnia (called Callie Vee) is the middle child and only girl among seven siblings. Fascinated with the natural world around her, Callie Vee rejects the corseted life of a proper young lady and spends much of her free time noting her observations of bugs, animals, plants, and river life in her Scientific Notebook. She is encouraged by her curmudgeonly grandfather, an educated amateur naturalist who introduces the preteen to the work of Charles Darwin, author of the groundbreaking and controversial *The Origin of Species*.

Calling Callie Vee "an instantly classic literary heroine," Jessica Rae Patton added in *E* magazine that *The Evolution of Calpurnia Tate* highlights how Darwin's

Cover of Jacqueline Kelly's middle-grade novel **The Evolution of Calpurnia Tate,** *featuring artwork by Beth White.* (Henry Holt & Company, 2009. Jacket illustration © 2009 by Beth White. Reproduced by permission.)

theory of evolution and "the notion of women in the sciences were [viewed as suspect] at the turn of the [twentieth] century." In *Horn Book,* Elissa Gershowitz also praised Kelly's fiction debut, writing that the novel introduces "a memorable, warm, spirited young woman who's refreshingly ahead of her time," while in *School Library Journal* Jennifer Schultz observed that Kelly "mix[es] gentle humor and pathos to great extent" in her "charming and inventive story." In *Booklist* Carolyn Phelan cited the "wry humor and . . . sharp eye for details" that are evidenced in *The Evolution of Calpurnia Tate,* and a *Kirkus Reviews* writer predicted that "readers will finish this witty, deftly crafted debut novel rooting for 'Callie Vee.'"

Biographical and Critical Sources

PERIODICALS

Booklist, May 1, 2009, Carolyn Phelan, review of *The Evolution of Calpurnia Tate,* p. 80.
E, July-August, 2009, Jessica Rae Patton, review of *The Evolution of Calpurnia Tate,* p. 47.

Horn Book, September-October, 2009, Elissa Gershowitz, review of *The Evolution of Calpurnia Tate,* p. 565.

Kirkus Reviews, April 1, 2009, review of *The Evolution of Calpurnia Tate.*

New York Times Book Review, June 14, 2009, Julie Just, review of *The Evolution of Calpurnia Tate,* p. 13.

Publishers Weekly, May 4, 2009, review of *The Evolution of Calpurnia Tate,* p. 51.

School Library Journal, May, 2009, Jennifer Schultz, review of *The Evolution of Calpurnia Tate,* p. 110.

ONLINE

Cynthia Leitich Smith Web log, http://cynthialeitichsmith. blogspot.com/ (May 15, 2010), interview with Kelly.

Jacqueline Kelly Home Page, http://www.jacquelinekelly. com (May 15, 2010).

*   *   *

KELSEY, Marybeth

Personal

Born in Arcadia, IN; married; children: three sons. *Education:* Indiana University, degree.

Addresses

Home—Bloomington, IN. *Agent*—Wendy Schmalz Agency, Box 831, Hudson, NY 12534.

Career

Writer. Owner of Moon Stones (jewelry store), Bloomington, IN. Has also worked as a telephone operator, hospital nurse, scriptwriter, and a writer of retail banking news.

Member

Society of Children's Book Writers and Illustrators.

Awards, Honors

One Hundred Titles for Reading and Sharing selection, New York Public Library, 2008, and Best Children's Book of the Year designation, Bank Street College of Education, 2009, both for *Tracking Daddy Down.*

Writings

NOVELS

Tracking Daddy Down, Greenwillow Books (New York, NY), 2008.

A Recipe 4 Robbery, Greenwillow Books (New York, NY), 2009.

Sidelights

Marybeth Kelsey is the author of two well-received novels for middle-grade readers, *Tracking Daddy Down* and *A Recipe 4 Robbery.* In the former, Kelsey tells the story of Billie Wisher, a spunky but sensitive eleven-year-old girl who learns that her ne'er-do-well father is on the run after robbing a bank. Although her father has often been absent from her life, Billie still clings to the hope that their relationship can be healed, and she becomes determined to locate him before the police do. Renee Steinberg, reviewing *Tracking Daddy Down* in *School Library Journal,* stated that Kelsey's tale "of adventure, family, love, and trust is a testament to how strong a child's need for fatherly attention . . . can be."

A Recipe 4 Robbery centers on Lindy Lou Phillips, who makes a most unusual discovery while attending a local festival. While dining on a plate of stewed cucumbers prepared by her neighbor, Granny Goose, Lindy spies a valuable locket in the gloppy meal. The youngster soon learns that the jewelry was stolen from the home of Mrs. Grimstone just days earlier, and that Granny is now a prime suspect. With her friends Margaret and Gus, Lindy sets out to prove Granny's innocence. "The novel is full of likable characters and fun twists and turns," Beth Cuddy wrote in *School Library Journal,* and a critic in *Kirkus Reviews* remarked that Kelsey's story "moves along at a good clip, [and is] narrated by Lindy with plenty of folksy humor."

Biographical and Critical Sources

PERIODICALS

Booklist, May 1, 2009, Carolyn Phelan, review of *A Recipe 4 Robbery,* p. 43.

Bulletin of the Center for Children's Books, June, 2009, Deborah Stevenson, review of *A Recipe 4 Robbery,* p. 404.

Kirkus Reviews, April 1, 2009, review of *A Recipe 4 Robbery.*

School Library Journal, December, 2008, Renee Steinberg, review of *Tracking Daddy Down,* p. 128; July, 2009, Beth Cuddy, review of *A Recipe 4 Robbery,* p. 86.

ONLINE

Mary Beth Kelsey Home Page, http://marybethkelsey.com (June 1, 2010).

Mary Beth Kelsey Web log, http://marybethkelsey. livejournal.com (June 1, 2010).*

KILWORTH, Garry 1941-
(Garry D. Kilworth, Garry Douglas Kilworth, F.K. Salwood)

Personal

Born July 5, 1941, in York, England; son of George (a Royal Air Force sergeant) and Joan (a bookkeeper) Kilworth; married Annette Bailey (a therapist and social worker); children: Richard, Chantelle. *Education:* King's College London, M.A. (English literature; with honors), 1975.

Addresses

Home—Ipswich, England. *Agent*—Maggie Noach, 21 Redan St., London; Ralph Vicinanza, 111 8th Ave., New York, NY 10011. *E-mail*—vequince@googlemail.com.

Career

Novelist and author of children's books. Royal Air Force, sergeant cryptographer worked on making and breaking codes in Singapore, Maldives, Germany, Aden, Bahrain, Kenya, Malta, and Cyprus, 1956-74; Cable & Wireless, London, England, executive, 1974-82; fiction writer, beginning 1977.

Awards, Honors

Gollancz/London *Sunday Times* Best Science Fiction Prize for a Short Story, 1974, for "Let's Go to Golgotha!"; (with Robert Holdstock) World Fantasy Award for Best Novella, 1992, and British Science Fiction Association Award, 1994, both for *The Ragthorn;* Carnegie Medal commendation, British Library Association, 1992, for *The Drowners;* World Fantasy Award nomination, 1994, for *Hogfoot Right and Bird Hands;* Children's Book of the Year Award, Lancashire County Library/National Westminster Bank, 1995, for *The Electric Kid;* Charles Whiting Award for Literature, 2008, for *Rogue Officer;* shortlisted for other literary awards, including Carnegie Medal.

Writings

FOR CHILDREN AND YOUNG ADULTS

The Wizard of Woodworld, Collins (London, England), 1987.

The Voyage of the Vigilance, Armada (London, England), 1988.

The Rain Ghost, Scholastic (London, England), 1989.

Dark Hills, Hollow Clocks: Stories from the Otherworld, Methuen (London, England), 1990.

The Third Dragon, illustrated by Mel Bramich, Hippo (London, England), 1991.

The Drowners, Methuen (London, England), 1991.

Billy Pink's Private Detective Agency, Methuen (London, England), 1993.

Garry Kilworth (Photograph by Annette Kilworth. Reproduced by permission.)

The Phantom Piper, Methuen (London, England), 1994.

(As Garry D. Kilworth) *The Electric Kid,* Bantam (New York, NY), 1994.

The Brontë Girls, Methuen (London, England), 1995.

Cybercats, Bantam (New York, NY), 1996.

The Raiders, Mammoth (London, England), 1996.

The Gargoyle, illustrated by Dan Williams, Heinemann (London, England), 1997.

Heavenly Hosts v. Hell United ("Epix" series), illustrated by Mark Oliver, Mammoth (London, England), 1998.

The Drummer Boy, Mammoth (London, England), 1998.

The Lantern Fox, illustrated by Chris Chapman, Mammoth (London, England), 1998.

Hey, New Kid!, illustrated by Stephen Player, Mammoth (London, England), 1999.

Soldier's Son ("Victorian Flashbacks" series), A. & C. Black (London, England), 2001.

Monster School, illustrated by Scoular Anderson, A. & C. Black (London, England), 2002.

Nightdancer, Dolphin (London, England), 2002.

Spiggot's Quest ("Knights of Liofwende" series), Atom (London, England), 2002.

Mallmoc's Castle ("Knights of Liofwende" series), Atom (London, England), 2003.

Boggart and Fen ("Knights of Liofwende" series), Atom (London, England), 2004.

The Silver Claw, Corgi Children's (London, England), 2005.

Attica, Atom (London, England), 2006.

Jigsaw, Atom (London, England), 2007.

The Hundred-towered City, Atom (London, England), 2008.

"WELKIN WEASELS" SERIES; MIDDLE-GRADE NOVELS

Thunder Oak, Corgi (London, England), 1997.

Castle Storm, Corgi (London, England), 1998.

Windjammer Run, Corgi (London, England), 1999.

Gaslight Geezers,, Corgi (London, England), 2001.

Vampire Voles,, Corgi (London, England), 2002.

Heastward Ho!,, Corgi (London, England), 2003.

FOR ADULTS; NOVELS

In Solitary, Faber & Faber (London, England), 1977.

The Night of Kadar, Faber & Faber (London, England), 1978.

Split Second, Faber & Faber (London, England), 1979.

Gemini God, Faber & Faber (London, England), 1981.

Theatre of Timesmiths, Gollancz (London, England), 1984.

Witchwater Country, Bodley Head (London, England), 1986.

Spiral Winds, Bodley Head (London, England), 1987.

Cloudrock, Unwin Hyman (London, England), 1988.

Abandonati, Unwin Hyman (London, England), 1988.

Hunter's Moon: A Story of Foxes, Unwin Hyman (London, England), 1989.

In the Hollow of the Deep-Sea Wave, Bodley Head (London, England), 1989.

Midnight's Sun, Unwin Hyman (London, England), 1990.

Standing on Shamsan, HarperCollins (London, England), 1992.

Frost Dancers: A Story of Hares, HarperCollins (London, England), 1992.

Angel, Gollancz (London, England), 1993, Forge (New York, NY), 1996.

(As Garry D. Kilworth) *Archangel,* Gollancz (London, England), 1994.

House of Tribes, Bantam (London, England), 1995.

The Roof of Voyaging (part one of "Navigator Kings" trilogy), Little, Brown (Boston, MA), 1996.

A Midsummer's Nightmare, Bantam (New York, NY), 1996.

The Princely Flower (part two of "Navigator Kings" trilogy), Little, Brown (Boston, MA), 1997.

Land-of-Mists (part three of "Navigator Kings" trilogy), Little, Brown (Boston, MA), 1997.

Shadow-hawk, Orbit (London, England), 1999.

ADULT NOVELS; AS GARRY DOUGLAS

Highlander (novelization of SF film), Grafton (London, England), 1986.

The Street, Grafton (London, England), 1988.

ADULT NOVELS; AS F.K. SALWOOD

The Oystercatcher's Cry, Headline Books (London, England), 1993.

The Saffron Fields, Headline Books (London, England), 1994.

The Ragged School, Headline Books (London, England), 1995.

"JACK CROSSMAN" NOVEL SERIES; AS GARRY DOUGLAS KILWORTH

(As Garry Douglas) *The Devil's Own* (historical novel), HarperCollins (London, England), 1997, published under name Garry Douglas Kilworth, Robinson (London, England), 2002.

The Valley of Death: Sergeant Jack Crossman and the Battle of Balaclava, HarperCollins (London, England), 1998.

Soldiers in the Mist, HarperCollins (London, England), 2000.

The Winter Soldiers, Constable (London, England), 2002, Carroll & Graf (New York, NY), 2003.

Attack on the Redan, Carroll & Graf (New York, NY), 2003.

Brothers of the Blade: Lieutenant Fancy Jack Crossman in India, Constable (London, England), 2004.

Rogue Officer, Severn House (Sutton, England), 2007.

Kiwi Wars, Severn House (Sutton, England), 2008.

OTHER

The Songbirds of Pain: Stories from the Inscape, Gollancz (London, England), 1984.

Tree Messiah (poetry), Envoi Poets (Newport, England), 1985.

In the Country of Tattooed Men (stories), HarperCollins (London, England), 1993, new edition, introduction by Brian Aldiss, Humdrumming (Bournemouth, England), 2006.

Hogfoot Right and Bird-Hands (stories), Edgewood Press, 1993.

Moby Jack and Other Tall Tales, introduction by Robert Holdstock, PS Publishing (Hornsea, England), 2006.

Contributor of stories to anthologies, including *Haunting Christmas Tales,* Scholastic, 1991, and to periodicals, including *Fantasy and Science Fiction, Interzone, Ad Astra,* and *Ambit.*

Author's works have been translated into fifteen languages.

Adaptations

The Drowners was adapted for a cassette tape by Chivers Audio, 1993; *Billy Pink's Private Detective Agency* was adapted for broadcast on BBC television's *Jackanory*; *The Winter Soldiers* was adapted as an audiobook, narrated by Terry Wale, Soundings Audiobooks, 2002.

Sidelights

Garry Kilworth joined the Royal Air Force as a young man, serving around the world for over fifteen years. After retiring from the British military and completing a business course, he became a senior executive at an international telecommunications company, but left a few years later to become a full-time writer. Beginning by writing for adults, the prolific Kilworth published science fiction, mystery, fantasy, military historical, horror, and family sagas before turning to younger readers with his novel *The Wizard of Woodworld*. Kilworth's many books for children and teens include standalone novels and multi-book series. Ranging in subject from ghosts to the Brontë sisters to a secret fantasy world, children's books continue to constitute a significant part of Kilworth's growing body of work. As he noted in *Books for Keeps,* "I believe writing for children to be more important than writing for adults. The formative years are a long, heady period in anyone's life, and writers who deal in them must do so with care . . . without appearing to preach or demand."

Kilworth was born in 1941, "to itinerant low-income parents, themselves from trawler fishing/farm labourer stock," as he once told *SATA*. His earliest childhood memories include both family adventures and near tragedies. Kilworth and his family were almost swept away in the floods of 1953 in southeastern England; while neighbors just across the road were drowned, the Kilworths were rescued by launch seven hours after their house was totally inundated. With his father a sergeant in the Royal Air Force (RAF), Kilworth attended over twenty schools while growing up and was raised partly in southern Arabia. There he and a school friend became lost in the Hadrahmaut Desert and were stranded without water for two days before they were finally located by an RAF rescue team.

As a child, Kilworth was heavily influenced by the writing of British author Richmal Crompton, herself an author of over forty books for adults, but forever remembered in England for her "William Brown" series, about the mid-century adventures of an adolescent boy. Kipling and Twain were other childhood favorites of Kilworth and the works of these authors instilled in him a lasting love for wit, adventure, and the well-turned phrase.

Kilworth left public school at age fifteen to attend RAF Training School, joining the force three years later as a senior aircraft telegraphist. Fifteen years later he left the RAF with the rank of sergeant cryptographer, having served in Europe, Africa, the Middle East, and on a remote coral island in the Maldives. During those years he also served as an RAF corporal "for the bloody withdrawal of British troops" from Aden in 1966-67, and found himself fighting against former Arab schoolmates. It was, Kilworth once explained to *SATA,* "a very disturbing and unhappy experience which still haunts me." Once retired from the RAF, Kilworth attended Southwest London Polytechnic, where he took a diploma in business studies. He then joined England's Cable & Wireless as an executive, travelling frequently to the United States and the Caribbean during the eight years he was with the company.

Kilworth still found time for his writing, and he was twenty years old when he completed his first full-length novel, a yet-unpublished children's book. He worked to perfect his craft, and in 1974 one of his science-fiction short stories won a prestigious British prize. Three years later Kilworth's novel *In Solitary* was published by Faber & Faber. He stayed with adult science fiction through a few more titles; then, as he later explained, "my natural bent took me towards the retelling of old mythologies and the inventing of new." Among these are animal fantasies, Polynesian tales, and a reworking of William Shakespeare's *A Midsummer Night's Dream.*

Kilworth's military background comes to the fore in his historical war novels, such as *The Devil's Own, The Winter Soldier,* and *Attack on the Redan,* which are set during the Crimean War and are part of his "Jack Crossman" novel series. Inspired by his home in rural

Jigsaw, *Kilworth's 2008 novel, mixes fantasy, science fiction, and mystery in its story of two brothers living on an exotic island.* (Atom/Little, Brown, 2008. Corbis, cover photographer. Reproduced by permission.)

England, Kilworth also writes what he calls "County Sagas," using the pen name F.K. Salwood, his grandmother's maiden name, while his novels *Angel* and *Archangel* mix police procedural with supernatural thriller in a saga about a pyromaniac who may or may not be an angelic avenger.

One of Kilworth's early teen novels, *The Rain Ghost,* uses the frame of a traditional ghost story to tell a story of alienation, peer pressure, and old-fashioned romance. Steve Winston, a teenager, is lost in the mountains on a school outing. While hunkering down in the bog to await rescue, Steve discovers an ornate antique dagger tangled in the heather. Strange feelings lead him to research the dagger, and this brings Steve to realize that he actually pulled the knife from the mummified fingers of one of an ancient tribe of Rain Warriors who were slaughtered on the mountain. That long-dead warrior is now haunting him. Susan R. Farber, writing in *Voice of Youth Advocates,* called *The Rain Ghost* "a nice horror story which has plenty of suspense but is not too terrifying."

A collection of ten tales, *Dark Hills, Hollow Clocks: Stories from the Otherworld* is geared for teens and includes "The Goblin Jag," "Warrior Wizards," "The Sleeping Giants," "The Hungry Ghosts," and "The Orkney Trows," among others. Killworth's stories are "told with exceptional imagination and verve," according to a *Junior Bookshelf* critic, while Margery Fisher concluded in *Growing Point* that the author's "almost conversational tone . . . makes for pleasurable reading while inventive plots and the constant reminiscences of true folk-tale give to this sparkling collection a certain justification."

Kilworth's award-winning *The Drowners* is another tale full of adventure and somewhat arcane knowledge, this time of an historical sort. "A fascinating byway of history," according to a *Junior Bookshelf* critic, the novel is set in the English county of Hampshire in the first half of the nineteenth century. The drowners of the title are actually early irrigation engineers who found that they could use a complicated system of sluices and channels to release the waters of a local river, flood the land in a controlled manner, and provide the conditions for grazing cattle that would allow them to get the herd to market early for the best prices. Tim, the youthful apprentice to the Master Drowner, is himself drowned while attempting to save a lady from the waters. Other complications follow: the absentee landlord is jealous of the other men's cattle and sends a tough to set matters right in Hampshire. Before the Master Drowner can teach Jem, the new apprentice, the complicated craft of "drowning," he also dies. Then Tim's ghost returns, helping local farmers and also teaching Jem how to control the flooding. The reviewer for *Junior Bookshelf* asserted that *The Drowner* "is a splendidly gripping story."

One of Kilworth's strengths as a writer is his ability to create the unexpected and give voice to the little known. His tales always feature an element of adventure, a holdover from the sort of book he enjoyed reading as a youth. In his novel *The Phantom Piper,* for example, the adults in the Scottish Highlands village of Canlish answer the call of a phantom piper to take to the hills, leaving their children behind to run the village and their own lives. The piper's appearance is the result of a tragic event: four centuries earlier, the village was decimated by a warring tribe after the efforts of a local piper to raise the alarm went unheeded. For a time the children of Canlish do well on their own. Then comes the arrival of Tyler and McFee, travelers who have been trapped in the snow. Their arrival introduces evil into the village, and now the children are on a desperate search for the music which will recall their parents and rid them of the two interlopers. A reviewer for *Junior Bookshelf* dubbed *The Phantom Piper* "a tense and frightening suspense story" featuring "fully rounded" characters and a theme that is an "affirmation of the human spirit."

The Electric Kid was inspired by the rubbish heaps in Manila, where Kilworth witnessed homeless children fighting over who will take first grab at the new trash.

Cover of Kilworth's middle-grade novel The Electric Kid, *featuring artwork by Greg Couch.* (Jacket illustration © 1995 by Greg Couch. Reproduced by permission of Orchard Books, an imprint of Scholastic, Inc.)

It is a harsh world in the year 2061 as Blindboy and Hotwire team up to survive the twenty-first century from their home in the city dump. Blindboy has compensatory hearing; he can hear so acutely as to pick up electronic impulses under mountains of trash. Hotwire, a girl, is something of an electronic genius and an expert at re-wiring discarded electronic wares for resale. What serve as survival skills for the two kids become a hot commodity for the crime syndicate, which kidnaps the pair and forces Blindboy and Hotwire to use their skills in perpetrating crime. "It's a thriller, a survival story, and science fiction all rolled into one tightly developed adventure," commented Heather McCammond-Watts in a review of *The Electric Kid* for the *Bulletin of the Center for Children's Books.* Sarah Guille, writing in *Horn Book,* noted that Kilworth's "action-filled tale, dripping with atmosphere, will please fans of sci-fi and detective stories alike," and in the *Voice of Youth Advocates* Jill Western dubbed *The Electric Kid* a "fast-paced and exciting book" and "a good choice for reluctant readers." An award-winning title in England as well as a break-through book for Kilworth in the United States, *The Electric Kid* was followed up with a sequel, *Cybercats,* which details the further adventures of Hotwire and Blindboy.

In *The Brontë Girls* Kilworth blends his interest in history and fantasy. His tale features the three remarkable Brontë sisters—Emily, Anne, and Charlotte—as the eighteenth-century writers live on a farm in the twentieth century. Past and present soon collide and ultimately force the reader to decide which of the two eras and societies are best. Kilworth originally planned the book as an adult title, but could not place it because it did not fit tidily into a genre box, so he subsequently sold it as a YA title, writing it exactly as if it were intended for the adult market. A *Books for Keeps* critic, in its review of the novel, noted that *The Brontë Girls* presents readers with a "thought-provoking reality."

Attica takes readers even further into the realm of fantasy through his story of three step-siblings. While exploring the new house chosen as the home of their blended family, Chloe, Alex, and Jordy discover that an overhead trap door is actually a portal into a dusty, shadowy, and strange world. In Attica the landscape is formed of cast-off objects ranging from coat hangers and manual typewriters to worn wooden boards and water tanks. As the three children realize, Attica is also a hostile place, and they encounter sinister creatures shaped like old dress forms while search for a way to return to their own world. Calling *Attica* "a rare find," Krista Hutley added in *Booklist* that "Kilworth doesn't skimp on his characterization or story."

Appraising the state of modern literature, Kilworth maintains that the hard and fast lines of genre and categories in adult fiction have ruined individuality in many writers, whereas the writer of children's literature is free simply to tell a story however he or she feels it should be told. Thus far, the smaller world of children's books has allowed for more autonomy. "Long may it remain uncontaminated," Kilworth concluded in *Books for Keeps.*

Biographical and Critical Sources

PERIODICALS

Booklist, January 1, 1996, Frances Bradburn, review of *The Electric Kid,* p. 814; May 15, 1996, Jennifer Henderson, review of *Angel,* p. 1572; May 1, 2006, Ray Olson, review of *Moby Jack and Other Tall Tales,* p. 77; September 1, 2007, Patty Engelmann, review of *The Rogue Officer,* p. 56; September 1, 2009, Patty Engelmann, review of *Kiwi Wars,* p. 48; April 15, 2009, Krista Hutley, review of *Attica,* p. 42.

Bookseller, December 16, 2005, Caroline Horn, interview with Kilworth, p. 27.

Books for Keeps, January, 1996, review of *The Brontë Girls,* p. 11; September, 1996, Garry Kilworth, "My Pal William Brown," pp. 6-7.

Bulletin of the Center for Children's Books, November, 1995, Heather McCammond-Watts, review of *The Electric Kid,* p. 95.

Horn Book, May-June, 1996, Sarah Guille, review of *The Electric Kid,* p. 336.

Junior Bookshelf, December, 1990, review of *Dark Hills, Hollow Clocks: Stories from the Otherwood,* p. 297; December, 1991, review of *The Drowners,* p. 264; December, 1994, review of *The Phantom Piper,* pp. 228-229.

Kirkus Reviews, December 15, 2002, review of *The Winter Soldiers,* p. 1791; September 1, 2003, review of *Attack on the Redan,* p. 1092; April 1, 2009, review of *Attica.*

Magazine of Fantasy and Science Fiction, July, 1996, Charles de Lint, review of *Angel,* p. 36.

Publishers Weekly, January 20, 2003, review of *The Winter Soldiers,* p. 56; August 11, 2008, review of *Kiwi Wars,* p. 28.

Voice of Youth Advocates, October, 1990, Susan R. Farber, review of *The Rain Ghost,* p. 229; December, 1995, Jill Western, review of *The Electric Kid,* p. 316.*

*   *   *

KILWORTH, Garry D.
See KILWORTH, Garry

*   *   *

KILWORTH, Garry Douglas
See KILWORTH, Garry

L

LEAL, Ann Haywood

Personal

Born in WA; daughter of teachers; married; husband's name Andy; children: Jessica, Holly. *Education:* B.A. (psychology and education); M.A. (education). *Hobbies and other interests:* Martial arts, running, playing guitar.

Addresses

Home—Waterford, CT. *Agent*—Daniel Lazar, Writers House, 21 W. 26th St., New York, NY 10010. *E-mail*—ann@annhaywoodleal.com.

Career

Teacher and writer. Teacher of first grade in Waterford, CT. Teacher of kickboxing and karate; community volunteer.

Member

Society of Children's Book Writers and Illustrators, Authors Guild.

Writings

Also Known as Harper, Henry Holt (New York, NY), 2009.
A Finders-Keepers Place, Henry Holt (New York, NY), 2010.

Sidelights

In her middle-grade novel *Also Known as Harper* Ann Haywood Leal captures the life of a budding writer, something she knows a great deal about. While growing up, Leal spent much of her time writing stories, often weaving characters modeled on family members into her fiction. She wrote her first novel in the sixth grade, and continued to write in her spare time while earning her teaching credential and starting a career as an elementary-school teacher. *Also Known as Harper* was inspired by Leal's work at a soup kitchen near her home in southern Connecticut, where she was confronted by the homelessness that confronts many families in crisis.

Named after writer Harper Lee, author of *To Kill a Mockingbird,* the heroine of *Also Known as Harper* uses poetry to express her feelings about the difficulties she and her family experiences when her alcoholic father abandons them after a new child is stillborn. Mama is now left with bills she cannot pay, and eviction from their home soon follows. The Morgan family is now forced to move into a small, run-down motel. Although fifth grader Harper had hoped to compete in her school's upcoming poetry contest, her mother must now go to work full time and relies on Harper to stay in the motel with her little brother, Hemingway. Surprisingly, the characters Harper meets at her new home prove to be an inspiration to the young writer, even as she worries about missing the chance to share her verses with her schoolmates.

While noting that the plot of *Also Known as Harper* contains "familiar elements," Ilene Cooper added in her *Booklist* review that Leal's novel features "sharply and sympathetically drawn" characters. Harper's poetry, in a "clear and natural" style, "will speak to readers and make them think," Cooper added. Calling Harper an "inspiring" young heroine, a *Publishers Weekly* critic added that the novel is enriched by "complex characters from various walks of life, and in *Kirkus Reviews* a critic deemed Leal's work "a poignant debut" that "will keep readers . . . enthralled." According to *School Library Journal* contributor Terrie Doric, *Also Known as Harper* is full of "realistic individuals whom readers will root for and celebrate with when their lives finally begin to improve."

"I have never known a time when I wasn't either dreaming of or working on a story," Leal told *SATA.* "I come from a long line of artists and musicians, and my parents knew early on that I wasn't myself if I wasn't either reading or creating a book of some kind. My grand-parents were singers and musicians and had a vaudeville act in the twenties. My mother was a beautiful painter, my father plays a mean saxophone, one of my brothers plays bass, and my other brother is a graphic designer. But I thought I was the first writer in the family. I didn't find out until just a short while ago how wrong I was.

"My cousin called one day last summer. 'I have some-thing for you,' she said. She wouldn't tell me what it was. All she would say was, 'I think it belongs to you.'

"She brought over an old brown manuscript box, tied with a piece of twine. It was our great-grandmother's stories! My great-grandmother, Ella, had been a hard-working farm woman in Washington State. That box contained three full manuscripts, typed and complete, and included several handwritten rough drafts. I always write story ideas and notes on any available scrap of paper, and I saw right away that so did she! A set of notes is written on the back of a milk receipt dated No-vember, 1933.

"Ella died before I could meet her, but I wish more than anything I could talk to her now. I don't know that she ever ventured much further than her dairy farm, but her stories are full of action and intrigue. I wonder if she ever dreamed of finding a publisher. But most of all, I wonder if she'd ever though that eighty years later, her great-granddaughter would be reading and cherishing her stories, and writing a few of her own."

Biographical and Critical Sources

PERIODICALS

Booklist, March 1, 2009, Ilene Cooper, review of *Also Known as Harper,* p. 43.
Kirkus Reviews, April 1, 2009, review of *Also Known as Harper.*
Publishers Weekly, May 25, 2009, review of *Also Known as Harper,* p. 58.
School Library Journal, June, 2009, Terrie Dorio, review of *Also Known as Harper,* p. 128.

ONLINE

Ann Haywood Leal Home Page, http://www.annhaywood leal.com (May 15, 2010).
Ann Haywood Leal Web log, http://www.annhaywoodleal. blogspot.com (May 31, 2010).
Class of 2k9 Web site, http://classof2k9.com/ (May 15, 2010), "Ann Haywood Leal."

*   *   *

LEIJTEN, Aileen

Personal

Born in Belgium; immigrated to United States; married John Rocco (a children's book illustrator and author);

Aileen Leijten (Reproduced by permission.)

children: one daughter. *Education:* California Institute of the Arts, degree (film animation). *Hobbies and other interests:* Reading, crafts.

Addresses

Home—Brooklyn, NY. *Agent*—Elizabeth Harding, Cur-tis Brown, Ltd., 10 Astor Pl., New York, NY 10003. *E-mail*—aileen@aleijten.com.

Career

Film animator, author, and artist. Freelance animator in Los Angeles, CA, for twelve years, with clients includ-ing Walt Disney Imagineering, Starbright Foundation, and Digital Domain; author and illustrator of picture books, beginning 2004.

Awards, Honors

Golden Kite Honor award, and Bank Street College Best Books designation, both 2009, for *Bella and Bean* by Rebecca Kai Dotlich.

Writings

SELF-ILLUSTRATED

Hugging Hour!, Philomel Books (New York, NY), 2009.

ILLUSTRATOR

Debbie Bertram and Susan Bloom, *City Hall: The Heart of Los Angeles,* Tallfellow Press (Los Angeles, CA), 2003.

Rebecca Kai Dotlich, *Bella and Bean,* Atheneum Books for Young Readers (New York, NY), 2009.

Sidelights

Belgian-born artist Aileen Leijten came to the United States to learn the art of film animation and worked in that field for more than a decade. A move from Los Angeles, California, to New York City in 2004 inspired Leijten to change her career goals—as did her marriage to artist and author John Rocco—and she now focuses her time on illustrating books for children. In 2009 she produced her first original picture-book text, pairing her story with original art to create *Hugging Hour!*

In *Hugging Hour!* a young girl named Drew (but called by her nickname "Drool") takes an important step toward independence when she spends her first night at Grandma's house. Missing her parents and unfamiliar with the new environment, Drool is gradually won over by the many wonderful things at Grandma's house, including Kip the chicken and tasty treats like fried ice cream, waffles, and marzipan cake. Praising the book's "cheerful, patterned artwork," which mixes "whimsical, comical details" and "familiar . . . settings," Shelle Rosenfeld added in *Booklist* that *Hugging Hour!* charms young readers with a beehive-hairdo-wearing granny who is "appealingly playful, indulgent, creative, and loving." While noting that the story is slightly overlong, a *Publishers Weekly* critic recommended *Hugging Hour!* for its "loopy worldview and comic earnestness," while a *Kirkus Reviews* writer praised the "winning intimacy" of the story and the "soft, subtly modulated" pencil and water-color images.

As an illustrator, Leijten has created artwork for Rebecca Kai Dotlich's award-winning picture book *Bella and Bean.* Focusing on the best-friendship between two mice who are as different as different can be, the picture book inspired a *Publishers Weekly* contributor to note that "Leijten . . . draws readers in immediately with her offbeat whimsy." A *Kirkus Reviews* critic, also reviewing the book, cited the engaging pairing of "lovely images and language play" in *Bella and Bean.*

Biographical and Critical Sources

PERIODICALS

Booklist, February 1, 2009, Shelle Rosenfield, review of *Hugging Hour!,* p. 46.

Bulletin of the Center for Children's Books, January, 2009, Deborah Stevenson, review of *Hugging Hour!,* p. 207; May, 2009, Jeannette Hulick, review of *Bella and Bean,* p. 358.

Kirkus Reviews, January 15, 2009, review of *Bella and Bean;* November 15, 2008, review of *Hugging Hour!*

Publishers Weekly, January 5, 2009, reviews of *Bella and Bean* and *Hugging Hour!,* both p. 48.

ONLINE

Aileen Leijten Home Page, http://www.aleijten.com (May 15, 2010).

Aileen Leijten Web log, http://aileen leijten.blogspot.com (May 15, 2010).

*   *   *

LEMNA, Don 1936-

Personal

Born 1936, in Canada; married; wife's name Deanna. *Hobbies and other interests:* Reading, music, planting flowers.

Addresses

Home—Canada.

Career

Writer. Canadian Armed Forces, career officer; retired as lieutenant colonel.

Writings

A Visit from Mr. Lucifer, Western Producer Prairie Books (Saskatoon, Saskatchewan, Canada), 1984.

Bubsy, illustrated by Sally J.K. Davies, Riverwood Publishers (Sharon, Ontario, Canada), 1993.

When the Sergeant Came Marching Home, illustrated by Matt Collins, Holiday House (New York, NY), 2008.

Has published both plays and children's books in Canada.

Sidelights

Canadian-born Don Lemna served in the Canadian Armed Forces, retiring as a lieutenant colonel. At that time, he began a second career as a writer, having discovered that his hobbies alone were insufficient to fill his days. In Canada, he has published works including *A Visit from Mr. Lucifer. When the Sergeant Came Marching Home,* an elementary-grade novel, was released in the United States in 2008.

When the Sergeant Came Marching Home, which is illustrated by Matt Collins, tells the story of a ten-year-old boy named Donald, who suddenly finds his life turned on its head when his father, a sergeant, returns from World War II. Reunited with his family, the sergeant moves them to a broken-down shack on a farm in the middle of rural Montana. Modern conveniences are left behind nof, for their new home has neither electricity nor running water. Angry and disappointed, Donald decides that the only answer is to run away, so he begins to make plans to leave for Hollywood. Life gets in the way, however, as Donald and his little brother start to discover aspects of their new home that they actually like. There is a horse on the farm that they can ride, and on the neighbor's land in the winter there is a frozen area that serves as a skating arena for ice hockey. They also get a dog, who makes a wonderful new companion for their adventures.

Told from Donald's point of view, *When the Sergeant Came Marching Home* recounts the boy's gradual acceptance of his new way of life and illustrates how rural surroundings help him tap his imagination. Donald describes the necessary work, as well, talking about the farm and all of the chores required to keep it running smoothly. As Donald gradually adjusts to his new life, he also begins to calm down in relation to his father. Bethany A. Lafferty, in a review for *School Library Journal,* noted that "the mood is light and playful throughout [*When the Sergeant Came Marching Home,*] with appropriately serious moments marking the maturity that Donald gains." *Booklist* contributor Hazel Rochman deemed the novel "timeless, each chapter resembling a short story, often with a quiet kick at the end," while a *Kirkus Reviews* writer concluded that "Lemna's first American publication is a welcome addition to the transplanted-city-boy genre."

Biographical and Critical Sources

PERIODICALS

Booklinks, July 1, 2008, Hazel Rochman, review of *When the Sergeant Came Marching Home,* p. 55.

Booklist, April 15, 2008, Rochman, review of *When the Sergeant Came Marching Home,* p. 57.

Bulletin of the Center for Children's Books, July 1, 2008, Elizabeth Bush, review of *When the Sergeant Came Marching Home.*

Kirkus Reviews, April 1, 2008, review of *When the Sergeant Came Marching Home.*

School Library Journal, July 1, 2008, Bethany A. Lafferty, review of *When the Sergeant Came Marching Home,* p. 103.*

*   *   *

LOVEGROVE, James 1965-
(Jay Amory, J.M.H. Lovegrove)

Personal

Born December 24, 1965, in Lewes, East Sussex, England; married; wife's name Lou; children: Monty, Theo. *Education:* Attended Radley College; St. Catherine's College Oxford, M.A. (English literature).

Addresses

Home—Eastbourne, Sussex, England. *E-mail*—jljimilu@aol.com.

Career

Novelist, beginning c. 1990.

Awards, Honors

Arthur C. Clarke Award shortlist, 1998, for *Days;* (with Peter Crowther) Bram Stoker Award nomination, and British Fantasy Society Award nomination, both for *The Hand That Feeds;* John W. Campbell Memorial Award shortlist, 2004, for *Untied Kingdom.*

Writings

FICTION

The Hope, Macmillan (London, England), 1990, White Wolf (Clarkston, GA), 1996.

(With Peter Crowther) *Escardy Gap,* Tor Books (New York, NY), 1996.

Days, Phoenix (England), 1998.

The Web: Computopia, Dolphin (England), 1998.

(As J.M.H. Lovegrove) *Krilov Continuum* (volume one in "Guardians" series), Gollancz (London, England), 1998.

(As J.M.H. Lovegrove) *The Berserker* (volume two in "Guardians" series), TV Books (New York, NY), 1999.

(With Peter Crowther) *The Hand That Feeds,* Maynard Sims Productions [England], 1999, included in *Foursight,* Gollancz (London, England), 2000.

The Foreigners, Gollancz (London, England), 2000.

How the Other Half Lives (novella), Millennium (London, England), 2000.

Imagined Slights (short-story collection), Gollancz (London, England), 2002.

Untied Kingdom, Gollancz (London, England), 2003.

Gig (novella), PS Publishing [England], 2004.

Worldstorm, Gollancz (London, England), 2004.

Provender Gleed, Gollancz (London, England), 2005.

Dead Brigade, Barrington Stoke (Edinburgh, Scotland), 2007.

The Age of Ra, Solaris (Oxford, England), 2009.

The Age of Zeus, Solaris (Oxford, England), 2010.

Contributor to anthology *Web 2028,* Millennium Books (England), 1999. Contributor of short fiction to periodicals, including *Crimewave.*

Author's work has been translated into several languages, including French, German, Italian, Japanese, Portuguese, Swedish, and Welsh.

MIDDLE-GRADE NOVELS

Wings, illustrated by Ian Miller, Barrington Stoke (Edinburgh, Scotland), 2001.

The House of Lazarus, Barrington Stoke (Edinburgh, Scotland), 2003.

Ant God, Barrington Stoke (Edinburgh, Scotland), 2005.

Cold Keep, Barrington Stoke (Edinburgh, Scotland), 2006.

Kill Swamp, Barrington Stoke (Edinburgh, Scotland), 2007.

Free Runner, Barrington Stoke (Edinburgh, Scotland), 2009.

"CLOUDED WORLD" SERIES; YOUNG-ADULT FANTASY NOVELS; UNDER NAME JAY AMORY

The Fledgling of Az Gabrielson, Gollancz (London, England), 2006.

Pirates of the Relentless Desert, Gollancz (London, England), 2007.

The Wingless Boy (includes *The Fledging of Az Gabrielson* and *Pirates of the Relentless Desert*), Gollancz (London, England), 2008.

Darkening for a Fall, Gollancz (London, England), 2008.

Empire of Chaos, Gollancz (London, England), 2008.

The Clouded World (includes *Darkening for a Fall* and *Empire of Chaos*), Gollancz (London, England), 2008.

"LORDS OF PAIN" SERIES; YOUNG-ADULT FANTASY NOVELS

The Lord of the Mountain, Barrington Stoke (Edinburgh, Scotland), 2010.

The Lord of the Void, Barrington Stoke (Edinburgh, Scotland), 2010.

The Lord of Tears, Barrington Stoke (Edinburgh, Scotland), 2010.

The Lord of the Typhoon, Barrington Stoke (Edinburgh, Scotland), 2010.

The Lord of Fire, Barrington Stoke (Edinburgh, Scotland), 2010.

OTHER

Contributor of reviews to periodicals, including *Financial Times.*

Sidelights

British author James Lovegrove's interest in writing transformed into a career track while he was attending Oxford University when one of his short stories won a college prize. After graduation he gave himself two years to write and successfully market a novel, and he accomplished this goal when *The Hope* was written, edited, and accepted for publication in two months flat. Ranging in focus from science fiction to fantasy to horror, Lovegrove now writes for a broad spectrum of readers, from adults to preteens, and his books have been praised for their entertaining plots, compelling characters, and the knowledge and research that underlies his stories.

The Hope is set on a gigantic ship, measuring five miles by two miles by one mile that has been sailing the oceans of the world for thirty years, never reaching port and never contacting another vessel. The passengers of *The Hope* are divided between the first-class ticket holders who occupy the upper levels of the ship, and the others, who berth precariously in the ship's lower regions. "Law is non-existent," Chris Gilmore asserted in the *St. James Guide to Horror, Ghost, and Gothic Writers,* "and order local at best." Although Lovegrove's book might in some ways be considered science fiction, it was classified by Gilmore as a horror story because the focus is more on the relationship between the ship's passengers and crew—all of whom are deranged to a degree—than on the condition of the ship itself. The *Hope,* added Gilmore, "recalls the [ill-fated cruise ship] *Titanic* in its layout, technology and class-structure. In mood it recalls the most angst-ridden passages of Brian Aldiss's *Non-Stop,* for its voyage is endless and purposeless, its construction a grandiose act of folly which beggared the billionaire whose hubris sponsored it, and who hanged himself as it set sail for the first and only time."

One of several collaborations between Lovegrove and writer/publishers Peter Crowther, *Escardy Gap* is set in "an explicitly fictional small town created by a nameless Manhattan writer," according to a *Publishers Weekly* reviewer. The town, a typically 1950s Midwestern hamlet, is visited by "a mysterious troupe of sideshow performers cut from the same cloth as Ray Bradbury's Cooger and Dark Traveling Pandemonium Show," the reviewer explained. According to a *Kirkus Reviews* contributor, the "old, self-pitying, burned-out Manhattan novelist" narrating the novel loses his planned storyline to the mayhem brought by Jeremiah Rackstraw, the leader of the troupe, and his companions. Members of The Company, as the troupe is known, "are deceptively pleasant before they begin maiming, disemboweling, or poisoning the innocent people who welcome them into their homes," the critic added. The putative heroine, Sara Sienkiewicz, and her male counterpart, Josh Knight, prove at first unable to deal with the troupe—in part because the narrator becomes jealous of their relationship and tries to keep Sara for himself. Although the *Publishers Weekly* reviewer maintained that Crowther and Lovegrove "pad the story with underdeveloped subplots and extended descriptions of characters and their quirks," the *Kirkus Reviews* contributor concluded by describing *Escardy Gap* as "lighthearted butchery, an intermittently lively dance around the maypole staged in an abattoir."

In *Provender Gleed* Lovegrove mixes word puzzles with "a lighthearted satire on the cult of the rich and famous," according to *School Library Journal* contributor Jackie Cassada. In the story, the young head of a powerful and influential dynasty is kidnaped and a pair of clever investigators must work quickly to assure that the man's fate is not a tragic one. The future is also the setting of *The Age of Ra,* which finds the pantheon of

Egyptian gods reining supreme: each god has a following among one or more regions, and the god's power grows as it gains more human worshipers. When a group of paratroopers arrive in the desert, they reach Freegypt, where a masked man called Lightbringer is determined to force the Egyptian gods from power. Readers who enjoy thoughtful and provocative futuristic stories will appreciate the "quirky and fascinating" story Lovegrove relates in *Provender Gleed,* Cassada noted, while in *Publishers Weekly* a contributor wrote that *The Age of Ra* weighs "social commentary on religion, family, love and war" on the scales balancing "theocracy [rule by gods] and humanism."

With his 2001 novel *Wings,* Lovegrove began to write for a young teen audience, particularly reluctant readers who would only turn the pages of a book if they were hooked by a compelling story. In the years since, he has continued to alternate books such as *Wings* with adult novels, entertaining younger readers with *The House of Lazarus, Ant God,* and the futuristic *Cold Keep,* all of which feature teen characters who bravely confront threats of epic proportions.

Under the pen name Jay Amory, Lovegrove has also penned the "Clouded World" series, which includes the novels *The Fledging of Az Gabrielson, Pirates of the Relentless Desert, Darkening for a Fall,* and *Empire of Chaos.* In the series opener, readers are introduced to the Clouded World, in which generations of humans living in cities built above the clouds have adapted by developing wings. Life here is sustained by elevators that bring food and other much-needed supplies up from the earth's surface, a place where the less-fortunate Groundlings toil. When the elevators begin arriving empty, sixteen-year-old Az Gabrielson is elected to go down to the surface and find out why. Az is the perfect choice to "pass" for a Groundling—he was born without wings. He discovers another way of life on the surface, a life full of conflict and hardship but also one of challenges and excitement. In *School Library Journal* Kristin Anderson noted that Lovegrove/Amory's novel transitions between science fiction and "a steampunk odyssey" in which "chases and explosions make for an action-filled read."

Biographical and Critical Sources

BOOKS

St. James Guide to Horror, Ghost, and Gothic Writers, St. James Press (Detroit, MI), 1998.

PERIODICALS

Kirkus Reviews, July 15, 1996, review of *Escardy Gap.*

Library Journal, August, 1996, Susan Hamburger, review of *Escardy Gap,* p. 119; January 1, 2007, Jackie Cassada, review of *Provender Gleed,* p. 100.

Publishers Weekly, July 29, 1996, review of *Escardy Gap,* p. 72; June 1, 2009, review of *The Age of Ra,* p. 38.

School Librarian, winter, 2006, Alison A. Maxwell-Cox, review of *The Fledging of Az Gabrielson,* p. 203; spring, 2009, Chris Brown, review of *The Clouded World,* p. 48.

School Library Journal, March, 2009, Kristin Anderson, review of *The Fledging of Az Gabrielson,* p. 104.

Times Literary Supplement, February 9, 1990, Peter Reading, review of *The Hope,* p. 149.

Voice of Youth Advocates, October, 2008, Sarah Flowers, review of *The Fledging of Az Gabrielson,* p. 326; December, 2009, Sarah Flowers, review of *Pirates of the Relentless Desert,* p. 417.

ONLINE

James Lovegrove Home Page, http://www.jameslovegrove. com (June 3, 2010).

Jay Amory Web site, http://www.jayamory.com (June 1, 2010).

*   *   *

LOVEGROVE, J.M.H.
See LOVEGROVE, James

M

MARINO, Nan

Personal

Born in Massapequa Park, NY; married. *Education:* Earned master's degrees in library science and education. *Hobbies and other interests:* Reading.

Addresses

Home—NJ. *Agent*—Rosemary Stimola, Stimola Literary Studio, 306 Chase Ct., Edgewater, NJ 07020. *E-mail*—nanmarino@yahoo.com.

Career

Librarian and author. Works as a librarian in NJ. Has also worked for a university, a public relations firm, a magazine publishing company, and an investment bank.

Member

Society of Children's Book Writers and Illustrators.

Awards, Honors

Golden Kite Award Honor Book for Fiction, Society of Children's Book Writers and Illustrators, 2010, and Best of the Best selection, Chicago Public Library, both for *Neil Armstrong Is My Uncle and Other Lies Muscle Man McGinty Told Me.*

Writings

Neil Armstrong Is My Uncle and Other Lies Muscle Man McGinty Told Me, Roaring Brook Press (New York, NY), 2009.

Contributor to *Authors Now!* Web site. Also contributor of scholarly articles to periodicals; contributor of short fiction to *Storyworks.*

Nan Marino (Reproduced by permission.)

Adaptations

Neil Armstrong Is My Uncle and Other Lies Muscle Man McGinty Told Me was adapted as an audio book, Brilliance Audio, 2009.

Sidelights

In her debut work, the middle-grade novel *Neil Armstrong Is My Uncle and Other Lies Muscle Man McGinty Told Me,* librarian and author Nan Marino explores the relationship between a lonely ten year old and the foster child who moves into her neighborhood.

Born and raised in Massapequa Park, New York, a suburb of Long Island, Marino longed for adventure as a child. "I was a daydreamer. And I wanted what I had in my dreams," she noted on her home page. "I spent a great part of my childhood searching for secret passages and magical places." Although she envisioned herself becoming a diplomat, a chef, or an architect, Marino graduated from college with degrees in library science and education, and then began penning stories. While serving as a librarian in New Jersey, she wrote what would become her first published novel. "I love writing," she remarked. "It's the perfect occupation for daydreamers. You can stare out the window. You can imagine. And you can share your dreams."

Set on Long Island during the summer of 1969, *Neil Armstrong Is My Uncle and Other Lies Muscle Man McGinty Told Me* centers on Tamara Ann Simpson, a sensitive youngster who feels distanced from her parents and whose best friend, Kebsie Grobser, has just moved away. When Douglas McGinty moves into a foster home down the street, Tamara comes to resent the scrawny boy who spins outrageous yarns, sarcastically dubbing him "Muscle Man," and she vows to expose his lies to the rest of her neighbors.

Critics offered praise for Marino's novel, particularly her fully realized portrait of Tamara. The author "paints a detailed portrait of the seeming gulf that surrounds a person after loss," observed Bethany Isaacson in *School Library Journal,* and Hazel Rochman, writing in *Booklist,* called it "rare to have a story told with sympathy from the view point of a bully." A critic in *Kirkus Reviews* also complimented Marino's ability to accurately capture the time period in *Neil Armstrong Is My Uncle and Other Lies Muscle Man McGinty Told Me,* stating that the details of 1960s life "combine with a poignant plot to reveal a depth unusual in such a straightforward first-person narrative."

Biographical and Critical Sources

PERIODICALS

Booklist, April 15, 2009, Hazel Rochman, review of *Neil Armstrong Is My Uncle and Other Lies Muscle Man McGinty Told Me,* p. 54.

Kirkus Reviews, April 1, 2009, review of *Neil Armstrong Is My Uncle and Other Lies Muscle Man McGinty Told Me.*

School Library Journal, June, 2009, Bethany Isaacson, review of *Neil Armstrong Is My Uncle and Other Lies Muscle Man McGinty Told Me,* p. 130.

ONLINE

Macmillan Web site, http://us.macmillan.com/ (May 1, 2010), "Nan Marino."

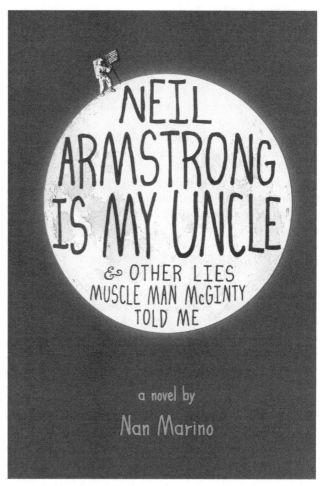

Cover of Marino's middle-grade novel **Neil Armstrong Is My Uncle and Other Lies Muscle Man McGinty Told Me** *which focuses on a summer of baseball and childhood rivalries.* (Roaring Brook Press, 2009. Reproduced by permission.)

Nan Marino Home Page, http://www.nanmarino.com (May 1, 2010).

Nan Marino Web log, http://nanmarino.blogspot.com (May 1, 2010).

*   *   *

MARRIOTT, Zoë 1982-
(Zoë Davina Marriott)

Personal

Born April 7, 1982.

Addresses

E-mail—zoe.marriott@ntlworld.com.

Career

Writer. Works as a civil servant.

Writings

The Swan Kingdom, Walker Books (London, England), 2007, Candlewick Press (Cambridge, MA), 2008.

Daughter of the Flames, Candlewick Press (Cambridge, MA), 2009.

Sidelights

British fantasy novelist Zoë Marriott first became interest in writing when she was a child. Marriott was afraid to sleep alone so her mother bought her *The Magic Faraway Tree* by Enid Blyton to help take her mind off of her fear. In addition to making her a reader, Blyton's story also influenced Marriott to become a writer. She began making her own books by copying pages from the published stories of others, then wrote her own story, an imaginative tale about a party held by a rabbit and a pig.

Based on Hans Christian Andersen's classic story "The Wild Swans," Marriott's first novel, *The Swan Kingdom,* tells the tale of Alexandra, a princess whose mother, the queen, is attacked by a beast in the woods. Although Alexandra has magical powers like her mother, she cannot save the queen, whose demise leads the king into despair as he spends all his time trying to track down the beast. Then one day he returns from a trip with a beautiful woman named Zella, who charms everyone but Alexandra and her brothers. The siblings believe that the woman is really a shape-shifting beast who is responsible for her mother's death. The king nevertheless marries Zella, and Alexandra is banished while her brothers are transformed into swans. As Alexandra grows older, her power becomes stronger and she eventually sets out to save her family and the kingdom.

Marriott's "use of language is distinctive and impressive," wrote Claire Rosser in a review of *The Swan Kingdom* for *Kliatt. School Library Journal* contributor Donna Rosenblum deemed the novel "well written with vivid details,"adding that the "rich tale has a little something for everyone—love, adventure, intrigue, betrayal, friendship, and murder." "Marriott's retelling . . . will certainly satisfy fans of Andersen's tale," wrote Norah Piehl in *Teenreads.com,* the critic adding that the author "skillfully weaves together elements of the original fairy story into her more complex narrative, making them suitable for a young adult narrative." A *Kirkus Reviews* contributor noted that "abundant visual details create richly evocative settings, and emotional connection is clear and tender."

Marriott's second fantasy novel, *Daughter of the Flames,* once again features a young heroine. The Rua people have been conquered by the Seedorne, people with a very different culture and religion. Zahira was an orphan raised by the Ruas and taught to hate the occupiers and to follow the Rua's religion. However, when the young woman now loses her adopted family and home due to violent upheavals in her land, she learns about her true origins as a Sedorne and sets out to bring about peace between the occupiers and the occupied. In the process, Zahira raises the ire of the Rua people,

who suspect her of treachery; this suspicion grows stronger when she falls in love with a Sedorne nobleman.

Citing *Daughter of the Flames* for its "complex history of civil war, racial struggles, and religious beliefs," *Booklist* contributor Debbie Carton added that Marriott's second novel serves up "a satisfying read for fantasy lovers." Also praising the story, John Lloyd commented on the *Bookbag* Web site that *Daughter of the Flames* "contains some good adventure . . ., is well peopled by the lead characters . . ., and also disarms us at times with things happening before we might expect, or just never predict in a thousand years."

Marriott once commented: "From a very young age I loved books and stories and idolized writers, who seemed like almost mythical beings to me (since I had never met or even seen one in real life). When I realized that I could tell stories too—that I really had the ability to create my own magical world just like the ones inside the pages of the books I borrowed from my local library—it changed my life. From that moment on, I never considered any other profession.

"All the books that I love have a huge influence on my writing, though mostly indirectly. Jane Austen and Agatha Christie probably have as much to answer for in my work as Garth Nix and Tamora Pierce, despite the fact that I write fantasy. However, my second novel was directly inspired by Diana Wynne Jones' nonfiction book *The Tough Guide to Fantasyland,* as I was driven to try and rework the fantasy clichés that she listed. Jones is an enduring delight to me, though her books and mine couldn't really be more different."

Of her writing process, Marriott stated: "It seems to change with every book, though some things stay the same. Mostly it begins when two or more unrelated things collide in my head (say, a character I've been toying with for a while and a setting that recently came to life in my imagination) and something lights up. At that point I try to scribble down as much detail as I can—often in the form of bullet points. Those scribbled notes are put away until I've finished whatever I'm already working on (because inspiration never strikes at a convenient time) and when they are retrieved I try to see if there's enough there for a plot to grow around. If there is, it's normally immediately apparent. The light comes back, brighter than ever, and I'll get a deluge of ideas that, again, I scribble down desperately as they begin to form into a story. This is my initial synopsis, but much of it may never actually make it into the book. It's really just trying to pin everything down so that the vital bits don't wriggle away. By the time I finish the synopsis I've become 'locked on' to this story, and that's when the notebook comes out. I have a collection of over fifty blank notebooks now, all of them different and waiting for 'their' book. I pick the right one based on my feelings about the story, and staple the rough synopsis into the front. From that moment on everything relating to the book goes in there—cut out pictures, research, snatches of dialogue that occur to me, sketches of characters, ideas and notes and, finally, when everything has formed together, I begin writing the story itself in the notebook. That book goes with me everywhere (onto the bus, into the dentist's waiting room, to parties, everywhere). It's especially important that it goes with me to my part-time job, because I try to write during my tea and lunch breaks. Whatever I've written during the day is typed up onto my laptop that evening or on my next day off, and is rewritten and re-drafted as it's typed. When I've gotten the full first draft down (though really it's the second draft by then, because of all the changes as I was typing) I put it aside for as long as I can bear to (my record is one week) and then get to my favorite part, which is revising. I print the whole manuscript out and go through it as quickly as I possibly can, picking out everything from spelling mistakes and typos to whole scenes that need to be removed, rewritten or rearranged. When all those changes are made in the electronic version it goes straight to my agent via e-mail before I can chicken out."

"My favorite book is always the one I'm working on right now, because I'm still full of hope and enthusiasm that I can make it match the vision in my head—and also because if I don't love it I won't be able to stand working on it every day for the next year. Once it leaves me, I have to sort of cut that love off, or I'll never be able to handle any of the editorial process. I'm proud of my finished works, but I don't yet have the necessary distance to love them. All I can see is all the things I wish I had done better."

"I hope my books bring people happiness," Marriott concluded. "That's all I want to achieve when I write—to give someone else the same joy that my favorite writers give me."

Biographical and Critical Sources

PERIODICALS

Booklist, January 1, 2008, Carolyn Phelan, review of *The Swan Kingdom,* p. 63; February 15, 2009, Debbie Carton, review of *Daughter of the Flames,* p. 71.

Bulletin of the Center for Children's Books, April, 2008, April Spisak, review of *The Swan Kingdom,* p. 343; May, 2009, Kate McDowell, review of *Daughter of the Flames,* p. 371.

Kirkus Reviews, January 15, 2008, review of *The Swan Kingdom.*

Kliatt, March, 2008, Claire Rosser, review of *The Swan Kingdom,* p. 17.

Publishers Weekly, January 28, 2008, review of *The Swan Kingdom,* p. 69.

School Librarian, autumn, 2007, Susan Elkin, review of *The Swan Kingdom,* p. 162.

School Library Journal, August, 2008, Donna Rosenblum, review of *The Swan Kingdom,* p. 130; August, 2009, Emily R. Brown, review of *Daughter of the Flames,* p. 110.

Voice of Youth Advocates, June, 2008, Leah Sparks, review of *The Swan Kingdom,* p. 162; April, 2009, Ann Welton, review of *Daughter of the Flames,* p. 66.

ONLINE

Bookbag, http://www.thebookbag.co.uk/ (October 24, 2008), John Lloyd, review of *Daughter of the Flames.*

Teenreads.com, http://www.teenreads.com/ (October 24, 2008), Norah Piehl, review of *The Swan Kingdom.*

Walker Books Web site, http://www.walker.co.uk/ (October 24, 2008), "Zöe Marriott."

Zoë Marriott Home Page, http://www.zoemarriott.com (June 10, 2010).

*   *   *

MARRIOTT, Zoë Davina
See MARRIOTT, Zoë

*   *   *

McGHEE, Holly M.
See DURAND, Hallie

*   *   *

MEBUS, Scott 1974-

Personal

Born November 28, 1974. *Education:* Attended Wesleyan University.

Addresses

Home—New York, NY. *Agent*—David Dunton, Harvey Klinger Inc., 301 W. 53rd St., New York, NY 10019.

Career

Television producer, music producer, writer, editor, novelist, playwright, and composer. Producer for Music Television (MTV) and Video Hits One (VH1), New York, NY; freelance writer. Performed as a stand-up comedian and with BAD SAM comedy performance group. Artist-in-residence, RPI University, 1998.

Writings

FOR CHILDREN

Gods of Manhattan, Dutton Juvenile (New York, NY), 2008.

The Hidden Light, Dutton Children's Books (New York, NY), 2008.

Spirits in the Park (sequel to *Gods of Manhattan*), Dutton Children's Books (New York, NY), 2009.

OTHER

Booty Nomad (adult novel), Miramax Books (New York, NY), 2003.

The Big Happy (adult novel; sequel to *Booty Nomad*), Miramax Books (New York, NY), 2006.

Author of plays, including *Tarnish* (rock musical), performed at International Fringe Festival.

Sidelights

Scott Mebus is a writer, television and music producer, and stand-up comedian who lives in New York City. He published his debut novel, *Booty Nomad,* in 2003, and has produced a sequel, *The Big Happy,* as well as entertaining younger readers with his young-adult novel *The Hidden Light* and the books in his "Gods of Manhat-

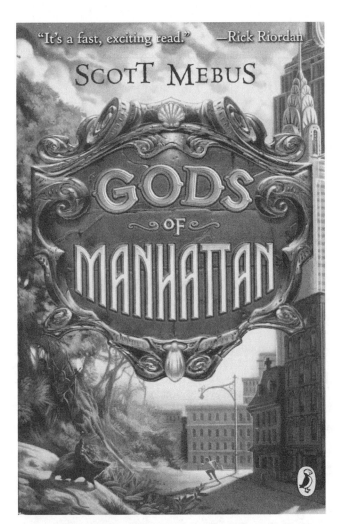

Cover of Scott Mebus's supernatural-tinged middle-grade adventure **Gods of Manhattan,** *featuring artwork by Brandon Dorman.* (Puffin Books, 2008. Cover art ©2008 by Brandon Dorman. Reproduced by permission.)

tan" trilogy of middle-grade novels. As a producer for MTV and VH1, Mebus has worked on projects such as *The Tom Green Show* and *The Real World.* He has also composed musical scores for MTV, VH1, and the Discovery Channel.

Mebus's interest in the arts began when he was a teenager; he first published his writing in the school newspaper. At age sixteen, he co-composed a theme song for a local theater, earning his first commission as a songwriter. As he grew older, Mebus continued to develop as an entertainer and writer, crafting plays and performing comedy.

In *Booty Nomad* Mebus follows twenty-something television producer David Holden, who breaks up with his girlfriend and begins to navigate the Manhattan dating scene. Featuring a mix of comedy, romance, and fiction that is designed to appeal to a predominantly male audience, *Booty Nomad* contains "flashes of sharp urban observation," according to a *Publishers Weekly* contributor. While *Booklist* contributor John Green found the novel to be "marred by awkward plot devices and gags that fall flat, it proves to have a surprisingly big heart (and the slapstick is often very funny)."

David Holden returns in *The Big Happy* and now he is falling for the neurotic Janey while trying to sabotage his friend Annie's wedding to Josh, a man David refers to as "Rat Boy." The novel's title refers to David's search for a state of perfect contentment. Allison Block, reviewing *The Big Happy* for *Booklist,* opined that "fans of the first novel will want to follow the story."

In *Gods of Manhattan,* Mebus changes course, transfixing younger readers with a tale of a spirit world named Mannahatta that coexists alongside modern Manhattan. When thirteen-year-old Rory Hennessy begins seeing Mannahatta after a magician's trick sparks an earthquake, he and his little sister, Bridget, find themselves entering the strange world. Here everyone who is worth remembering still lives, from notables such as Alexander Hamilton and Babe Ruth to famous criminals such as Captain Kidd. Mannahatta is also populated by several strange creatures, and here cockroaches are respected animal warriors. Rory and Bridget soon learn that all is not right in Mannahatta, however, as the world's heroes have lost their luster and the Munsee tribe—Manhattan's original residents—are caged in a place called the Trap. Learning that he is a Light, a rare human who is able to see this spirit world, the teen sets about trying to help the displaced Native American spirits.

Citing the first "Gods of Manhattan" novel for its "surprising depth and freshness," *Kliatt* contributor Cara Chancellor added that Mebus creates "historical characters who . . . are far more interesting than their dry, textbook counterparts." A *Kirkus Reviews* contributor called *Gods of Manhattan* an "uncommonly entertaining crossover debut," while in *Booklist* Krista Hutley cited the author's "comic timing and sense of absurdity."

Rory and Bridget return in *Spirits in the Park* as they attempt to find out why the Munsee people are entering the real world and haunting Manhattan's Central Park. As Rory researches the history of the Mannahatta tribe, he learns that the spiritual unrest will not end until a centuries-old wrong is set right. Reviewing *Spirits in the Park, School Library Journal* contributor Cara von Wrangel Kinsey remarked that Mebus "builds to a hectic and satisfying conclusion" in a story that will appeal to both lovers of fantasy and "history buffs."

Biographical and Critical Sources

PERIODICALS

Booklist, November 15, 2003, John Green, review of *Booty Nomad,* p. 576; April 15, 2006, Allison Block, review of *The Big Happy,* p. 29; May 15, 2008, Krista Hutley, review of *Gods of Manhattan,* p. 59.
Journal of Adolescent and Adult Literacy, October, 2009, Hannah Jarvis, review of *Gods of Manhattan,* p. 181.
Kirkus Reviews, December 15, 2003, review of *Booty Nomad,* p. 1417; March 15, 2006, review of *The Big Happy,* p. 257; March 1, 2008, review of *Gods of Manhattan.*
Kliatt, May, 2008, Cara Chancellor, review of *Gods of Manhattan,* p. 13.
Publishers Weekly, February 2, 2004, review of *Booty Nomad,* p. 61; April 10, 2006, review of *The Big Happy,* p. 43.
School Library Journal, April, 2008, Sharon Rawlins, review of *Gods of Manhattan,* p. 146; September, 2009, Cara von Wrangel Kinsey, review of *Spirits in the Park,* p. 167.

ONLINE

Dark Fantasy Web site, http://www.darkfantasy.org/ (January 15, 2008), Amanda Kilgore, review of *Gods of Manhattan.*
Green Man Review Online, http://www.greenmanreview.com/ (June 5, 2008), Christopher White, review of *Gods of Manhattan.*
Nerve Web site, http://www.nerve.com/ (June 5, 2008), interview with Mebus.
Scott Mebus Home Page, http://www.scottmebus.com (June 1, 2010).
SF Site, http://www.sfsite.com/ (June 1, 2010), Nathan Brazil, review of *Gods of Manhattan.**

*　　　*　　　*

MICHAEL, Jan 1947-

Personal

Born 1947, in Yorkshire, England. *Education:* Attended college.

Addresses

Home—Amsterdam, Netherlands; Settle, North Yorkshire, England.

Career

Novelist and literary agent.

Awards, Honors

Vlag en Wimpel award (Netherlands).

Writings

Flying Crooked: A Story of Cancer, Acceptance, and Hope (memoir), Greystone Books (Berkeley, CA), 2005.
Leaving Home (adult novel), Andersen (London, England), 2008.
City Boy (middle-grade novel), Clarion Books (New York, NY), 2009.

Also author of adult novels *The Lost Lover* and *Amsterdam Blues.*

Author's work has been translated into several languages, including Dutch, Germany, Italian, and Japanese.

Sidelights

Jan Michael was born and raised in Yorkshire, England, but traveled throughout Africa and Asia during summers off from boarding school. A writer and literary agent who now makes her home in the Netherlands, she has published the adult novels *Leaving Home,* as well as sharing her knowledge of life in rural Africa with younger readers in the middle-grade novel *City Boy.* Another book by Michael, the inspiring memoir *Flying Crooked: A Story of Cancer, Acceptance, and Hope,* chronicles her efforts to come to terms with a life-threatening illness.

In *City Boy* a boy must make the transition from living in urban Malawi to life in a rural village. After both his parents die of AIDS-related illnesses, Sam Sangala is taken in by his Aunt Mercy, who lives in a hut without electricity. This is a shock for the grieving preteen, who now also loses his friends from private school, his computer, and many other modern conveniences. When the last vestige of his former life—a pair of expensive blue running shoes—disappears, the boy is devastated. Slowly, however, Sam finds acceptance in the village and learns the value of extended family and rich cultural traditions. In her re-creation of Sam's narrative, Michael avoids "condescension or sentimentality," noted *Booklist* contributor Hazel Rochman, while in *School Library Journal* Kathleen Isaacs dubbed *City Boy* a "moving story" that introduces readers to "traditional village ways." The author "subtly layers detail" into her

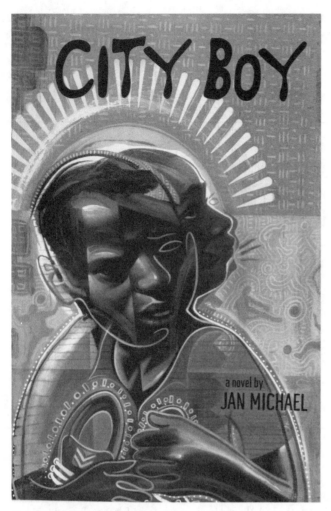

Cover of Jan Michael's middle-grade novel City Boy, *featuring artwork by Rudy Gutierrez.* (Illustration cooopyright © 2009 by Rudy Gutierrez. All rights reserved. Reprinted by permission of Clarion Books, an imprint of Houghton Mifflin Harcourt Publishing Company. All rights reserved.)

rich descriptions of village life, noted a *Kirkus Reviews* writer, making *City Boy* "a powerful portrait of poverty and hardship" that is balanced by "shades of hope." In *Horn Book* Elissa Gershowitz maintained that Michael's novel powerfully captures the resilience of people within Africa, "a country besieged by a devastating epidemic while its people press on with their daily lives."

Biographical and Critical Sources

BOOKS

Michael, Jan, *Flying Crooked: A Story of Cancer, Acceptance, and Hope* (memoir), Greystone Books (Berkeley, CA), 2005.

PERIODICALS

Booklist, May 1, 2009, Hazel Rochman, review of *City Boy,* p. 77.

Horn Book, September-October, 2009, Elissa Gershowitz, review of *City Boy,* p. 568.
Kirkus Reviews, April 1, 2009, review of *City Boy.*
School Library Journal, August, 2009, Kathleen Isaacs, review of *City Boy,* p. 110.

ONLINE

R Books Web site, http://www.rbooks.co.uk/ (June 1, 2010), "Jan Michael."*

* * *

MILLER, Allan 1978-
(Miller Brothers, a joint pseudonym)

Personal

Born 1978; son of Christian booksellers. *Education:* College degree (computer animation).

Addresses

Home—Auburn, WA. *E-mail*—amiller@lumination studios.com.

Career

Author and illustrator. Lumination Studios, cofounder and computer animator; animator, with brother Allen Miller, for children's video series "Juniors Giants." Presenter at schools.

Awards, Honors

(With Christopher Miller) Moonbeam Bronze Medal for Preteen Fiction, and Clive Staples Award for Christian Speculative Fiction short list, both 2009, both for *Hunter Brown and the Secret of the Shadow.*

Writings

"HEROES OF PROMISES" PICTURE-BOOK SERIES

(And illustrator, with Christopher Miller, as The Miller Brothers) *The Legend of Gid the Kid and the Black Bean Bandits,* Warner Press (Anderson, IN), 2007.
(And illustrator, with Christopher Miller, as The Miller Brothers) *Ten-Gallon Sam and the Perilous Mine,* Warner Press (Anderson, IN), 2008.

"CODEBREAKERS" ELEMENTARY-GRADE NOVEL SERIES

(With Christopher Miller, as The Miller Brothers) *Hunter Brown and the Secret of the Shadow,* Warner Press (Anderson, IN), 2008.
(With Christopher Miller, as The Miller Brothers) *Hunter Brown and the Consuming Fire,* Warner Press (Anderson, IN), 2009.

Biographical and Critical Sources

PERIODICALS

School Library Journal, March, 2009, Jake Pettit, review of *Hunter Brown and the Secret of the Shadow,* p. 148.
Voice of Youth Advocates, October, 2008, Laura Panter, review of *Hunter Brown and the Secret of the Shadow,* p. 354.

ONLINE

Christopher Miller Home Page, http://www.lumination studios.com (May 31, 2010).
Codebearers Web site, http://www.codebearers.com/ (May 31, 2010).
Miller Brothers Web log, http://themillerbrothers.blogspot. com/ (April 15, 2010).*

MILLER BROTHERS
See MILLER, Allan

*   *   *

MILUSICH, Janice

Personal
Married; children: three.

Addresses
Home—Port Jefferson, NY. *E-mail*—jan.milusich@gmail.com.

Career
Author and educator. Teacher of visually impaired students. Member, Smithtown Township Arts Council.

David Gordon creates the artwork for Janice Milusich's toddler-friendly picture book Off Go Their Engines, Off Go Their Lights. (Dutton Children's Books, 2008. Illustration ©2008 by David Gordon. Reproduced by permission.)

Member

Long Island Children's Writers & Illustrators (co-chair, 2010).

Awards, Honors

Huntington Arts Council grant, 2009.

Writings

Off Go Their Engines, Off Go Their Lights, illustrated by David Gordon, Dutton Children's Books (New York, NY), 2008.

Sidelights

A teacher of visually impaired students, Janice Milusich is the author of *Off Go Their Engines, Off Go Their Lights,* a bedtime tale featuring artwork by David Gordon. Set in a busy city, the work follows a mother and son as they board a yellow taxi cab to head home at the end of the day. As the cab winds its way through the crowded streets, it passes a number of equally colorful vehicles—including a blue ice-cream truck, a black-and-white police car, and a red pumper truck—that are also preparing to wind down after a day filled with activity.

Off Go Their Engines, Off Go Their Lights earned praise from critics, who noted Milusich's spare but soothing narrative. "The simple rhyming text induces listeners to relax and become sleepy," observed *School Library Journal* reviewer Linda Staskus, and Carolyn Phelan, writing in *Booklist,* commented that young readers will enjoy "the nicely cadenced refrain that ends each section of the story." According to a contributor in *Kirkus Reviews,* "Milusich combines colors and vehicles and turns the resulting mixture into a volume perfect for bedtime."

Biographical and Critical Sources

PERIODICALS

Booklist, June 1, 2008, Carolyn Phelan, review of *Off Go Their Engines, Off Go Their Lights,* p. 91.
Kirkus Reviews, May 15, 2008, review of *Off Go Their Engines, Off Go Their Lights.*
School Library Journal, August, 2008, Linda Staskus, review of *Off Go Their Engines, Off Go Their Lights,* p. 98.
Tribune Books (Chicago, IL), June 28, 2008, Mary Harris Russell, review of *Off Go Their Engines, Off Go Their Lights,* p. 7.

ONLINE

Long Island Children's Writers & Illustrators Web site, http://www.licwi.org/ (June 1, 2010), "Janice Milusich."

Smithtown Township Arts Council Web site, http://www.stacarts.org/ (June 1, 2010), "Janice Milusich."

*   *   *

MOBIN-UDDIN, Asma

Personal

Born in FL; married; has children. *Education:* Ohio State University, B.S., M.D. *Hobbies and other interests:* Traveling, public speaking, spending time with family.

Addresses

Home—Dublin, OH. *E-mail*—asmamu@columbus.rr.com.

Career

Pediatrician and writer.

Member

Society of Children's Book Writers and Illustrators, Council on American-Islamic Relations (past president of Ohio chapter), Interfaith Association of Central Ohio (past member of education committee).

Awards, Honors

Paterson Prize for Books for Young People, and Bank Street College of Education Best Children's Book designation, both 2006, both for *My Name Is Bilal;* Bank Street College of Education Best Children's Book designation, Middle East Outreach Council Book Award honorable mention, and *Skipping Stones* Honor designation, all 2008, and *Storytelling World* Resources Awards Honor designation, 2009, all for *The Best Eid Ever;* Parent's Choice Award, 2009, and Bank Street College of Education Best Children's Book designation, and CCBC Best Book designation, both 2010, all for *A Party in Ramadan.*

Writings

My Name Is Bilal, illustrated by Barbara Kiwak, Boyds Mills Press (Honesdale, PA), 2005.
The Best Eid Ever, illustrated by Laura Jacobsen, Boyds Mills Press (Honesdale, PA), 2007.
A Party in Ramadan, illustrated by Laura Jacobsen, Boyds Mills Press (Honesdale, PA), 2009.

Contributor of articles to *Columbus Dispatch* and *Religion News Service.*

Sidelights

An American of Pakistani descent, Asma Mobin-Uddin is also a pediatrician who took a sabatical from her career to focus on parenting her children. While a full-time mother, Mobin-Uddin made her publishing debut with *My Name Is Bilal,* in which she inspires young readers to be true to themselves and cherish their identity instead of being afraid of what others might think of them. Other books have followed, including *The Best Eid Ever* and *A Party in Ramadan.* In addition to writing for children, Mobin-Uddin also visits schools, leads workshops within interested communities, and is a contributor on Muslim topics to the *Columbus (OH) Dispatch.*

On her home page, Mobin-Uddin explained that the search for suitable reading materials for her own children inspired her to become a writer. "I had difficulty finding good books about Muslim kids to read to them," she recalled. "Many of the books I found in local libraries about Muslims were stereotypical and many of them were about camels or sultans or something else that is as foreign to the Muslim-American experience as it is to any other American experience. Even when the books were written in a sensitive way, they were almost always set in some far-away location, not in America. . . . So I had two main reasons for starting to write books for children. I wanted to introduce accurate books about the Muslim-American experience to the general American community, and I wanted to write books that Muslim-American kids would see themselves in."

My Name Is Bilal follows brother and sister Bilal and Ayesha, who start a new school in a U.S. town. As the only Muslim children, they are greeted with teasing from some bullies due to Ayesha's headscarf. However, their teacher, Mr. Ali, is also Muslim, and with his support and reassurance the children learn that they have an important place in the local culture and gain the self-confidence to stand up for themselves. Carolyn Phelan, writing in *Booklist,* commented that Mobin-Uddin's book provides "a good starting place for discussions of cultural differences, prejudice, and respect for the beliefs of others," while Kathleen E. Gruver stated in *School Library Journal* that with its "well-done treatment of a subject not often seen in children's picture books," *My Name Is Bilal* "will enhance discussions of cultural diversity and understanding." The Council on Islamic Education and the Islamic Networks Group both endorsed the book and included it on their recommended reading lists for educators.

Featuring graphite-and-pastel artwork by Laura Jacobsen, *The Best Eid Ever* introduces children to the biggest holiday of the Muslim year: Eid-ut-Adha, which is similar to Thanksgiving in its focus on sharing food with family, friends, and those less fortunate. While her parents are on a pilgrimage in the Middle East, Aneesa is at home in the United States, under the care of her grandmother, Nonni. During a holiday visit to their mosque, Aneesa sees a family of refugees and focuses her attention away from her loneliness and toward helping these struggling displaced people. Noting that the book's "pictures illustrate the story with warmth,"

Phelan added that Mobin-Uddin's "clearly written story will interest many children." *School Library Journal* critic Fawia Gilani-Williams wrote of *The Best Eid Ever* that Mobin-Uddin's "beautifully composed story straddles two worlds" in its "heartwarming tale of a child's generosity."

In *A Party in Ramadan* Mobin-Uddin once again collaborates with Jacobsen to create an engaging Muslim-centered story. Leena's family is preparing for the month-long celebration of Ramadan, a special time in which Muslims spend time in fasting and reflection. During the holiday, Leena is invited to a friend's party, and while she enjoys the gathering, she also honors the Muslim holiday by passing on lemonade, chocolate cake, and ice cream until fasting is over and the iftar feast is before her. The "blend of the upbeat and challenging moments" in *A Party in Ramadan* "will spark discussion," predicted *Booklist* contributor Hazel Rochman, and Gilani-Williams recommended Mobin-Uddin's "engaging" story as "a perfect resource for teaching about choices, sharing, and empathy." Calling the book "a slice of the Muslim-American experience," a *Kirkus Reviews* writer praised *A Party in Ramadan* "a compassionate family story" that serves "as both mirror for Muslim-American children and window for their non-Muslim friends."

Biographical and Critical Sources

PERIODICALS

Booklist, August, 2005, Carolyn Phelan, review of *My Name Is Bilal,* p. 2029; January 1, 2008, Carolyn Phelan, review of *The Best Eid Ever,* p. 86; March 15, 2009, Hazel Rochman, review of *A Party in Ramadan,* p. 67.

Kirkus Reviews, July 1, 2005, review of *My Name Is Bilal,* p. 739; April 1, 2009, review of *A Party of Ramadan.*

Ohioana Quarterly, Jennifer Zaranek, review of *My Name Is Bilal,* p. 547.

Publishers Weekly, August 29, 2005, review of *My Name Is Bilal,* p. 61.

School Library Journal, August, 2005, Kathleen E. Gruver, review of *My Name Is Bilal,* p. 103; December, 2007, Fawzia Gilani-Williams, review of *The Best Eid Ever,* p. 96; April, 2009, Fawzia Gilani-Williams, review of *A Party in Ramadan,* p. 114.

ONLINE

Asma Mobin-Uddin Home Page, http://www.asmamobin uddin.com (May 31, 2010).

*   *   *

MOON, Lily
See WARNES, Tim

MOSS, Marissa 1959-

Personal

Born September 29, 1959; daughter of Robert (an engineer) and Harriet Moss; married Harvey Stahl (a professor); children: Simon, Elias, Asa. *Education:* University of California, Berkeley, B.A. (art history); attended California College of Arts and Crafts.

Addresses

Home—Berkeley, CA.

Career

Author and illustrator.

Member

Authors Guild, PEN West, Society of Children's Book Writers and Illustrators, Screenwriters Guild.

Awards, Honors

Parent Council Outstanding Award for informational book, 2000, for *My Notebook (with Help from Amelia);* Parent's Guide to Children's Media Award, 2001, and Children's Choice Award, 2002, both for *Oh Boy, Amelia!*

Writings

SELF-ILLUSTRATED PICTURE BOOKS

Who Was It?, Houghton (Boston, MA), 1989.
Regina's Big Mistake, Houghton (Boston, MA), 1990.
Want to Play?, Houghton (Boston, MA), 1990.
After-School Monster, Lothrop (New York, NY), 1991.
Knick Knack Paddywack, Houghton (Boston, MA), 1992.
But Not Kate, Lothrop (New York, NY), 1992.
In America, Dutton (New York, NY), 1994.
Mel's Diner, BridgeWater Books (Mahwah, NJ), 1994.
The Ugly Menorah, Farrar, Straus (New York, NY), 1996.
Galen: My Life in Imperial Rome ("Ancient World Journal" series), Harcourt (San Diego, CA), 2002.

"AMELIA'S NOTEBOOK" SERIES; SELF-ILLUSTRATED

Amelia's Notebook, Tricycle Press (Berkeley, CA), 1995.
Amelia Writes Again, Tricycle Press (Berkeley, CA), 1996.
My Notebook (with Help from Amelia), Tricycle Press (Berkeley, CA), 1997.
Amelia Hits the Road, Tricycle Press (Berkeley, CA), 1997.
Amelia Takes Command, Tricycle Press (Berkeley, CA), 1998, published as *Amelia's Bully Survival Guide,* Simon & Schuster Books for Young Readers (New York, NY), 2006.

Dr. Amelia's Boredom Survival Guide, Pleasant Company (Middleton, WI) 1999, published as *Amelia's Boredom Survival Guide: First Aid for Rainy Days, Boring Errands, Waiting Rooms, Whatever!,* Simon & Schuster Books (New York, NY), 2006.
The All-New Amelia, Pleasant Company (Middleton, WI), 1999.
Luv Amelia, Luv Nadia, Pleasant Company (Middleton, WI), 1999.
Amelia's Family Ties, Pleasant Company (Middleton, WI), 2000.
Amelia's Easy-as-Pie Drawing Guide, Pleasant Company (Middleton, WI), 2000.
Amelia Works It Out, Pleasant Company (Middleton, WI), 2000.
Madame Amelia Tells All: (Except Fortunes and Predictions), Pleasant Company (Middleton, WI), 2001, published as *Amelia Tells All,* Simon & Schuster Bools for Young Readers (New York, NY), 2007.
Oh Boy, Amelia!, Pleasant Company (Middleton, WI), 2001.
Amelia Lends a Hand, Pleasant Company (Middleton, WI), 2002.
Amelia's Best Year Ever: Favorite Amelia Stories from American Girl Magazine, Pleasant Company (Middleton, WI), 2003.
Amelia's Sixth-Grade Notebook, Simon & Schuster (New York, NY), 2004.
Amelia's Most Unforgettable Embarrassing Moments, Simon & Schuster (New York, NY), 2005.
Amelia's Book of Notes and Note Passing, Simon & Schuster (New York, NY), 2006.
Amelia Writes Again, Simon & Schuster Books for Young Readers (New York, NY), 2006.
Amelia's Are-we-there-yet, Longest Ever Car Trip, Simon & Schuster Books for Young Readers (New York, NY), 2006.
Amelia's Guide to Gossip: The Good, the Bad, and the Ugly, Simon & Schuster Books for Young Readers (New York, NY), 2006.
Amelia's Longest Biggest Most-fights-ever Family Reunion, Simon & Schuster Books for Young Readers (New York, NY), 2006.
Amelia's School Survival Guide, Simon & Schuster Books for Young Readers (New York, NY), 2006.
Amelia's Seventh-Grade Notebook, Simon & Schuster Bools for Young Readers (New York, NY), 2007.
Vote 4 Amelia, Simon & Schuster Books for Young Readers (New York, NY), 2007.
Amelia's Itchy-twitchy, Lovey-dovey Summer at Camp Mosquito, Simon & Schuster Books for Young Readers (New York, NY), 2008.

"MAX DISASTER" SERIES; SELF-ILLUSTRATED

Max's Logbook, Scholastic, Inc. (New York, NY), 2003, revised and expanded as *Alien Eraser to the Rescue,* Candlewick Press (Somerville, MA), 2009.
Max's Mystical Notebook, Scholastic, Inc. (New York, NY), 2004, revised and expanded as *Alien Eraser Unravels the Mystery of the Pyramids,* Candlewick Press (Somerville, MA), 2009.

Alien Eraser Reveals the Secrets of Evolution, Candlewick Press (Somerville, MA), 2009.

FOR CHILDREN

True Heart, illustrated by Chris F. Payne, Harcourt (San Diego, CA), 1998.

Rachel's Journal: The Story of a Pioneer Girl ("Young American Voices" series), Harcourt (San Diego, CA), 1998.

Emma's Journal: The Story of a Colonial Girl ("Young American Voices" series), Harcourt (San Diego, CA), 1999.

Hannah's Journal: The Story of an Immigrant Girl ("Young American Voices" series), Harcourt (San Diego, CA), 2000.

Rose's Journal: The Story of a Girl in the Great Depression ("Young American Voices" series), Harcourt (San Diego, CA), 2001.

Brave Harriet: The First Woman to Fly the English Channel, illustrated by C.F. Payne, Harcourt (San Diego, CA), 2001.

Mighty Jackie: The Strike-out Queen, illustrated by C.F. Payne, Harcourt (San Diego, CA), 2002.

Sky High: The True Story of Maggie Gee, illustrated by Carl Angel, Tricycle Press (Berkeley, CA), 2009.

The Pharaoh's Secret, Amulet Books (New York, NY), 2009.

ILLUSTRATOR

Catherine Gray, *One, Two, Three, and Four—No More?,* Houghton (Boston, MA), 1988.

Dr. Hickey, adapter, *Mother Goose and More: Classic Rhymes with Added Lines,* Additions Press (Oakland, CA), 1990.

Bruce Coville, *The Lapsnatcher,* BridgeWater Books (Mahwah, NJ), 1997.

David M. Schwartz, *G Is for Googol: A Math Alphabet Book,* Tricycle Press (Berkeley, CA), 1998.

Sidelights

An author and illustrator who has produced picture books and chapter books that range in focus from humorous contemporary stories to historical fiction, Marissa Moss is best known for her series of beginning readers featuring a young writer named Amelia. In the "Amelia's Notebooks" series, which includes *Amelia Hits the Road, Amelia's Most Unforgettable Embarrassing Moments,* and *Amelia's Guide to Gossip: The Good, the Bad, and the Ugly,* Moss's spunky elementary-grade heroine chronicles her adventures in enthusiastic, entertaining journals. The books share Moss's belief in the importance of story-telling; as she once explained to *SATA,* "When you write or tell about something, you have a kind of control over it, you shape the events, you sort them through, you emphasize some aspects, omit others. . . . Besides the flights of pure fancy, the imaginative leaps that storytelling allows, it was this sense of control, of finding order and meaning that mattered most to me as a child."

Born in 1959, Moss earned a degree in art history from the University of California at Berkeley. As she once recalled, "I could say I never thought I'd be a writer, only an illustrator and writing was forced upon me by a lack of other writers' stories to illustrate. Or I could say I always wanted to be a writer, but I never thought it was really possible. As a voracious reader, it seemed too much of a grown-up thing to do, and I'd never be mature enough to do it. Or I could say I've been writing and illustrating children's books since I was nine. It just took me longer than most to get published. All these stories are true, each in their own way."

Moss began her career as a picture-book illustrator, working with author Catherine Gray, as well as creating art to pair with her own simple texts. One of her first published books as both writer and illustrator, *Who Was It?,* depicts young Isabelle's quandary after she breaks the cookie jar while attempting to sneak a between-meals snack. Praising Moss's watercolor illustrations for this book, *Booklist* reviewer Denise Wilms also noted that the story's "moral about telling the truth is delivered with wry, quiet humor."

In *Regina's Big Mistake* a young artist's frustration with her own lack of ability compared to that of the rest of her classmates is counteracted by a sensitive art teacher, as Regina is shown how to "draw around" a lumpy sun, transforming it into a moon. Readers "will enjoy the solace of having another child struggling to achieve, and succeeding," maintained Zena Sutherland in the *Bulletin of the Center for Children's Books.* Also reviewing *Regina's Big Mistake, School Library Journal* contributor Ruth Semrau concluded that "Moss's crayon cartoons are exactly what is needed to depict the artistic endeavors of very young children."

In *After-School Monster* Luisa returns home from school to find a sharp-toothed creature waiting in her kitchen. Although scared, the girl stands up to the monster, turning the tables on the creature and evicting it from her house before her mother gets home. While noting that the theme of *After-School Monster* could frighten very small children who are contemplating being left alone, a *Junior Bookshelf* contributor nonetheless praised Moss's "striking" full-page illustrations, which feature "an imaginative use of changing sizes."

In another imaginative picture-book offering, Moss updates the traditional nursery rhyme "Knick Knack Paddywack" with what Sheilamae O'Hara described in *Booklist* as a pairing of "rollicking, irreverent verse" and "colorful, action-filled" pictures. The author/illustrator's "use of language will tickle all but the tongue tied," added Jody McCoy in an appraisal of *Knick Knack Paddywack* for *School Library Journal.*

"The character of Amelia came to me when I opened a black and white mottled composition book and started to write and draw the way I remembered I wrote and drew when I was nine," Moss once recalled about the first of her popular "Amelia's Notebook" beginning readers. The series follows the spunky Amelia through a series of daily adventures as she changes schools, makes new friends, and copes with an annoying older sister. Hand-lettered and bound in a manner that resembles a black-and-white school composition book, each series installment is "chock-full of personal asides and tiny spot drawings" and features a story-line that "rings true with third-grade authenticity," according to *School Library Journal* contributor Carolyn Noah.

"Amelia is droll and funny and not too sophisticated for her years," noted *Booklist* reviewer Stephanie Zvirin, the critic observing that the diarist has an emotional side too, missing her old friends and full of childhood aspirations about her future. In *Amelia Writes Again* Amelia has turned ten and begins a new notebook. In doodles, sketches, and snippets of thoughts, she comments on such things as a fire at school and her inability to pay attention during math class. Everything Moss includes in Amelia's notebooks is true, as Moss tells the school groups she visits, "or is based on the truth. Names have all been changed, because my older sister is mad enough at me already, and some details are altered to make for a better story. So, yes, there really was a fire in my school, but the idea of putting treasures in the newly poured pavement didn't occur to me at the time." Moss wishes it had, and she lets Amelia do it in *Amelia Writes Again.*

In *Amelia Works It Out* the adventurous heroine tries to start her own business so she can buy a pair of expensive glow-in-the-dark shoes, while in *Oh Boy, Amelia!* she takes a life-skills class and discovers that she is handy with tools. In *Amelia's Guide to Gossip* she takes time out to educate the uninformed reader on the ways amazing stories make their way through the fourth-grade rumor mill, while a summer with friend Carly at Camp Runamucka mixes fun with romantic tensions in *Amelia's Itchy-twitchy, Lovey-dovey Summer at Camp Mosquito.* In *School Library Journal,* Maryann H. Owen dubbed the colorfully illustrated *Amelia's Itchy-twitchy, Lovey-dovey Summer at Camp Mosquito* "another entertaining 'notebook' from a seasoned writer."

Writing in Amelia's voice allows Moss a flexibility that conventional picture-book writing does not. "I can go back and forth between different kinds of writing—the pure invention of storytelling, the thoughtful searching of describing people and events, and the explorations Amelia takes when she writes about noses or numbers, things she notices and writes down to figure out what it is that she's noticing," the author once told *SATA.* "In the same way that I can go from describing a new teacher to making a story about clouds, Amelia allows me to move freely between words and pictures. I can draw as Amelia draws or I can use *tromp l'oeil* for the objects she tapes into her notebook. . . . The notebook format allows me to leap from words to images and this free flowing back and forth is how I work best. It reflects the way I think—sometimes visually, sometimes verbally—with the pictures not there just to illustrate

the text, but to replace it, telling their own story. . . . Kids often ask me which comes first, the words or the pictures. With Amelia, it can be either, and I love that fluidity."

In addition to noting their value as entertaining stories, critics often praise the "Amelia's Notebooks" series for leading younger readers into the art of journal writing, a result about which Moss could not be happier. "The many letters I get from kids show that, inspired by Amelia, they, too, are discovering the magic of writing," she once noted. "When readers respond to Amelia by starting their own journals, I feel I've gotten the highest compliment possible—I've made writing cool."

Giving equal time to boys, Moss uses the journal format to focus on an equally engaging character in her "Max Disaster" series, which include the quirkily titled *Alien Eraser to the Rescue, Alien Eraser Unravels the Mystery of the Pyramids,* and *Alien Eraser Reveals the Secrets of Evolution.* In *Alien Eraser to the Rescue* readers meet Max, who uses journals to chronicle the scientific advances he makes in his "experiments" as well as flights of his imagination cast as cartoon drawings, experiments, and running commentary. The "funny, kid-savvy montage" Moss creates in *Alien Eraser to the Rescue* also has an emotional side, according to a *Publishers Weekly* contributor; Max's career ambitions—to become a scientist like his parents—sometimes take a back seat to worries over his parents'

Marissa Moss's self-illustrated "Amelia's Notebook" series begins with the imaginatively illustrated beginning reader **Amelia's Notebook.** *(Si-mon & Schuster, 2006. © 1995 by Marissa Moss. Reproduced by permission.)*

Readers follow Moss in her walk through the ancient world in **Galen: My Life in Imperial Rome.** (Illustration © 2002 by Marisa Moss. Reproduced by permission of Harcourt, Inc.)

separation and issues with his older brother. A comic strip about the time-spanning exploits of an eraser from outer space that has purportedly taken control of Max's mind weaves throughout the "Max Disaster" books, prompting Melinda Piehler to recommend Moss's "eye-catching transitional readers" to "both reluctant and avid readers." As the *Publishers Weekly* contributor concluded, "Moss is a master at verbalizing kids' anxieties and channeling their astute observations of family life."

In addition to her "Amelia's Notebooks" and "Max Disaster" stories, Moss has created a series focusing on young writers from different historical periods, featuring the same realistic appearance created by a patchwork of drawings and inserted objects. The first book in the series, *Rachel's Journal: The Story of a Pioneer Girl,* is set in 1850 and accompanies a family to California along the Oregon Trail. Moss spent many hours doing research, reading histories, exploring library archives, and pouring over the actual letters and diaries of people who traversed the United States by covered wagon. "It was, for the most part, riveting reading and I was impressed with what an enormous undertaking, what a leap of faith it was for pioneers to come" to the West coast, she once noted. "It was a dangerous trip. Indians, river crossings, storms, and especially sickness were all feared. But I was struck by the difference between how men and women viewed the journey and how children saw it. To kids, it was a great adventure, troublesome at times, tedious and terrifying at others, but ultimately exciting. These children showed tremendous courage and strength of character, and I tried to capture some of that, as well as the exhilaration of travelling into the unknown, in Rachel's journal."

Moss has completed several other works in the "Young American Voices" series, among them *Emma's Journal:*

The Story of a Colonial Girl, Hannah's Journal: The Story of an Immigrant Girl, and *Rose's Journal: The Story of a Girl in the Great Depression. Hannah's Journal* concerns a ten-year-old Lithuanian girl who immigrates to the United States in 1901. Reviewing the work in *School Library Journal,* Jane Marino remarked that "Moss does give her readers a real sense of the time in which the protagonist lived." *Rose's Journal,* which is set on a Kansas farm in 1935, prompted *School Library Journal* contributor Roxanne Burg to recommend the story to young history buffs because "there is quite a bit of historical information packed into [Moss's] . . . short book."

Moss delves even further into the past, profiling a twelve-year-old slave in the self-illustrated *Galen: My Life in Imperial Rome.* The first book in Harcourt's "Ancient World Journal" series, *Galen* blends fact and fiction in describing Galen's world, living and works in the home of the Roman Emperor Augustus. According to a reviewer in *Publishers Weekly,* Moss provides "a clear, intriguing portrait of ancient Roman life," and *Booklist* contributor GraceAnne A. DeCandido wrot that the "delightful book is rich in detail."

Another trip into the ancient world awaits readers in Moss's middle-grade novel *The Pharaoh's Secret,* as two siblings of Egyptian ancestry travel to Cairo and become involved in a mystery surrounding the disappearance of an ancient pharaoh's chief architect. Fourteen-year-old Talibah is guided by a mysterious voice, which may be that of her deceased mother or something more sinister; meanwhile, younger brother Adom helps by finding a talisman that protects the wearer. Including sketches capturing Talibah's impressions of the tombs and temples she explores during her adventure, *The Pharaoh's Secret* features "believable" protagonists, according to *School Library Journal* contributor Kathleen Isaacs. A *Kirkus Reviews* writer described the novel as a mix of "historical intrigue, family issues, and a brief episode of time travel."

Moss looks at U.S. aviator Harriet Quimby in *Brave Harriet: The First Woman to Fly the English Channel.* Quimby, the first woman to become a licensed pilot, flew from England to France on April 16, 1912. Her historic solo flight was overshadowed by another event that occurred the same day: the sinking of the luxury ocean liner *Titanic.* Quimby's "contemplation of the glory that might have been . . . is sensitively portrayed," wrote *School Library Journal* reviewer Ann Chapman Callaghan in her review of *Brave Harriet..*

Another young woman takes to the skies in *Sky High: The True Story of Maggie Gee,* which is based on the life of a young Chinese-American pilot who joined the Women Air-Force Service Pilots (WASPs) during World War II. While growing up in the 1930s, Maggie Gee dreamed of flying airplanes, and her wartime flight missions allowed her to fulfill those dreams, as Moss shows in her inspiring picture book. The story is brought to life in detailed acrylic-and-colored pencil images by Carl Angel that "vibrantly depict the settings and events" in Moss's first-person narration, according to *School Library Journal* critic Donna Atmur, while a *Kirkus Reviews* writer described *Sky High* as "an inspirational tale of an inspirational woman." In *Booklist,* Ilene Cooper noted that the inclusion of social themes such as racial discrimination do not darken Gee's uplifting story, and Moss's ability to base her text on interviews with her subject gives *Sky High* "a lovely, personal feel."

Mighty Jackie: The Strike-out Queen tells the true story of Jackie Mitchell, a seventeen year old who pitched

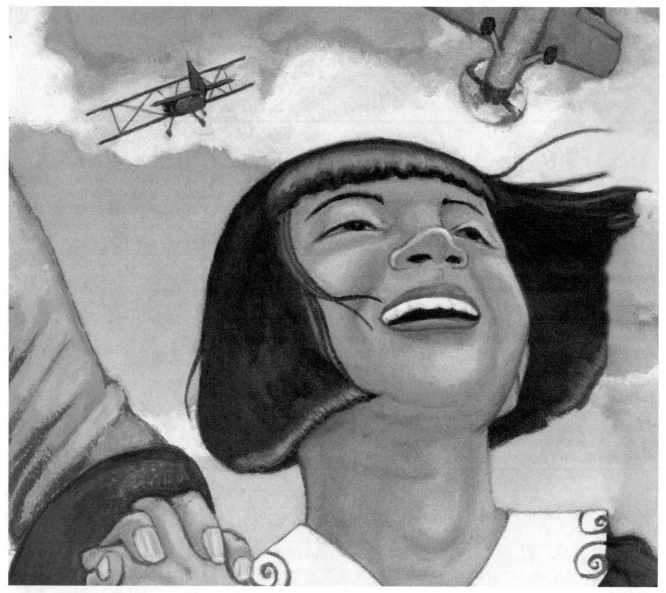

Moss's illustrated biography Sky High *captures the life of female pilot Maggie Gee in artwork by Carl Angel.* (Illustration © 2009 by Carl Angel. Used by permission of Tricycle Press, an imprint of Random House Children's Books, a division of Random House, Inc.)

for the Chattanooga Lookouts, a minor-league baseball team. Moss describes how Mitchell received coaching and encouragement at a young age from both her father and Dazzy Vance, a major-league pitcher. In 1931, the Lookouts played an exhibition game against the New York Yankees, who were then led by superstars Babe Ruth and Lou Gehrig, and Mitchell made baseball history by striking out the legendary duo. "Moss relays the details . . . with the blow-by-blow breathless of a sportscaster and the confidence of a seasoned storyteller," wrote a critic in _Publishers Weekly,_ and _School Library Journal_ contributor Grace Oliff observed that "The narrative captures the tension and excitement, and has the air of an experience remembered."

Biographical and Critical Sources

PERIODICALS

Booklist, November 1, 1989, Denise Wilms, review of _Who Was It?,_ p. 555; July, 1992, Sheilamae O'Hara, review of _Knick Knack Paddywack,_ p. 1941; April 1, 1995, Stephanie Zvirin, review of _Amelia's Notebook,_ p. 1391; November 1, 1999, Carolyn Phelan, reviews of _The All-New Amelia_ and _Luv Amelia, Luv Nadia,_ both p. 530; February 15, 2000, Carolyn Phelan, review of _Amelia's Family Ties,_ p. 1113; September 1, 2000, Carolyn Phelan, review of _Amelia Works It Out,_ p. 115; October 1, 2000, Carolyn Phelan, review of _Hannah's Journal: The Story of an Immigrant Girl,_ p. 340; July, 2001, Carolyn Phelan, review of _Brave Harriet: The First Woman to Fly the English Channel,_ p. 2009; August, 2001, Susan Dove Lempke, review of _Madame Amelia Tells All,_ p. 2121; January 1, 2002, Carolyn Phelan, review of _Oh Boy, Amelia!,_ p. 859; March 1, 2002, Ilene Cooper, review of _Brave Harriet,_ p. 1146; December 15, 2002, GraceAnne A. DeCandido, review of _Galen: My Life in Imperial Rome,_ p. 760; October 15, 2003, Todd Morning, review of _Max's Logbook,_ p. 412; January 1, 2004, GraceAnne A. DeCandido, review of _Mighty Jackie: The Strikeout Queen,_ p. 868; June 1, 2009, Ilene Cooper, review of _Sky High: The True Story of Maggie Gee,_ p. 84.

Bulletin of the Center for Children's Books, October, 1990, Zena Sutherland, review of _Regina's Big Mistake,_ p. 40.

Junior Bookshelf, April, 1993, review of _After-School Monster,_ p. 62.

Kirkus Reviews, September 15, 2002, review of _Galen,_ p. 1396; January 15, 2004, review of _Mighty Jackie,_ p. 87; April 1, 2009, review of _Alien Eraser to the Rescue;_ July 15, 2009, review of _Sky High;_ October 1, 2009, review of _The Pharaoh's Secret._

Publishers Weekly, August 31, 1998, Sally Lodge, "Journaling Back through Time with Marissa Moss," p. 20; July 16, 2001, review of _Brave Harriet,_ p. 180; October 21, 2002, review of _Galen,_ p. 76; July 14, 2003, review of _Max's Logbook,_ p. 76; January 19, 2004, review of _Mighty Jackie,_ p. 76; May 25, 2009, review of _Alien Eraser to the Rescue,_ p. 57.

Reading Today, April, 2001, Lynne T. Burke, review of "Amelia" series, p. 32; August, 2001, Lynne T. Burke, review of _Amelia Works It Out,_ p. 30.

School Library Journal, January, 1991, Ruth Semrau, review of _Regina's Big Mistake,_ p. 79; June, 1992, Jody McCoy, review of _Knick Knack Paddywack,_ p. 100; July, 1995, Carolyn Noah, review of _Amelia's Notebook,_ p. 79; October, 1999, Lisa Gangemi Kropp, review of _The All-New Amelia,_ p. 121; December, 1999, Susan Hepler, review of _Emma's Journal: The Story of a Colonial Girl,_ p. 108; June, 2000, Holly Belli, _Amelia's Family Ties,_ p. 122; September, 2000, Wendy S. Carroll, review of _Amelia Works It Out,_ p. 206; November, 2000, Jane Marino, review of _Hannah's Journal,_ p. 129; July, 2001, Leslie S. Hilverding, review of _Madame Amelia Tells All,_ p. 86; September, 2001, Ann Chapman Callaghan, review of _Brave Harriet,_ p. 220; October, 2001, Debbie Stewart, review of _Oh Boy, Amelia!,_ p. 126; December, 2001, Roxanne Burg, review of _Rose's Journal: The Story of a Girl in the Great Depression,_ p. 108; October, 2002, Lynda S. Poling, review of _Galen,_ pp. 168-169; October, 2003, Elaine Lesh Morgan, review of _Max's Logbook,_ p. 132; February, 2004, Grace Oliff, review of _Mighty Jackie,_ pp. 134-135; May, 2005, Jennifer Ralston, review of _Amelia Takes Command,_ p. 50; December, 2006, Elaine Lesh Morgan, review of _Amelia's Guide to Gossip: The Good, the Bad, and the Ugly,_ p. 151; July, 2008, Maryann H. Owen, review of _Amelia's Itchy-twitchy, Lovey-dovey Summer at Camp Mosquito,_ p. 106; August, 2009, Melinda Piehler, reviews of _Alien Eraser to the Rescue_ and _Alien Eraser Unravels the Mystery of the Pyramids,_ both p. 80; September, 2009, Donna Atmur, review of _Sky High,_ p. 145; November, 2009, Kathleen Isaacs, review of _The Pharaoh's Secret,_ p. 115.

ONLINE

Harcourt Books Web site, http://www.harcourtbooks.com/ (June 1, 2004), interview with Moss.*

P

PARTRIDGE, Elizabeth 1951-

Personal

Born 1951, in CA; daughter of Rondal Partridge (a photographer); married; husband's name Tom; children: several sons. *Education:* University of California—Berkeley, degree (women's studies), 1974; studied Chinese medicine in Oxford, England, Licentiate of Acupuncture, 1978.

Addresses

Home—San Francisco, CA. *Agent*—Ken Wright, Writer's House, 21 W. 26th St., New York, NY 10010. *E-mail*—elizabeth@elizabethpartridge.com.

Career

Writer. Practiced acupuncture and herbal medicine in San Francisco, CA, beginning late 1970s. Co-producer, with sister Meg Partridge, of documentary film *Dorothea Lange: A Visual Life.* Speaker at conferences, writing programs, and conventions.

Awards, Honors

Judy Lopez Memorial Honor Award for Children's Literature, Women's National Book Association, 1996, for *Clara and the Hoodoo Man;* Jane Addams Honor Book Award, Golden Kite Honor Award for Nonfiction, Society of Children's Book Writers and Illustrators, Best Book for Young Adult selection and Notable Children's Book selection, both American Library Association (ALA), Bay Area Reviewer's Award for children's literature, and Lasting Connections selection, *Book Links* magazine, all c. 1998, all for *Restless Spirit;* National Book Award finalist, *Boston Globe/Horn Book* Award for Nonfiction, Golden Kite Award for Nonfiction, 100 Titles for Reading and Sharing designation, New York Public Library, ALA Best Books for Young Adults and Notable Book designations, and several Best Books designations, all c. 2001, all for *This Land Was Made for You and Me;* Michael L. Printz Honor Book designation, ALA Best Books for Young Adults designation, and several other Best Books designations, all c. 2006, all for *John Lennon;* Jane Addams Children's Book Award, *Boston Globe/Horn Book* Award for Nonfiction, and *Los Angeles Times* Book Prize, all 2009, and Notable Social Studies Trade Book designation, Notable Books for a Global Society designation, Capitol Choices Noteworthy Books for Children designation, ALA Notable Children's Book and Best Books for Young Adult designations, New York Public Library 100 Titles for Reading and Sharing selection, and California Book Award Young-Adult finalist, all 2010, all for *Marching for Freedom.*

Writings

FOR CHILDREN

Clara and the Hoodoo Man (novel), Dutton (New York, NY), 1996.

Restless Spirit: The Life and Work of Dorothea Lange (photobiography), Viking (New York, NY), 1998.

Pig's Eggs, illustrated by Martha Weston, Golden Books (New York, NY), 2000.

Oranges on Golden Mountain, illustrated by Aki Sogabe, Dutton (New York, NY), 2001.

This Land Was Made for You and Me: The Life and Music of Woody Guthrie, Viking (New York, NY), 2001.

Annie and Bo and the Big Surprise, illustrated by Martha Weston, Dutton (New York, NY), 2002.

Moon Glowing, illustrated by Joan Paley, Dutton (New York, NY), 2002.

Whistling, illustrated by Anna Grossnickle Hines, Greenwillow (New York, NY), 2003.

(Adaptor) *Kogi's Mysterious Journey,* illustrated by Aki Sogabe, Dutton Children's Books (New York, NY), 2003.

John Lennon: All I Want Is the Truth, Viking (New York, NY), 2005.

Big Cat Pepper, illustrated by Lauren Castillo, Blooms-
bury Children's Books (New York, NY), 2009.
*Marching for Freedom: Walk Together, Children, and Don't
You Grow Weary,* Viking (New York, NY), 2009.

OTHER

(Editor) *Dorothea Lange: A Visual Life,* Smithsonian
(Washington, DC), 1993.
(With Sally Stein) *Quizzical Eye: The Photography of
Rondal Partridge,* Heyday Books (Berkeley, CA),
2002.

Sidelights

California-based writer Elizabeth Partridge is the author
of a range of books, from historical fiction and biographies to stories for young children. She is also the author of *Annie and Bo and the Big Surprise,* an easy
reader about two mice who are friends, and the picture
books *Oranges on Golden Mountain, Moon Glowing,*
and *Big Cat Pepper.* Commenting on *Annie and Bo* in
Booklist, Gillian Engberg appreciated Partridge's use of
"simple, descriptive language," which the critic deemed
"just right for beginning readers." Similarly, a *Kirkus
Reviews* contributor called *Annie and Bo* a "sweet and
gentle" story that provides "fast-clipping exercise" for
new readers.

Partridge's father was a photographer, as was her pater-
nal grandmother, Imogen Cunningham. Prior to his marriage her father, Rondal, was fortunate to have the opportunity to apprentice with family friend Dorothea
Lange, a noted documentary photographer who remains
best known for her work done on the behest of the
Farm Security Administration during the Great Depression of the 1930s. After Rondal married, his family
continued to associate with Lange's family until her
death in 1965, when Partridge was a young teen, and
Lange also became Elizabeth's godmother.

As one of several children who were raised by artistic,
bohemian parents, Partridge spent many of her childhood summers traveling around the country with her
family. "Sometimes money ran out," Partridge recalled
of her childhood on her home page. "My parents
scrambled, borrowed, traded, made do. Food was basic,
and in lean times, sparse. Hand-me-down clothes were
the norm. I was both proud of my family and acutely
aware of being different. At times, I longed for my father to put on a suit and go to a regular job like other
fathers did. But nobody ever said 'you can't' to me. In
the freeform swirl, we were always encouraged to become whoever we wanted to be."

After Elizabeth's sister Meg Partridge made a film about
Grandmother Cunningham, the Partridge sisters collaborated on a one-hour documentary about Lange.
Called *Dorothea Lange: A Visual Life,* the film was accompanied by a book with the same title, which Elizabeth edited. Partridge was then contracted to write a

children's biography about Lange that was published as
Restless Spirit: The Life and Work of Dorothea Lange.
Writing in *School Library Journal,* Jackie Gropman
lauded *Dorothea Lange* as a "magnificently reproduced
collection of photos and insightful essays" that interweaves Lange's personal history with a large selection
of her photographic achievements. Mary M. Burns
wrote in *Horn Book* that Partridge makes a "thoughtful
presentation" about Lange's life in *Restless Spirit,* including photographs and personal details about Lange's
life. Similarly, *Booklist* critic Hazel Rochman appreciated the combined presentation of Lange's work and
life events in *Restless Spirit,* characterizing it as a "fine
photo-essay that will interest adults as much as teens."

Writing *Restless Spirit* inspired Partridge to profile other
noted individuals in a similar fashion. In *This Land Was
Made for You and Me: The Life and Music of Woody
Guthrie* she brings to life the world of noted American
folk singer, while *John Lennon: All I Want Is the Truth*
captures the insights and activism of perhaps the most
famous Beatle. Noting that Partridge's photobiography
does not minimize the controversy surrounding Lennon,
a *Booklist* contributor added that *John Lennon* treats
readers to an "engrossing biography of an edgy and
enigmatic figure," and in *Horn Book* Betsey Hearne
recommended the book for the author's "masterful job
of placing Lennon's music in the context of his times."

To write her biography of Guthrie, Partridge interviewed
two of the songwriter's children, as well as his col-
league, folksinger Pete Seeger, and she also did research into the historic backdrop that inspired the man's
work. In the *New York Times Book Review,* a critic noted
that Partridge's "excellent, photo-studded biography"
reinjects Guthrie's most famous legacy—the song of
the book's title—with "its [original] undercurrent of
irony." A *Publishers Weekly* critic dubbed *This Land
Was Made for You and Me* "a lucid, affecting portrait"
of Guthrie, and in *Horn Book* Betty Carter praised the
book for presenting "a full picture of a man who defined . . . the second quarter of the twentieth century."

Turning to another aspect of twentieth-century culture,
*Marching for Freedom: Walk Together, Children, and
Don't You Grow Weary* captures the civil-rights movement through Partridge's focus on the children and
young adults who marched in the Reverend Martin
Luther King's historic march from Selma to Montgomery in March of 1965. The book also features dozens of
photographs of the march, and captures the determination of the young crusaders, many of whom Partridge
was able to interview in the course of researching her
book. "In chronicling this episode primarily from the
young participants' perspective," wrote *New York Times
Book Review* critic Leonard S. Marcus in a review of
the book, ". . . Partridge takes the past off its pedestal
and shows how ordinary people, children among them,
can sometimes tip the balance and help determine the
outcome of events." Praising *Marching for Freedom* as
"a sharply focuses historical narrative," Jonathan Hunt

added in *Horn Book* that Partridge mixes "almost peerless . . . photo selection" with a "dramatic and harrowing" account of the march that is framed by "enough context of the Jim Crow South to orient readers."

In addition to her biographical and historical works, Partridge has also authored several fiction works for children. Based on a true incident, *Clara and the Hoo-Doo Man* tells the story of Clara and her family's life in the hills of Tennessee during the late nineteenth century. The work is noteworthy, wrote Nancy Vasilakis in *Horn Book,* not just because of its period setting but also because the "characters are convincingly drawn," while a *Publishers Weekly* reviewer remarked on Partridge's "luminescent writing."

Other books by Partridge include *Oranges on Golden Mountain,* a picture book that charts the struggle of a Chinese boy who immigrates to the United States during the late 1800s and must find his place in the new home he has adopted. Reviewing the work for the *New York Times Book Review,* Laurence Downes noted that "this is a fresh subject for a picture book, and Partridge . . . tells it with vividness, grace and exquisite restraint." Engberg, writing in *Booklist,* dubbed *Oranges on Golden Mountain* "beautifully written" and also remarked on the cut-paper artwork by Aki Sogabe. Sogabe and Partridge also collaborate on *Kogi's Mysterious Journey,* pairing the author's retelling of a medieval Japanese folktale about an artist's attempt to capture the beauty of nature with "traditional cut-paper Japanese motifs," according to a *Publishers Weekly* critic. In *School Library Journal* Margaret A. Chang cited Partridge's "spare, poetic" retelling, and described *Kogi's Mysterious Journey* as an "enticing version of a Japanese tale" that will treat youngsters to "a compelling read-aloud."

Featuring mixed-media artwork by Lauren Castillo, *Big Cat Pepper* features a rhyming text in which Partridge describes a young boy's love for his tabby cat and the way he deals with Pepper's death from old age. Noting that comprehending a pet's death is one of childhood's most difficult passages, Daniel Kraus added in *Booklist* that the poignant story in *Big Cat Pepper* "is buoyed by a stirring ending," while *School Library Journal* contributor Kara Schaff noted that Castillo's illustrations "reinforc[e] . . . the idea that [the cat's] . . . death is part of a natural cycle."

Another picture-book offering by Partridge, *Whistling* features an unusual form of illustration: quilted designs in greens and blues by artist Anna Grossnickle Hines. In the story, a father and son spend time together on a camping trip and enjoy the coming of dawn. Again turning to rhyme, Partridge exhibits "a poetic flair that adds texture and engages all the senses," according to *School Library Journal* critic Laurie Edwards, the reviewer describing *Whistling* as "a compelling and seemlessly woven collage of art and text." In *Kirkus Reviews*

a critic predicted that the "gentle rhythms of both story and pictures" will inspire young listeners with a "magical sense of family love and devotion to the natural world."

Biographical and Critical Sources

PERIODICALS

Booklist, October 15, 1998, Hazel Rochman, review of *Restless Spirit: The Life and Work of Dorothea Lange,* p. 417; March 1, 2000, Stephanie Zvirin, review of *Restless Spirit,* p. 1249; January 1, 2001, Gillian Engberg, review of *Oranges on Golden Mountain,* p. 970; November 1, 2001, Gillian Engberg, review of *Annie and Bo and the Big Surprise,* p. 487; April 1, 2002, Gillian Engberg, review of *This Land Was Made for You and Me: The Life and Music of Woody Guthrie,* p. 1338; October, 2005, review of *John Lennon: All I Want Is the Truth;* April 15, 2009, Daniel Kraus, review of *Big Cat Pepper,* p. 45; August 1, 2009, Hazel Rochman, review of *Marching for Freedom: Walk Together, Children, and Don't You Grow Weary,* p. 67.

Horn Book, November-December, 1996, Nancy Vasilakis, review of *Clara and the HooDoo Man,* p. 739; March, 1999, Mary M. Burns, review of *Restless Spirit,* p. 228; March-April, 2002, Betty Carter, review of *This Land Was Made for You and Me,* p. 230; September-October, 2005, Betsy Hearne, review of *John Lennon,* p. 606; November-December, 2009, Jonathan Hunt, review of *Marching for Freedom,* p. 699.

Kirkus Reviews, November 1, 2001, review of *Annie and Bo and the Big Surprise,* p. 1555; March 1, 2003, review of *Whistling,* p. 394.

News Photographer, July, 1995, C. Zoe Smith, review of *Dorothea Lange: A Visual Life,* p. A18.

New York Times Book Review, October 21, 2001, Laurence Downes, "Young Man Goes East to the West"; July 14, 2002, review of *This Land Was Made for You and Me;* January 17, 2010, Leonard S. Marcus, review of *Marching for Freedom,* p. 12.

Publishers Weekly, June 17, 1996, review of *Clara and the HooDoo Man,* p. 65; January 17, 2000, review of *Pig's Eggs,* p. 56; February 25, 2002, review of *This Land Was Made for You and Me,* p. 68; September 9, 2002, review of *Moon Glowing,* p. 66; December 15, 2003, review of *Kogi's Mysterious Journey,* p. 72; October 3, 2005, review of *John Lennon,* p. 72; April 27, 2009, review of *Big Cat Pepper,* p. 130; October 12, 2009, review of *Marching for Freedom,* p. 52.

School Library Journal, July, 1995, Jackie Gropman, review of *Dorothea Lange,* p. 106; March, 2001, Margaret A. Chang, review of *Oranges on Golden Mountain,* p. 218; April, 2002, Ginny Gustin, review of *This Land Was Made for You and Me,* p. 180; November, 2002, Carol Ann Wilson, review of *Moon Glowing,* p. 133; April, 2003, Laurie Edwards, review of *Whistling,* p. 134; November, 2003, Margaret A. Chang, review of *Kogi's Mysterious Journey,* p. 128; October, 2005, Ginny Gustin, review of *John Lennon,*

p. 192; June, 2009, Kara Schaff, review of *Big Cat Pepper,* p. 97; October, 2009, Margaret Auguste, review of *Marching for Freedom,* p. 150.

ONLINE

Elizabeth Partridge Home Page, http://www.elizabeth partridge.com (June 1, 2010).

* * *

PON, Cindy 1973-

Personal

Born 1973, in Taipei, Taiwan; immigrated to United States, 1980; married; children: two. *Education:* University of California, San Diego, B.A.; New York University, M.A. *Hobbies and other interests:* Traveling, watching films, reading fantasy and historical fiction.

Addresses

Home—San Diego, CA. *Agent*—Bill Contardi, Brandt & Hochman Literary Agents, 1501 Broadway, Ste. 2310, New York, NY 10036. *E-mail*—pon.cindy@gmail.com.

Career

Author and artist. *Exhibitions:* Pon's Chinese brush paintings have been exhibited in San Diego, CA.

Member

Society of Children's Book Writers and Illustrators, Chinese Brush Painting Society.

Writings

Silver Phoenix: Beyond the Kingdom of Xia (fantasy novel), Greenwillow Books (New York, NY), 2009.

Sidelights

In her debut novel *Silver Phoenix: Beyond the Kingdom of Xia,* Cindy Pon offers "an appealing magical adventure set in a refreshingly non-Western milieu," observed a critic in *Kirkus Reviews.* Taking place in an ancient land that resembles China, the work centers on a young woman's quest for her father, who is held prisoner by a corrupt emperor. Pon's fantasy tale is a reflection of her own literary tastes, as she remarked to Lee & Low Books online interviewer Stacy Whitman. "When I read," Pon stated, "I love escapism, and if I can learn something about a different culture or become immersed in the author's world and characters, that is the best experience for me."

Born in Taipei, Taiwan, Pon moved to the United States when she was six years old. Entering the public school system without a background in English proved difficult for the author. "I remember going into the class and not understanding anything," she recalled to *Cynsations* online interviewer Cynthia Leitich Smith. "It made a deep impression on me—when a child cannot comprehend what's being said. I remember my first grade teacher writing my name on the board because I didn't know the alphabet, much less how to spell."

With the help of both her ESL (English as a Second Language) teacher and her mother, who tutored her at home, Pon eventually learned to read and write, and her English skills then surpassed those of her mother. Pon became a voracious reader, devouring the works in Noel Streatfeild's classic "Shoes" series of career novels, and she also read and reread *A Little Princess* by Frances Hodgson Burnett and *Island of the Blue Dolphins* by Scott O'Dell. As a teenager, Pon gravitated to fantasy, counting Tad Williams, Terry Brooks, J.R.R. Tolkien, and Madeleine L'Engle among her favorite authors. "I honestly wonder if there will be a day when I can write a novel without fantastic elements in it," she told Whitman. "I think fantasy (and speculative fiction) is so liberating. You are only limited by your own imagination in the worlds and stories you create."

Pon is also a student of Chinese brush painting, and she notes that her efforts as an artist informed her writing. "When the idea of this novel came to me," the author told Whitman, "I had just begun studying Chinese brush painting and becoming more interested in learning about the art and culture. (I did take classes in Chinese studies in university but that was more recent times, like the Cultural Revolution, etc.) Fantasy has and always will be my first love. . . . So I thought I'd write a story that combined these two interests."

Silver Phoenix focuses on the adventures of Ai Ling, a seventeen year old from the land of Xia who undertakes a dangerous journey to locate her father, who disappeared months earlier while visiting the emperor's palace. Along the way, Ai Ling is joined by Chen Yong, a young man of mixed race who is searching for clues to his origins, and Chen's brother, Li Rong. As the trio traverses a mysterious landscape, they face a host of demons and predators, and Ai Ling discovers that she possesses fantastic powers. "Strong characters and lyrical writing make this story compelling," Christina Fairman remarked in *Voice of Youth Advocates.* In *Booklist* Ilene Cooper also complimented Pon's novel, maintaining that the author's prose, "both fluid and exhilarating, shines whether she's describing a dinner delicacy or what it feels like to stab an evil spirit in the gut."

Biographical and Critical Sources

PERIODICALS

Booklist, April 1, 2009, Ilene Cooper, review of *Silver Phoenix: Beyond the Kingdom of Xia,* p. 39.

Bulletin of the Center for Children's Books, June, 2009, Kate McDowell, review of *Silver Phoenix,* p. 414.

Kirkus Reviews, April 1, 2009, review of *Silver Phoenix.*

School Library Journal, December, 2009, Christi Esterle, review of *Silver Phoenix,* p. 129.

Voice of Youth Advocates, August, 2009, Christina Fairman, review of *Silver Phoenix,* p. 242.

ONLINE

Cindy Pon Home Page, http://cindypon.com (May 1, 2010).

Cindy Pon Web log, http://cindypon.com/blog/ (May 1, 2010).

Cynsations Web log, http://cynthialeitichsmith.blogspot.com/ (May 7, 2009), Cynthia Leitich Smith, "New Voice: Cindy Pon on *Silver Phoenix: Beyond the Kingdom of Xia.*"

HarperTeen Web site, http://www.harperteen.com/ (May 1, 2010), "Cindy Pon."

Lee & Low Books Web site, http://www.leeandlow.com/ (May 1, 2010), Stacy Whitman, "Cindy Pon on Reading beyond Reality."*

*   *   *

POSESORSKI, Sherie

Personal

Female. *Education:* Columbia University, M.F.A.

Addresses

Home—Toronto, Ontario, Canada; FL.

Career

Author, editor, and book reviewer. Former editor for Harlequin Enterprises.

Awards, Honors

Moonbeam Children's Book Award, 2009, for *Shadow Boxing.*

Writings

Escape Plans (novel), Shaw Street Press (Toronto, Ontario, Canada), 1991.

Shadow Boxing (novel), Coteau Books (Regina, Saskatchewan, Canada), 2009.

Contributor of reviews and essays to periodicals, including *Books in Canada, Quill & Quire,* and *New York Times Book Review.*

Sidelights

Sherie Posesorski, a writer, editor, and book reviewer based in Canada, is the author of two novels for young-adult readers, *Escape Plans* and *Shadow Boxing.* In *Es-*cape Plans Posesorski relates the story of Becky Makowiecki, the daughter of Holocaust survivors who have relocated to Canada. During the Cuban Missile Crisis of 1962, Becky decides to construct a bomb shelter in her yard, an action that triggers unpleasant memories for her father.

Shadow Boxing centers on Alice Levitt, a sixteen year old who is grieving the loss of her mother, who died after a long illness. Unable to connect with her emotionally distant father, who had a series of affairs, Alice begins cutting herself to cope with her pain while turning to her equally troubled best friend and cousin Chloe for support. Alice also finds solace in her job at an antiquarian bookstore, where her boss teaches her to appreciate the value of traditions, as well as through her work at a fertility clinic, where she befriends an understanding young woman. "How one deals with memory is crucial here," Marnie Parsons noted in the Toronto *Globe & Mail.* Alice, Parsons continued, "has made the mementos of her mother's life a haven, but until she learns to use things to build her own life, she is unable to move forward."

Biographical and Critical Sources

PERIODICALS

Canadian Review of Materials, November 27, 2009, Karen Rankin, review of *Shadow Boxing.*

Globe & Mail (Toronto, Ontario, Canada), September 28, 2009, Marnie Parsons, review of *Shadow Boxing.*

Kirkus Reviews, April 1, 2009, review of *Shadow Boxing.*

School Library Journal, July, 2002, Renee Steinberg, review of *Escape Plans,* p. 124.

ONLINE

Coteau Books Web site, http://coteaubooks.com/ (June 1, 2010), "Sherie Posesorski."*

*   *   *

POSTGATE, Daniel 1964-

Personal

Born, 1964, in Whitstable, England; son of Richard "Oliver" Postgate (a television producer); married; children: Florence, Harry.

Addresses

Home—Whitstable, England. *Agent*—Celia Catchpole, 56 Gilpin Ave., London SW14 8QY, England. *E-mail*—daniel@danpostgate.com.

Career

Cartoonist, author, and illustrator. *Sunday Times,* London, England, former cartoonist; formerly worked as a chef.

Awards, Honors

Nottingham Children's Book Award, 2008, for *Smelly Bill.*

Writings

SELF-ILLUSTRATED

It's a Dog's Life (collected cartoon strips), Pendulum Gallery (Alton, England), 1991.
Kevin Saves the World, David Bennett (St. Albans, England), 1994.
Super Molly and the Lolly Rescue, Puffin (London, England), 1998.
Wild West Willy, Collins (London, England), 1999.
Ghost Train, Penguin (London, England), 2000.
Cats, Dogs, and Crocodiles, Puffin (London, England), 2001.
Cosmo and the Pirates (sequel to *Ghost Train*), Puffin (London, England), 2002.
The Richest Crocodile in the World, Collins (London, England), 2003.
Engelbert Sneem and His Dream Vacuum Cleaner, Meadowside Children's (London, England), 2006, published as *Engelbert Sneem and His Dream Vacuum Machine,* North-South Books (New York, NY), 2007.
Smelly Bill, NorthSouth Books (New York, NY), 2007, published in *Dig the Dog, and Other Stories,* Meadowside Children's (London, England), 2007.
Smelly Bill Stinks Again, Meadowside Children's (London, England), 2007.
There's a Yeti in My Shed!, Meadowside Children's (London, England), 2008.
The Snagglerollop, illustrated by Nick Price, Chicken House (New York, NY), 2009.

Creator of cartoon strips, including "A Dog's Life," "Bugs," and "AndtheDayBurnsCold." Also author/illustrator of *Big Mum Plum.*

ILLUSTRATOR

Kjartan Poskitt, *The Gobsmacking Galaxy,* Hippo (London, England), 1997.
The Hairy Toe, Walker (London, England), 1998.
Amanda Loverseed, *I Think My Mum's a Witch,* Walker (London, England), 1998.
Tony Mitton, *Spooky Hoo-haa!,* Walker (London, England), 1998.
Tony Mitton, *There's No Such Thing!: A Flip-flap Book,* Candlewick Press (Cambridge, MA), 1999.
Kjartan Poskitt, *The Essential Arithmetrics,* Hippo (London, England), 1999, published as *Awesome Arithmetrics,* Scholastic (London, England), 2008.
Lindsay Camp, *The Grumpy Little Girls and the Bouncy Ferret,* Collins (London, England), 2000.
Lindsay Camp, *The Grumpy Little Girls and the Naughty Little Boy,* Collins (London, England), 2000.
Lindsay Camp, *The Grumpy Little Girls and the Princess Party,* Collins (London, England), 2000.
Lindsay Camp, *The Grumpy Little Girls and the Wobbly Sleepover,* Collins (London, England), 2000.
Martin Oliver, *Dead Dinosaurs,* Scholastic (London, England), 2000.
Stephen Law, *The Philosophy Files,* Orion (London, England), 2000, published as *Philosophy Rocks!,* Hyperion (New York, NY), 2002.
Kjartan Poskitt, *The Mean and Vulgar Bits: Fractions and Averages,* Hippo (London, England), 2000.
Stephen Law, *The Outer Limits,* Dolphin (London, England), 2003, published as *The Philosophy Files 2,* Orion Children's (London, England), 2006.
Jane Bingham, reteller, *The Billy Goats Gruff,* Usborne (London, England), 2004.
Alec Silifant, *Scary Edwin Page,* Meadowside Children's (London, England), 2004.
Mike Goldsmith, *Fantastic Future,* Hippo (London, England), 2004.
Michaela Morgan, *The Spooks,* Oxford University Press (Oxford, England), 2006.
Jonathan Meres, *Diary of a Trainee Rock God,* Barrington Stoke (Edinburgh, Scotland), 2006.
Martin Waddell, *Charlie's Tasks,* Picture Window Books (Minneapolis, MN), 2007.
Sheila May Bird, *My Auntie Susan,* Crabtree Pub. Co. (New York, NY), 2008.

Sidelights

Daniel Postgate is a self-trained artist who mastered his cartooning technique while training to become a chef. Eventually hired by the London *Sunday Times,* he cre-

Daniel Postgate's **The Snagglerollop** *features a fun-more-than-scary monster that is brought to life in Nick Price's art.* (Illustration ©2009 by Nick Price. Reproduced by permission of Scholastic, Inc.)

ated cartoon strips such as "It's a Dog's Life" before turning to children's-book illustration with easy readers featuring texts by writers such as Tony Mitton, Lindsay Camp, Kjartan Poskitt, and Martin Waddell. Stephen Law's *Philosophy Rocks!,* one of several books featuring Postgate's art, introduces middle-grade readers to eight questions that great thinkers continue to ponder, mixing a serious discussion of philosophy with real-world examples, quotes from well-known children's books, and Postgate's "whimsical illustrations," which *School Library Journal* contributor Joel Shoemaker asserted "break up [Law's] . . . text and provide some think time."

With books such as *Engelbert Sneem and His Dream Vacuum Machine, The Richest Crocodile in the World,* and *Smelly Bill,* Postgate takes on the task of both artist and author, mixing rhyming texts with his watercolor-and-ink illustrations. Described by *School Library Journal* contributor Linda M. Kenton as "one of those treasured picture books that has a fresh concept, beautiful poetry, and appealing illustrations," *Engelbert Sneem and His Dream Vacuum Machine* tells the story of an elfin creature who flies about in the night and steals children's dreams in order to enjoy them himself. When Sneem realizes that his theft of happy dreams has left children only with nightmares, he has a change of heart, however, and decides to relieve children of their nightmares instead. A story of a wealthy reptile who learns that all his riches are nothing compared to the happiness of good friends is told in *The Richest Crocodile in the World,* an amusing animal-filled tale that features "childlike themes. . ., urbane cartooning, and comic chemistry" between central characters, according to a *Publishers Weekly* critic.

A story that will resonate with all children who dislike bath time, *Smelly Bill* focuses on a dog that avoids its human family's many efforts to bathe it. However, when the very determined Great-Aunt Bleach comes to dog-sit during a family vacation, cleaning the stinky pup becomes her primary goal. Bill hides out in the smelliest place a dog can find, but no avail. "Postgate's . . . cartoons pull out all the stops," announced a *Publishers Weekly* critic in reviewing the story, the critic asserting that the author/illustrator's watercolor-and-ink illustrations "provide the perfect complement to his rollicking verse." *Smelly Bill*—which Postgate has followed up with the equally humorous *Smelly Bill Stinks Again*—earned praise from Martha Simpson in *School Library Journal,* the critic predicting that the book's "bright, energetic pictures . . . are sure to tickle youngsters' funny bones." In *Kirkus Reviews* a contributor described Postgate's canine hero as "a wily, scraggly, snaggle-toothed mongrel" and praised the author's "delightful rhymes" as highlights of a book that "is truly tail-wagging fun."

In another original picture book, *The Snagglerollop,* illustrations by Nick Price bring to life Postgate's easy-reading, sing-song text. In the story, young Sam is not allowed to have a pet, but when he comes home with the imaginary Snagglerollop his mom and dad approve. Soon the large, imaginary creature is joining the family on outings, and when Sam's friend Emily bemoans the lack of a pet kitten, the boy suggests that she bring home an equally exotic imaginary creature. In *School Library Journal* Mary Jean Smith predicted that *The Snagglerollop* "will resonate with youngsters" of various reading abilities.

Biographical and Critical Sources

PERIODICALS

Kirkus Reviews, March 1, 2007, review of *Smelly Bill,* p. 230; April 1, 2009, review of *The Snagglegrollop.*
Publishers Weekly, June 16, 2003, review of *The Richest Crocodile in the World,* p. 70; May 7, 2007, review of *Smelly Bill,* p. 58.
School Library Journal, October, 2002, Joel Shoemaker, review of *Philosophy Rocks!,* p. 187; August, 2007, Martha Simpson, review of *Smelly Bill,* p. 88; November, 2007. Linda M. Kenton, review of *Englebert Sneem and His Dream Vacuum Machine,* p. 99; September, 2008, Susan Lissim, review of *My Auntie Susan,* p. 138; May, 2009, Mary Jean Smith, review of *The Snagglegrollop,* p. 85.

ONLINE

Daniel Postgate Home Page, http://www.danpostgate.com (May 15, 2010).
Walker Books Web site, http://www.walker.co.uk/ (May 15, 2010), "Daniel Postgate."*

* * *

POTTER, Alicia

Personal

Female. *Education:* Simmons College, B.A. (English); Vermont College of Fine Arts, M.F.A. (writing for children and young adults).

Addresses

Home—Boston, MA. *Agent*—Prospect Agency, 551 Valley Rd., PMB 377, Upper Montclair, NJ 07043. *E-mail*—apotter@tiac.net.

Career

Journalist and author of books for children. Presenter at schools and conferences.

Awards, Honors

Award from PEN New England; Oppenheim Toy Portfolio Gold Award, 2009, for *Fritz Danced the Fandango.*

Writings

Fritz Danced the Fandango, illustrated by Ethan Long, Scholastic, Inc. (New York, NY), 2009.
Mrs. Harkness and the Panda, Alfred A. Knopf (New York, NY), 2011.

Contributor of articles and reviews to *Boston Phoenix, Family Fun,* and *Health.*

Biographical and Critical Sources

PERIODICALS

Booklist, May 15, 2009, Julie Cummins, review of *Fritz Danced the Fandango,* p. 44.
Kirkus Reviews, April 1, 2009, review of *Fritz Danced the Fandango.*
School Library Journal, May, 2009, Marge Loch-Wouters, review of *Fritz Danced the Fandango,* p. 86.

*   *   *

PROSEK, James 1975-

Personal

Born May 23, 1975, in Stamford, CT; son of Louis Prosek (an astronomy teacher) and Christina Willinger. *Ethnicity:* "White" *Education:* Yale University, B.A., 1997. *Religion:* "Angling." *Hobbies and other interests:* Fishing, playing guitar, singing.

Addresses

Home and office—Easton, CT. *Agent*—Elaine Markson, 44 Greenwich Ave., New York, NY 10011.

Career

Artist, writer, activist, and naturalist. Cofounder, with Yvon Chouinard, of World Trout (conservation initiative), 2004—. Producer and host of *The Complete Angler* (documentary), ESPN, 2002. Songwriter and guitarist for Troutband. *Exhibitions:* Paintings have been shown at galleries and museums, including Beinecke Rare Book and Manuscript Library, Yale University, New Haven, CT, 1996; Cincinnati Museum Center, Cincinnati, OH, 1999; Gerald Peters Gallery, New York, NY, 2000, 2003; Galerie Larock-Granoff, Paris, France, 2002; Aldrich Contemporary Art Museum, Ridgefield, CT, 2008; Center for Contemporary Printmaking, Norwalk, CT, 2009; Beverly Reynolds Gallery, Richmond, VA, 2009; and Tanya Bonakdar Gallery, New York, NY, 2010.

Awards, Honors

Peabody Award, 2003, for documentary *The Complete Angler;* Cooperative Children's Book Council Choices selection, for *A Good Day's Fishing;* Teachers' Choices selection, International Reading Association, and Best Children's Books of the Year designation, Bank Street College of Education, both for *Bird, Butterfly, Eel.*

Writings

(Self-illustrated) *Trout: An Illustrated History,* Knopf (New York, NY), 1996.
Joe and Me: An Education in Fishing and Friendship (memoir), Rob Weisbach Books (New York, NY), 1997.
The Complete Angler: A Connecticut Yankee Follows in the Footsteps of Walton (also see below), HarperCollins (New York, NY), 1999.
(Self-illustrated) *Early Love and Brook Trout,* Lyons Press (New York, NY), 2000.
(And producer and host) *The Complete Angler* (documentary), ESPN, 2002.
(Self-illustrated) *Fly-fishing the 41st: Around the World on the 41st Parallel,* HarperCollins (New York, NY), 2003, published as *Fly-fishing the 41st: From Connecticut to Mongolia and Home Again: A Fisherman's Odyssey,* 2004.
(Self-illustrated) *Trout of the World,* Stewart, Tabori & Chang (New York, NY), 2003.
(Self-illustrated) *A Good Day's Fishing,* Simon & Schuster (New York, NY), 2004.
The Day My Mother Left (young-adult novel), Simon & Schuster (New York, NY), 2007.
(Editor, with Joseph Furia; and illustrator) *Tight Lines: Ten Years of the Yale Anglers' Journal,* Yale University Press (New Haven, CT), 2007.
(Self-illustrated) *Bird, Butterfly, Eel,* Simon & Schuster (New York, NY), 2009.

Cofounder of *Yale Anglers' Journal,* 1996. Contributor to periodicals, including *New York Times* and *Sports Afield.*

OTHER

(Illustrator) Stephen Sloan, editor, *Fly Fishing Is Spoken Here: The Most Prominent Anglers in the World Talk Tactics, Strategies, and Attitudes,* Lyons Press (Guilford, CT), 2003.

Adaptations

The Day My Mother Left was adapted as an audio book.

Sidelights

An accomplished author and artist, James Prosek has earned recognition for creating spectacular watercolor paintings that examine humankind's relationship with nature. An avid fisherman, Prosek shares his love of the sport in such books as *Joe and Me: An Education in Fishing and Friendship* and *A Good Day's Fishing,* the latter a self-illustrated title for young readers.

Prosek also works as an activist and naturalist; in 2004, he cofounded World Trout, an organization dedicated to preserving native trout species around the globe. In addition to his other endeavors, he plays guitar, sings, and writes songs for Troutband, an acoustic trio. "Prosek is a young man of incredible talent—artistic, literary, and musical," Meredith E. Lewis stated in a *Watercolor* profile. "His prose is graceful, engaging, and fresh, and provides an articulate and gently persuasive argument for living a contemplative life."

Prosek's interest in the natural world was fueled by the art of John James Audubon and Louis Agassiz Fuertes, which he discovered at the age of five. "My fascination with the idea of capturing a living, ecstatically colorful creature within the pages of a book," Prosek told Robert H. Boyle in *Sports Illustrated,* "was born out of my love for both Audubon and Fuertes." He began fishing at the urging of a classmate, and the experiences helped the future artist stave off bouts of loneliness. "Fishing helped me discover myself, to find my own footing, in the wake of my mother leaving home when I was nine," he remarked in a *Children's Literature* interview. "When my mother left, I started going off into the woods by

Cover of James Prosek's **The Day My Mother Left,** *a middle-grade novel following the coming of age of a young boy.* (Cover photographs ©2009 by Little Blue Wolf Productions/Corbis. Reproduced by permission.)

myself with a fishing rod. It gave me a certain power to know that I had this skill to catch fish that not a lot of my friends did."

During the years that most teenagers spend struggling with rebellion and identity, Prosek drew pictures and went fishing. His parents encouraged him, pushing him in math and science in school and paying for private art lessons. Prosek kept a journal, sketching each fish he caught, describing where he caught them and in what weather. His father, Louis, interviewd for *Yankee* magazine by Jim Collins, described him as "extraordinarily focused" on his twin passions of painting and fishing.

Prosek's hard work paid off, and he began to gain a reputation as a naturalist at the surprisingly young age of twenty, when he published *Trout: An Illustrated History.* The idea for this book came early to Prosek. When he was fourteen, he searched the library for an illustrated encyclopedia on trout that was equivalent to Audubon's famous works on birds. No such book existed, so Prosek decided to create one. The work, which *New York Times* reviewer Christopher Lehmann-Haupt called a "dazzlingly brilliant collection," contains seventy-one watercolor plates of American trout and their European relative, the brown trout. "The finished paintings," declared John Balzar in the *Los Angeles Times Book Review,* "are so evocative that he [Prosek] has been compared favorably to the man who inspired him, John James Audubon, which is as much praise as any young artist could ever hope for."

In creating *Trout* Prosek painted each fish four times to be sure he correctly captured all their patterns and colors. When he could, he based his work on photographs, but in some cases the trout he was painting had become extinct, or had hybridized with other trout. In these cases, Prosek based his work on detailed descriptions in what he calls "insanely hard-to-find old books written before trout were tampered with on a large scale." *Trout* includes natural histories of each species and variant, and, as Balzar noted, is "an eloquent testimony to, and plea for, the diversity of these streamlined marvels." "For me," Prosek commented, "the trout in its stream is the essence of life—encompassing survival and beauty, death and rebirth."

When Prosek was fifteen years old, he was caught fishing without a license by game warden Joe Haines. Instead of sending Prosek to juvenile court, Haines gave him a second chance and an education on legal fishing, and their friendship is described in Prosek's memoir, *Joe and Me.* Haines taught Prosek to be an outdoorsman with style, passing along lessons in generosity, humor, curiosity, having a good heart, and doing the right thing, as well as the location of secret fishing spots and special fishing techniques. Although Joe had no education beyond high school, he had the wisdom that can only be gained through long observation of nature, and Prosek was a willing student. As Lehmann-Haupt wrote in his *New York Times* review of the book, "What the older man mainly taught the author was how to observe the minute details of nature."

A *Kirkus Reviews* critic described Prosek's watercolors in *Joe and Me* as "sweet, innocent, if not particularly artful" and noted that "Prosek . . . may be well on his way to becoming a fine writer of the outdoors." A *Publishers Weekly* critic concurred that Prosek's writing style needs refinement, but called the book "engaging" and "appealing." Lehmann-Haupt deemed *Joe and Me* "a charming, physically attractive memoir," then added: "Here [is] a young man of unusual gifts, not the least of them being the capacity to understand what it is like not to be so young anymore."

In *The Complete Angler: A Connecticut Yankee Follows in the Footsteps of Walton,* Prosek recounts his travels through England as a college undergraduate at Yale University. During his trip he fished in the same waters as Izaak Walton, author of *The Compleat Angler,* a classic work first published in 1653. "The book's charm . . . lies in its quiet realism, both in Prosek's honest reflections and in his vivid paintings, which accompany the text," remarked a contributor in *Publishers Weekly,* and Lehmann-Haupt noted that the memoir's "prose makes you see the special greenness of English foliage and feel the gentle current of its streams." Prosek followed *The Complete Angler* with *Early Love and Brook Trout,* a personal work also illustrated with his watercolor paintings. Prosek's "writing at its best is simple, earnest and resonant," a critic in *Publishers Weekly* stated of the book.

A travelogue filled with Prosek's watercolors, *Fly-Fishing on the 41st* chronicles the fisherman artist's journeys along the 41st parallel, the latitude line that contains the city of Easton, Connecticut, where he lives, as well as New York, Madrid, Istanbul, and Beijing. Dennis Dodge, writing in *Booklist,* noted that the author's "enthusiasm for fish by no means blinds him to the charms and eccentricities of the places he goes," and a *Publishers Weekly* reviewer concluded of *Fly-Fishing on the 41st* that "Prosek's passion and earnest investigation more than make up for any absence of tall fish tales."

A young angler describes his love for a favorite pastime in Prosek's *A Good Day's Fishing,* his first children's book. While searching through his tackle box for his most essential items, the narrator acquaints readers with a variety of lures and hooks, all which are depicted in Prosek's accompanying illustrations. *A Good Day's Fishing* "is a special treat that may lure to the surface the ever-hopeful fisherperson lurking in youngsters' inner depths," Patricia Manning noted in *School Library Journal,* and Ed Sullivan, critiquing the title in *Booklist,* remarked that "the wonderfully detailed, gentle watercolor illustrations of fish and gear offer a lovely introduction."

In his award-winning children's title *Bird, Butterfly, Eel* Prosek explores the migration patterns of a barn swallow, a monarch butterfly, and an American eel, all of which begin their life on a New England farm. The unusual page layout employs three horizontal panels, allowing readers to view all three creatures simultaneously. "You can tell Prosek understands that in factual books we want not only to be entertained but to build on our body of knowledge," Lisa Von Drasek observed in the *New York Times Book Review.* "Jewellike colors, skilled draftsmanship and intelligent composition bring readers right into the world" of the animals, a *Publishers Weekly* critic wrote, and Von Drasek complimented the artwork by stating that "Prosek's detailed watercolor paintings bring us into the landscape."

The Day My Mother Left, Prosek's debut young-adult novel, focuses on Jeremy Vrabec, a nine year old who is devastated after his mother abandons their family for another man. With the help of a caring uncle, Jeremy turns to sketching wildlife for solace and begins learning how to cope with his unresolved feelings for his estranged parent. "Prosek's story is the sort English teachers would love to assign. It is a fine book, with a quality of excellence we don't frequently see," Claire Rosser noted in *Kliatt.* The semi-autobiographical tale also earned praise from a *Publishers Weekly* reviewer, who maintained that "readers will feel hopeful for the hero, even if he cannot yet recognize his own strength."

Despite his success in a number of artistic fields, Prosek is modest about his accomplishments. "I've been lucky to find an audience for the things I do," he told *Watercolor* reporter Lewis. "I've found that the times when things work best for me are the times when I'm doing what my heart tells me to do. I've been trying to live more in my imagination and less in what's really out there, because what's really out there isn't necessarily real either. What you create can become real."

Biographical and Critical Sources

PERIODICALS

Audubon, July, 1996, review of *Trout: An Illustrated History,* p. 113.

Booklist, April 15, 1999, John Rowen, review of *The Complete Angler: A Connecticut Yankee Follows in the Footsteps of Wisdom,* p. 1501; June 1, 2000, John Rowen, review of *Early Love and Brook Trout* p. 1834; February 15, 2003, Dennis Dodge, review of *Fly-Fishing the 41st: Around the World on the 41st Parallel,* p. 1031; February 15, 2004, Ed Sullivan, review of *A Good Day's Fishing,* p. 1063; April 15, 2007, Hazel Rochman, review of *The Day My Mother Left,* p. 40; January 1, 2009, Carolyn Phelan, review of *Bird, Butterfly, Eel,* p. 90.

Country Living, April, 1999, Matthew Holm, "Watercolors and Fish Tales," p. 92.

Inc., October, 1999, "What Makes James Prosek's Business Plan So Different from Yours Is That He's Not Just Going into Business for Himself. He's Going into Business as Himself," p. 52.

Kirkus Reviews, May 1, 1997, review of *Joe and Me: An Education in Fishing and Friendship,* p. 703.

Kliatt, January, 2007, Claire Rosser, review of *The Day My Mother Left,* p. 17.

Library Journal, June 15, 2000, Jeff Grossman, review of *Early Love and Brook Trout,* p. 92; February 1, 2003, Larry R. Little, review of *Fly-Fishing the 41st,* p. 97.

Los Angeles Times Book Review, June 9, 1996, John Balzar, review of *Trout,* p. 8.

New York Times, July 31, 1994, James Lomuscio, "A Fair Bid to Become the Audubon of the Fishing World;" July 7, 1997, Christopher Lehmann-Haupt, review of *An Education in Fishing and Friendship;* May 13, 1999, Christopher Lehmann-Haupt, review of *The Complete Angler;* November 12, 2000, Pete Bodo, "A Portrait of the Artist as a Young Fly-fisherman," p. 45; January 13, 2008, Susan Hodara, "Interpreting a Blueprint for Birds," p. 10.

New York Times Book Review, June 1, 2003, Adam Clymer, review of *Fly-Fishing the 41st,* p. 11; May 10, 2009, Lisa Von Drasek, "Bird on a Wire, Eel in a Pond," p. 17.

Outdoor Life, April, 1996, review of *Trout,* p. 21.

People, July 1, 1996, "Scaled Models: Reelist James Prosek Puts His Catch on Canvas," p. 62.

Publishers Weekly, February 19, 1996, review of *Trout,* p. 200; May 26, 1997, review of *Joe and Me,* p. 77; April 12, 1999, review of *The Complete Angler,* p. 63; April 24, 2000, review of *Early Love and Brook Trout,* p. 75; February 17, 2003, review of *Fly-Fishing the 41st,* p. 66; January 22, 2007, review of *The Day My Mother Left,* p. 185; February 16, 2009, review of *Bird, Butterfly, Eel,* p. 128.

School Library Journal, May, 2004, Patricia Manning, review of *A Good Day's Fishing,* p. 122; March, 2007, Terrie Dorio, review of *The Day My Mother Left,* p. 217; February, 2009, Kathy Piehl, review of *Bird, Butterfly, Eel,* p. 84.

Sports Illustrated, April 29, 1996, Robert H. Boyle, "All the Colors of a Rainbow," p. A4.

Watercolor, fall, 2003, Linda S. Price, "A Symbiotic Relationship: A Talented Painter and Writer, James Prosek Has Discovered How the Two Disciplines Can Work Together Both Creatively and Commercially," p. 102; summer, 2005, Meredith E. Lewis, "Nature, Imagination Itself," p. 100.

Yankee, July, 1997, Jim Collins, profile of Prosek, pp. 38-42, 112-114.

ONLINE

Children's Literature Web site, http://www.childrenslit.com/childrenslit/ (June 1, 2010), "Q&A with James Prosek."

James Prosek Home Page, http://www.troutsite.com (June 1, 2010).

Yale University Press Web site, http://yalepress.yale.edu/ (June 1, 2010), interview with Prosek.*

R

RAYNOR, Gemma 1985-

Personal

Born 1985, in Sheffield, England. *Education:* North Wales School of Art and Design, degree (illustration; first class), 2006. *Hobbies and other interests:* Making jewelry, collecting postcards.

Addresses

Home—Chester, England. *Agent*—Eunice McMullen, Low Ibbotsholme Cottage, Off Bridge La., Troutbeck Bridge, Windermere, Cumbria LA23 1HU, England.

Career

Illustrator of books and greeting cards.

Awards, Honors

Young Designers Illustration Award, and Award for Design Excellence in Illustration, New Designers Exhibition, both 2006.

Illustrator

Lucy M. George, *What's the Time Mr Wolf?*, Meadowside Children's (London, England), 2007.
Gillian Shields, *Tom's Tree,* Good Books (Intercourse, PA), 2009.

Also illustrator of *Mimi Make-Believe.*

Biographical and Critical Sources

PERIODICALS

Booklist, May 1, 2009, Randall Enos, review of *Tom's Tree,* p. 90.
Kirkus Reviews, April 1, 2009, review of *Tom's Tree.*

School Library Journal, June, 2009, Marilyn Ackerman, review of *Tom's Tree,* p. 99.

ONLINE

Eunice McMullen, Ltd., Web site, http://www.eunice mcmullen.co.uk/ (June 1, 2010), "Gemma Raynor."
Walker Books Australia and New Zealand Web site, http://www.walkerbooks.com.au/ (June 1, 2010), "Gemma Raynor."*

*   *   *

RAYYAN, Omar 1968-

Personal

Born 1968; married: wife's name Sheila (an artist).

Addresses

Home—MA. *E-mail*—omar@studiorayyan.com.

Career

Studio Rayyan, artist and illustrator.

Writings

ILLUSTRATOR

Cathy Spagnoli, *The Greedy Crows: A Tale from Northern India,* Wright Group (Bothell, WA), 1995.
Eric A. Kimmel, *Rimonah of the Flashing Sword: A North African Tale,* Holiday House (New York, NY), 1995.
Suhaib Hamid Ghazi, *Ramadan,* Holiday House (New York, NY), 1996.
Eric A. Kimmel, *Count Silvernose: A Story from Italy,* Holiday House (New York, NY), 1996.

Teresa Bateman, *The Ring of Truth: An Original Irish Tale,* Holiday House (New York, NY), 1997.

Evangeline Nicholas, *Lilacs, Lotuses and Ladybugs,* Wright Group (Bothell, WA), 1997.

John Warren Stewig, *King Midas: A Golden Tale,* Holiday House (New York, NY), 1999.

Kathleen Duey, *Moonsilver,* Aladdin Paperbacks (New York, NY), 2001.

Kathleen Duey, *The Mountains of the Moon,* Aladdin (New York, NY), 2002.

Kathleen Duey, *The Silver Bracelet,* Aladdin (New York, NY), 2002.

Kathleen Duey, *The Sunset Gates,* Aladdin (New York, NY), 2002.

Ann Downer, *Hatching Magic,* Simon & Schuster (New York, NY), 2003.

Kathleen Duey, *True Heart,* Aladdin (New York, NY), 2003.

Kathleen Duey, *The Journey Home,* Aladdin (New York, NY), 2003.

Kathleen Duey, *Castle Avamir,* Aladdin Paperbacks (New York, NY), 2003.

M.I. McAllister, *Urchin of the Riding Stars,* Miramax Books/Hyperion Books for Children (New York, NY), 2005.

Mary Casanova, *Dog-napped,* Aladdin Paperbacks (New York, NY), 2006.

Mary Casanova, *Trouble in Pembrook,* Aladdin Paperbacks (New York, NY), 2006.

M.I. McAllister, *Urchin and the Heartstone,* Hyperion Books for Children (New York, NY), 2006.

Judy Cox, *The Mystery of the Burmese Bandicoot,* Marshall Cavendish (New York, NY), 2007.

M.I. McAllister, *The Urchin and the Raven War,* Hyperion Books for Children (New York, NY), 2008.

Peter Howe, *Waggit's Tale,* HarperCollins (New York, NY), 2008.

Mary Casanova, *The Turtle-Hatching Mystery,* Simon & Schuster (New York, NY), 2008.

Ann Downer, *The Dragon of Never-Was,* Simon & Schuster (New York, NY), 2008.

Judy Cox, *The Case of the Purloined Professor,* Marshall Cavendish (New York, NY), 2009.

Peter Howe, *Waggit Again,* HarperCollins (New York, NY), 2009.

Sidelights

Born 1968, Omar Rayyan is a studio artist and illustrator as well as owner of the Studio Rayyan along with his wife and fellow artist, Sheila Rayyan. Rayyan has illustrated numerous books geared toward younger audiences of varying ages, bringing to life texts by writers such as Teresa Bateman, Judy Cox, and John Warren Stewig.

King Midas: A Golden Tale, a retelling of the classic tale by Stewig, provides ample contextual material for Rayyan to include in his illustrations, such as the richly designed interiors and architecture and the mysterious mythological creatures that are cast in Stewig's tale. As in the classic story, Midas is gifted with the ability to turn items into gold with a simple touch, and the man tests his newfound ability by wandering around and stroking things into gold. However, at breakfast he realizes the limitations of his new talent, when, sitting down to coffee and a bowl of breakfast cereal—Poseidon Puffs—he proceeds to turn his daughter Marygold into a gold statue. Fortunately for Midas, the stranger who gifted him with the golden touch reappears to take away the special talent and also restore Marygold to normal. John Peters, reviewing *King Midas* for *Booklist,* declared that "children will pore over the plethora of comic detail in Rayyan's swirling illustrations."

Rayyan provides the art work for a series of early reader stories by Kathleen Duey that follow the adventures of a young girl named Heart Avamir. First introduced to readers in *Moonsilver,* Heart has apparently been abandoned, and to make things more complicated, she cannot seem to remember where she came from or why she is alone. A grumpy man found her wandering, and despite his cantankerous mood he took her in, but Heart was given a name by Ruth, the local apothecary, who has taken a more personal interest in the girl. Catherine Threadgill, in a review for *School Library Journal,* praised the book for early readers, citing Rayyan's "moody, evocative black-and-white illustrations."

Heart is on the run in *The Mountains of the Moon.* Discovered by gypsies while she hides a young unicorn, Heart protects the magical animal by pretending that it's horn is not real, but instead is attached with a bit of tree gum. The gypsies fall for her trick and end up taking both Heart and the unicorn along with them as they travel on. While Heart enjoys being part of a "family", she realizes soon enough that by staying with the gypsies she puts them in danger. As she continues her own travels in *The Silver Bracelet*, it gradually becomes apparent to Heart that she has some link to the unicorns. Susan Dove Lempke, in a review for *Booklist,* commented of *The Mountains of the Moon* that "Rayyan's illustrations, one per chapter, are old-fashioned and luscious."

Biographical and Critical Sources

PERIODICALS

Booklist, March 1, 1995, Ilene Cooper, review of *Rimonah of the Flashing Sword: A North African Tale,* p. 1245; March 15, 1996, Susan Dove Lempke, review of *Count Silvernose: A Story from Italy,* p. 1263; October 1, 1996, Susan Dove Lempke, review of *Ramadan,* p. 337; July 1, 1997, Karen Morgan, review of *The Ring of Truth: An Original Irish Tale,* p. 1817; February 15, 1999, John Peters, review of *King Midas: A Golden Tale,* p. 1073; January 1, 2002, Susan Dove Lempke, review of *Moonsilver,* p. 856; September 1, 2002, Susan Dove Lempke, review of *The Mountains of the Moon,* p. 123; September 1, 2002, review of

The Silver Bracelet, p. 123; March 1, 2003, Susan Dove Lempke, review of *The Sunset Gates,* p. 1197; March 1, 2003, review of *True Heart,* p. 1197; October 1, 2005, GraceAnne A. DeCandido, review of *Urchin of the Riding Stars,* p. 59; June 1, 2006, Carolyn Phelan, review of *The Dragon of Never-Was,* p. 70; October 1, 2007, Kristen McKulski, review of *The Mystery of the Burmese Bandicoot,* p. 59; July 1, 2008, Anne O'Malley, review of *Waggit's Tale,* p. 68.

Bulletin of the Center for Children's Books, July 1, 1996, review of *Count Silvernose,* p. 377; December 1, 1996, review of *Ramadan,* p. 134; May 1, 1997, review of *The Ring of Truth,* p. 313; March 1, 1999, review of *King Midas,* p. 258.

Childhood Education, September 22, 1999, Linda J. Gibbs, review of *King Midas,* p. 47.

Horn Book, July 1, 1996, Elizabeth S. Watson, review of *Count Silvernose*; July 1, 2006, Anita L. Burkam, review of *The Dragon of Never-Was.*

Instructor, September 1, 1997, review of *The Ring of Truth,* p. 22.

Kirkus Reviews, July 1, 2005, review of *Urchin of the Riding Stars,* p. 739; June 1, 2006, review of *The Dragon of Never-Was,* p. 571; August 15, 2007, review of *The Mystery of the Burmese Bandicoot.*

Magpies, May 1, 2005, review of *Urchin of the Riding Stars,* p. 36.

Publishers Weekly, February 13, 1995, review of *Rimonah of the Flashing Sword,* p. 78; February 24, 1997, review of *The Ring of Truth,* p. 91; June 27, 2005, review of *Urchin of the Riding Stars,* p. 63; June 23, 2008, review of *Waggit's Tale,* p. 55.

Reading Teacher, May 1, 1998, Evelyn B. Freeman, review of *The Ring of Truth,* p. 684.

School Library Journal, March 1, 1995, Donna L. Scanlon, review of *Rimonah of the Flashing Sword,* p. 198; March 1, 1996, Donna L. Scanlon, review of *Count Silvernose,* p. 189; October 1, 1996, Celia A. Huffman, review of *Ramadan,* p. 113; May 1, 1997, Beth Tegart, review of *The Ring of Truth,* p. 92; March 1, 1999, Patricia Lothrop-Green, review of *King Midas,* p. 201; December 1, 2001, Catherine Threadgill, review of *Moonsilver,* p. 99; August 1, 2003, Eva Mitnick, review of *Hatching Magic,* p. 158; February 1, 2004, Elaine E. Knight, review of *Castle Avamir,* p. 111; November 1, 2005, Caitlin Augusta, review of *Urchin of the Riding Stars,* p. 141; December 1, 2006, Mara Alpert, review of *The Dragon of Never-Was,* p. 136; December 1, 2006, Kristin Anderson, review of *Urchin and the Heartstone,* p. 150; December 1, 2007, Sheila Fiscus, review of *The Mystery of the Burmese Bandicoot,* p. 120; August 1, 2008, Kathleen E. Gruver, review of *Waggit's Tale,* p. 122.

Social Education, April 1, 1998, review of *Ramadan,* p. 214.

Teacher Librarian, May 1, 1999, Jessica Higgs, review of *Ramadan,* p. 51.

Voice of Youth Advocates, February 1, 2006, Teresa Copeland, review of *Urchin of the Riding Stars,* p. 500.

ONLINE

Studio Rayyan Web site, http://www.studiorayyan.com (June 1, 2010).*

ROLLINS, James 1961-
[A pseudonym]
(James Clemens, James Czajkowski)

Personal

Born James Czajkowski, August 20, 1961, in Chicago, IL. *Education:* University of Missouri, D.V.M., 1985. *Hobbies and other interests:* Amateur spelunking and SCUBA diving.

Addresses

Home—Sacramento, CA. *Agent*—Russell Galen, Scovil Galen Ghosh Literary Agency, 276 5th Ave., Ste. 708, New York, NY 10001. *E-mail*—authorjamesrollins@me. com.

Career

Novelist. Owned a veterinary clinic in Sacramento, CA, for ten years.

Member

International Thriller Writers (co-president, 2009).

Writings

"BANNED AND THE BANISHED" FANTASY SERIES; UNDER PSEUDONYM JAMES CLEMENS

Wit'ch Fire, Del Rey (New York, NY), 1998.
Wit'ch Storm, Del Rey (New York, NY), 1999.
Wit'ch War, Del Rey (New York, NY), 2000.
Wit'ch Gate, Del Rey (New York, NY), 2001.
Wit'ch Star, Del Rey (New York, NY), 2002.

"GODSLAYER CHRONICLES" FANTASY SERIES; UNDER PSEUDONYM JAMES CLEMENS

Shadowfall, Roc (New York, NY), 2005.
Hinterland, Roc (New York, NY), 2006.

NOVELS

Subterranean, Avon (New York, NY), 1999.
Excavation, HarperTorch (New York, NY), 2000.
Amazonia, Morrow (New York, NY), 2002.
Ice Hunt, Morrow (New York, NY), 2003.
Indiana Jones and the Kingdom of the Crystal Skull (movie novelization), Del Rey (New York, NY), 2008.
Jake Ransom and the Skull King's Shadow, HarperCollins (New York, NY), 2009.
Altar of Eden, Morrow (New York, NY), 2010.

"SIGMA FORCE" SERIES

Sandstorm, Morrow (New York, NY), 2004.
Map of Bones, Morrow (New York, NY), 2005.
Black Order, Morrow (New York, NY), 2006.

The Judas Strain, Morrow (New York, NY), 2007.
The Last Oracle, Morrow (New York, NY), 2008.
The Doomsday Key, Morrow (New York, NY), 2009.

Adaptations

The Doomsday Key was adapted as an audio book, HarperAudio, 2009.

Sidelights

James Rollins, a veterinarian-turned-writer, is the author of such best-selling adventure novels as *Sandstorm, The Doomsday Key,* and several novels in his "Sigma Force" series. Rollins—whose real name is James Czajkowski—is also the creator of the "Godslayer" and "Banned and the Banished" fantasy novels, published under the pseudonym James Clemens. "My goal when I set out to write is not to examine the human condition or explore the trials and tribulations of modern society," Rollins noted on his home page. "When I set out to write, I aim for pure balls-to-the-wall adventure, pure escape and entertainment."

Rollins developed an appreciation for reading and writing in high school, but ultimately followed his interest in medicine by earning a doctorate of veterinary medicine from the University of Missouri. "I wrote a lot in junior high and high school and took some creative writing classes, but I was set on being a veterinarian," he remarked in a *Writers Digest* interview with Maria Schneider. "I always read voraciously, and I always wanted to be a writer, but it didn't seem like a career." Rollins opened a veterinary clinic in Sacramento, California, writing short fiction in his spare time before graduating to book-length manuscripts. At the Maui Writers Conference in 1996, he entered a manuscript into a writers' contest and earned the attention that led to the publishing of his first novel, *Wit'ch Fire.* Rollins, who counts Jules Verne, H.G. Wells, and H. Rider Haggard among his literary influences, eventually gave up his veterinary clinic to become a full-time novelist.

Published under his Clemens pseudonym, *Wit'ch Fire* is also the first book in Rollins' "Banned and the Banished" series. The book and series focus on Elena, a young woman searching for the answer to why she suddenly developed magical powers. After her parents are killed and her brother captured, Elena is pursued by villains looking to steal her magic and cause her harm. She is helped along the way by a host of fantastic companions that includes a nymph, a giant, and an ogre. Many reviewers welcomed *Wit'ch Fire* as an enjoyable read, sometimes commenting on Rollins's imaginative characters and plot. Others appreciated the author's development of a multidimensional story with an exciting premise. Rollins "demonstrates considerable skill at combining swift pacing with character development in this gracefully written beginning to a projected high fantasy quest," observed *Library Journal* contributor Jackie Cassada in a review of *Wit'ch Fire.*

Rollins went on to write four more books in his "Banned and the Banished" series. In *Wit'ch Storm* Elena ventures to A'loa Glen, a legendary lost city that holds the key to defeating a powerful dark lord. "There's a lot of character building—much of it expert" in the novel, wrote a *Publishers Weekly* critic. With the help of her allies, Elena prepares to invade A'loa Glen in *Wit'ch War.* The narrative "revolves around strong women and an abundantly detailed world," noted a contributor in *Publishers Weekly.*

Wit'ch Gate, the fourth series installment, continues to follow the witch Elena as she searches for the weirgates, which must be destroyed in order to relieve the blight brought on by the Dark Lord. Elena and her friends split up, and each group pursues one of the four weirgates, encountering many hazards along their respective paths. *Wit'ch Gate* is "a solid addition to the growing body of panoramic fantasy," commented Cassada in another review for *Library Journal.* "The author supplies enough plot twists to keep the reader guessing what will happen next," remarked a *Publishers Weekly* contributor. In *Wit'ch Star,* the conclusion to the "Banned and the Banished" series, Elena and her companions reunite to destroy the remaining weirgate.

Also published under the Clemens pseudonym, Rollins' "Godslayer Chronicles" begins with *Shadowfall.* Here the author tells the story of Tylar de Noche, a knight who witnessed the murder of one of the hundred gods of the Nine Lands. Now on the run, Tylar also searches for the creature that is responsible for the murder, and he joins forces with several outcasts who are willing to help him. In *Hinterland,* Tylar must enter a barren world to save the Nine Lands. Roland Green noted in *Booklist* that in *Shadowfall* Clemens has "developed at great, possibly excessive, length how . . . aspects [of darkness] affect the world and the characters he creates." Writing in *Library Journal,* Jackie Cassada described the same novel as "a compelling tale filled with richly developed characters" and dubbed *Hinterland* "a gripping, tautly constructed tale."

Rollins is also the author of several stand-alone novels that blend science fiction and suspense. In *Subterranean* a team of specialists led by paleoanthropologist Ashley Carter explores a mysterious world beneath Antarctica. The novel "is enjoyable in its loving embrace of adventure-novel traditions," according to a *Publishers Weekly* critic. In *Amazonia* he tells the story of a group of scientists trekking through the jungles of the Amazon in search of a missing biopharmaceutical exploratory expedition. They also seek the answer to why a U.S. Special Forces agent from that expedition emerged from the jungle in mutated form before dying, harboring a disease that could devastate the American population. *Amazonia* "reads like an adventure flick with breakneck pacing and lots of gory details," wrote Gavin Quinn in a review for *Booklist,* while a *Publishers Weekly* contributor called the book an "old-fashioned, rugged adventure in the tradition of Haggard and Crichton, told with energy, excitement and a sense of fun."

Rollins followed up the success of *Amazonia* with *Ice Hunt,* which finds another group of U.S. scientists uncovering the secrets stored in an abandoned World War

II-era Russian base in the Arctic. While the U.S. military finds itself in a covert power struggle over the Russian base, a mythical and frightening creature hunts the people living around the base. Rollins "writes with intelligence, clarity, and a refreshing sense of humor," attested a *Kirkus Reviews* contributor, and Quinn predicted that "new readers will be delighted and established fans will find exactly what they have come to expect: a fun and fast-paced story that is full of suspense."

Sandstorm, the first volume in Rollins' "Sigma Force" series, begins when a major explosion in the British Museum destroys a giant portion of the antiquities wing. A team made up of Safia al-Maaz, her wealthy friend Lady Kara Kensington, scientist Omaha Dunn, and American Painter Crowe, who has links to the government agency behind Sigma Force, set out to discover the cause and the culprits behind the explosion. Their search takes them as far as Arabia and the legendary city of Ubar. Having determined that the explosion was caused by antimatter, they must now discover its source. Pam Johnson, in a review for *School Library Journal,* commented of *Sandstorm* that "the characters tend to be a bit stereotypical at first, but fit into the plot and support the action. And they evolve."

Rollins' "Sigma Force" series continues with *Map of Bones.* With a plot that revolves around Vatican spies and a secret religious order, as well as a biblical object shrouded in mystery, the novel drew more than one comparison to Dan Brown's best-selling novel *The Da-Vinci Code.* When a break-in at the Cologne Cathedral results in the theft of the bones reputedly belonging to the Three Wise Men, Sigma Force assigns one of its top agents, Grayson Pierce, to investigate. Pierce takes a team with him and heads to Rome, where he then joins forces with Italian police lieutenant Rachel Verona. The plot thickens as the missing bones turn out to be a deadly substance capable of starting the planet on the road to Armageddon. A reviewer for *Publishers Weekly* found the dialogue in *Map of Bones* appropriately believable and remarked that "Rollins has few peers in the research department, which makes the historical material fascinating."

In *Black Order,* the next of the "Sigma Force" novels, strange events begin occurring around the globe. A disturbing plague spreads like wildfire through a monastery in Nepal, and in a nearby cave, a swastika is found on the wall. Meanwhile, in Denmark, all available artifacts once owned by select Victorian scientists, such as Charles Darwin, are being amassed, some purchased legitimately, others secured using deadly force. In South Africa, animals are being hunted by a mythical beast come to life. Sigma Force sets out to unravel these mysteries, and the group quickly finds itself searching for a much broader answer: the origin of life. *Library Journal* contributor Jeff Ayers observed that in *Black Order* "all of these diverse elements blend seamlessly in Rollins's hands," while David Pitt opined in *Booklist* that "Rollins keeps getting better with every novel, and his fast-paced thrillers are feasts for the imagination."

The Judas Strain, the fourth book in the "Sigma Force" series, finds the members of the team facing the resurgence of an ancient and deadly virus known as the Judas Strain, which has the potential to wipe out all life on the planet. Scientists have reason to suspect this particular virus was responsible for huge dips in the population during previous eras, and they are adamant that it be stopped. Sigma Force faces opposition from a terrorist group called the Guild. The Guild is just as anxious as Sigma Force to put a halt to the spread of the virus, but its motives are far less altruistic. While the government agency seeks to save lives, the members of the Guild intend to harness the power of the virus in order to rule the planet. Robert Conroy, in a review for *Library Journal,* commented that, "as with all Rollins books, [*The Judas Strain*] . . . is great good fun, if readers suspend their disbelief and sense of logic." In *Booklist* Pitt praised the novel for "characters rendered in broad strokes, punchy dialogue, short paragraphs that propel us headlong through the story."

In *The Last Oracle* Sigma Force contends with dangers that include radioactive poisoning, genetically engineered wolves and tigers, rogue spies, and a group of strange gypsy children with implants behind their ears. The action starts when Pierce, on his way to Sigma's underground laboratory beneath the Smithsonian Institute in Washington, DC, encounters an apparently homeless man who gives him a coin and then dies in his arms. Pierce brings the corpse to the lab and runs some tests, only to discover that the coin is from ancient Greece, the man was a neurology professor, and his corpse contains high amounts of radioactivity. With his Sigma teammates, Pierce sets out to learn who killed the professor, and their path leads to a Russian who had been involved in the massacre of a Romanian village years earlier. Meanwhile, Monk Bryant, presumed dead, comes out of an amnesiac coma in Ukraine where he is besieged by children begging for his help. All of them have cranial implants—and Monk now has one, too. Praising *The Last Oracle* as a "fabulous mix of history, science, and adventure," Jeff Ayers wrote in *Library Journal* that the book stands as Sigma's "most compelling and perilous adventure" to date. A *Publishers Weekly* reviewer also rated the book highly, citing Rollins' skillful use of scientific information and his fast-paced prose.

The safety of the world's food supply is just one of the problems facing Sigma in *The Doomsday Key.* Sent to Africa to investigate after an experimental agricultural site is attacked and all its staff, including the son of a U.S. senator, are killed, Pierce and his team learn that the answer may be tied to a secret from ancient Egypt. In the days of the pharaohs, a "Doomsday key" purportedly holding strange new healing powers, was brought from Egypt to the British Isles. The lore it contained passed to the ancient Celts and then to the early Christian inhabitants of the isles, whose writings were encoded in *The Domesday Book.* Sigma now studies this tome in hopes of finding the antidote to the devastating crop fungus that is rampant across the planet, but meanwhile he must contend with the terrorist group the Guild, as well as with obstacles put in Sigma's way by the Vatican. Rollins' "prose explodes off the page in a twisty and compelling thriller," noted Ayers, and Pitt remarked that in *The Domesday Book* the author "creates imaginative puzzles for his characters to solve."

For several critics, the appeal of the "Sigma Force" series lies in its engaging characters. Indeed, Rollins stated in an interview posted on his home page that he considers three-dimensional characters essential to a good mystery, even when the book is intended as pure entertainment. Explaining that the focus in his books is "murder, magic, and mayhem," Rollins went on to say that "I don't think any adventure story will work unless you do indeed engage the reader on a level deeper than pure popcorn-entertainment. He must care about the characters, or why join you on this journey? She must be invested in the characters to care about their fate."

In his first foray into juvenile fiction, *Jake Ransom and the Skull King's Shadow,* Rollins recounts the perilous adventures of eighth-grader Jake and his older sister Kady, whose archaeologist parents disappeared three years earlier while exploring Mayan artifacts. Invited to a British show of these artifacts, the siblings are magically transported to Calypso, a jungle land whose inhabitants include not only Mayans, but also ancient Romans, Neanderthals, and even dinosaurs. These beasts live within Calypso's volcanoes, which contain crystals with alchemical powers. When alchemist Kalvernum Rex attacks Calypso, Jake joins with the local inhabitants to fend off the threat. A critic in *Publishers Weekly* noted that in *Jake Ransom and the Skull King's Shadow,* Rollins "presents a wide range of interesting historical information while telling a rollicking good story," and a writer for *Kirkus Reviews* remarked that, while the book begins as a realistic adventure story, it "takes a big left turn into fantasy without abandoning the thrills."

Though he is best known for stories that feature nonstop action and suspenseful narratives, Rollins hopes that his works are thought provoking as well. "My main goal is to entertain," he remarked on his home page, "but I think the best entertainment also strives to make us think and to challenge our view of history or the world around us. It's important to leave readers with something to contemplate after they turn that last page. When I hear a reader say that a certain novel intrigued them enough to explore a detail raised in a book, I know I've done my job well: to entertain, to intrigue, but also to leave something to explore afterward."

Biographical and Critical Sources

PERIODICALS

Booklist, February 15, 2002, Gavin Quinn, review of *Amazonia,* p. 971; June 1, 2003, Gavin Quinn, review of *Ice Hunt,* p. 1746; December 15, 2003, Barbara Baskin, review of *Ice Hunt,* p. 762; May 1, 2005, David Pitt, review of *Map of Bones,* p. 1534; July, 2005, Roland Green, review of *Shadowfall,* p. 1911; March 15, 2006, David Pitt, review of *Black Order,* p. 6; February 1, 2007, David Pitt, review of *The Judas Strain,* p. 36; March 15, 2009, Ilene Cooper, review of *Jake Ransom and the Skull King's Shadow,* p. 58; May 15, 2009, David Pitt, review of *The Doomsday Key,* p. 4.

Kirkus Reviews, September 15, 2001, review of *Wit'ch Gate,* p. 1331; February 1, 2002, review of *Amazonia,* p. 135; May 15, 2003, review of *Ice Hunt,* p. 711; June 1, 2008, review of *The Last Oracle,*; April 1, 2009, review of *Jake Ransom and the Skull King's Shadow.*

Library Journal, June 15, 1998, Jackie Cassada, review of *Wit'ch Fire,* p. 111; May 15, 1999, Jackie Cassada, review of *Wit'ch Storm,* p. 131; August, 1999, Denise Dumars, review of *Wit'ch Fire,* p. 176; July, 2000, Jackie Cassada, review of *Wit'ch War,* p. 147; November 15, 2001, Jackie Cassada, review of *Wit'ch Gate,* p. 100; June 15, 2005, Jackie Cassada, review of *Shadowfall,* p. 65; June 15, 2006, Jeff Ayers, review of *Black Order,* p. 59; March 1, 2007, Robert Conroy, review of *The Judas Strain,* p. 78; June 15, 2005, Jackie Cassada, review of *Shadowfall,* p. 65; November 15, 2006, Jackie Cassada, review of *Hinterland,* p. 62; May 15, 2008, Jeff Ayers, review of *The Last Oracle,* p. 93; June 1, 2009, Jeff Ayers, review of *The Doomsday Key,* p. 92.

Publishers Weekly, November 4, 1996, Paul Nathan, "Deep-sea Adventure," p. 23; April 12, 1999, review of *Wit'ch Storm,* p. 59; May 3, 1999, review of *Subterranean,* p. 73; July 3, 2000, review of *Wit'ch War,* p. 53; October 8, 2001, review of *Wit'ch Gate,* p. 50; March 4, 2002, review of *Amazonia,* p. 58; June 30, 2003, review of *Ice Hunt,* p. 54; June 21, 2004, review of *Sandstorm,* p. 44; May 16, 2005, review of *Map of Bones,* p. 39; June 13, 2005, review of *Shadowfall,* p. 37; May 12, 2008, review of *The Last Oracle,* p. 36; April 27, 2009, review of *The Doomsday Key,* p. 108 May 11, 2009, "PW Talks with James Rollins: Inside the Cardboard Box," p. 33; May 18, 2009, review of *Jake Ransom and the Skull King's Shadow,* p. 56.

Sacramento Bee, June 29, 2007, Allen Pierleoni, "Not One but Two Alter Egos for Veterinarian as Novelist"; June 26, 2008, Allen Pierleoni, "Thriller Author Lives Much of What He Writes"; July 21, 2008, Allen Pierleoni, "Novelist James Rollins Weaves Mind-boggling 'What-Ifs' into His Thrillers."

School Library Journal, November, 2004, Pam Johnson, review of *Sandstorm,* p. 177; September, 2009, Kelley Siegrist, review of *Jake Ransom and the Skull King's Shadow,* p. 172.

Seattle Post-Intelligencer, June 17, 2005, Jeff Ayers, "Author Sets Team on Trail of Religious Relics in 'Map of Bones.'"

Writers Digest, July 10, 2008, Maria Schneider, interview with Rollins.

ONLINE

James Clemens Home Page, http://www.jamesclemens.com (November 20, 2005).

James Rollins Home Page, http://www.jamesrollins.com (October 1, 2009).

Writers Write Web site, http://www.writerswrite.com/ (December 20, 2005), Claire E. White, interview with Rollins.

*   *   *

ROTH, Ruby 1983(?)-

Personal

Born c. 1983; has children.

Addresses

Home—Los Angeles, CA.

Career

Artist and author. Teacher of art to children. *Exhibitions:* Works exhibited at Museum of Children's Art, Oakland, CA.

Writings

That's Why We Don't Eat Animals: A Book about Vegans, Vegetarians, and All Living Things, North Atlantic Books (Berkeley, CA), 2009.

Sidelights

In her original stylized, digital full-color images, California writer and artist Ruby Roth presents the reasons why some people opt not to eat meat, poultry, and/or fish in her book *That's Why We Don't Eat Animals: A Book about Vegans, Vegetarians, and All Living Things.* Roth's picture-book introduction to a well-known alternative lifestyle is cast with chickens, turtles, pigs, cows, and even dolphins. The book explains the difference between a vegetarian and a vegan (a vegan does not use or consume any animal products, whether they be milk, eggs, feathers or down, wool, fur, or leather) and provides resources for readers interested in finding out more about the topic.

Ruby Roth introduces children to an important social concept in her self-illustrated picture book **That's Why We Don't Eat Meat.** (North Atlantic Books, 2009. Illustration ©2009 by Ruby Roth. Reproduced by permission.)

Beginning with the connections among all living creatures, Roth then attempts to humanize animals by accounting for the many animal behaviors that mimic those of man. For example, turkeys dance in groups and seem to exhibit a human-like sadness, according to Roth. She then draws attention to the suffering of creatures raised as food, noting that when poultry and cattle raised for human consumption are housed in restrictive quarters away from their natural environments. In addition, Roth argues that the farming of livestock and other animals leads to the depletion of natural resources forests and endangered species.

While noting that "some may consider this an attempt to indoctrinate the young," *Booklist* contributor Daniel Kraus called *That's Why We Don't Eat Animals* "a courageous stab at a serious topic." Also addressing Roth's somewhat controversial picture book, a *Publishers Weekly* critic maintained that while the work "is sure to raise awareness," younger children "may find the heart-tugging descriptions and images . . . a little overwhelming." In *Kirkus Reviews* a writer observed that Roth makes her case for vegetarianism by showing that "animals are very like people and too cute to eat." While inappropriate for youngsters who are unaware of the nutritional debate surrounding vegetarianism, *That's Why We Don't Eat Animals* is suitable "for children in already vegan or vegetarian households," the critic added.

Biographical and Critical Sources

PERIODICALS

Booklist, April 15, 2009, Daniel Kraus, review of *That's Why We Don't Eat Animals: A Book about Vegans, Vegetarians, and All Living Things*, p. 40.
Kirkus Reviews, April 1, 2009, review of *That's Why We Don't Eat Animals*.
Publishers Weekly, May 25, 2009, review of *That's Why We Don't Eat Animals*, p. 57.

ONLINE

Ruby Roth Home Page, http://www.wedonteatanimals.com (June 1, 2010).
North Atlantic Books Web site, http://www.northatlantic books.wordpress.com/ (February 18, 2009), "Ruby Roth."*

*　　*　　*

RUNHOLT, Susan

Personal

Children: Annalisa.

Addresses

Home—Saint Paul, MN.

Career

Writer. Worked as a bank clerk, au pair, waitress, maid, motel desk clerk, laundress, caterer, and director of programming for South Dakota Public Television; fund-raising consultant for social service and arts organizations.

Awards, Honors

Debut Dagger Award, 2005, for *The Mystery of the Third Lucretia*.

Writings

"LARI AND LUCAS" MYSTERY SERIES

The Mystery of the Third Lucretia, Viking Children's Books (New York, NY), 2008.
Rescuing Seneca Crane, Viking Children's Books (New York, NY), 2009.

Sidelights

Susan Runholt is the author of the teen novels *The Mystery of the Third Lucretia* and *Rescuing Seneca Crane*. Both of these books are part of her "Kari and Lucas" mystery series.

Published in 2008, *The Mystery of the Third Lucretia* introduces best friends Kari Sundgren and Lucas Stickney, teenagers from St. Paul, Minnesota, who share a love for art and travel. During a trip to the Minneapolis Institute of Art, the girls encounter a mysterious man painting in the room where Rembrandt's famous painting of Lucretia is hung. A year later, they see the same man in the National Gallery in London, busily copying another painting by Rembrandt. Not long after, Kari and Lucas stumble on an article in the *International Herald Tribune* that talks about the discovery of a new Rembrandt painting in Amsterdam. Convinced that the mysterious man they encountered at the museums has forged this painting, the two friends set out to locate him.

Most reviewers were impressed with Runholt's debut, *Kliatt* contributor Claire Rosser noting: "Lots of action, authentic emotions, friendship strains, mother-daughter conflicts . . . Runholt gets it all just right in this novel." *Armchair Interviews* online reviewer Andrea Sisco praised *The Mystery of the Third Lucretia* and hoped "that this is just the first in a long series of Kari and Lucas adventures." In *School Library Journal* Emma Runyan noted the story's "continuous action and likable characters," but added that "the mystery . . . remains a bit flat, without many twists." "Readers will no doubt look forward to reading more adventures of these teen detectives," remarked a *Kirkus Reviews* critic, and *Booklist* reviewer Gillian Engberg was impressed with Kari's "authentic narration, her strong realistic friendship with Lucas, the cosmopolitan settings, and the carefully plotted mystery."

On her home page, Runholt cited her daughter, Annalisa, as a source of inspiration for the book. Just like Kari and her mom, Runholt and her daughter visited the Minneapolis Institute of Arts, where they saw Rembrandt's paintings of Lucretia. Years later, when she decided to write the book, Runholt remembered how much her daughter had loved Rembrandt's work and decided to revolve her novel around it. Completed in the mid-1990s, *The Mystery of the Third Lucretia* won a Debut Dagger Award in 2005.

Biographical and Critical Sources

PERIODICALS

Booklinks, July 1, 2008, Gillian Engberg, review of *The Mystery of the Third Lucretia,* p. 54.

Booklist, May 1, 2008, Gillian Engberg, review of *The Mystery of the Third Lucretia,* p. 46.

Bulletin of the Center for Children's Books, April 1, 2008, Deborah Stevenson, review of *The Mystery of the Third Lucretia,* p. 352.

Kirkus Reviews, April 1, 2008, review of *The Mystery of the Third Lucretia.*

Kliatt, March 1, 2008, Claire Rosser, review of *The Mystery of the Third Lucretia,* p. 18.

School Library Journal, March 1, 2008, Emma Runyan, review of *The Mystery of the Third Lucretia,* p. 209.

Voice of Youth Advocates, April 1, 2008, Christina Fairman, review of *The Mystery of the Third Lucretia,* p. 53.

ONLINE

Armchair Interviews Web site, http://reviews.armchair interviews.com/ (January 5, 2009), Andrea Sisco, review of *The Mystery of the Third Lucretia.*

Loft Literary Center Web site, http://www.loft.org/ (January 5, 2009), "Susan Runholt."

Susan Runholt Home Page, http://www.susanrunholt.com (January 5, 2009).*

S

SALAS, Laura Purdie 1966-

Personal

Born 1966, in FL; married; husband's name Randy; children: Annabelle, Maddie. *Education:* B.A. (English). *Hobbies and other interests:* Racquetball, reading, Scrabble, board games, Rock Band, reading, trying new things (like running a half-marathon—ack!), "and did I mention reading?"

Addresses

Home—Minneapolis, MN. *E-mail*—lpsalas@bitstream. net.

Career

Author and educator. Former magazine editor; taught middle-grade English for two years. Speaker at schools and young author conferences.

Awards, Honors

Minnesota Book Award finalist, 2010, for *Stampede!*

Writings

FOR CHILDREN; NONFICTION

Canoeing, Capstone High-Interest Books (Mankato, MN), 2002.

China, Bridgestone Books (Mankato, MN), 2002.

Forest Fires, Capstone High-Interest Books (Mankato MN), 2002.

Germany, Bridgestone Books (Mankato, MN), 2002.

Ice Fishing, Capstone High-Interest Books (Mankato, MN), 2002, revised edition, 2008.

Snowmobiling, Capstone High-Interest Books (Mankato, MN), 2002, revised edition, 2008.

The Trail of Tears, 1838 ("Let Freedom Ring" series), Bridgestone Books (Mankato, MN), 2003.

The Wilderness Road, 1775 ("Let Freedom Ring" series), Bridgestone Books (Mankato, MN), 2003.

Discovering Nature's Laws: A Story about Isaac Newton, illustrated by Emily C.S. Reynolds, Carolrhoda Books (Minneapolis, MN), 2004.

Saltwater Fishing, Capstone Press (Mankato, MN), 2004, revised edition, 2008.

Taking the Plunge: A Teen's Guide to Independence, Child & Family Press (Washington, DC), 2004.

Charles Drew: Pioneer in Medicine, Capstone Press (Mankato, MN), 2006.

Phillis Wheatley: Colonial American Poet, Capstone Press (Mankato, MN), 2006.

Whose Coat Is This?: A Look at How Workers Cover Up: Jackets, Smocks, and Robes, illustrated by Amy Bailey Muehlenhardt, Picture Window Books (Minneapolis, MN), 2006.

Whose Gloves Are These?: A Look at Gloves Workers Wear: Leather, Cloth, and Rubber, illustrated by Amy Bailey Muehlenhardt, Picture Window Books (Minneapolis, MN), 2006.

Whose Shoes Are These?: A Look at Workers' Footwear: Flippers, Sneakers, and Boots, illustrated by Amy Bailey Muehlenhardt, Picture Window Books (Minneapolis, MN), 2006.

Deserts: Thirsty Wonderlands, illustrated by Jeff Yesh, Picture Window Books (Minneapolis, MN), 2007.

Oceans: Underwater Worlds, illustrated by Jeff Yesh, Picture Window Books (Minneapolis, MN), 2007.

Rain Forests: Gardens of Green, illustrated by Jeff Yesh, Picture Window Books (Minneapolis, MN), 2007.

Temperate Deciduous Forests: Lands of Falling Leaves, illustrated by Jeff Yesh, Picture Window Books (Minneapolis, MN), 2007.

Wetlands: Soggy Habitat, illustrated by Jeff Yesh, Picture Window Books (Minneapolis, MN), 2007.

Do Crocodiles Dance?: A Book about Animal Habits, illustrated by Jeff Yesh, Picture Window Books (Minneapolis, MN), 2007.

Do Lobsters Leap Waterfalls?: A Book about Animal Migration, illustrated by Todd Ouren, Picture Window Books (Minneapolis, MN), 2007.

Do Pelicans Sip Nectar?: A Book about How Animals Eat, illustrated by Todd Ouren, Picture Window Books (Minneapolis, MN), 2007.

Do Polar Bears Snooze in Hollow Trees?: A Book about Animal Hibernation, illustrated by Todd Ouren, Picture Window Books (Minneapolis, MN), 2007.

Do Turtles Sleep in Treetops?: A Book about Animal Homes, illustrated by Jeff Yesh, Picture Window Books (Minneapolis, MN), 2007.

Does an Elephant Fit in Your Hand?: A Book about Animal Sizes, illustrated by Jeff Yesh, Picture Window Books (Minneapolis, MN), 2007.

Grasslands: Fields of Green and Gold, illustrated by Jeff Yesh, Picture Window Books (Minneapolis, MN), 2007.

Scrapbooking for Fun!, Compass Point Books (Minneapolis, MN), 2008.

Write Your Own Poetry, Compass Point Books (Minneapolis, MN), 2008.

Coral Reefs: Colorful Underwater Habitats, illustrated by Jeff Yesh, Picture Window Books (Minneapolis, MN), 2009.

From Mealworm to Beetle: Following the Life Cycle, illustrated by Jeff Yesh, Picture Window Books (Minneapolis, MN), 2009.

From Seed to Maple Tree: Following the Life Cycle, illustrated by Jeff Yesh, Picture Window Books (Minneapolis, MN), 2009.

Tundras: Frosty, Treeless Lands, illustrated by Jeff Yesh, Picture Window Books (Minneapolis, MN), 2009.

Amphibians: Water-to-land Animals, illustrated by Kristin Kest, Picture Window Books (Minneapolis, MN), 2010.

Mammals: Hairy, Milk-making Animals, illustrated by Rosiland Solomon, Picture Window Books (Minneapolis, MN), 2010.

Reptiles: Scaly-skinned Animals, illustrated by Rosiland Solomon, Picture Window Books (Minneapolis, MN), 2010.

(With Francha Roffé Meinhard) *The Facts about Inhalants,* Marshall Cavendish Benchmark (New York, NY), 2010.

Contributor to periodicals, including *Spider* and *Highlights for Children.*

POETRY; FOR CHILDREN

And Then There Were Eight: Poems about Space, Capstone Press (Mankato, MN), 2008.

Do Buses Eat Kids?: Poems about School, Capstone Press (Mankato, MN), 2008.

Flashy, Clashy, and Oh-so Splashy: Poems about Color, Capstone Press (Mankato, MN), 2008.

Seed Sower, Hat Thrower: Poems about Weather, Capstone Press (Mankato, MN), 2008.

Shrinking Days, Frosty Nights: Poems about Fall, Capstone Press (Mankato, MN), 2008.

Tiny Dreams, Sprouting Tall: Poems about the United States, Capstone Press (Mankato, MN), 2008.

A Fuzzy-fast Blur: Poems about Pets, Capstone Press (Mankato, MN), 2009.

Always Got My Feet: Poems about Transportation, Capstone Press (Mankato, MN), 2009.

Chatter, Sing, Roar, Buzz: Poems about the Rain Forest, Capstone Press (Mankato, MN), 2009.

Lettuce Introduce You: Poems about Food, Capstone Press (Mankato, MN), 2009.

Stampede!: Poems to Celebrate the Wild Side of School, illustrated by Steven Salerno, Clarion Books (New York, NY), 2009.

"SCIENCE SONGS" SERIES

Are You Living?: A Song about Living and Non-living Things, illustrated by Viviana Garofoli, Picture Window Books (Minneapolis, MN), 2009.

From Beginning to End: A Song about Life Cycles, illustrated by Viviana Garofoli, Picture Window Books (Minneapolis, MN), 2009.

Home on the Earth: A Song about Earth's Layers, illustrated by Viviana Garofoli, Picture Window Books (Minneapolis, MN), 2009.

Move It! Work It!: A Song about Simple Machines, illustrated by Viviana Garofoli, Picture Window Books (Minneapolis, MN), 2009.

Eight Great Planets!: A Song about the Planets, illustrated by Sergio De Giorgi, Picture Window Books (Minneapolis, MN), 2010.

I'm Exploring with My Senses: A Song about the Five Senses, illustrated by Sergio De Giorgi, Picture Window Books (Minneapolis, MN), 2010.

Many Creatures: A Song about Animal Classifications, illustrated by Sergio De Giorgi, Picture Window Books (Minneapolis, MN), 2010.

There Goes the Water: A Song about the Water Cycle, illustrated by Sergio De Giorgi, Picture Window Books (Minneapolis, MN), 2010.

"ALPHABET FUN" SERIES

A Is for Arrr!: A Pirate Alphabet, Capstone Press (Mankato, MN), 2010.

C Is for Cake!: A Birthday Alphabet, Capstone Press (Mankato, MN), 2010.

P Is for Pom Pom!: A Cheerleading Alphabet, Capstone Press (Mankato, MN), 2010.

S Is for Score!: A Sports Alphabet, Capstone Press (Mankato, MN), 2010.

Y Is for Yowl!: A Scary Alphabet, Capstone Press (Mankato, MN), 2010.

Z Is for Zoom!: A Race Car Alphabet, Capstone Press (Mankato, MN), 2010.

J Is for Jingle Bells: A Christmas Alphabet, Capstone Press (Mankato, MN), 2011.

Y Is for Yak: A Zoo Alphabet, Capstone Press (Mankato, MN), 2011.

Sidelights

Using engaging rhyme, Laura Purdie Salas shares her many interests with young readers in books that include *Y Is for Yowl!: A Scary Alphabet, Stampede!: Poems to*

Celebrate the Wild Side of School, and *A Fuzzy-fast Blur: Poems about Pets.* The natural world figures prominently in most of Salas's picture-book texts, and the diversity of the world's animals and environments joins weather and other scientific subjects as her subjects. Comparing Salas's writing to that of noted children's author Jane Yolen, Donna Cardon wrote in *School Library Journal* that the author's "language flows naturally and none of the poems [in *A Fuzzy-fast Blur*] feels awkward or forced." *And Then There Were Eight,* which focuses on astronomy, is characteristic of Salas's work in its use of a range of poetic forms, such as limerick, free verse, cinquain, and acrostic. Praising the descriptive verses in *Booklist,* John Peters added that *And Then There Were Eight* is a "versatile" work that could be used in "both science and language-arts" studies.

In *Stampede!* Salas's poetry pairs with Steve Salerno's cartoon drawings to play on the similarity of habits between young schoolchildren and animals. Like a swarm of bees, children buzz around on the playground while waiting for the school doors to open, and they arrive at lunch as hungry as bears, Salas observes. Her eighteen "wild" poems "are positively shot through with simile and metaphor," according to Peters, and in *School Li-*

Steve Salerno captures the energy in Laura Purdie Salas's rhyming picture book **Stampede!** (Illustration © 2009 by Steven Salerno. Reprinted by permission of Clarion Books, an imprint of Houghton Mifflin Harcourt Publishing Company. All rights reserved.)

brary Journal Marilyn Taniguchi cited the pairing of Salerno's "whimsical pictures" with Salas's "child-friendly verses."

Referencing Salas's "Science Songs" series, which includes *Are You Living?: A Song about Living and Non-living Things, Home on the Earth: A Song about Earth's Layers,* and *Move It! Work It!: A Song about Simple Machines,* Ragan O'Malley explained in *School Library Journal* that each volume presents "basic science concepts" and reinforces them using "the tunes of well-known songs." For example, *Are You Living?* is set to the tune of "Are You Sleeping?" and features digital artwork by Viviana Garofoli. The book's lyrics reveal the characteristics of a living organism, while fact boxes provide science-hungry readers with more detailed information. In her review for *Booklist,* Kristen McKulski recommended *Are You Living?* for its ability to "inject a little life and creativity into beginning science studies."

Salas's "Alphabet Fun" series includes *P Is for Pom Pom!: A Cheerleading Alphabet, S Is for Score!: A Sports Alphabet,* and *Y Is for Yowl!* In the last-named book, the author pairs photographs of unsettling objects—ranging from aliens and bats to quicksand and lightning—with a brief, child-friendly text. According to *Booklist* critic Daniel Kraus, with its "impressive grimness," *Y Is for Yowl!* "could inspire creative ideas around Halloween time."

"I always knew I loved to read, but I never even knew as a kid that writing was something you could do for a living!," Salas told *SATA.* "I meet so many writers who knew they were writers practically from when they were in diapers. Not me! I didn't really discover how much I loved writing until I was in college. I was in the veterinary medicine program, but my first creative-writing class set me on the track to becoming a writer.

"I wrote for adults for a while, but later I discovered that kids are a much better audience! Books were the world I lived in as a kid, and I love writing books for today's kids. I write lots of nonfiction and enjoy that, but poetry is my absolute favorite thing to write. One of the things I love about poetry is that it's short and accessible for every kid. Whether you like silly or serious or scary stuff, there are poems out there that are just right for you!"

Biographical and Critical Sources

PERIODICALS

Booklist, April 1, 2009, Kristen McKulski, review of *Are You Living?: A Song about Living and Non-living Things,* p. 62; May 1, 2009, John Peters, review of *Stampede!: Poems to Celebrate the Wild Side of School,* p. 84; October 1, 2009. Daniel Kraus, review of *Y Is for Yowl!: A Scary Alphabet,* p 82.

Kirkus Reviews, April 1, 2009, review of *Stampede!*
School Library Journal, December, 2003, Carol Fazioli, review of *The Trail of Tears, 1838,* p. 174; January, 2008, Nancy Kunz, review of *Scrapbooking for Fun!,* p. 142; May, 2008, John Peters, review of *And Then There Were Eight: Poems about Space,* p. 117; January, 2009, Donna Cardon, review of *Chatter, Sing, Roar, Buzz: Poems about the Rain Forest,* p. 94; May, 2009, Ragan O'Malley, review of *Are You Living?,* and Marilyn Taniguchi, review of *Stampede!,* both p. 97.

ONLINE

Laura Purdie Salas Home Page, http://www.laurasalas. com (May 15, 2010).
Laura Purdie Salas Web log, http://laurasalas.livejournal. com (May 15, 2010).

* * *

SALWOOD, F.K.
See KILWORTH, Garry

* * *

SANDLER, Martin W.

Personal

Married; wife's name Carol.

Addresses

Home—Cotuit, MA.

Career

Writer, educator, and producer of television programs. Instructor at schools, including University of Massachusetts—Amherst and Smith College, and at middle schools and high schools. Producer of television programs, including *Excellence in the Public Sector, American Image, American Treasure,* and *The Entrepreneurs.*

Awards, Honors

Boston Globe/Horn Book Award, c, 1979, for *The Story of American Photography;* Notable Children's Trade Book in the Field of Social Studies designation, National Council for the Social Studies/Children's Book Council, 1997, for *Inventors;* Award for Excellence in Nonfiction, Young Adult Library Services Association, and Outstanding Science Trade Books for Children designation, National Science Teachers Association, both 2009, both for *Secret Subway;* seven Emmy awards; two Pulitzer Prize nominations; Golden Cine award.

Writings

NONFICTION

The Way We Lived: A Photographic Record of Work in a Vanished America, Little, Brown (Boston, MA), 1977.

(With T.S. Bronson) *This Was Connecticut: Images of a Vanished World,* Little, Brown (Boston, MA), 1977.
This Was New England: Images of a Vanished Past, New York Graphic Society (Boston, MA), 1977.
The Story of American Photography: An Illustrated History for Young People, Little, Brown (Boston, MA), 1979.
As New Englanders Played, Globe Pequot Press (Chester, CT), 1979.
This Was America (based on the television series), Little, Brown (Boston, MA), 1980.
Changing Channels: Living (Sensibly) with Television, Addison-Wesley (Reading, MA), 1983.
American Image: Photographing 150 Years in the Life of a Nation, Contemporary Books (Chicago, IL), 1989.
Celebrating the American Family, Entrepreneurial Management Co. (Washington, DC), 1992.
(With Deborah A. Hudson, Carol Weiss, and Neil de-Guzmán) *Beyond the Bottom Line: How to Do More with Less in Nonprofit and Public Organizations,* Oxford University Press (New York, NY), 1998.
America!: A Celebration, foreword by Walter Cronkite, Dorling Kindersley (New York, NY), 2000.
Vaqueros: America's First Cowmen, Henry Holt (New York, NY), 2001.
Against the Odds: Women Pioneers in the First Hundred Years of Photography, Rizzoli (New York, NY), 2002.
Photography: An Illustrated History, Oxford University Press (New York, NY), 2002.
America's Great Disasters, HarperCollins (New York, NY), 2003.
Island of Hope: The Story of Ellis Island and the Journey to America, Scholastic, Inc. (New York, NY), 2004.
America through the Lens: Photographers Who Changed the Nation, Henry Holt (New York, NY), 2005.
Resolute: The Epic Search for the Northwest Passage and John Franklin, and the Discovery of the Queen's Ghost Ship, Sterling Publishing (New York, NY), 2006.
Trapped in Ice!: An Amazing True Whaling Adventure, Scholastic, Inc. (New York, NY), 2006.
Lincoln through the Lens: How Photography Revealed and Shaped an Extraordinary Life, Walker & Company (New York, NY), 2008.
The Dust Bowl through the Lens: How Photography Revealed and Helped Remedy a National Disaster, Walker & Company (New York, NY), 2008.
Secret Subway: The Fascinating Tale of An Amazing Feat of Engineering, National Geographic (Washington, DC), 2009.
Lost To Time: Unforgettable Stories That History Forgot, Sterling Publishing (New York, NY), 2010.

TEXTBOOKS

(With Edwin C. Rozwenc and Edward C. Martin) *The People Make a Nation,* Allyn & Bacon (Boston, MA), 1971.
(Editor, with Edwin C. Rozwenc and Edward C. Martin) *The Restless Americans: The Challenge of Change in American History,* illustrated by Judy Poe, Ginn (Lexington, MA), 1972.

In Search of America, Ginn (Lexington, MA), 1975.

"LIBRARY OF CONGRESS YOUNG PEOPLE'S AMERICAN HISTORY" SERIES

Pioneers, introduction by James Billington, HarperCollins (New York, NY), 1994.

Cowboys, introduction by James Billington, HarperCollins (New York, NY), 1994.

Presidents, introduction by James Billington, HarperCollins (New York, NY), 1995.

Immigrants, introduction by James Billington, HarperCollins (New York, NY), 1995.

Civil War, introduction by James Billington, HarperCollins (New York, NY), 1996.

Inventors, introduction by James Billington, HarperCollins (New York, NY), 1996.

"TRANSPORTATION IN AMERICA" SERIES

Straphanging in the USA: Trolleys and Subways in American Life, Oxford University Press (New York, NY), 2003.

Galloping across the USA: Horses in American Life, Oxford University Press (New York, NY), 2003.

Riding the Rails in the USA: Trains in American Life, Oxford University Press (New York, NY), 2003.

Driving around the USA: Automobiles in American Life, Oxford University Press (New York, NY), 2003.

On the Waters of the USA: Ships and Boats in American Life, Oxford University Press (New York, NY), 2003.

Flying over the USA: Airplanes in American Life, Oxford University Press (New York, NY), 2004.

SCREENPLAYS

(With Sherry Reisner and Steve Schlow) *This Was America* (television series), Boston Broadcasters Inc., 1978–1979.

Odyssey: The Art of Photography at National Geographic, WETA-TV (Washington, DC), 1990.

Author of screenplays for television programs, including *Excellence in the Public Sector, American Image, American Treasure,* and *The Entrepreneurs.*

Sidelights

An Emmy Award-winning television producer, Martin W. Sandler is also the author of numerous works of nonfiction for children and young adults, among them

Martin W. Sandler gifts horse lovers with a richly illustrated historical study of their favorite animal in **Galloping across the USA: Horses in American Life.** (Oxford University Press 2003. Reproduced by permission.)

The Story of American Photography: An Illustrated History for Young People, a recipient of the *Boston Globe/Horn Book* Award. His series include the "Library of Congress Young People's American History" books and the "Transportation in America" series. For the former, Sandler drew on the archives of the Library of Congress, making use of that organization's many historical photographs and primary sources to teach middle-grades students about the history of the United States. These books span a wide range of subjects, from presidents to immigrants to cowboys, but all are notable for the many photographs and other period illustrations that they contain. This "multitude of illustrations," as Janice Del Negro noted in a *Booklist* review of *Immigrants,* "is nicely designed for browsing." A *Publishers Weekly* contributor praised the format of both *Cowboys* and *Pioneers,* calling these books "crisply written, beautifully designed and blessed with an abundance of art" as well as "a valuable addition to American history for the middle grades."

Sandler's "Transportation in America" books cover many ways people have transported themselves around the United States throughout the nation's history, from horses and dugout canoes through modern supertankers, airplanes, and cars. Like the "Library of Congress Young People's American History" series, the books that make up "Transportation in America" contain "many well-captioned photographs, documents, and prints from various periods," Carolyn Phelan noted in a *Booklist* review of both *Galloping across the USA: Horses in American Life* and *Riding the Rails in the USA: Trains in American Life.* The books also consider the wider effects of the technologies they discuss, explaining, for example, how the invention of the car made both life in the suburbs and the modern tourism industry possible and how transcontinental railroads helped to tie a younger United States together. *Driving around the USA: Automobiles in American Life* is "brief but entertaining," as well as "logically organized and readable," Jeffrey A. French wrote in *School Library Journal,* while in the same publication Pamela K. Bomboy described *Straphanging in the USA: Trolleys and Subways in American Life* as a "fascinating narrative."

Sandler has a special interest in photography; his books on the history of this art include *The Story of American Photography, American Image: Photographing 150 Years in the Life of a Nation, Photography: An Illustrated History,* and *Against the Odds: Women Pioneers in the First Hundred Years of Photography. Photography* is an "authoritative history" of the subject, Joel Shoemaker declared in *School Library Journal,* the critic adding that it is also "compact . . . engaging and literate." *Photography* covers the technical side of the process, explaining the innovations that led from the early daguerreotype to digital photography and "Photoshopping", and also the artists who worked and work in this medium. All in all, Gillian Engberg concluded in *Booklist,* Sandler's book is a "well-done, clearly written overview."

In *America through the Lens: Photographers Who Changed the Nation,* Sandler examines the work of such notable individuals as U.S. Civil War photographer Matthew Brady, social documentarian Jacob Riis, and fashion photographer Toni Frissell. The biographies are "carefully presented to highlight the ways their work served to change both the art and science of photography and their subjects," a critic in *Kirkus Reviews* stated, and Engberg praised "the informative chapters that combine compelling biographical narratives with a larger view of the photographers' legacies." Containing more than one hundred images, *Lincoln through the Lens: How Photography Revealed and Shaped an Extraordinary Life* offers a biography of the sixteenth president, noting his use of the new medium of photography to achieve his political goals. According to a contributor in *Kirkus Reviews,* "Sandler's informative and accessible text moves thematically through time," and Barbara Auerbach, writing in *School Library Journal,* remarked that the "appealing, accessible title will be savored from beginning to end." In *The Dust Bowl through the Lens: How Photography Revealed and Helped Remedy a National Disaster* Sandler argues that the images produced by Walker Evans, Dorothea Lange, and other documentary photographers helped shape the nation's response to the early-twentieth-century's ecological catastrophe. In the words of a *Kirkus Reviews* critic, the author "offers an interesting perspective on the power photography has to shape public opinion and inspire social change."

America's Great Disasters combines "dramatic material, archival photography, and an accessible text to create an appealing title," Edith Ching explained in *School Library Journal.* The disasters Sandler covers include well-known events such as the Johnstown Flood of 1889, the Galveston, Texas, hurricane of 1900, and the 1906 San Francisco earthquake. However, he also includes more-obscure catastrophes, including the explosion of the Sultana riverboat during the Civil War and the Blizzard of 1888. "The accounts are competently written, ascribing blame, where appropriate, to human greed or negligence," noted a *Kirkus Reviews* contributor, and Sandler also discusses the lessons that policymakers learned from each event. In addition to its educational aspects, *America's Great Disasters* is a "rousing reading for disaster buffs," John Peters concluded in *Booklist.*

Sandler is also the author of *Island of Hope: The Story of Ellis Island and the Journey to America.* The book follows immigrants as they disembark at Ellis Island, the major immigrant processing center in the United States from 1892 through 1954. He then explains where many of these people wound up after being admitted to the United States: living in crowded city tenements, going West to stake their claim on a farm, or working as laborers building the railroads or in other heavy industries. Of particular interest to young readers, noted a *Publishers Weekly* contributor, is that Sandler's book "emphasizes the role of children and teens, who often learned the language and customs more quickly than their parents and assumed great responsibility in families." In telling the tales of these young immigrants and their parents the author "seamlessly blends factual information with the moving words and stories of those passing through Ellis Island," Diane S. Marton declared in *School Library Journal,* the critic calling *Island of Hope* a "lucid, well-composed work."

Sandler turns his attention to one of the most unusual expeditions in history in *Resolute: The Epic Search for the Northwest Passage and John Franklin, and the Discovery of the Queen's Ghost Ship.* Sir John Franklin, a British explorer hoping to discover a route from the Atlantic Ocean to the Pacific, set sail from England in 1845; he was never heard from again. The British government mounted a number of efforts to locate Franklin, one of them involving HMS *Resolute,* which became locked in Arctic ice, was abandoned by its crew, and was later found adrift by U.S. whalers. "Sandler expertly weaves letters, logs, and other sources from crew members and various key players into an immensely readable book," as *Library Journal* reviewer Susanne Markgren commented. Similarly, *Trapped in Ice!: An*

Cover of Sandler's adventure filled history Resolute, *which chronicles the search for the Northwest Passage.* (Cover photograph ©National Archives of Canada. Used with permission from Sterling Publishing Co., Inc.)

Amazing True Whaling Adventure describes a real-life adventure from 1871, when more than 1,000 men battled incredibly harsh conditions in the Arctic after leaving their stranded vessels to begin an eighty-mile journey to safety. Writing in *School Library Journal,* Janet S. Thompson called *Resolute* "a gripping combination of survival story and history."

In *Secret Subway: The Fascinating Tale of an Amazing Feat of Engineering* Sandler offers a portrait of *Scientific American* magazine founder Alfred Ely Beach, an inventor who designed a successful air-driven, underground transportation system in New York City, despite the objections of corrupt and powerful politician William W. "Boss" Tweed. A contributor to *Kirkus Reviews* described *Secret Subway* as "a grand tale of 19th-century American enterprise," and Hazel Rochman observed in *Booklist* that audiences "will be held as much by the gripping, personal story as by the engineering details of Beach's plan."

Biographical and Critical Sources

PERIODICALS

Booklist, February 1, 1994, Carolyn Phelan, review of *Cowboys,* p. 1004; March 1, 1995, Chris Sherman, review of *Presidents,* p. 1238; April 15, 1995, Janice Del Negro, review of *Immigrants,* p. 1496; December 15, 2000, Brad Hooper, review of *America!: A Celebration,* p. 777; January 1, 2001, Anne O'Malley, review of *Vaqueros: America's First Cowmen,* p. 937; April 15, 2002, Gillian Engberg, review of *Photography: An Illustrated History,* p. 1394; June 1, 2003, John Peters, review of *America's Great Disasters,* p. 1770; September 15, 2003, Carolyn Phelan, reviews of *Galloping across the USA: Horses in American Life* and *Riding the Rails in the USA: Trains in American Life,* both p. 234; April 15, 2004, John Peters, review of *Island of Hope: The Story of Ellis Island and the Journey to America,* p. 1442; September 1, 2005, Gillian Engberg, review of *America through the Lens: Photographers Who Changed the Nation,* p. 109; October 15, 2006, Gilbert Taylor, review of *Resolute: The Epic Search for the Northwest Passage and John Franklin, and the Discovery of the Queen's Ghost Ship,* p. 18; June 1, 2009, Hazel Rochman, review of *The Secret Subway: The Fascinating Tale of an Amazing Feat of Engineering,* p. 48.

Children's Digest, December, 1997, review of *Inventors,* p. 10.

Curriculum Review, September, 2003, "U.S. History on Four Feet," review of *Galloping across the USA,* p. 12.

Horn Book, January, 2001, review of *Vaqueros,* p. 116.

Kirkus Reviews, April 15, 2003, review of *America's Great Disasters,* p. 611; March 15, 2004, review of *Island of Hope,* p. 276; July 15, 2005, review of *America through the Lens,* p. 796; September 1, 2008, review of *Lincoln through The Lens: How Photography Revealed and Shaped an Extraordinary Life;* April 1, 2009, review of *The Secret Subway;* September 1, 2009, review of *The Dust Bowl through the Lens: How Photography Revealed and Helped Remedy a National Disaster.*

Library Journal, March 15, 2001, David Bryant, review of *America!,* p. 80; June 1, 2002, Shauna Frischkorn, review of *Against the Odds: Women Pioneers in the First Hundred Years of Photography,* p. 144; October 1, 2006, Susanne Markgren, review of *Resolute,* p. 90.

New York Times Book Review, November 8, 2009, Jessica Bruder, "Blowin' in the Wind," review of *The Dust Bowl through the Lens,* p. 18.

Publishers Weekly, January 17, 1994, review of *Cowboys,* p. 440; November 27, 2000, review of *Presidents* and *Civil War,,* p. 78; March 22, 2004, review of *Island of Hope,* p. 88.

School Library Journal, January, 2001, Coop Renner, review of *Vaqueros,* p. 154; June, 2002, Joel Shoemaker, review of *Photography,* p. 168; August, 2003, Edith Ching, review of *America's Great Disasters,* p. 184; November, 2003, Pamela K. Bomboy, review of *Riding the Rails in the USA,* p. 166; January, 2004, Pamela K. Bomboy, review of *Straphanging in the USA: Trolleys and Subways in American Life,* p. 156; April, 2004, Jeffrey A. French, review of *Driving around the USA: Automobiles in American Life,* p. 180; June, 2004, Diane S. Marton, review of *Island of Hope,* p. 174; July, 2004, Anne Chapman Callaghan, review of *On the Waters of the USA: Ships and Boats in American Life,* p. 127; November, 2005, Jodi Kearns, review of *America through the Lens,* p. 170; June, 2006, Janet S. Thompson, review of *Trapped in Ice!: An Amazing True Whaling Adventure,* p. 184; October, 2008, Barbara Auerbach, review of *Lincoln through the Lens,* p. 174; October, 2009, Ann Welton, review of *The Dust Bowl through the Lens,* p. 152.

ONLINE

HarperCollins Children's Book Web site, http://www.harpercollinschildrens.com/ (June 1, 2010), "Martin W. Sandler."

Oxford University Press Web site, http://www.oup.com/ (June 1, 2010), "Martin W. Sandler."*

* * *

SHAHAN, Sherry 1949-

Personal

Born August 14, 1949, in Los Angeles, CA; daughter of Frank Webb and Sylvia Brunner Benedict; married Ed Shahan (a rancher); children: Kristina O'Connor, Kyle Beal. *Education:* California Polytechnic State University, B.S.; Vermont College of Fine Arts, M.F.A. (writing for children and young adults). *Hobbies and other interests:* Travel.

Sherry Shanan (Reproduced by permission.)

Addresses

Home and office—2603 Richard Ave., Cayucos, CA 93430. *E-mail*—kidbooks@thegrid.net.

Career

Freelance travel journalist, photographer, and children's book author. University of California—Los Angeles, instructor in online writing course; lecturer at schools and libraries; presenter at conferences.

Member

Society of Children's Book Writers and Illustrators, Society of American Travel Writers, Authors Guild.

Writings

FICTION

Frozen Stiff, Delacorte Press (New York, NY), 1998.
Fountain of Weird, Avon (New York, NY), 1998.
Working Dogs, Troll Communications (Mahwah, NJ), 1999.

(And illustrator) *The Little Gardener,* Random House (New York, NY), 1999.

The Jazzy Alphabet, illustrated by Mary Thelen, Philomel (New York, NY), 2002.

Mirounga's Pup, Richard C. Owen (Katonah, NY), 2002.

Soccer Is Fun, Peachtree Publishers (Atlanta, GA), 2004.

Spicy Hot Colors!/¡Colores picantes!, illustrated by Paula Barragán, August House LittleFolk (Little Rock, AR), 2004.

Cool Cats Counting, illustrated by Paula Barragán, August House LittleFolk (Little Rock, AR), 2005.

Death Mountain, Peachtree (Atlanta, GA), 2005.

That's Not How You Play Soccer, Daddy, illustrated by Tatjana Mai-Wyss, Peachtree (Atlanta, GA), 2007.

¡Fiesta!: A Celebration of Latino Festivals, illustrated by Paula Barragán, August House LittleFolk (Atlanta, GA), 2009.

Purple Daze (young-adult verse novel), Running Press Kids, 2011.

Author's work has been translated into Italian, Dutch, German, and Danish.

NONFICTION

(And photographer) *Barnacles Eat with Their Feet: Delicious Facts about the Tide Pool Food Chain,* Millbrook Press (Brookfield, CT), 1995.

(And photographer) *Dashing through the Snow: The Story of Alaska's Jr. Iditarod,* Millbrook Press (Brookfield, CT), 1997, second edition, Mondo Publishing (New York, NY), 2006.

(And photographer) *The Little Butterfly,* Random House (New York, NY), 1998.

(And photographer) *Feeding Time at the Zoo,* Random House (New York, NY), 2000.

Willie Covan Loved to Dance, Mondo Publishing (New York, NY), 2004.

OTHER

(Photographer) Cherie Winner, *The Sunflower Family,* Carolrhoda Books (Minneapolis, NM), 1996.

(Photographer) Jonathan London, *Tell Me a Story,* Richard C. Owen (Katonah, NY), 1998.

(Photographer) Laura Joffe Numeroff, *If You Give an Author a Pencil,* Richard C. Owen Publishers (Katonah, NY), 2002.

(Photographer) Mike Thaler, *Imagination,* Richard C. Owen Publishers (Katonah, NY), 2002.

Contributor to national and international periodicals, including *Writer.*

Sidelights

In addition to her work as a travel writer, Sherry Shahan is the author of both picture-book texts and middle-grade novels that mix her interest in adventure with her love of poetry. Shanan's novel *Death Mountain* is based on a true story and finds two girls struggling to survive on a mountain top in the Sierra Nevadas during a severe electrical storm, while *Cool Cats Counting* pairs Shahan's simple rhyming text with colorful artwork by Ecuadorean illustrator Paula Barragán. Citing the well-studied depiction of "survival techniques" in *Death Mountain,* Vicki Reutter wrote in *School Library Journal* that Shahan exhibits "a level of technical detail [that] rivals" that of popular adventure novelist Will Hobbs. In addition to featuring an "independent" preteen heroine with a "self-sufficient attitude," *Death Mountain* ranks as "a great addition to the adventure-survival genre," Reutter maintained.

"As a travel writer and photographer my assignments for international and national magazines have taken me on horseback into Africa's Maasailand, hiking a leech-infested rain forest in Australia, paddling a kayak in Alaska, riding horseback with gauchos in Argentina, and hiking Ayer's Rock in Australia," Shahan once told *SATA.* "And those are just the A's." "Isn't that part of the fun of being a writer?," she asks readers of *Writer* magazine. "Taking risks, then, if one survives, putting fingers to keyboards so less-worldly souls can have a vicarious thrill while seated in a BarcaLounger?"

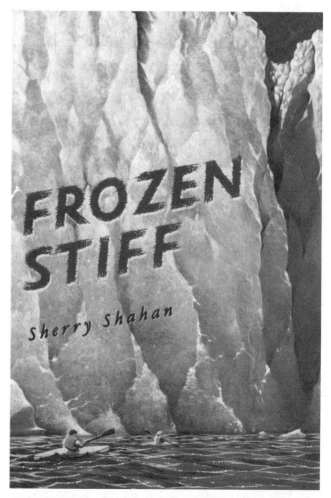

Cover of Shahan's adventure novel Frozen Stiff, *featuring artwork by Wayne McLoughlin.* (Jacket cover ©1998 by Delacorte Books. Used by permission of Delacorte Press, an imprint of Random House Children's Books, a division of Random House, Inc.)

Filled with information about the sled-dog race it imitates on a smaller scale, Shahan's *Dashing through the Snow: The Story of Alaska's Jr. Iditarod* introduces to young readers the Junior Iditarod competition. Here teen competitors lead a pack of dogs for two days through the harsh Alaskan winter, racing their sleds through the snow and ice in their attempt to be the first team to cross the finish line. In her book, Shahan shares with readers all of the elements of the race, including how youngsters prepare, the provisions they pack, how they care for their animals, and some of the difficulties they might face along the trail. *School Library Journal* critic Mollie Bynum offered enthusiastic words for the "interesting, informative book" and cited the author's photography as among its many strengths. Calling *Dashing through the Snow* a visual "masterpiece," Bynum predicted that readers "will find the subject fascinating, and the presentation pleasing."

The forty-ninth state also is the setting of Shahan's adventure novel *Frozen Stiff*, a "compelling adventure story with a highly realized Alaskan setting," according to *Booklist* contributor Shelley Townsend-Hudson. Sneaking off for a kayaking trip without permission, cousins Cody and Derek anticipate a weekend of fun in the Alaskan outdoors. However, the teens have little experience kayaking. They soon find themselves in serious danger when they lose one kayak and almost all of their supplies to a sudden flood. After Cody experiences a temporary bout of snow-blindness, she notices a strange man lurking near their camp and fears that her cousin may have been kidnapped. Describing the action in *Frozen Stiff* as "rapid and mostly realistic," a *Kirkus Reviews* critic added that Shahan "describes the natural beauty" of Alaska "with authority." In her review, Townsend-Hudson claimed that the novel "has all the elements a good survival story should have."

Shahan turns to younger readers in *Spicy Hot Colors!/ ¡Colores Picantes!* The first of several collaborations with Barragán, the book teaches children the name of nine colors in a bilingual text that is paired with "appealing and attention grabbing" paintings that incorporate elements of well-know works of art, according to *School Library Journal* writer Rosalyn Pierini. In her text for the book, Shahan employs a variety of rhyme schemes, focusing reader attention on interactive sounds such as tapping, clapping, and banging. Praising the book's ability to inspire "reader/listener's participation," a *Kirkus Reviews* writer added that Barragán's detailed images "echo the exuberance of the verse." "Learning a foreign language has never been so much fun," asserted Pierini, while in *Booklist* Ilene Cooper characterized *Spicy Hot Colors!* as "a brilliant fest of color that will entice children as it helps them learn a few Spanish words."

Other titles by Shahan and Barragán include *Cool Cats Counting* and *¡Fiesta!: A Celebration of Latino Festivals,* the latter which introduces readers to a year's worth of holidays, one for every month. From January's

Shahan teams up with Ecuadorean artist Paula Barragán in the vibrant concept book Spicy Hot Color!/¡Colores picantes! (August House Little Folk, 2004. Illustration ©2004 by Paula Barragan. Reproduced by permission.)

Fiesta de San Antonio Abad to May's Cinco de Mayo, Shahan's free-verse text in *¡Fiesta!* is augmented by a paragraph that discusses each special day in greater detail, while Barragán's cut-paper collage images "dance across the pages" in "stunning" succession, according to a *Kirkus Reviews* writer. *Cool Cats Counting* treats readers to the "rhythmically jazzy beats" of Shahan's rhyming verse, according to a *Kirkus Reviews* writer, and here Barragán depicts dancing animals sporting jaunty hats, fringed skirts, and high-heeled dancing shoes. In *School Library Journal* Maura Bresnahan dubbed *Cool Cats Counting* a must for "libraries looking to jazz up their counting books."

Biographical and Critical Sources

PERIODICALS

Booklist, February 1, 1996, Carolyn Phelan, review of *Barnacles Eat with Their Feet: Delicious Facts about the Tide Pool Food Chain,* p. 931; March 1, 1997, Carolyn Phelan, review of *Dashing through the Snow,* p. 1158; July, 1998, Shelley Townsend-Hudson, review of *Frozen Stiff,* p. 1883; June 1, 2002, GraceAnne A. DeCandido, review of *The Jazzy Alphabet,* p. 1744; September 15, 2004, Ilene Cooper, review of *Spicy*

Hot Colors!/¡Colores picantes!, p. 247; September 1, 2007, Hazel Rochman, review of *That's Not How You Play Soccer, Daddy!,* p. 137; April 1, 2009, Andrew Medlar, review of *¡Fiesta!: A Celebration of Latino Festivals,* p. 42.

Bulletin of the Center for Children's Books, May, 1998, Deborah Stevenson, review of *Frozen Stiff,* p. 339.

Children's Book Review Service, April, 1997, review of *Dashing through the Snow,* p. 106.

Kirkus Reviews, June 1, 1998, review of *Frozen Stiff,* p. 817; August 1, 2004, review of *Spicy Hot Colors!/ ¡Colores picantes!,* p. 749; April 1, 2009, review of *¡Fiesta!*

Kliatt, September 15, 2005, review of *Cool Cats Counting,* p. 1033; November, 2005, Janis Flint-Ferguson, review of *Death Mountain,* p. 10.

Publishers Weekly, May 6, 2002, review of *The Jazzy Alphabet,* p. 56.

School Library Journal, September, 1989, Janet E. Gelfand, review of *There's Something in There,* p. 257; April, 1996, Karey Wehner, review of *Barnacles Eat with Their Feet,* p. 150; October, 1996, Steve Matthews, review of *The Sunflower Family,* p. 142; April, 1997, Mollie Bynum, review of *Dashing through the Snow,* p. 132; August, 1998, Arwen Marshall, review of *Frozen Stiff,* p. 165; July, 2002, Helen Foster James, review of *The Jazzy Alphabet,* p. 99; November, 2004, Rosalyn Pierini, review of *Spicy Hot Colors!,* p. 130; October, 2005, Maura Bresnahan, review of *Cool Cats Counting,* p. 149; November, 2005, Vicki Reutter, review of *Death Mountain,* p. 148; October, 2007, Blair Christolon, review of *That's Not How You Play Soccer, Daddy!,* p. 128; April, 2009, Sandra Welzenbach, review of *¡Fiesta!,* p. 126.

Writer, June, 2009, Sherry Shanan, "From a Fierce Storm, a Published Novel," p. 33.

ONLINE

Sherry Shanan Home Page, http://www.sherryshanan.com (June 1, 2010).*

*   *   *

SHOULDERS, Michael 1954-

Personal

Born August 19, 1954; married, 1974; wife's name Debbie (a writer and educator); children: Jason, Ryan, Meghann. *Education:* Austin Peay State, B.A. (elementary education), 1976; attended Governor's Academy for Teachers of Writing, 1995; Tennessee State University, Ed.D., 2004. *Hobbies and other interests:* Tennis.

Addresses

Home—Clarksville, TN. *E-mail*—mshoulders@charter. net.

Career

Educator and writer. Clarksville-Montgomery County School System, teacher, then Title I supervisor, 1976-2005; freelance writer, 1995—. Presenter at schools; in-service trainer focusing on literacy and discipline.

Member

International Reading Association.

Writings

V Is for Volunteer: A Tennessee Alphabet, illustrated by Bruce Langton, Sleeping Bear Press (Chelsea, MI), 2001.

Count on Us: A Tennessee Number Book, illustrated by Bruce Langton, Sleeping Bear Press (Chelsea, MI), 2003.

M Is for Magnolia: A Mississippi Alphabet, illustrated by Rick Anderson, Sleeping Bear Press (Chelsea, MI), 2003.

N Is for Natural State: An Arkansas Alphabet, illustrated by Rick Anderson, Sleeping Bear Press (Chelsea, MI), 2003.

1 Mississippi, 2 Mississippi: A Mississippi Number Book, illustrated by Rick Anderson, Sleeping Bear Press (Chelsea, MI), 2004.

(With wife, Debbie Shoulders) *D Is for Drum: A Native American Alphabet,* illustrated by Irving Toddy, Sleeping Bear Press (Chelsea, MI), 2006.

Natural Numbers: An Arkansas Number Book, illustrated by Rick Anderson, Sleeping Bear Press (Chelsea, MI), 2008.

Say Daddy!, illustrated by Teri Weidner, Sleeping Bear Press (Chelsea, MI), 2008.

The ABC Book of American Homes, illustrated by Sarah S. Brannen, Charlesbridge (Watertown, MA), 2008.

(With Debbie Shoulders) *G Is for Gladiator: An Ancient Rome Alphabet,* illustrated by Victor Juhasz, Sleeping Bear Press (Ann Arbor, MI), 2010.

Goodnight Baby Bear, illustrated by Teri Weidner, Sleeping Bear Press (Ann Arbor, MI), 2010.

E Is for Eucharist: A Catholic Alphabet Book, illustrated by Rick Anderson, Sleeping Bear Press (Ann Arbor, MI), 2010.

Author of column "Story Time," published in *Clarkville (TN) Leaf-Chronicle,* 1997-2003.

Sidelights

In his many picture books, educator and literacy consultant Michael Shoulders has parlayed the twenty-six letters of the English alphabet into everything from a trip back in time to ancient Rome to a study of American architecture to a visit to the state of Mississippi. He teams up with illustrator Sarah S. Brannen to create *The ABC Book of American Homes,* while *D Is for Drum: A Native American Alphabet* finds Shoulders teaming with his wife, Debbie Shoulders, to create the text that is brought to life in Irving Toddy's artwork. In *School Library Journal* Anne Chapman Callaghan noted the variety of dwellings covered in *The ABC Book of American Homes* and suggested Shoulder's book as "a jumping-off point for further study." Carolyn Phelan commented favorably on "the variety of houses . . . , the readability of the text, and the quality of the illustrations" in her review of the same book for *Booklist,* while a *Kirkus Reviews* writer praised the "elegant simplicity" evoked due to the illustrator's use of "precise architectural details and clean, straight lines."

D Is for Drum uses a rhyming text to introduce young children to the diversity of Indian cultures present in North America at the time the first Europeans came ashore. Calling the Shoulders' text "significant" due to their ability to include interesting facts in their "poetic rhyme," Ken Marantz added in *School Arts* that the detailed warm-toned images of Native Americans in Toddy's illustrations for *D Is for Drum* "are a precise alignment with the text."

In addition to alphabet books, Shoulders has also written *Say Daddy!* and *Goodnight Baby Bear,* two picture books illustrated with Terry Weidner's pastel-toned water-color images. In *Say Daddy!* an infant bear recounts its first days of life as it is welcomed by its parents and hugged and read to by various loving friends and relatives. Baby Bear returns in *Goodnight Baby Bear,* as the many special adventures it shares with family members all end with a cozy bedtime story and an home-made oatmeal-raisin cookie. Recommending *Say Daddy!* for "literacy and wellness programs" focusing on parenting, Linda Staskus added in *School Library Journal* that Weidner's illustrations "heighten the dreamy, sweet, and cheerful atmosphere" of Shoulder's story.

Biographical and Critical Sources

PERIODICALS

Booklist, August 1, 2008, Carolyn Phelan, review of *The ABC Book of American Homes,* p. 74.

Kirkus Reviews, June 1, 2008, review of *The ABC Book of American Homes.*

Michael Shoulders teams up with artist Sarah S. Brannen in the unique picture book **The ABC Book of American Homes.** (Illustration ©2008 by Sarah S. Brannen. All rights reserved. Used with permission by Charlesbridge Publishing, Inc.)

School Arts, November, 2006, Ken Marantz, review of *D Is for Drum: A Native American Alphabet,* p. 48.

School Library Journal, September, 2006, Jayne Damron, review of *D Is for Drum,* p. 196; May, 2008, Linda Staskus, review of *Say Daddy!,* p. 108; October, 2008, Anne Chapman Callaghan, review of *The ABC Book of American Homes,* p. 136.

ONLINE

Michael Shoulders Home Page, http://www.michael shoulders.com (May 15, 2010).

Sleeping Bear Press Web site, http://www.sleepingbear press.com/ (May 15, 2010), "Michael Shoulders."

* * *

SILVER, Jago
See JAGO

* * *

SILVER, Maggie

Personal

Born in England; married. *Education:* Royal College of Art, degree (natural history illustration).

Addresses

Home—Richmond Park, England.

Career

Illustrator and author. Illustrator for London Zoo and Kew Gardens, London, England.

Writings

SELF-ILLUSTRATED

Who Lives Here? (lift-the-flap book), Sierra Club Books for Children (San Francisco, CA), 1995, reprinted, Mathew Price (Denton, TX), 2009.

Who's at Home? (lift-the-flap book), Lutterworth Press (Cambridge, England), 1995, Mathew Price (Denton, TX), 2009.

ILLUSTRATOR

(With others) Mike Poulton, *Patrick and the Fox,* Oxford University Press (Oxford, England), 1988.

David Oakden, *Anna's Eggs,* Oxford University Press (Oxford, England), 1988.

(With others) Mike Poulton, *William and the Mouse,* Oxford University Press (Oxford, England), 1988.

John Norris Wood, *Nature Hide and Seek: Woods and Forests,* Random House (New York, NY), 1993, reprinted, Mathew Price Limited (Denton, TX), 2008.

Rolfe Green, *The Birds of Regent Park,* Royal Parks (London, England), 1999.

(With Uwe Mayer) Emma Helbrough, *How Flowers Grow,* new edition, Usborne (London, England), 2006.

Biographical and Critical Sources

PERIODICALS

Kirkus Reviews, April 1, 2009, review of *Who's at Home?*

Publishers Weekly, August 2, 1993, review of *Nature Hide and Seek: Woods and Forests,* p. 80.*

* * *

SMALL, David 1945-

Personal

Born February 12, 1945, in Detroit, MI; son of Edward Pierce (a doctor) and Elizabeth Small; married Sarah Stewart (a writer), September, 1980; children: (previous marriages) five. *Education:* Wayne State University, B.F.A., 1968; Yale University, M.F.A., 1972. *Hobbies and other interests:* Swimming, traveling, sketching out-of-doors.

Addresses

Home—Mendon, MI. *Agent*—Holly McGhee, Pippin Properties, 155 E. 38th St., Ste. 2H, New York, NY 10016.

Career

Author and illustrator of children's books; freelance artist. State University of New York—Fredonia College, assistant professor of art, 1972-78; Kalamazoo College, Kalamazoo, MI, assistant professor of art, 1978-83, artist-in-residence, 1983-86. *Exhibitions:* Works included in numerous exhibits, including a touring show sponsored by the National Center for Children's Illustrated Literature.

Awards, Honors

Children's Books of the Year listee, Library of Congress, and Parents' Choice Remarkable Book designation, Parents' Choice Foundation (PCF), both 1982, both for *Eulalie and the Hopping Head;* Notable Book for Children in the Field of Social Studies designation, National Council of Social Studies/Children's Book Council, 1983, for *Mean Chickens and Wild Cucumbers;* Best Books designations, *School Library Journal*

David Small (Photograph by Doug Hren. Reproduced by permission of Pippin Properties, Inc.)

and *Booklist,* both 1984, both for *Anna and the Seven Swans;* Children's Books of the Year listee, Child Study Association of America, 1985, for *The Christmas Box;* Parents' Choice Award for Literature, 1985, for *Imogene's Antlers; Redbook* Award, and Notable Book designation, American Library Association (ALA), both 1988, both for *Company's Coming;* Parents' Choice Award for picture books, 1989, for *As: A Surfeit of Similes,* and 1990, for *Box and Cox;* Caldecott Honor Book designation, ALA, Christopher Award, ALA Notable Book designation, ABBY Award Honor Book designation, and New York Public Library 100 Titles for Reading and Sharing inclusion, all c. 1998, all for *The Gardener* by Sarah Stewart; Caldecott Medal, 2001, and Garden State Children's Book Award, 2003, both for *So You Want to Be President?* by Judith St. George; Gold Medal, Society of Illustrators, for *The Mouse and His Child* by Russell Hoban; Heartland Award, Great Lakes Booksellers Association, 2001, for *The Journey* by Stewart; International Reading Association/Children's Book Center Choice designation, 2004, for *The Friend* by Stewart; ALA Notable Book designation, 2007, and E.B. White Read-aloud Award, American Booksellers for Children, 2008, both for *When Dinosaurs Came with Everything* by Elise Broach; National Book Award in Young People's Literature finalist, 2008, and Newbery Honor Book designation, 2009, both for *The Underneath* by Kathi Appelt; Christopher Award, 2009, for *That Book Woman* by Heather Henson; National Book Award finalist 2009, and Young-Adult Non-

fiction Indie Book Award finalist, Michigan Notable Books designation, ALA Notable Book designation, and numerous notable book designations, all 2010, all for *Stitches.*

Writings

SELF-ILLUSTRATED PICTURE BOOKS

Eulalie and the Hopping Head, Macmillan (New York, NY), 1982.

Imogene's Antlers, Crown (New York, NY), 1985.

Paper John, Farrar, Straus (New York, NY), 1987.

Ruby Mae Has Something to Say, Crown (New York, NY), 1992.

George Washington's Cows, Farrar, Straus (New York, NY), 1994.

Hoover's Bride, Crown (New York, NY), 1995.

Fenwick's Suit, Farrar, Straus (New York, NY), 1996.

ILLUSTRATOR

Nathan Zimelman, *Mean Chickens and Wild Cucumbers,* Macmillan (New York, NY), 1983.

Jonathan Swift, *Gulliver's Travels,* Morrow (New York, NY), 1983.

Burr Tillstrom, *The Kuklapolitan Players Present: The Dragon Who Lived Downstairs,* Morrow (New York, NY), 1984.

Maida Silverman, *Anna and the Seven Swans,* translated from the Russian by Natasha Frumin, Morrow (New York, NY), 1984.

Eve Merriam, *The Christmas Box,* Morrow (New York, NY), 1985.

Arthur Yorinks, *Company's Coming,* Crown (New York, NY), 1988.

Peggy Thomson, *The King Has Horse's Ears,* Simon & Schuster (New York, NY), 1988.

Milton Meltzer, *American Politics: How It Really Works,* Morrow (New York, NY), 1989.

Norton Juster, *As: A Surfeit of Similes,* Morrow (New York, NY), 1989, revised edition published as *As Silly as Knees, as Busy as Bees: An Astounding Assortment of Similes,* Beech Tree (New York, NY), 1998.

Grace Chetwin, *Box and Cox,* Bradbury (New York, NY), 1990.

Sarah Stewart, *The Money Tree,* Farrar, Straus (New York, NY), 1991.

Eve Merriam, *Fighting Words,* Morrow (New York, NY), 1992.

Beverly Cleary, *Petey's Bedtime Story,* Morrow (New York, NY), 1993.

Sarah Stewart, *The Library,* Farrar, Straus (New York, NY), 1995.

Sarah Stewart, *The Gardener,* Farrar, Straus (New York, NY), 1997.

Bonny Becker, *The Christmas Crocodile,* Simon & Schuster (New York, NY), 1998.

Carl Sandburg, *The Huckabuck Family and How They Raised Popcorn in Nebraska and Quit and Came Back,* new edition, Farrar, Straus (New York, NY), 1999.

Judith St. George, *So You Want to Be President?,* Philomel (New York, NY), 2000, revised and updated, 2004.

Sarah Stewart, *The Journey,* Farrar, Straus (New York, NY), 2001.

Russell Hoban, *The Mouse and His Child,* Arthur A. Levine Books (New York, NY), 2001.

Judith St. George, *So You Want to Be an Inventor?,* Philomel (New York, NY), 2002.

Linda Ashman, *The Essential Worldwide Monster Guide,* Simon & Schuster (New York, NY), 2003.

Sarah Stewart, *The Friend,* Farrar, Straus (New York, NY), 2004.

Judith St. George, *So You Want to Be an Explorer?,* Philomel (New York, NY), 2005.

Senator Edward M. Kennedy, *My Senator and Me: A Dog's-Eye View of Washington, DC,* Scholastic, Inc. (New York, NY), 2006.

Elise Broach, *When Dinosaurs Came with Everything,* Atheneum (New York, NY), 2006.

Jennifer Armstrong, *Once upon a Banana,* Simon & Schuster (New York, NY), 2006.

Heather Henderson, *That Book Woman,* Atheneum Books for Young Readers (New York, NY), 2008.

Kathi Appelt, *The Underneath,* Atheneum Books for Young Readers (New York, NY), 2008.

Jane Yolen, *Elsie's Bird,* Philomel (New York, NY), 2010.

Naomi Howland, *The Princess Says Goodnight,* HarperCollins (New York, NY), 2011.

OTHER

Stitches: A Memoir (graphic novel), W.W. Norton & Co. (New York, NY), 2009.

Contributor of illustrations to periodicals, including *New York Times* and *New Yorker.*

Sidelights

Caldecott medalist David Small is the author and illustrator of children's books which, with their offbeat stories, clever texts, and pictures, entertain readers both young and old. His original self-illustrated stories, which include *Eulalie and the Hopping Head, Imogene's Antlers, George Washington's Cows,* and *Hoover's Bride,* feature engaging line drawings that bring to life his lighthearted, whimsical tales while his graphic-novel-style *Stitches: A Memoir* is rich with "visual and rhetorical metaphors" and "evocative and beautifully detailed" pen-and-ink art, according to *School Library Journal* contributor Francisca Goldsmith. As an illustrator, Small is equally well known for his contributions to award-winning books by children's authors such as Beverly Cleary, Judith St. George, Eve Merriam, and Russell Hoban, as well as those by his own wife, author Sarah Stewart.

Born in Detroit, Michigan, Small did not intend to become an artist. Although he enjoyed creating cartoons as a child, as a teenager he found himself attracted to literature and intending to make his living as a playwright. Setting out on his chosen career path, Small enrolled at Wayne State University. During his sophomore year, realizing that his artistic talents then exceeded his literary ones, Small transferred to the university's art school. In 1968, he graduated with a bachelor's of fine arts degree, and then moved to Yale University where he also earned an M.F.A. in fine arts.

After finishing his university education, Small remained connected to the academic world, first teaching at the State University of New York—Fredonia College, and then at Kalamazoo College. The same year he stopped teaching, 1982, his first self-illustrated children's book, *Eulalie and the Hopping Head,* was published to critical acclaim.

Other early works authored and illustrated by Small were also well received by critics, among them *Imogene's Antlers,* a fanciful story about a young girl who wakes up one morning to find that her forehead has sprouted a handsome rack of antlers. *Paper John* tells the story of a simple man who uses his paper-folding skills to outwit the devil, while *Ruby Mae Has Something to Say* features a tongue-tied woman who wishes to share the word of peace at the United Nations. In a

Small's illustration projects include his award-winning collaboration with author Judith St. George on So You Want to Be President. (Illustration © 2000 by David Small. Used by permission of Philomel Books, an imprint of Penguin Putnam Books for Young Readers, a division of Penguin Putnam Inc. All rights reserved.)

review of *Paper John, Booklist* reviewer Ilene Cooper called Small "one of the most inventive illustrators around today."

Other original tales have continued to appear, albeit not frequently enough for fans of Small's quietly subversive humor. "Witty and silly in equal measure, Small's . . . cheeky expose about the real reason the father of our country went into politics works on a number of conceptual levels," wrote a *Publishers Weekly* in a review of *George Washington's Cows,* which finds Washington fleeing from his rural home in Mount Vernon because of demanding bovines, petulant pigs, and well-read sheep. A reading of *Hoover's Bride* inspired Leone McDermott to note in *Booklist* that Small's "exuberantly loopy romance will delight the silly" with its story of a sloppy bachelor who cleans up his house with the aid of a vacuum cleaner and finds love in the process. A lonely boy decides that his nerdy wardrobe may be the reason he has no friends in *Fenwick's Suit,* and in the book's splashy, 1930s-style artwork Small plays on the truth behind the old adage that "the clothes wear the man."

Small began illustrating books by other authors at the same time that he began writing and illustrating his own stories. From the beginning, his talent for bringing to life humorously quirky characters was tapped by publishers, as can be seen by his list of assignments: a new edition of Jonathan Swift's classic satire *Gulliver's Travels,* Nathan Zimelman's *Mean Chickens and Wild Cucumbers,* Burr Tillstrom's *The Kuklapolitan Players Present: The Dragon Who Lived Downstairs,* and Peggy Thomson's *The King Has Horse's Ears.* More recent works include illustrations for *Fighting Words,* a text by the late poet Eve Merriam that finds country-boy Dale and city-girl Leda engaging in a word fight that becomes so enjoyable that they both agree to resume their verbal wars another day. In *School Library Journal* Luann Toth remarked that Merriam's characters "take center stage in the quirky pen-and-ink and watercolor drawings with perfect facial expressions to match each verbal assault." Calling the book "an original," *Booklist* reviewer Carolyn Phelan wrote that "Small's captivating ink-and-watercolor artwork sets the war in a variety of entertaining settings."

Another book featuring Small's art, *The Huckabuck Family and How They Raised Popcorn in Nebraska and Quit and Came Back* is taken from American poet Carl Sandburg's classic 1922 book *Rootabaga Stories.* In this newly illustrated version (the original featured art by Maud and Miska Petersham) a farmer named Jonas Jonas Huckabuck, together with his wife, Mama Mama, and his daughter, Pony Pony, live on a Nebraska farm, raising corn, until one day, when Pony Pony discovers a silver buckle while weeding the squash. Her parents warn that the buckle is a sign of luck, but they are unsure if the shiny object signifies good luck or bad. A fire the next day that turns all of their harvest into popcorn reveals to the Huckabucks that their fortunes have

Readers share the small-scale adventures in Russell Hoban's **The Mouse and His Child** *through Small's detailed art.* (Illustration © 2001 by David Small. Reproduced by permission of Scholastic, Inc.)

turned for the worse, so the family decides to leave until the blizzard of popcorn clears itself. Many cities later, the family finds a second buckle matching the first and so sets off for home, realizing that their farm is ready to welcome them back. Several reviewers applauded Small for introducing *Rootabaga Stories* to a new audience as well as for his accompanying illustrations. Writing in *Horn Book,* a critic predicted that "with a new treatment by David Small in picture book format, this particular selection . . . should reach a contemporary audience." Small "depicts the family's peripatetic lifestyle with wry wit and droll details," claimed a *Publishers Weekly* reviewer, "leading readers of this engaging book to feel they've met with the good kind of luck."

In his work for Linda Ashman's *The Essential Worldwide Monster Guide* Small brings to life thirteen creatures that range from Scotland's Loch Ness monster to India's Ravana, the Greek Sirenes, and the North American Sasquatch. The artist's "energetic and wacky" ink-and-watercolor images add to the fun, according to *School Library Journal* reviewer Nina Lindsay, the critic going on to note that they combine with Ashman's "enchanting and excellent" rhyming text to produce "a beautifully designed volume." In Elise Broach's humorous *When Dinosaurs Came with Everything,* Small's art brings to life the story of a modern boy who winds up with a free dinosaur. In her *School Library Journal* review of Broach's story, Marge Loch-Wouters praised the "sketchy, tongue-in-cheek watercolor-and-ink" images that illuminate "the boy's exuberance, the dinosaurs' mass, and the hubbub that a city full of these reptiles would create."

The "sprightly artwork, executed in ink and watercolor, is just made for a second look," wrote Cooper in a *Booklist* review of Small's illustrations for Jennifer Armstrong's *Once upon a Banana.* Also appraising Armstrong's book, a *Kirkus Reviews* contributor dubbed the work "a tour de force of visual sequencing" in which the illustrator "sets up a hilarious chain of events along a busy city street." Noting the presence of Small's characteristic "huge, motley cast" of engaging characters, a *Publishers Weekly* reviewer noted of *Once upon a Banana* that "the pages overflow with enough pratfalls and comic asides to reward many readings."

Small's award-winning collaborations include his work with writer Judith St. George on *So You Want to Be President?, So You Want to Be an Explorer?,* and *So You Want to Be an Inventor? So You Want to Be Presi-*

Small and St. George reunite to share inspiring stories about great innovators in the picture book So You Want to Be an Inventor? (Illustration ©2002 by David Small. Used by permission of Philomel Books, a Division of Penguin Young Readers Group, a Member of Penguin Group (USA) Inc., 345 Hudson Street, New York, NY 10014. All rights reserved.)

dent? offers young readers lighthearted information about the men who have held the highest political office in the United States. Ranging from trivia about how many presidents have been named James (six) to how many presidents have been born in a log cabin (eight), the fact-filled book gives readers a humorous look at the many occupants of the White House. Small's award-winning illustrations include depictions of Richard Nixon flashing a "V" for victory sign in the White House bowling lanes, a rotund William H. Taft being hoisted by a crane into a bathtub, and the somber Woodrow Wilson doing a little jig, each image based in part on a real-life incident. In *Booklist* Phelan claimed that "Small's delightful illustrations, usually droll and sometimes hilarious, will draw children to the book and entertain them from page to page," while a *Publishers Weekly* critic felt that "the comical caricatured artwork emphasizes some of the presidents' best known qualities and amplifies the playful tone of the text."

According to *U.S. News & World Report* writer Marc Silver, Small found the illustrations for *So You Want to Be President?* challenging to create. He had only five months to capture the essence of forty-two U.S. presidents, and as Small told Silver, he quickly discovered that "the handsomer they are, the harder they are to draw." However, "sketching freely, wildly at times," as *Horn Book* contributor Patricia Lee Gauch observed, Small finished the pictures for the book, going on to earn the highest award in children's book illustration, the Caldecott Medal, for his efforts.

Small and St. George continue their collaboration with an introduction to the lives of visionaries ranging from ship's captain Christopher Columbus and paleontologist Mary Kingsley to aviatrix Amelia Earhart and test pilot Chuck Yeager in *So You Want to Be an Explorer?* and technology innovators ranging from printing-press inventor Johannes Gutenberg to Alexander Graham Bell and beyond in *So You Want to Be an Inventor?* The artist's "larger than life, extravagantly wrought caricatures" fully balance St. George's humorous and "inspirational" text in *So You Want to Be an Explorer?,* according to a *Kirkus Reviews* contributor, and Lucinda Snyder Whitehurst concluded of the companion volume that "the snappy tone of the text and the richly drawn illustrations" will entertain young readers. *Booklist* reviewer GraceAnne A. DeCandido proclaimed of the series that "lively energy infuses the work of this award-winning team."

Featuring a rhyming text by Heather Henson, *That Book Woman* also benefits from Small's contributions. In Henson's tale, the hard-working, no-nonsense oldest child in a rural family gradually begins to see the value of books, thanks to the librarian who, as part of the WPA's Pack Horse Library project, visits his Appalachian Mountain home during the hardship years of the 1930s. Bringing to life the story's "carefully honed text," Small's "deft, rough-edged" watercolor, pastel, and ink images "convey even more," noted Joanna Rudge Long in *Horn Book,* while Julie Just observed in the *New York Times Book Review* that his "illustrations . . . unfold at times almost as in a graphic novel." Another illustration project, Kathi Appelt's evocative middle-grade novel *The Underneath,* mixes hope and heartbreak in its story of a lost and pregnant cat that finds a refuge under the floor of the hovel of a bitter old man. Echoing what Rudge described as Appelt's "lyrical, circling narrative, Homeric in its cadenced repetitions," Small's detailed drawings capture the story's "endearing characters," resulting in a book that is "a natural for reading aloud." Jennifer Mattson also praised the creative collaboration in *The Underneath,* concluding that the "fluid lines" in Small's illustrations make them "a perfect match for the book's saturated settings and Appelt's ebbing, flowing lyricism."

Among Small's growing list of illustration credits are several books written by his wife, children's author Sarah Stewart. In each of the couple's collaborations, which include *The Money Tree, The Gardener, The Journey, The Library,* and *The Friend,* Stewart crafts her story from a combination of letters, diary entries, and rhyme. Her texts are brought to life in Small's large watercolor illustrations, making the books perfect for use during story hours.

In *The Money Tree* Stewart and Small relate the story of a tree growing in Miss McGillicuddy's yard that bears leaves shaped like dollar bills. All summer long townsfolk and strangers alike greedily pick currency from the tree and even ask for branches of the tree to plant on their own land. Busy making quilts, tending her garden, and flying kites, Miss McGillicuddy seems unaffected by all the attention her new tree receives, but when fall comes and all the tree's leaves are gone, she taps into another value of the tree: she cuts down the strange specimen and burns its wood in her fireplace during the cold winter months. Describing Small's images as "reminiscent of the art of Carl Larsson," a *Publishers Weekly* critic added that the book's "evocative, pastel-filled watercolors echo the hushed, mysterious tone" of Stewart's story. Noting that *The Money Tree* provides a starting point for discussions about "contemporary values," *Horn Book* reviewer Hanna B. Zeigler added that "Small's charming and detailed illustrations portray a strong, independent woman whose life is graceful and meaningful."

The couple's Caldecott Honor-winning *The Gardener,* as well as *The Journey* and *The Friend,* each tell the story of a young girl though a series of letters and diary entries. In *The Gardener* Lydia Grace Finch must help her unemployed parents during the Great Depression of the 1930s by working in her uncle's bakery. Lydia does not mind working in the city, though she misses her favorite past time, tending her beloved plants and flowers. Through Lydia's letters to her country-dwelling family, readers learn how the girl adapts to city life by turning her uncle's apartment and rooftop into a beautiful garden. "Small controls the action with dramatic

angles," wrote *Horn Book* contributor Susan P. Bloom, the critic adding that "objects placed close up . . . afford deep perspective to a page bustling with detail." Although the illustrator's paintings "are a bit more softly focused than usual," *Booklist* reviewer Stephanie Zvirin added that "they are still recognizably [Small's], with wonderfully expressive characters, ink-line details, and patches of pastel."

The Journey relates the story of a young Amish girl, Hannah, as she visits Chicago for the first time. In diary entries, Hannah describes all the wonders she sees in the city and compares them to life in the country. Although she is amazed by the tall skyscrapers, the elevated train system, and the many shops in the city, by trip's end she realizes how much she misses her family and the activities on the farm. Accompanying Hannah's recollections are Small's double-page illustrations, one spread showing the young girl amid the hustle and bustle of Chicago, and the next one offering a bucolic view of her rural Amish home. *School Library Journal* contributor Wendy Lukehart found that the book's "design perfectly meld[s] to its subtle message," and a *Publishers Weekly* critic wrote that "Small effectively depicts the spare, serene Amish lifestyle and . . . underscores the sharp contrast between the two settings."

Also told in Stewart's gentle rhyme, *The Friend* focuses on privileged young carrot-top Annabelle Bernadette Clementine Dodd, the only daughter of wealthy parents who lives in a large seaside home. The family housekeeper, Beatrice Smith, is the girl's only friend, and the two spend almost all their time together exploring the nearby beach. When Annabelle ventures out into the ocean alone one day, she becomes caught in the undertow, but the diligent Beatrice is there to save her. In *Publishers Weekly* a critic dubbed *The Friend* the couple's "most personal work to date," noting that the story is based on an incident from Stewart's own childhood. Praising Small's artistic accompaniment, Roger Sutton wrote in *Horn Book* that his "tender but scrupulously individualized portraits and glorious double-page spreads" evoke the close relationship between child and caregiver that grounds Stewart's spare text.

In *The Library,* Small and Stewart introduce a woman who loves to read. Since childhood Elizabeth Brown has collected and read books, intending to read every volume ever published. While other girls played with dolls and skates, Elizabeth occupied herself with piles and piles of books. As a grown woman, she continues to buy and consume books until she notices that she has no room for even one more volume in her overstuffed house. To solve her problem, the bookworm shares her passion by donating her book collection to the town and creating a library for all to enjoy. *New York Times Book Review* critic Rebecca Pepper Sinkler commented on how well Small's illustrations mesh with Stewart's text. "He . . . grounds the action of the story in time and place," note the critic, concluding of *The Library:* "It's a joy to look at, from its delicately framed full-page illustrations to the witty doodads that fill the white spaces around the smaller ones." A *Publishers Weekly* contributor noted that "Small's . . . airy illustrations charm with historical touches and soothing pastel hues," while *Booklist* reviewer Ilene Cooper wrote that with the "wonderfully unique perspectives" incorporated into Small's "framed pastel artwork," "reading has never looked quite so delicious."

Biographical and Critical Sources

BOOKS

Children's Literature Review, Volume 53, Gale (Detroit, MI), 1999.
Merriam, Eve, *Fighting Words,* Morrow (New York, NY), 1992.
Small, David, *Stitches: A Memoir,* W.W. Norton (New York, NY), 2009.

PERIODICALS

Booklist, June 15, 1987, Ilene Cooper, review of *Paper John,* p. 1608; May 15, 1992, Carolyn Phelan, review of *Fighting Words,* p. 1688; November 1, 1994, Kathy Broderick, review of *George Washington's Cows,* p. 510; March 15, 1995, Ilene Cooper, review of *The Library,* p. 1338; February 1, 1996, Leone McDermott, review of *Hoover's Bride,* p. 939; June 1, 1997, Stephanie Zvirin, review of *The Gardener,* p. 1722; September 15, 1999, Linda Perkins, review of *The Huckabuck Family and How They Raised Popcorn in Nebraska and Quit and Came Back,* p. 270; July, 2000, Carolyn Phelan, review of *So You Want to Be President?,* p. 2034; March 15, 2001, Ellen Mandel, review of *The Journey,* p. 1399; August, 2002, review of *So You Want to Be an Inventor?,* p. 1954; November 1, 2003, Jennifer Mattson, review of *The Essential Worldwide Monster Guide,* p. 498; September 15, 2005, Jennifer Mattson, review of *So You Want to Be an Explorer?,* p. 69; November 1, 2006, Ilene Cooper, review of *Once upon a Banana,* p. 58; September 15, 2007, Ilene Cooper, review of *When Dinosaurs Came with Everything,* p. 73; May 15, 2008, Jennifer Mattson, review of *The Underneath,* p. 54; July 1, 2009, Ian Chipman, review of *Stitches,* p. 6.
Horn Book, January-February, 1992, Hanna Zeigler, review of *The Money Tree,* p. 62; July-August, 1995, Ann A. Flowers, review of *The Library,* p. 454; November-December, 1997, Susan P. Bloom, review of *The Gardener,* p. 673; September, 1999, review of *The Huckabuck Family and How They Raised Popcorn in Nebraska and Quit and Came Back,* p. 600; March, 2001, review of *The Journey,* p. 202; July, 2001, Patricia Lee Gauch, "David Small," p. 421; September-October, 2002, Betty Carter, review of *So You Want to Be an Inventor?,* p. 601; September-October, 2004, Roger Sutton, review of *The Friend,* p. 575; August 1, 2006, John Peters, review of *My Sena-tor and Me: A Dog's-Eye View of Washington, DC,* p. 81; January-February, 2007, Lolly Robinson, review of *Once upon a Banana,* p. 55; May-June, 2008, Joanna Rudge Long, review of *The Underneath,* p. 303; November-December, 2008, Joanna Rudge Long, review of *That Book Woman,* p. 691.
Kirkus Reviews, July 15, 2002, review of *So You Want to Be an Inventor?,* p. 1044; August 15, 2003, review of *The Essential Worldwide Monster Guide,* p. 1069; July 1, 2004, review of *The Friend,* p. 637; August 1, 2005, review of *So You Want to Be an Explorer?,* p. 858; October 1, 2006, review of *Once upon a Banana,* p. 1009.
New York Times Book Review, June 4, 1995, Rebecca Pepper Sinkler, review of *The Library,* p. 25; May 20, 2001, review of *The Journey;* February 15, 2009, Julie Just, review of *That Book Woman,* p. 15; September 6, 2009, Eric Konigsberg, "Finding a Voice in a Graphic Memoir."
Publishers Weekly, August 30, 1991, review of *The Money Tree,* p. 83; August 29, 1994, review of *George Washington's Cows,* p. 78; April 18, 1995, review of *The Library,* p. 61; June 2, 1997, review of *The Gardener,* p. 70; July 26, 1999, review of *The Huckabuck Family and How They Raised Popcorn in Nebraska and Quit and Came Back,* p. 89; July 17, 2000, review of *So You Want to Be President?,* p. 193; January 8, 2001, review of *The Journey,* p. 66; October 13, 2003, review of *The Essential Worldwide Monster Guide,* p. 79; June 7, 2004, review of *The Friend,* p. 50; May 1, 2006, review of *My Senator and Me,* p. 62; October 2, 2006, review of *Once upon a Banana,* p. 61; August 6, 2007, review of *When Dinosaurs Came with Everything,* p. 187; August 10, 2009, review of *Stitches,* p. 42.
School Library Journal, June, 1992, Luann Toth, review of *Fighting Words,* p. 99; March, 2001, Wendy Luke-hart, review of *The Journey,* p. 220; September, 2003, Grace Oliff, review of *The Gardener,* p. 85, and Nina Lindsay, review of *The Essential Worldwide Monster Guide,* p. 194; August, 2004, Marianne Saccardi, review of *The Friend,* p. 96; September, 2005, Lucinda Snyder Whitehurst, review of *So You Want to Be an Explorer?,* p. 196; August, 2006, Wendy Lukehart, review of *My Senator and Me,* p. 106; December, 2006, Susan Weitz, review of *Once upon a Banana,* p. 94; September, 2007, review of *When Dinosaurs Came with Everything,* p. 158; October, 2008, Angela J. Reynolds, review of *That Book Woman,* p. 110; September, 2009, Francisca Goldsmith, review of *Stitches,* p. 193.
U.S. News & World Report, January 29, 2001, Marc Silver, "The Cartoonist in Chief," p. 8.

ONLINE

David Small Home Page, http://davidsmallbooks.com (May 31, 2010).
Pippin Properties Web site, http://www.pippinproperties.com/ (October 27, 2007), "David Small."*

SMITH, Danna
(Danna Kessimakis Smith)

Personal

Born in Murray, UT; married; husband's name Dave; children: Boston, Olivia. *Education:* College degree. *Hobbies and other interests:* Reading, golfing, gardening, watercolor painting.

Addresses

Home—Woodbridge, CA. *Agent*—Kendra Marcus, BookStop Literary Agency, 67 Meadow View Rd., Orinda, CA 94563; kendra@bookstopliterary.com. *E-mail*—danna@dannasmithbooks.com.

Career

Writer.

Member

Society of Children's Book Writers and Illustrators.

Awards, Honors

Creative Child Seal of Excellence award, 2004, for *A Wild Cowboy;* 2x2 Reading List, Texas Library Association, for *Two at the Zoo.*

Writings

(As Danna Kessimakis Smith) *A Wild Cowboy,* illustrated by Laura Freeman, Hyperion/Jump at the Sun (New York, NY), 2004.

(As Danna Kessimakis Smith) *A Brave Spaceboy,* illustrated by Laura Freeman, Hyperion/Jump at the Sun (New York, NY), 2005.

Two at the Zoo: A Counting Book, illustrated by Valeria Petrone, Clarion Books (New York, NY), 2009.

Contributor of stories to periodicals, including *Spider.*

Sidelights

Danna Smith is the author of such highly regarded works for young readers as *A Wild Cowboy* and *Two at the Zoo: A Counting Book.* "A picture book is more than a book to me, it's an experience," Smith remarked on her home page. "It's art and story wrapped up in a neat little package that children and adults can enjoy over and over again. Being a part of the picture book world is extremely rewarding."

The author's debut title, *A Wild Cowboy,* was published under the name Danna Kessimakis Smith and celebrates the power of imagination. Told in verse, the work centers on a cowboy-loving youngster's trip to his grand-

Danna Smith (Reproduced by permission.)

mother's apartment, where he enjoys campfire "grub" (hot dogs and popcorn) and rounds up a "herd" of puppies. According to *School Library Journal* critic Mary Elam, Smith's tale "has a natural flow, like a child's stream of consciousness, and the rhyming text reads aloud smoothly," and a contributor in *Kirkus Reviews* noted that *A Wild Cowboy* "does justice to a child's ability to use what's at hand to feed inventiveness." In a companion tale, *A Brave Spaceboy,* a boy and his younger brother, having just moved into a new house, imagine themselves venturing into outer space to discover new worlds. "Smith's rhythmic language contributes spirited movement to a tale that explores the ambivalent feelings that many children experience during relocation," Rebecca Sheridan commented in *School Library Journal.*

A young boy and his grandfather don safari hats and gaze upon a variety of exotic animals, including warthogs, alligators, and parrots, in Smith's *Two at the Zoo,* a counting story. Linda M. Kenton, writing in *Booklist,* called the work "an engaging read-aloud," and a critic in *Kirkus Reviews* observed that the author's "rollicking, rhyming text scans well."

Biographical and Critical Sources

PERIODICALS

Booklist, April 1, 2004, Karin Snelson, review of *A Wild Cowboy,* p. 1370.

Kirkus Reviews, March 1, 2004, review of *A Wild Cowboy,* p. 230; April 1, 2005, review of *A Brave Spaceboy,* p. 425; January 15, 2009, review of *Two at the Zoo: A Counting Book.*

Smith introduces counting skills in her entertaining text for **Two at the Zoo,** *a picture book featuring artwork by Valeria Petrone.*

Publishers Weekly, May 3, 2004, review of *A Wild Cowboy,* p. 190.

School Library Journal, May, 2004, Mary Elam, review of *A Wild Cowboy,* p. 124; May, 2005, Rebecca Sheridan, review of *A Brave Spaceboy,* p. 97; February, 2009, Linda M. Kenton, review of *Two at the Zoo,* p. 86.

ONLINE

California Readers Web site, http://www.californiareaders. com/ (May 10, 2010), Bonnie O'Brian, "Meet Danna Smith."

Danna Smith Home Page, http://www.dannasmithbooks. com (May 1, 2010).

Danna Smith Web log, www.dannasmith.blogspot.com/ (May 1, 2010).

*   *   *

SMITH, Danna Kessimakis
See SMITH, Danna

*   *   *

SMITHSON, Ryan 1985-

Personal

Born 1985, in CO; married; wife's name Heather. *Education:* Hudson Valley Community College, A.A.S. (criminal justice), 2007; currently attending Empire State College. *Hobbies and other interests:* Martial arts, downhill skiing, hiking, white-water rafting.

Addresses

Home—East Greenbush, NY.

Career

American Red Cross, Albany, NY, mobile unit assistant. Has also worked at an after-school program for children. *Military service:* U.S. Army Reserves, served in Iraq, 2005.

Awards, Honors

John L. Buono Award for Civic Engagement.

Writings

Ghosts of War: The True Story of a Nineteen-year-old GI (memoir), HarperCollins (New York, NY), 2009.

Sidelights

In his critically acclaimed memoir *Ghosts of War: The True Story of a Nineteen-year-old GI* Ryan Smithson recounts his experiences as a U.S. Army engineer stationed in Iraq. Raised in East Greenbush, New York, Smithson joined the Army Reserves at the age of seventeen, in response to the terrorist attacks of September 11, 2001. "I'd heard all about September 11th," he writes in *Ghosts of War*. "I'd watched it happen on television. I'd heard the theories and discussions about foreign policy that were way over my head. I'd bowed my head during tributes and moments of silence. I knew all about 9/11, but I felt like it was my generation's responsibility to do something about it."

Trained as a heavy-equipment operator, Smithson was deployed to Iraq in 2005. *Ghosts of War* offers his observations on basic training and also describes his platoon's missions, which included bulldozing earth berms and repairing roads damaged by improvised explosive devices, at times while under mortar attack. Smithson also describes his sometimes difficult readjustment to civilian life. A critic in *Kirkus Reviews* called *Ghosts of War* "a remarkable, deeply penetrating read that will compel teens to reflect on . . . duty, patriotism and sacrifice," and Eric Norton described the memoir in *School Library Journal* as "a tough but powerful look at one man's experience." A *Publishers Weekly* contributor offered similar praised, heralding Smithson's book as "a fascinating, often humorous—and occasionally devastating—account of the motivations and life of a contemporary soldier."

Biographical and Critical Sources

BOOKS

Smithson, Ryan, *Ghosts of War: The True Story of a Nineteen-year-old GI* (memoir), HarperCollins (New York, NY), 2009.

PERIODICALS

Booklist, July 1, 2009, John Peters, review of *Ghosts of War,* p. 49.
Kirkus Reviews, April 1, 2009, review of *Ghosts of War.*
Publishers Weekly, May 25, 2009, review of *Ghosts of War,* p. 59.
School Library Journal, March, 2009, Eric Norton, review of *Ghosts of War,* p. 169.

ONLINE

HarperCollins Web site, http://www.harpercollins.com/ (June 1, 2010), "Ryan Smithson."*

*   *   *

STEWART, Trenton Lee 1970-

Personal

Born 1970; married; children: two sons. *Education:* University of Iowa, M.F.A. *Hobbies and other interests:* Reading, movies, playing music, taking walks, playing chess and poker, visiting art museums, spending time with family.

Addresses

Home—Little Rock, AR.

Career

Author and educator. Former creative-writing teacher.

Writings

Flood Summer (novel), Southern Methodist University Press (Dallas, TX), 2005.

"MYSTERIOUS BENEDICT SOCIETY" SERIES; MIDDLE-GRADE NOVELS

The Mysterious Benedict Society, illustrated by Carson Ellis, Little, Brown (Boston, MA), 2007.
The Mysterious Benedict Society and the Perilous Journey, illustrated by Diana Sudyka, Little, Brown (Boston, MA), 2008.
The Mysterious Benedict Society and the Prisoner's Dilemma, illustrated by Diana Sudyka, Little, Brown (New York, NY), 2009.

Sidelights

A former teacher of creative writing, Alabama native Trenton Lee Stewart became a full-time author with the publication of *Flood Summer,* a novel set in small-town Arkansas that finds misfit loners Abe and Marie brought together during a torrential downpour. Stewart has since turned to younger readers, producing the "Mysterious Benedict Society" series. Geared for middle graders and compared by critics to works by J.K. Rowling, Roald Dahl, and Lemony Snicket, Stewart's series includes *The Mysterious Benedict Society, The Mysterious Benedict Society and the Perilous Journey,* and *The Mysterious Benedict Society and the Prisoner's Dilemma.*

The Mysterious Benedict Society was inspired by Stewart's love of puzzles. "I'd long had an image in mind of a child taking a difficult test that was more than it appeared to be," he explained in an interview for the Hachette Book Group Web site. "To me that seemed the beginning of an intriguing story. When a similar idea occurred to me later, I thought of it as a possible addition to the first one. From there the story began to take shape. So although the book might work without the puzzles, it would not exist without them."

The Mysterious Benedict Society introduces readers to four special young people who respond to an unusual newspaper advertisement seeking gifted children who have ambition. Answering the ad are orphaned Reynie

Cover of Trenton Lee Stewart's middle-grade novel **The Mysterious Benedict Society, *featuring artwork by* Carson Ellis.** (Little, Brown & Company, 2008. Cover art ©Carson Ellis. Reproduced by permission.)

Muldoon, tomboy Kate Wetherall, the recalcitrant Constance Contraire, and Reynie's friend George "Sticky" Washington. The preteens meet Mr. Benedict, who asks them to take a difficult, problem-solving test along with a group of other applicants. After passing the challenge, the four children are sent on a special mission to infiltrate the Learning Institute for the Very Enlightened. Here they must foil the wicked plot of Ledroptha Curtain, who intends to enslave the world by broadcasting brainwashing messages to people's homes through use of his Whisperer machine. Puzzle solving is a key to their success, and each child approaches problems from a unique angle. Constance, for example, uses her sheer stubbornness to get results; Kate is adept at using tools; Sticky possesses a memory like a bear trap; and Reynie, who becomes their chosen leader, is simply an expert at finding solutions to puzzles. Noting the fast pace of Stewart's prose, *Booklist* contributor Ilene Cooper added that the author "writes with . . . attention to the intricacies of plot and personality." The inclusion of "underlying themes . . . and hints of more adventures to come" make Stewart an "author . . . to remember," concluded Beth L. Meister in her review of *The Mysterious Benedict Society* for *School Library Journal.*

In *The Mysterious Benedict Society and the Perilous Journey* Mr. Benedict and his loyal sidekick are kidnaped by Mr. Curtain, but have time to leave tantalizing clues as to their location for Reynie, Constance, Kate, and Sticky. As his adventure plays out, Stewart weaves in themes on such topics as the potential dangers of the media, the importance of education and intelligence, and the potential of children when they are not underestimated. Citing the author's use of "wordplay . . . , literary allusions, ingenious escapes, and light-handed terror," Judith A. Hayn added in her *Journal of Adolescent & Adult Literacy* review that *The Mysterious Benedict Society and the Perilous Journey* contains enough "just plain fun [to] take this tale beyond the obvious comparisons with Harry Potter." Writing in *School Library Journal,* Beth L. Meister predicted that the book's mix of "coincidences, . . . unusual characters, threatening villains, and dramatic plot twists will grab and hold readers' attention," while Eva Mitnick praised Stewart's novel in the same periodical as "a rip-roaring adventure" as well as "a warm and satisfying tale about friendship."

Featuring artwork by Diane Sudyka, *The Mysterious Benedict Society and the Prisoner's Dilemma* finds the evil Mr. Curtain still intent on his plan to control all of humanity by tracking down his missing Whisperer machine. With their powers more controlled, Constance, Reynie, and company now set their minds to thwarting this dastardly scheme, but things look grim when they fall into Mr. Curtain's trap. Although Caitlin Augusta noted in *School Library Journal* that the third novel in the "Mysterious Benedict Society" series "lacks the facile agility of its predecessors," she added that the characters still engage readers in a tale buoyed by "rollicking metaphors." Praising the "well-delineated characters" of Stewart's four young heroes, *Horn Book* contributor Anita L. Burkam added that the "thumping good action scenes" in *The Mysterious Benedict Society and the Prisoner's Dilemma* will keep readers transfixed.

Biographical and Critical Sources

PERIODICALS

Booklinks, March, 2007, Ilene Cooper, review of *The Mysterious Benedict Society,* p. 12.

Booklist, January 1, 2007, Ilene Cooper, review of *The Mysterious Benedict Society,* p. 93; March 15, 2008, Ilene Cooper, review of *The Mysterious Benedict Society and the Perilous Journey,* p. 51.

Bulletin of the Center for Children's Books, May, 2007, Karen Coats, review of *The Mysterious Benedict Society,* p. 357.

Children's Bookwatch, September, 2007, review of *The Mysterious Benedict Society.*

Choice, March, 2006, S.F. Klepetar, review of *Flood Summer,* p. 1230.

Christian Science Monitor, June 20, 2008, Jenny Sawyer, review of *The Mysterious Benedict Society and the Perlious Journey,* p. 25.

Horn Book, March 1, 2007, Anita L. Burkam, review of *The Mysterious Benedict Society,* p. 203; May-June, 2008, Anita L. Burkham, review of *The Mysterious*

Benedict Society and the Perilous Journey, p. 328; November-December, 2009, Anita L. Burkam, review of *The Mysterious Benedict Society and the Prisoner's Dilemma,* p. 687.

Journal of Adolescent & Adult Literacy, October, 2007, Judith A. Hayn, review of *The Mysterious Benedict Society,* p. 189.

Publishers Weekly, December 18, 2006, review of *The Mysterious Benedict Society,* p. 63.

School Library Journal, March, 2007, Beth L. Meister, review of *The Mysterious Benedict Society,* p. 219; April, 2007, review of *The Mysterious Benedict Society,* p. 59; May, 2008, Eva Mitnick, review of *The Mysterious Benedict Society and the Perilous Journey,* p. 140; October, 2009, Caitlin Augusta, review of *The Mysterious Benedict Society and the Prisoner's Dilemma,* p. 138.

Voice of Youth Advocates, February, 2007, Donna Scanlon, review of *The Mysterious Benedict Society,* p. 547.

ONLINE

Hachette Book Group Web site, http://www.hachettebookgroupusa.com/ (January 18, 2008), interview with Stewart.

Kidsreads.com, http://www.kidsreads.com/ (January 18, 2008), Norah Piehl, review of *The Mysterious Benedict Society.**

T-V

TALLIS, Robyn
See COVILLE, Bruce

*   *   *

TAYLOR, G.P. 1958(?)-
(Graham Peter Taylor)

Personal
Born c. 1958, in Scarborough, North Yorkshire, England; father a shoemaker, mother a food server; married c. 1983; wife's name Kathy (a nurse); children: Lydia, Hannah, Abigail.

Addresses
Home—Cloughton, England.

Career
Author, 2002—. Roadie for musical acts, including the Sex Pistols and Elvis Costello, c. 1974-79; glass washer at a nightclub in Yorkshire, England, c. 1979; CBS Records, London, England, band promoter, early 1980s; social worker in Yorkshire, early 1980s; North Yorkshire Police Department, beat officer, 1986-96; vicar for Church of England, Cloughton, 1995-2004.

Awards, Honors
Yorkshire Awards Arts and Entertainment Award, 2007.

Writings

FANTASY NOVELS

Shadowmancer, privately published, 2002, Faber & Faber (London, England), 2003, Putnam (New York, NY), 2004.

Wormwood, Putnam (New York, NY), 2004.

Tersias, Faber & Faber (London, England), 2005, published as *Tersias the Oracle,* Putnam (New York, NY), 2006.

The Curse of Salamander Street, Faber & Faber (London, England), 2006, published as *The Shadowmancer Returns: The Curse of Salamander Street,* Putnam (New York, NY), 2007.

Mariah Mundi: The Midas Box, Faber & Faber (London, England), 2007, Putnam (New York, NY), 2008.

Mariah Mundi and the Ghost Diamonds, Faber & Faber (London, England), 2008.

Mariah Mundi and the Ship of Fools, Faber & Faber (London, England), 2009.

"DOPPLE GANGER CHRONICLES" NOVEL SERIES

The Twizzle Sisters and Erik, Markonia Enterprises (East Barnet, England), 2006, published as *The First Escape,* Tyndale House (Carol Stream, IL), 2008.

The Secret of Indigo Moon, illustrated by Daniel Boultwood and others, Tyndale House (Carol Stream, IL), 2009.

OTHER

(With Bob Smietana) *G.P. Taylor: Sin, Salvation, and Shadowmancer,* Zondervan (Grand Rapids, MI), 2006.

(Author of introduction) Mark Denton, *The Yorkshire Coast,* Frances Lincoln (London, England), 2006.

Contributor to London *Times.*

Adaptations
Shadowmancer and *Wormwood* were optioned for film by Fortitude Films; *Shadowmancer* was adapted as an audiobook.

Sidelights
At the age of forty-two, English vicar G.P. Taylor decided that if he wanted to realize his dream of being an author, it was now or never. Drawing on his surround-

ings—the vicarage of Cloughton, in Yorkshire, England—as well as his former vocations, which included work as a policeman, social worker, and rock-band promoter, he produced the novel *Shadowmancer.* Working from his kitchen table, Taylor self-published and distributed his novel beginning in 2002; after receiving a copy from one of Taylor's parishioners and noting the popularity of the book, London publisher Faber & Faber reissued *Shadowmancer* nationwide a year later. By 2004 the bestselling novel had made its way across the Atlantic to North American readers, and its author had become something of a celebrity in his native England.

Taylor was born around 1958 in Scarborough, England, to deaf parents, and his family often communicated using sign language. His father was employed as a cobbler and shoe repairer while his mother worked as an assistant at a canteen. A poor student, Taylor was twice expelled from school, once for setting a teacher's desk on fire. "I was just a rebel and didn't really appreciate what people were doing for me and thought I knew better than anybody else," he later admitted to Chris Bond in the *Yorkshire Post.* "I was my own worst enemy." Taylor ran away from home as a teen and went to London where he got involved with the punk scene and the music business. While working as a roadie for musical acts such as the Sex Pistols and Elvis Costello, he succumbed to the temptations of the rock-and-roll lifestyle. "I was a very heavy drinker and I experimented with drugs because it was part of the culture, and some of my friends became heroin addicts," he remarked to Bond of the "Godless time in my life."

When Taylor was twenty-one years old, he left London and eventually returned to Yorkshire. As he told Bond, "I woke up one morning and looked out my bedroom window and Brixton was on fire. I went and looked in the mirror and what was staring back was a very old man and something inside me said 'Go home, I'll find you a job and I'll find you a wife.' So I packed my bags and left that day." While working as a glass washer in a night club, he received some training as a social worker and began working at a center for the deaf and elderly. Through this new job, Taylor came into contact with a group of Christians who helped him investigate their faith. "Very gently and very slowly they dismissed every argument I had," he told *New York Times* interviewer Dinitia Smith. "I didn't become a born-again Christian. It wasn't like Saul on the road to Damascus. Over a period, I realized this was the way I should follow."

While working at the center, Taylor met his wife, Kathy, whom he married in 1983. Taylor later joined the North Yorkshire police, serving as a beat officer from 1986 to 1996. His career in law enforcement ended after he was viciously assaulted by a gang outside a pub. The attack left him deaf in one ear. He had also been kicked in his throat, which left him with a benign growth, and he was forced to resign his position. By this time, Taylor was already training to become an Anglican minister. In

Cover of **Shadowmancer,** *the fantasy novel that started G.P. Taylor's writing career.* (Firebird, 2004. Photograph ©2004 by Deborah Vess. All rights reserved. Reproduced by permission of Firebird, a division of Penguin Putnam Books for Young Readers.)

1995, he entered the clergy and became vicar of Whitby. Taylor later transferred to Cloughton, near his birthplace of Scarborough, where he was appointed vicar of St. Mary's. As the church developed its well-known ministry of healing through prayer, Taylor became known for his exorcism-like activities in homes, something he called "house prayers."

Around 2002, a woman heard Taylor speak at his church and suggested that he write a book. As he told *Yorkshire Post* contributor Catherine Scott, "I was in Hull one time talking about the growing trends of the occult in children's literature and saying how there was a need for someone to write books that meet our desire for a good story and show a God who is involved in people's lives. A woman came up to me at the end and said, 'If you've got so many concerns, why don't you write a book yourself?,' and I thought, 'Well, why don't I?'"

Inspired by the parishioner's words and his interest in the occult, Taylor wrote what became *Shadowmancer* in about nine months. Set in the history-filled lands along England's northeast coast, *Shadowmancer* draws readers back to the 1700s. Power-hungry Obadiah Demurral, vicar of the remote parish of Thorpe, begins to secretly explore the black arts, having long since lost his faith and concern over his soul in his lust for godlike power. Demurral's efforts are aided by a powerful gold artifact called the Keruvim, which he acquired from thieves who stole it from an African temple to the gods. Together with its mate, the magic artifact will allow its owner to gain control over all things. When African traveler Raphah traces the Keruvim to Demurral's parish, he hopes to reacquire it for the temple. Instead, he finds himself engaged in a battle with the ruthless vicar, as well as with dead spirits capable of such awful things as cursing humans with perpetual nightmares. Aided by two children, Kate Cogland and the homeless Thomas Barrick, Raphah fights the greedy Demurral, who has no qualms about robbery and murder in attempting to gain absolute power over nature.

Reviewing *Shadowmancer* for *Library Journal,* Tamara Butler described the novel as "steeped in English folklore" and added that, while the book is geared for teen readers, "it is complex enough to hold the interest of

Cover of Taylor's Wormwood, *which draws readers into a Victorian-era mystery leading to a forbidding villain and features photography by* **Deborah Vess.** (Cover photograph ©Ghost Design, 2004. Reproduced by permission of Firebird, a division of Penguin Putnam Books for Young Readers.)

adults." While finding the story, with its religious parables, "a dark and weighty morality tale," a *Publishers Weekly* reviewer concluded that *Shadowmancer* contains "enough surprises to keep readers madly turning the pages."

In *The Shadowmancer Returns: The Curse of Salamander Street,* a sequel to Taylor's debut work, Kate and Thomas escape the clutches of Obadiah Demurral with the help of smuggler Jacob Crane, only to find themselves trapped by a corrupt alchemist. Meanwhile, Raphah accompanies Beadle, a former servant of Demurral, on a journey to London, where they uncover a secretive plan that involves the Holy Grail. "From a *Hound of the Baskervilles*-style subplot in dark, wild fairy magic, Taylor writes arrestingly of evil's many guises," wrote Mattson.

Taylor's second novel, *Wormwood,* was published in 2004. In eighteenth-century London, Dr. Sabian Blake receives a mysterious gift—the Nemorensis, an ancient volume of prophecy that foretells the arrival of Wormwood, a comet that threatens to devastate the city. When Blake's housemaid, Agetta, steals the Nemorensis, she comes under the spell of a fallen angel who wants to possess the book's magic. The author's "writing is sensuous and spellbinding, drawing readers into a place where masked dark angels battle over human souls and immortality," noted *Kliatt* reviewer Michele Winship.

In *School Library Journal* Carolyn Lehman noted Taylor's inclusion of "exquisitely detailed scenes of violence and mayhem," all of which make *Wormwood* "unremittingly dark." Other critics remarked that *Wormwood* is much more violent and gruesome than its predecessor. "Readers of many faiths will appreciate the spectacular ringside view of hand-to-hand combat between immortals," *Booklist* contributor Jennifer Mattson stated, while a *Kirkus Reviews* critic deemed the novel "relentlessly horrific." In *Publishers Weekly* a reviewer noted that Taylor is "even more explicit . . . about his allegory's tether to Christianity" in *Wormwood*, with its battle between fallen and true angels, but added that *Wormwood* "brings some cohesion and depth" to Taylor's body of work.

While moving out of his vicarage in the fall of 2004, Taylor accidentally threw the hand-edited manuscript of his next novel, *Tersias,* into the fire. Fortunately, he had another, unedited copy of the manuscript to work from. Published in the United States as *Tersias the Oracle,* the novel follows the adventures of Jonah Ketch, a highwayman who has stolen a magical knife from the sinister Lord Malpas, and Tersias, a blind prophet who receives his visions from a supernatural creature known as the Wretchkin. "Taylor's imagination is as ripe as a rotting corpse," noted Suzi Feay in the London *Independent on Sunday,* and *Booklist* contributor Holly Koelling stated that "the story's gritty setting, moody tone, and brisk action in *Tersias the Oracle* will appeal to many."

Cover of Taylor's historical fantasy **Tersias the Oracle,** *featuring art-work by Cliff Nielsen.* (Firebird, 2006. Illustration ©2006 by Cliff Nielsen. All rights reserved. Reproduced by permission of Firebird, a division of Penguin Putnam Books for Young Readers.)

An orphaned schoolboy works as a magician's assistant at a Victorian resort in *Mariah Mundi: The Midas Box.* Life at the Prince Regent holds many surprises for fifteen-year-old Mariah, who learns that each of the five lads preceding him mysteriously disappeared and that the hotel's basement contains an Egyptian sarcophagus surrounded by a host of squirming sea creatures. Taylor "has a terrific gift for storytelling," wrote Toby Clements in the London *Daily Telegraph,* and in *Booklist,* Ian Chipman dubbed *Mariah Mundi* "an atmospheric, diabolically inventive thriller." Also reviewing the novel, Connie Tyrrell Burns observed in *School Library Journal* that repeated readings from sophisticated readers will "uncover new levels of meaning" in Taylor's story.

The first volume in Taylor's illustrated "Dopple Ganger Chronicles," *The First Escape* follows orphaned twins Sadie and Saskia Dopple, who are separated when Saskia is adopted from the orphanage by a rich but reclusive writer. Soon Sadie finds a way to escape and follow her sister, aided by a former burglar named Erik Ganger. Caught up in a powerful web of magic created by a former magician, Sadie and Eric work to extricate themselves while Sadie and her adopted guardian are threatened by a band of criminals. In *Booklist,* Chipman remarked on the religious elements that tint Taylor's story, but noted that the transitions between prose and illustrated panel are sometimes "arbitrary and disjointed." Commenting on the "intriguing" combination of "prose, panels, and pictures" in Taylor's self-styled "illustronovella," in her *School Library Journal* review, Alana Abbott added that *The First Escape* may appeal to fans of Roald Dahl or Lemony Snicket.

Eric Ganger and the Dopple twins continue their adventures in *The Secret of Indigo Moon,* as a villain from *The First Escape* returns to plot again. Bouncing between a traditional narrative and graphic-novel-like segments, Taylor's second "Dopple Ganger Chronicles" installment "plumbs . . . religious undertones . . . a little more deeply," according to Chipman. The "gorgeous design" of *The Secret f the Indigo Moon,* as well as its "creepy illustrations," will assure it a readership, the critic added.

Taylor has come a long way since his days as a troubled teen. His views on relationships and religion have also changed dramatically, and a heart condition has also impacted his perspective. "My health problems have completely changed my life," he remarked to Scott. "It has made me realise that every day is important and how important it is to tell my children that I love them every single day. My daughter Lydia helped me realise that my view of God was like tunnel vision, now I realise he is everywhere."

Biographical and Critical Sources

BOOKS

Taylor, G.P., and Bob Smietana, *G.P. Taylor: Sin, Salvation, and Shadowmancer,* Zondervan (Grand Rapids, MI), 2006.

PERIODICALS

Booklist, April 15, 2004, Jennifer Mattson, review of *Shadowmancer,* p. 1451; September 1, 2004, Jennifer Mattson, review of *Wormwood,* p. 109; March 15, 2006, Holly Koelling, review of *Tersias the Oracle,* p. 45; May 15, 2007, Jennifer Mattson, review of *The Shadowmancer Returns: The Curse of Salamander Street,* p. 56; May 1, 2008, Ian Chapman, review of *Mariah Mundi: The Midas Box,* p. 50; October 1, 2008, Ian Chapman, review of *The First Escape,* p. 49; September 1, 2009, Ian Chipman, review of *The Secret of Indigo Moon,* p. 93.

Christianity Today, June, 2004, Greg Taylor, "A Christian Harry Potter?," p. 63; January, 2005, Cindy Crosby, review of *Wormwood,* p. 718.

Daily Telegraph (London, England), July 25, 2003, Nigel Bunyan, "Vicar's Debut Novel Is 'The Next Big Thing' for Literary Investors," p. 10; August 13, 2005, James Francken, "A Writer's Life: G.P. Taylor," p. 1; August 25, 2007, Toby Clements, review of *Mariah Mundi: the Midas Box.*

Entertainment Weekly, May 28, 2004, Troy Patterson, "Has G.P. Taylor Written the Next Harry Potter?," p. 78.

Horn Book, July-August, 2004, Anita L. Burkham, review of *Shadowmancer,* p. 461.

Independent (London, England), June 19, 2003, Nicholas Tucker, review of *Shadowmancer,* p. 13.

Independent on Sunday (London, England), June 15, 2003, James Morrison, "Move over Harry Potter and Make Way for the Vicar," p. 11; August 15, 2004, "This Cultural Life: G.P. Taylor," p. 54; August 7, 2005, Suzi Feay, review of *Tersias,* p. 19.

Kirkus Reviews, March 1, 2004, review of *Shadowmancer,* p. 230; September 1, 2004, review of *Wormwood,* p. 874; March 15, 2006, review of *Tersias the Oracle,* p. 301; April 15, 2008, review of *Mariah Mundi.*

Kliatt, March, 2004, Michele Winship, review of *Shadowmancer,* p. 16; September, 2004, Michele Winship, review of *Wormwood,* p. 16.

Library Journal, April 1, 2004, Tamara Butler, review of *Shadowmancer,* p. 82.

National Review, December 31, 2004, Andrew Stuttaford, "The Trouble with Harry," p. 46.

Newsweek, March 29, 2004, Tara Pepper, "Hotter than Potter?," p. 16.

New York Times, July 24, 2004, Dinitia Smith, "*Harry Potter* Inspires a Christian Alternative," p. B7.

New York Times Book Review, November 14, 2004, Elizabeth Devereaux, review of *Wormwood,* p. 20.

Publishers Weekly, April 5, 2004, review of *Shadowmancer,* p. 63; April 19, 2004, James Bickers, "The Vicar and the Bestseller," p. 25; August 16, 2004, review of *Wormwood,* p. 64; April 23, 2007, review of *The Shadowmancer Returns,* p. 54.

School Library Journal, October, 2004, Jane P. Fenn, review of *Shadowmancer,* p. 86, and Carolyn Lehman, review of *Wormwood,* p. 180; October, 2006, Sharon Grover, review of *Tersias the Oracle,* p. 174; September, 2007, Christi Voth, review of *The Shadowmancer Returns,* p. 209; August, 2008, Connie Tyrrell Burns, review of *The Midas Box,* p. 135; November, 2008, Alana Abbott, review of *The First Escape,* p. 153.

Times (London, England), June 14, 2003, Jane Dickson, "The First Book of Graham, Chapter I," p. 3; September 23, 2006, Amanda Craig, review of *The Curse of Salamander Street,* p. 15.

Yorkshire Post (Yorkshire, England), August 24, 2005, Chris Bone, "Fantasy and Reality of Literary Fame"; September 27, 2006, Catherine Scott, "A Writer's New Life of Dreams and Nightmares."

ONLINE

British Broadcasting Corporation Web site, http://www.bbb.co.uk/blast/ (December 3, 2004), transcript of interview with Taylor.

G.P. Taylor Home Page, http://www.gptaylor.info (June 1, 2010).*

* * *

TAYLOR, Graham Peter
See TAYLOR, G.P.

* * *

VEGA, Denise 1962-

Personal

Born December 10, 1962, in Seattle, WA; married Matt Perkins; children: Zachary, Jesse, Rayanne. *Education:* Attended Colorado State University; University of California, Los Angeles, B.A. (motion-picture television); Harvard University, Ed.M. *Hobbies and other interests:* Fishing, hiking, camping, swimming, watching movies, reading.

Addresses

Home—Denver, CO.

Career

Writer.

Member

International Reading Association (member, Colorado Council), Authors Guild, Colorado Authors League, Society of Children's Book Writers and Illustrators (Rocky Mountain chapter, co-regional advisor).

Awards, Honors

Lee & Low Books New Voices Honor Award for unpublished manuscript, 2001, for *Superhombre;* Colorado Book Award for Young-Adult Literature, 2005, and Books for the Teen Age selection, New York Public Library, both for *Click Here (to Find out How I Survived Seventh Grade);* Colorado Top Hand Award, and Colorado Book Award for Young Adult Literature, both for *Fact of Life No. 31;* Living in Color Literary Award, Multicultural Literature Advocacy Group, for *Grandmother, Have the Angels Come?*

Writings

JUVENILE FICTION

Click Here (to Find out How I Survived Seventh Grade), Little, Brown (New York, NY), 2005.

Build a Burrito: A Counting Book in English and Spanish, illustrated by David Diaz, Scholastic, Inc. (New York, NY), 2008.

Fact of Life No. 31, Knopf (New York, NY), 2008.

Access Denied (and Other Eighth-Grade Error Messages) (sequel to *Click Here [to Find out How I Survived Seventh Grade]*), Little, Brown (New York, NY), 2009.

Grandmother, Have the Angels Come?, illustrated by Erin Eitter Kono, Little, Brown (New York, NY), 2009.

Contributor of short fiction to periodicals, including *Pockets.*

NONFICTION

WordPerfect for Legal Professionals, Version 5.1, CFMS (Jacksonville, FL) 1992.

Groupwise for Windows 3.1 on the Job Essentials, Que Corporation (Indianapolis, IN), 1996.

Groupwise for Windows 3.1 on the Job Essentials Instructor's Manual, Que Corporation (Indianapolis, IN), 1996.

WordPerfect 101 for the Law Office: A Guide to Basic Document Production, ABA Section of Law Practice Management (Chicago, IL), 1996.

WordPerfect 201 for the Law Office: A Guide to Advanced Document Production, ABA Section of Law Practice Management (Chicago, IL), 1996.

Discover WordPerfect Suite 8, IDG Books Worldwide (Foster City, CA), 1997.

WordPerfect 7 for Windows '95 Essentials, Level II, Que E & T (Indianapolis, IN), 1997.

WordPerfect 7 for Windows '95 Essentials Level III, Que E & T (Indianapolis, IN), 1997.

(With Shelley O'Hara and Julia Kelly) *Discover Office '97,* IDG Books Worldwide (Foster City, CA), 1997.

Learning the Internet for Kids: A Voyage to Internet Treasures, DDC (New York, NY), 1998.

Word Processing for Kids, illustrated by Ryan Sather, DDC (New York, NY), 1999.

Sidelights

A former technical writer, Denise Vega is the author of a number of well-received novels for adolescents, including *Fact of Life No. 31,* as well as picture books for younger readers. Literature has always played an important role in Vega's life, as she noted on her home page, and her interest in storytelling also influenced her decision to become a writer. "I read a lot as a kid and beyond and wanted to be able to create stories that readers could relate to, just as I related to the books I read," she stated. "I wanted to entertain, but also maybe give readers insights, too."

Although Vega wrote her first novel when she was fifteen years old, she had to wait for many years to see her first work of fiction published. By the time that book, the middle-grade novel *Click Here (to Find out How I Survived Seventh Grade),* reached bookstore shelves, Vega was no stranger to the publishing process; she had already made a success out of writing instructional books for popular computer programs, and had

even penned a few computer books for young readers. In *Click Here* she focuses on a preteen protagonist who shares Vega's own interest in computers. Self-conscious Erin Swift thinks her feet are too big; in evaluating her life she believes the only thing she is good at is working on the computer and writing on her secret blog. Entering middle school, she immediately encounters disappointment when she realizes that her best friend, Jilly, is in another class. To make matters worse, Erin is forced into a dreaded confrontation with her arch nemesis, a classmate named Serena. As romance develops and jealousy and heartache follow, Erin vents her rollercoaster emotions on her blog, but when the confidential e-diary is accidentally posted online for friends and classmates to see, her honesty threatens the relationships she values most.

In a review of *Click Here* for *School Library Journal,* Linda L. Plevak commented that Vega's "characters and situations are believable, and readers will relate to and

Cover of Denise Vega's humorous preteen novel Facts of Life, *featuring artwork by Michael Storrings.* (Cover art ©2008 by Michael Storrings. ©2009 by Laurel-Leaf, an imprint of Random House Children's Books, a division of Random House, Inc.)

sympathize with Erin's dilemmas." A *Publishers Weekly* contributor called the story "a heartfelt book about a girl becoming her own person," while in *Kirkus Reviews* a critic praised the "the blog segments and first-person narration" as "immediate and funny."

Erin makes a return appearance in *Access Denied (and Other Eighth Grade Error Messages),* a sequel to *Click Here.* Despite being a year older, the spunky blogger still faces a host of humorously embarrassing situations, including dealing with her overprotective mother, surviving her first breakup, and coping with a wild new classmate who wants to remake Erin as a "bad girl." When a personal tragedy ensues, however, the teen is forced to confront her grief and loss. "Erin's ups and downs are humanizing, entertaining and real," a contributor in *Kirkus Reviews* stated, and Nora G. Murphy, writing in *School Library Journal,* also offered praised for the novel, maintaining that "it is fun to read about a computer-and gadget-loving girl protagonist."

Fact of Life No. 31, a young-adult novel, centers on Kat Flynn, a sixteen-year-old free spirit who practices yoga, trains for a triathlon, and assists her mother, Abra, at a midwifery. After Kat strikes up an unlikely relationship with classmate Manny Cruz, she finds herself confused by Manny's insistence that they keep the budding romance a secret, but she is unable to share her pain with her distant and controlling mother. When Libby Giles, one of the most popular students at Kat's school, arrives pregnant at the midwifery, Kat learns to see her classmate—and her mother—in a new light. "Kat is an unusual protagonist who doesn't easily fit into type," Gillian Engberg stated in *Booklist,* and *Kliatt* reviewer Myrna Marler maintained that "Kat navigates through [a] maze of pain and jealousy with her self-identity intact."

In *Grandmother, Have the Angels Come?,* a picture book inspired by her own maternal grandmother, Vega examines the wonders of the aging process. The work focuses on a little girl's love for her grandparent, who addresses the youngster's concerns about her diminishing senses with kindness and compassion. "The affection that pours from the pages is strong and believable," a *Publishers Weekly* critic observed, and Shelle Rosenfeld noted in *Booklist* that *Grandmother, Have the Angels Come?* "recasts ageing with positive and poetic imagery and reassurances of eternal love."

Biographical and Critical Sources

PERIODICALS

Booklist, May 15, 2008, Gillian Engberg, review of *Fact of Life No. 31,* p. 38; March 1, 2009, Shelle Rosenfeld, review of *Grandmother, Have the Angels Come?,* p. 50.

Girls' Life, April-May, 2005, review of *Click Here (to Find out How I Survived Seventh Grade),* p. 36.

Kirkus Reviews, March 1, 2005, review of *Click Here (to Find out How I Survived Seventh Grade),* p. 297; April 15, 2008, review of *Fact of Life No. 31;* December 1, 2008, review of *Grandmother, Have The Angels Come?;* June 15, 2009, review of *Access Denied (and Other Eighth Grade Error Messages).*

Kliatt, May, 2008, Myrna Marler, review of *Fact of Life No. 31,* p. 18.

Publishers Weekly, April 4, 2005, review of *Click Here (to Find out How I Survived Seventh Grade),* p. 60; January 26, 2009, review of *Grandmother, Have the Angels Come?,* p. 118.

School Library Journal, May, 2005, Linda L. Plevak, review of *Click Here (to Find out How I Survived Seventh Grade),* p. 140; October, 2009, Nora G. Murphy, review of *Access Denied,* p. 140.

Voice of Youth Advocates, June, 2005, Arlene Garcia, review of *Click Here (to Find out How I Survived Seventh Grade),* p. 140.

ONLINE

Bildungsroman Web log, http://slayground.livejournal.com/ (June 10, 2008), interview with Vega.

Denise Vega Home Page, http://www.denisevega.com (June 1, 2010).

Hatchette Book Group Web site, http://www.hachettebook group.com/ (June 1, 2010), "Denise Vega."*

*   *   *

VILELA, Fernando 1973-

Personal

Born 1973, in Brazil. *Education:* University of Campinas, B.F.A., 1995; University of São Paulo, M.A., 2008.

Addresses

Home—São Paulo, Brazil. *E-mail*—fe.vilela@uol.com. br; fevilela@gmail.com.

Career

Illustrator, graphic artist, and author. Teacher at Tomie Ohtake Institute, São Paulo, Brazil, beginning 2005; lecturer. *Exhibitions:* Works exhibited in numerous galleries in Brazil, and at Mexican Cultural Institute, Washington, DC, 2004; International Illustration Biannual, Bratislava, 2005; Golobortko Studio, New York, NY, 2006; American Cultural Institute, Washington, DC, 2006; and International Children's Illustration Bienna, Barreiros, Portugal, 2007.

Awards, Honors

São Simão Art Fair Acquisition Prize, 1994; Sesc Macapaá Art Fair Acquisition Prize, 2002; Contemporary Art Fiar of Santo André Acquisition Prize, 2004; Premio Ilustrador revelação-FNLIJ, 2004, for *Ivan Filho-de-boi.*

Writings

SELF-ILLUSTRATED; FOR CHILDREN

Lampião y Lancelote, Editora Cosac & Naify (São Paulo, Brazil), 2006.
Le chemin, Éditor Autremement (France), 2007.
A Toalha Vermelha (title means "The Red Towel"), Editoral Brinque-Book, 2007.
Tapajós, Editora Ática, 2007.
Olemac e Melô, Cia das Letrinhas, 2007.
Comilança, Editora DCL, 2008.
O Barqueiro e o canoeiro, Editor Scipione, 2008.

ILLUSTRATOR; FOR CHILDREN

Marina Tenório, *Ivan Filho-de-boi (Mitos Russos),* Editora Cosac & Naify (São Paulo, Brazil), 2004.
Sulami Katy, *Meu lugar no mundo,* Editora Ática, 2004.
Daniel Munduruki, *Sabedoria das águas,* Editora Global, 2004.
Ilan Brenman, *A dobradura do Samurai,* Editora Cia das Letrinhas, 2005.
Ilan Breneman, *As narrativas preferidas de um contador de histórias,* Editora Landy, 2005.
Antonio Oliveira, adaptor, *Prometeu acorrentado (de ésquilo),* Editora F.T.D., 2005.
Rogério de Andrade Barbosa, *A vingança do Falcão,* Editorial Brinque Book, 2006.
Ilan Brenman, *Hermes o Motoboy,* Editora DCL, 2006.
Stela Barbieri, *A menina do fio,* Girafinha (São Paulo, Brazil), 2006.
Stela Barbieri, *O que cabe num livro,* Girafinha (São Paulo, Brazil), 2006.
Stela Barbieri, *Bumba-meu-boi,* Girafinha (São Paulo, Brazil), 2007.
Rudyard Kipling, *O elefante infante* (title means "The Infant Elephant"), Editora Musa, 2007.
Joel Franz Rosell, *A lenda de Taita Osongo,* Edições SM, 2007.
Inglês de Sousa, *O rebelde e outros contos Amazônicos,* Editora Scipione, 2007.
Jacques Prévert, *Contos para crianças impossiveis,* Editora Cosac & Naify (São Paulo, Brazil), 2007.

Ilan Brenman, *A festa de aniversário,* Editora DCL, 2007.
Bráulio Tavares, *A invecão do mundo pelo Deus curumim,* Editora 34, 2008.
Stela Barbieri, *ABC do Japão,* Editora SM, 2008.
Stela Barbieri, *Pedro Malasartes,* Editora Moderna, 2008.
Sean Taylor, *The Great Snake: Stories from the Amazon,* Frances Lincoln (New York, NY), 2008.
Judith Maida, *O nascimento do Universo,* Editor Atica, 2009.

Contributor to books, including *We Are All Born Free,* Frances Lincoln (New York, NY), 2008, to book series "8 jeitos de mudar o munto," by Stela Barbieri, and *Machado de Assis,* and *Contador de histórias de Bolso,* by Ian Brenman, all 2008.

ILLUSTRATOR; OTHER

Francisco Vilella, *Ave Cachaça! Nascimento, vida, reza e glória,* Editora do Autor, 2008.
Álvaro Faleiros, *Meio mundo,* Editora Ateliê, 2008.

Also illustrator of *Da morte odes mínimas,* by Hilda Hist; *Pelo corpo,* by Donizete Galvão and Ronald Polito; and *Antologia poética da geracão 60,* edited by Álvaro Alves and Carolos Felipe Moisés.

Biographical and Critical Sources

PERIODICALS

Kirkus Reviews, October 15, 2008, review of *The Great Snake: Stories from the Amazon.*
School Library Journal, December, 2008, Mary Jean Smith, review of *The Great Snake,* p. 116.

ONLINE

Fernando Vilela Home Page, http://www.artebr.com (May 15, 2010).*

WANG, Shaoli

Personal

Born in Qingdao, China; immigrated to Canada, 1995. *Education:* Qindao Normal College, degree (children's book illustration, painting), 1988.

Addresses

Home—Vancouver, British Columbia, Canada. *E-mail*—slw@shaoliwang.com.

Career

Art teacher and illustrator. Painting teacher in Vancouver, British Columbia, Canada, beginning c. 1996. *Exhibitions:* Works included in China National Fine Arts Exhibition, 1992, 1995, and exhibited at Central Fine Arts College, Beijing, China, 1993, Plaza of Nations, Vancouver, British Columbia, Canada, 1996-99, Dr. Sun Yat Sen Chinese Gardens, Vancouver, 1997, and Yaletown Gallery, Vancouver, 2008.

Awards, Honors

City of Qingdao Children and Young Adults' Art Education Award, 1989; City of Qingdao Ten Best Young Artists Award, 1991, 1993; Province of Shandang Art Exhibition Silver Award, 1992; China National Children and Young Adults' Art Competition Best Teacher Award, 1992, 1995; Province of Shandang Children's Creativity Essay Competition, First Prize, 1993; China National Best Art Teacher Award, 1994; British Columbia Book Prize for Illustrated Books, 2006, for *Bamboo* by Paul Yee.

Illustrator

(With others) *Zhan Zheng De Li Cheng,* Guo fang da xue chu ban she (Beijing, China), 2001.

Paul Yee, *Bamboo,* Tradewind Books (Vancouver, British Columbia, Canada), 2006.

Paul Yee, *Shu-Li and Tamara,* Tradewind Books (Vancouver, British Columbia, Canada), 2008.

Sidelights

Born in the People's Republic of China, Shaoli Wang grew up under the strictures of Chairman Mao Zedong's Cultural Revolution. Wang's artistic talents were recognized early on, and she eventually graduated from Qingdao Normal College with a degree in painting and book illustration. She worked as an illustrator and teacher in China until 1995, when she immigrated to western Canada. Now living in Vancouver, British Columbia, Wang continues to teach and exhibit her award-winning art. She has also illustrated picture books for noted Canadian children's author Paul Yee, among them *Bamboo* and *Shu-Li and Tamara.*

In *Bamboo* Yee adapts a Chinese folktale in his story of a young couple who plant a grove of bamboo as a sym-

Chinese-born artist Shaoli Wang creates engaging illustrations for Paul Yee's picture book **Shu-Li and Tamara.** (Tradewind Books, 2007. Illustration ©2007 by Shaoli Wang. Reproduced by permission.)

bol of their love. In the ensuing years, the couple are separated and the wife, Ming, is left to live with her brother-in-law and his jealous wife, Jin. Although Jin makes every effort to undermine Ming, including giving her poor land to farm and making baseless accusations, the woman thrives with the help of the magical bamboo. Ultimately, despite numerous hardships, Ming reunites with her husband, again with the help of the bamboo. Calling Yee's retelling "well told" and rich with "elements of magic and trickery," Anne Burke added in *Resource Links* that Wang's "very beautiful" folk-style illustrations bring to life "life in a small Chinese village." The artist's juxtaposition of rural life and panoramic scenes "contribut[e] . . . to the story's magical dimension through wild, off-kilter perspectives," asserted *Booklist* contributor Jennifer Mattson, and in *Quill & Quire* Bridget Donald noted that Wang's "vibrantly coloured" images incorporate "details from old, rural China" and "skillfully bridge the traditional and the modern."

A chapter book featuring a contemporary story about friendship, Yee's *Shu-Li and Tamara* finds Chinese-Canadian immigrant Shu-Li hoping to fit in among her fourth-grade classmates. Tamara becomes her first and best friend and is often invited to eat at Shu-Li's family's Chinese restaurant when she is hungry. Due to her own family's poverty, Tamara becomes the brunt of class rumors and Shu-Li's father eventually urges his daughter to stay clear of the girl. However, Shu-Li determines to discover the truth and remain true to her friend. Noting the stylized pencil drawings Wang contributes to *Shu-Li and Tamara, Canadian Review of Materials* contributor Huai-Yang Lim wrote that they "complement the story by highlighting key points of action and conflict as well as significant settings and objects."

Biographical and Critical Sources

PERIODICALS

Booklist, June 1, 2006, Jennifer Mattson, review of *Bamboo,* p. 78; April 1, 2008, Carolyn Phelan, review of *Shu-Li and Tamara,* p. 57.
Canadian Review of Materials, October 13, 2006, Huai-Yang Lim, review of *Bamboo;* December 7, 2007, Huai-Yang Lim, review of *Shu-Li and Tamara.*
Quill & Quire, January, 2006, Bridget Donald, review of *Bamboo.*
Resource Links, February, 2006, Anne Burke, review of *Bamboo,* p. 14; December, 2007, Michelle Gowans, review of *Shu-Li and Tamara,* p. 36.
School Library Journal, September, 2008, Teri Markson, review of *Shu-Li and Tamara,* p. 161.

ONLINE

Shaoli Wang Home Page, http://www.shaoliwang.com (May 15, 2010).*

WARNES, Tim
(Lily Moon, Timothy Warnes)

Personal

Born in London, England; son of Michael (a paper conservator) and Julia Warnes; married Jane Chapman (an illustrator); children: Noah, Levi. *Education:* Kingston Polytechnic, diploma, 1990; Brighton University, B.A. (illustration; with honors), 1993. *Religion:* Christian. *Hobbies and other interests:* The natural world, photography, gardening, "walking, beachcombing, and going to the cinema, being a dad."

Addresses

Home—Somerset, England.

Career

Illustrator and author of children's books, beginning 1993.

Member

Royal Society for the Protection of Birds, National Trust.

Awards, Honors

Nottinghamshire Children's Book Award, Benjamin Franklin Award finalist, and Dutch Libraries Association Children's Book Prize, all 1997, all for *I Don't Want to Go to Bed!* by Julie Sykes; Nottinghamshire Children's Book Award, 1998, for *I Don't Want to Have a Bath!* by Sykes; Nottingham Experian Big Three Book Award finalist, 2000, for *It Could Have Been Worse* by A.H. Benjamin; Sheffield Children's Book Award commended title, 2003, for *Scaredy Mouse* by Alan MacDonald.

Writings

SELF-ILLUSTRATED, UNLESS OTHERWISE NOTED

We Love Preschool, Millbrook Press (Brookfield, CT), 1998.
Ollie's 123, Walker (London, England), 1999.
Ollie's Colours, Walker (London, England), 1999.
Ollie's ABC, Walker (London, England), 2000.
Ollie's Opposites, Walker (London, England), 2000.
Can't You Sleep, Dotty?, Tiger Tales (Wilton, CT), 2001.
Happy Birthday, Dotty!, Tiger Tales (Wilton, CT), 2003.
Mommy Mine, illustrated by wife, Jane Chapman, HarperCollins (New York, NY), 2005.
Daddy Hug, illustrated by Jane Chapman, HarperCollins (New York, NY), 2007.
Chalk and Cheese, Simon & Schuster Books for Young Readers (New York, NY), 2008.

Tim Warnes (Reproduced by permission.)

ILLUSTRATOR

Linda Jennings, *Tom's Tail,* Little, Brown (Boston, MA), 1995.

Ragnhild Scamell, *Who Likes Wolfie?,* Little, Brown (Boston, MA), 1995.

Jane Chapman, *Peter and Pickle's Puzzling Presents,* Little Tiger Press (London, England), 1995.

Julie Sykes, *I Don't Want to Go to Bed!,* Little Tiger Press (London, England), 1996.

A.H. Benjamin, *The Clumsy Elephant,* Golden Press (New York, NY), 1996.

Julie Sykes, *Sssh!,* Little Tiger Press (London, England), 1996.

Hiawyn Oram, *Counting Leopard's Spots: Animal Stories from Africa,* Orchard (London, England), 1996.

Julie Sykes, *I Don't Want to Have a Bath!,* Magi (London, England), 1997.

Christine Leeson, *Max and the Missing Mice,* Golden Press (New York, NY), 1997.

Christine Leeson, *Davy's Scary Journey,* Little Tiger Press (London, England), 1997.

Hiawyn Oram, *Not-so-Grizzly Bear Stories,* Orchard (London, England), 1997.

Julie Sykes, *Hurry Santa!,* Little Tiger Press (London, England), 1998.

James Riordan, *Little Bunny Bobkin,* Little Tiger Press (London, England), 1998.

A.H. Benjamin, *It Could Have Been Worse . . . ,* Little Tiger Press (London, England), 1998.

Julie Sykes, *Little Tiger Goes to School,* Little Tiger Press (London, England), 1999.

Julie Sykes, *Santa's Busy Day!,* Little Tiger Press (London, England), 1999.

Julie Sykes, *Little Tiger's Big Surprise!,* Little Tiger Press (London, England), 1999, Tiger Tales (Wilton, CT), 2001.

Judy West, *Have You Got My Purr?,* Little Tiger Press (London, England), 1999.

Dick King-Smith, *Dinosaur School,* Puffin (Harmondsworth, England), 1999.

Michael Coleman, *You Noisy Monkey,* Rigby (London, England), 2000.

Michael Coleman, *George and Sylvia: A Tale of True Love,* Little Tiger Press (London, England), 2000.

Julie Sykes, *Wake up, Little Tiger,* Little Tiger Press (London, England), 2000.

Julie Sykes, *Time for Bed, Little Tiger,* Little Tiger Press (London, England), 2000.

Isobel Gamble, *Who's That?,* Barron's (Hauppauge, NY), 2001.

Julie Sykes, *Wait for Me, Little Tiger!,* Tiger Tales (Wilton, CT), 2001.

Julie Sykes, *That's Not Fair, Hare!,* Barron's Educational (Hauppauge, NY), 2001.

Dick King-Smith, *The Great Sloth Race,* Puffin (London, England), 2001.

Judith Nicholls, *Inky-Pinky Blot,* Ladybird (London, England), 2001.

Julie Sykes, *Careful, Santa!,* Tiger Tales (Wilton, CT), 2002.

Alan MacDonald, *Scaredy Mouse,* Tiger Tales (Wilton, CT), 2002.

Hiawyn Oram, *Pudge's Play,* Puffin (London, England), 2002.

Hiawyn Oram, *Pudge's House,* Puffin (London, England), 2002.

Julie Sykes, *Bless You, Santa!,* Tiger Tales (Wilton, CT), 2004.

Nicola Grant, *Don't Be So Nosy, Posy!,* Tiger Tales (Wilton, CT), 2004.

Julia Rawlinson, *A Surprise for Rosie,* Tiger Tales (Wilton, CT), 2005, published as *Rosie's Special Surprise,* Little Tiger Press (London, England), 2005.

Jesus Loves Me!, Simon & Schuster (New York, NY), 2005.

Ian Whybrow, *Say Hello to the Animals!,* Macmillan Children's (London, England), 2005.

David Bedford, *I've Seen Santa!,* Tiger Tales (Wilton, CT), 2005, published with CD ROM, Little Tiger Press (London, England), 2007.

Steve Smallman, *Bumbletum,* Tiger Tales (Wilton, CT), 2006.

Rise and Shine!, Simon & Schuster (New York, NY), 2006.

Gillian Lobell, *Little Honey Bear and the Smiley Moon,* Tiger Tales (Wilton, CT), 2006.

Carrie Weston, *Oh, Boris!,* Oxford University Press (Oxford, England), 2007.

David van Buren, *I Love You as Big as the World,* Good Books (Intercourse, PA), 2008.

Carrie Weston, *The New Bear at School,* Scholastic Press (New York, NY), 2008.

Norbert Landa, *Sorry!,* Good Books (Intercourse, PA), 2009.

Norbert Landa, *The Great Monster Hunt,* Good Books (Intercourse, PA), 2010.

Books illustrated by Warnes have been translated into seventeen languages.

ILLUSTRATOR, UNDER PSEUDONYM LILY MOON

Kenneth Steven, *The Bearer of Gifts,* Dial (New York, NY), 1998.

Kenneth Steven, *The Song of the Trees,* Little Tiger Press (London, England), 2002.

Adaptations

The "Little Tiger" series by Julie Sykes, featuring Warnes's illustrations, has been adapted into other book formats.

Sidelights

British artist and author Tim Warnes brings to life the works of a number of children's book authors through his vibrant, cartoon-like drawings and his whimsical take on life. Working with writers such as Julie Sykes, Judy West, Dick King-Smith, and Hiawyn Oram, Warnes has collaborated on several award-winning picture-book efforts, among them Sykes's humorous *I Don't Want to Go to Bed!* and *I Don't Want to Take a Bath!,* both which reverberate with the adamant stance taken by children everywhere. Describing Oram's *Counting Leopard's Spots: Animal Stories from Africa* as a "handsome offering," *School Library Journal* contributor Tom S. Hurlburt added that Warnes' "paintings . . . are expressive, nicely capturing the characters and their environs," and his "expressive, comical illustrations add even more whimsy" to Alan Macdonald's *Scaredy Mouse,* in the opinion of a *Kirkus Reviews* critic. As his career has progressed, Warnes has also taken on the role of author, creating texts for both self-illustrated books such as *Happy Birthday Dotty* and *Chalk and Cheese.*

While growing up in London, England, Warnes "used to spend hours drawing, making little illustrated books and cartoon strips," as he once revealed to *SATA*; consequently "my career is essentially a natural and happy progression of my main lifelong interest." Among his favorite illustrations were the cartoon characters featured in animated films, particularly those by Walt Disney, and his early training in drawing was gained by copying those characters. "I love reading 'The Making of . . .'-type books to major animated feature films; the process behind character and stylistic development is especially revealing and feeds my work probably more than any other one particular source."

In college Warnes worked primarily in black-and-white media, such as pen and ink, but his work since has exhibited an increasingly sophisticated use of color. "In my first books I used a limited palette of just one red, one yellow, one blue and white," he once explained to *SATA,* "but now I actively enjoy seeking out new combinations of process colors. I work in acrylic paint, with oil pastel and pencil details and Chinese ink outlines (my Dad gave me the solid ink stone when I was thirteen, and I'm still using it today)."

The Christmastime book *Shhh!* is one of many collaborations between Warnes and author Sykes; others include *That's Not Fair, Hare!,* Sykes's "Little Tiger" picture-book series, and the "Santa" books *Hurry Santa, Bless You Santa!,* and *Santa's Busy Day.* In *Shhh!* the artist/illustrator wanted to provide something in each of his drawings for young readers to hunt for, so he drew a small mouse into every two-page illustration. "The publisher and [Sykes] developed this idea and gave me a voice on the last spread—now Mouse is as much a part of our Santa books as Santa himself," Warnes once told *SATA.* Praising Warnes' use of "bright colors" in *Shhh!,* a *School Library Journal* contributor commented of the finished product: The "lively illustrations show a round-faced, button-eyed Santa, . . . [whose] constant state of surprise and confusion . . . will delight young readers." Praising the artwork in *Hurry Santa!, Booklist*

Warnes' illustration projects include Julie Sykes's holiday-themed picture book **Hurry, Santa!** (Little Tiger Press, 1998. Illustration © 1998 by Tim Warnes. Reproduced by permission.)

reviewer Ilene Cooper noted that Warnes "mixes the right amount of frenetic energy and laughs," creating art work that "attracts attention with its bright colors and cute characterizations." *That's Not Fair, Hare!* "strikes a nice balance between expressive illustrations and a read-aloud text," concluded Piper L. Nyman in a *School Library Journal* review.

Containing ten stories based on tales from around the world, Oram's *Not-so-Grizzly Bear Stories* shares a wealth of tales with universal themes, such as the trickster tale. Reflecting these themes, Warnes' color-filled cartoon-like illustrations "represent an endearing array of animals from pandas to polar bears," commented Shelley Woods in her *School Library Journal* review of the work. Animals also feature prominently in Ragnhild Scamell's *Who Likes Wolfie?,* as a wolf tries to become more popular with the animals around him. Warnes' illustrations for Scamell's book successfully mirror Wolfie's dreams of popularity, "maintain[ing] a certain naive playfulness," according to a *Publishers Weekly* contributor. Commenting on the illustrator's technique, *Booklist* reviewer Ilene Cooper cited Warnes' "eye-catching . . . thick paintings with elements so well defined that at first glance" they appear "to be collage."

As in *Not-so-Grizzly Bear Stories,* bears are cast in many of Warnes' picture-book illustrations, often in human roles. In bringing to life a popular hymn in *Jesus Loves Me!,* the artist was inspired by his own wife and son to cast a bear family that gardens, celebrates holidays, goes fishing, and reads stories together. Their activities are captures in ink, crayon, and acrylic images that are "suffused with the gentle light of a spring morning," according to *School Library Journal* contributor Linda L. Walkins, the critic adding that Warnes' art "tell[s] a story of a loving and reverent family" featuring "friendly characters." The bear family returns in

Rise and Shine!, which shares another hymn in which "these happy ursine characters serve as inviting hosts to the hymn," according to a *Publishers Weekly* critic. Reviewing his work for David Bedford's *I've Seen Santa!,* *School Library Journal* contributor Lisa Falk concluded that Warnes' warm-toned images "convey the coziness and really carry the appeal" of Bedford's tale, while in *Horn Book* Jennifer M. Brabander cited the "soft illustrations of the large, lumbering bears and their cozy cave." Rabbit joins Bear in Warnes' illustrations for Norbert Landa's *Sorry!,* and here the artist's "soft colors, [and] expressive characters . . . make this a highly appealing story," according to *School Library Journal* critic Linda Staskus. Reviewing Landa's story in *Booklist,* Cooper concluded that Warnes' "oversize artwork features simple shapes and soft colors and has friendly appeal for a young audience."

In *Mommy Mine* and *Daddy Hug* Warnes' text is paired with illustrations by his wife, artist Jane Chapman. Reviewing *Mommy Mine* in *School Library Journal,* Linda M. Kenton praised the "creative wording and joyful imagery," while a *Kirkus Reviews* contributor wrote that the "sing-song cadence" Warnes weaves into his rhyming text "is naturally suited for read-aloud sessions" and ranked the volume "high on the exuberance scale."

In *Chalk and Cheese,* another original story, author/illustrator Warnes tells a story of friendship that prompted *School Library Journal* contributor Kate McClelland to recall "many of the most endearing friendships in children's literature." Cheese is a British-born country mouse whose holiday allows him to join longtime pen pal Chalk, a city dog, on a tour of Chalk's New York City turf. Cheese is animated and chatty, while Chalk is quiet and sedate, and the two remain friends despite these differences. "The contrast between the friends is heightened by Warnes's watercolor and pencil cartoons," added McClelland, the critic observing that the diminutive mouse is given a large mouth and the white-furred Chalk is portrayed as "large and pleasant." In *Kirkus Reviews* a critic noted that the "watercolor-and-pencil illustrations" in *Chalk and Cheese* "have a humorous appeal."

For Warnes, developing well-defined characters is his favorite part of being a children's book illustrator. "When I come to a new project," he once explained to *SATA,* "I really enjoy researching picture reference for it, and I'm very proud of my extensive collection of reference material gleaned over years from various magazines and newspapers, etc! Without a source of reference I feel very out of my depth; as it is, each new project is always daunting."

Warnes begins each of his book projects by sketching page after page of character drawings, sometimes using photographs, "sometimes taking inspiration from people that I know, especially children, even if it is an elephant that I'm drawing!" He then reviews these drawings, picking out the ones that best fit the author's text. "At this stage I may make minor suggestions to the original text if I have a particular idea in mind, which may or may not be incorporated, and add my own incidental characters or actions."

In addition to working under his own name, Warnes has also coined the pseudonym Lily Moon, under which he illustrated the christian-themed picture book *The Bearer of Gifts,* a story written by Kenneth Steven that retells the story of Santa Claus. "I was delighted to receive this commission," Warnes explained of the 1998 picture book, "since it gave me the opportunity to express my [Christian] faith in my work; I also happen to love wintry landscapes which always seem so magical to me." Warnes's inspiration for *The Bearer of Gifts* was "largely drawn from my imagination, textiles, and

primitive art, and any source of color reference that grabbed me, [among them] . . . my rug and a painting by Paul Klee," he told *SATA.* Praising the folk art-style and "deep, rich hues" apparent in Warnes's work, *Booklist* reviewer Lauren Peterson noted that the illustrations, "in a variety of sizes and shapes and with patterned borders and intriguing compositions, add interest."

Using a pseudonym "gives me a new identity and the freedom to express ideas . . . that wouldn't be possible in my usual style," Warnes once explained to *SATA.* "It has also fed my other work: the technique of using oil pastel on top of acrylic that was a distinguishing feature of my Lily Moon work has now crept into some of 'my own' work." As Lily Moon, Warnes has designed greeting cards and Christmas cards, as well as illustrating another book by Steven, *The Song of the Trees.*

In his work as an illustrator, Warnes continues to expand his skills as an artist. In addition to the technical aspects of his job, he also has dreams of expanding his work beyond the printed page. "I suppose my ideal dream would be for something of mine to be properly animated as a feature," he told *SATA,* "or to be involved in the character designs for such a film."

Biographical and Critical Sources

PERIODICALS

Booklist, April 15, 1996, Ilene Cooper, review of *Who Likes Wolfie?,* p. 1447; September 1, 1998, Ilene Cooper, review of *Hurry Santa!,* p. 134; October 15, 1998, Lauren Peterson, review of *The Bearer of Gifts,* p. 429; August 1, 2009, Ilene Cooper, review of *Sorry!,* p. 82.

Warnes collaborates with his wife, artist Jane Chapman, to create picture books such as **Mommy Mine.** (Illustration © 2005 by Jane Chapman. Used by permission of HarperCollins Children's Books, a division of HarperCollins Publishers.)

Horn Book, November-December, 2006, Jennifer M. Brabander, review of *I've Seen Santa!,* p. 688.

Kirkus Reviews, February 15, 2002, review of *Scaredy Mouse,* p. 261; February 15, 2005, review of *Mommy Mine,* p. 237; September 15, 2006, review of *Little Honey Bear and the Smiley Moon,* p. 960; December, 2006, review of *Rise and Shine!,* p. 1274; April 1, 2008, review of *I Love You as Big as the World;* June 15, 2008, review of *The New Bear at School;* October 1, 2008, review of *Chalk and Cheese.*

Publishers Weekly, April 8, 1996, review of *Who Likes Wolfie?,* p. 68; May 29, 2000, review of *Have You Got My Purr?,* p. 81; February 11, 2002, review of *Scaredy Mouse,* p. 186; November 28, 2005, review of *Jesus Loves Me!,* p. 54; September 25, 2006, review of *I've Seen Santa!,* p. 69; November 27, 2006, review of *Rise and Shine!,* p. 54.

School Library Journal, April, 1996, Jacqueline Elsner, review of *Who Likes Wolfie?,* p. 117; October, 1996, review of *Shhh!,* p. 41; December, 1998, Tom S. Hurlburt, review of *Counting Leopard's Spots: Animal Stories from Africa,* p. 112; April, 1999, Shelley Woods, review of *Not-so-Grizzly Bear Stories,* p. 106; February, 2002, Piper L. Nyman, review of *That's Not Fair, Hare!,* p. 114; April, 2003, Heather Miller, review of *Happy Birthday, Dotty!,* p. 142; June, 2002, Roxanne Burg, review of *Scaredy Mouse,* p. 102; July, 2005, Linda M. Kenton, review of *Mommy Mine,* p. 84; March, 2006, Linda L. Walkins, review of *Jesus Loves Me!,* p. 209; October, 2006, Lisa Falk, review of *I've Seen Santa!,* p. 94; November, 2006, Andrea Tarr, review of *Little Honey Bear and the Smiley Moon,* p. 99; May, 2008, review of *Daddy Hug,* p. 111; June, 2008, Linda Staskus, review of *I Love You as Big as the World,* p. 115; July, 2008, Heidi Estrin, review of *The New Bear at School,* p. 83; November, 2008, Kate McClelland, review of *Chalk and Cheese,* p. 102; June, 2009, Linda Staskus, review of *Sorry!,* p. 94.

ONLINE

HarperCollins Publishers Web site, http://www.harper collins.com/ (May 25, 2010), "Tim Warnes."

*   *   *

WARNES, Timothy
See WARNES, Tim

*   *   *

WOLFE, Frances

Personal

Born in Halifax, Nova Scotia, Canada; married.

Addresses

Home—Portuguese Cove, Nova Scotia, Canada. *Agent*—c/o Writers' Federation of Nova Scotia, 1113 Marginal Rd., Halifax, Nova Scotia B3H 4P7, Canada. *E-mail*—fran.wolfe@ns.sympatico.ca.

Career

Author, illustrator, storyteller, and puppeteer. Halifax Public Library, Halifax, Nova Scotia, Canada, children's library employee, 1972-2003. Muralist; presenter at schools.

Member

Writers' Federation of Nova Scotia.

Awards, Honors

Amelia Frances Howard-Gibbon Illustrator's Award, Canadian Library Association, and Ann Connor Brimmer Award for Children's Literature, both 2002, both for *Where I Live;* Mayor's Award for Excellence in Illustration, Halifax Regional Municipality, 2005, for *One Wish.*

Writings

SELF-ILLUSTRATED PICTURE BOOKS

Where I Live, Tundra Books (Plattsburgh, NY), 2001.
One Wish, Tundra Books (Plattsburgh, NY), 2004.
The Little Toy Shop, Tundra Books (Plattsburgh, NY), 2008.

Sidelights

Frances Wolfe is a self-taught Canadian painter whose picture books are notable for their "beautiful, impressive art," as Be Astengo described it in a *School Library Journal* review of Wolfe's award-winning first book, *Where I Live.* Wolfe worked as a storyteller and children's programmer in the Youth Services department of the Halifax, Nova Scotia, Regional Library system for nearly thirty years before she published her first book. A well-known artist in her region, she lives in Portuguese Cove, Nova Scotia, in a house she and her husband built on land that has been in her family for over a century. Her paintings and murals can be found in several Halifax libraries.

Both *Where I Live* and Wolfe's second book, *One Wish,* are odes to the Canadian seashore, a place where Wolfe's family has lived for generations. In *Where I Live* the young narrator describes her environment "in spare, poetic prose," as Astengo explained. Although the narrator does not say where she lives until the end of the book, Wolfe's "strikingly larger than life" illustrations, as Fern Kory described them in the *Bulletin of the Center for Children's Books,* provide plenty of obvious clues. "The end result," Denise Parrott concluded in *Resource Links,* "is an East Coast anthem that will speak to any child about the sea."

Frances Wolfe's artwork pairs with her gentle text in the picture book **Where I Live.** (Tundra Books, 2001. Copyright © 2001 by Frances Wolfe. Reproduced by permission.)

Although it is still a picture book, *One Wish* is perhaps of more interest to adults than children, according to some critics. The narrator, again a little girl, talks about her one wish in life: to own a cottage by the sea. She explains all of the things she would see and do if she could live by the ocean, such as feeding seagulls, collecting seashells, and sailing. Finally, Wolfe reveals that the narrator has her wish: at the end of the book a spread depicts an old woman sitting on her porch watching the ocean. The "breathtaking" and "magnificent illustrations," as Judy Cottrell described them in *Resource Links,* may be the true draw of *One Wish,* especially for younger readers. "Stunning, light-filled paintings dominate each spread," Lee Bock noted in *School Library Journal,* and *Booklist* contributor Ilene Cooper commented upon an image showing the narrator's beach-combing finds—"shells, a starfish, a feather—so carefully depicted that every detail can be seen."

In *The Little Toy Shop* Wolfe turns her attention to the Christmas season in her story about a special toy shop run by the kindly Mr. Kringle. The toys in this shop are fortunate because Mr. Kringle has a reputation for selecting the perfect toy for each gift-giving customer. When a small toy rabbit arrives at his store, it learns about Christmas and dreams of being a Christmas gift for a special boy or girl. Then a little girl falls in love with the stuffed bunny, and promises to return to purchase it. When the toy is sold to another customer by accident, all are distraught until Mr. Kringle manages to set things right and the bunny gains its wish after all. Praising Wolfe's gentle story, Diane Olivo-Posner added that the author/artist's "vibrant oil-on-masonite paintings bring life to this heartwarming tale." While a *Kirkus Reviews* writer found *The Little Toy Shop* to be some-

what sentimental, Wolfe's "attractive illustrations exhibit sophisticated perspectives" and feature "a dear little bunny" at the center of it all.

Biographical and Critical Sources

PERIODICALS

Booklist, May 1, 2001, Carolyn Phelan, review of *Where I Live,* p. 1694; June 1, 2004, Ilene Cooper, review of *One Wish,* p. 1750.

Bulletin of the Center for Children's Books, May, 2001, Fern Kory, review of *Where I Live,* p. 356.

Kirkus Review, November 1, 2008, review of *The Little Toy Shop.*

Resource Links, April, 2001, Denise Parrott, review of *Where I Live,* p. 9; April, 2004, Judy Cottrell, review of *One Wish,* p. 56.

School Library Journal, April, 2001, Be Astengo, review of *Where I Live,* p. 136; June, 2004, Lee Bock, review of *One Wish,* p. 122; October, 2008, Diane Olivio-Posner, review of *The Little Toy Shop,* p. 99.

ONLINE

Canadian Children's Book Centre Web site, http://www.bookcentre.ca/ (May 31, 2010), "Frances Wolfe."

Canadian Library Association Web site, http://www.cla.ca/ (June 26, 2002), "Frances Wolfe, Winner of the 2002 Amelia Frances Howard-Gibbon Illustrator's Medal."

Random House Web site, http:// www.randomhouse.com/ (May 31, 2010), "Frances Wolfe."

Tundra Books Web site, http://www.tundrabooks.com/ (May 31, 2010), "Frances Wolfe."

Writers' Federation of Nova Scotia Web site, http://www.writers.ns.ca/ (May 31, 2010), "Frances Wolfe."